THE *Christian*
*Traveler's*
*Companion:*

*Western*
*Europe*

# THE *Christian Traveler's Companion:*

# *Western Europe*

## AMY S. ECKERT
## AND WILLIAM J. PETERSEN

Fleming H. Revell
A Division of Baker Book House Co
Grand Rapids, Michigan 49516

Published by Fleming H. Revell
a division of Baker Book House Company
P.O. Box 6287, Grand Rapids, MI 49516-6287

Printed in the United States of America

**Library of Congress Cataloging-in-Publication Data**

Eckert, Amy S.
    The Christian traveler's companion. Western Europe / Amy S. Eckert and William J. Petersen.
      p.   cm.
    ISBN 0-8007-5741-6
    1. Europe, Western—Guidebooks. 2. Christians—Travel—Europe, Western—Guidebooks. I. Petersen, William J. II. Title.
D967.E28 2001
914.04′56—dc21                                  00-067323

The sidebars written by Charles Huttar in the United Kingdom section are used with permission of the author.

For current information about all releases from Baker Book House, visit our web site:

           http://www.bakerbooks.com

# Contents

# Introduction

Christian travel is for everyone. Honest—everyone. To do Christian travel you don't have to be a minister or priest or even a member of church leadership. You don't have to be a senior citizen or a parent trying to set a good example. You don't have to be a member of a particular denomination or adhere to certain religious beliefs. You don't need to have "arrived" spiritually or be a daily Bible reader or be a member in the church choir or a Sunday school teacher, and you don't even have to attend church each and every Sunday without fail.

Christian travel is not necessarily a trip with a religious theme, like a vacation to the Holy Land or a pilgrimage tour. It doesn't have to be a service trip, where you participate in mission work—building hospitals and churches for the disadvantaged. And you don't have to go on a spiritual retreat unless you want to.

What we mean by Christian travel is travel that rejuvenates your spirit as well as your body, travel that does not leave your spiritual life behind on the coffee table, travel that helps families talk about their faith and that of others in history, travel that encourages appreciation for what God has done and thankfulness for his great gifts. We don't mean to imply that you need to turn your vacation time into an around-the-clock church service. But there are many small things you can do along the way to make all of your travels Christian.

With a little preplanning, you can make faith a focal point of any vacation. Add small side trips to your family's vacation plans. Are you planning to visit family in the Netherlands this summer? Take time to visit the Museum Amstelkring in Amsterdam, and learn about the secret attic churches that sprang up in the city during the 16th century. You'll acquire a new appreciation for the difficulties that Catholics suffered during the time of the Reformation and for the religious tolerance and love that their Protestant neighbors provided them.

It is inspiring to learn of the faith of the Christians who lived before us. In the early 15th century Jan Hus and his followers braved great dangers as they attempted to worship according to their own consciences. Hus was eventually burned at the stake for his beliefs, but the Hussites, who would later be called Moravians, continued, eventually sending missionaries to the rest of Europe and North America. Your family will benefit from visiting sites associated with these great Christian leaders and will learn to appreciate the religious freedom that most of us take for granted.

Even business trips can include an element of Christian travel. Are you attending a conference in London? Why not take time to view the sacred art collections in the British Museum? Take advantage of a free Sunday morning and visit a local church. Is there a historic cathedral nearby or a church that is noted for its stunning architecture, artwork, or music? *The Christian Traveler's Companion: Western Europe* includes listings that will help you find these places.

By noting places in your travels that are associated with Christianity, you create natural topics for family conversation that focuses on God and what he has done. For instance, did you know that "Silent Night" was written in Oberndorf, Austria? Did you know that St. Patrick herded swine as a youngster near Antrim, Northern Ireland? Or that you can visit the site of St. Paul's shipwreck in Malta?

Many Christians say they feel closest to God when they are out in nature. And it is true that the handiwork of humans cannot compare with God's creation, whether it is Norway's fjord country or the rocky beauty of Portugal's Atlantic seacoast. What better way to add a spiritual element to your trip than to marvel at God's amazing creation? Including every scenic area in Europe would have been outside the scope of this book, but we point out the must-see locations.

## TRAVEL WITH A PURPOSE

Throughout history travel has been an important element of a life of faith. Centuries ago Abraham began the tradition, picking up and moving when God called him. Abraham packed up all of his possessions, his family, and his servants and traveled to a new land. The journey itself was an important part of Abraham's spiritual life. Along the way he encountered trials through which God was able to teach him valuable lessons. And since Abraham had no idea where his destination would be and no familiarity with the land or its inhabitants, each day must have been a new adventure in his faith walk, relying on God for his every need.

The Israelites learned a similar lesson. Their journeys took much longer, lasting 40 years. Notice that, following the Israelites' disobedience, God commanded his people not simply to camp or to settle and wait for 40 years, but to wander, to travel. It must be that God's lessons would be learned through the travel itself, not simply through the waiting.

Christ spent the majority of his ministry traveling and teaching, and when life became too much for him, he headed out into the countryside, walking in the desert of Judea or traveling by boat on the Sea of Galilee. And the disciples followed suit, traveling throughout their world spreading the gospel, visiting believers, and assisting with local projects. Although travel in that day was not only difficult but even perilous, the disciples saw travel as an unavoidable part of spreading the Good News.

For centuries the early church viewed faith-related travel as an important part of Christian life. The faithful would find someone

## The World's First Travel Guidebooks

In writing a book like this it was often reassuring to the authors to remember that the world's first travel guidebooks were written by monks specifically for Christian travelers.

In 333 a traveler known simply as the Bordeaux Pilgrim wrote a detailed travel guide on Jerusalem to pilgrims who made their way to the holy city from Europe. About 800 years later in 1130 a more extensive guide, *The Pilgrim Guide,* was written by Almeri Picaud, a Poitou monk who detailed a variety of routes to Santiago de Compostela. He described the inhabitants, climate, and customs of the territory that pilgrims would traverse, including the most interesting routes, interesting side trips, minor shrines, and places to stay along the way.

Amy and Bill consider themselves among good company.

to care for their businesses or farms while they headed off to the shrine of a saint in the hope of receiving a blessing. Travelers were often gone for months at a time, but while the way was difficult and accommodations meager, the journey was not without its pleasures. Family members strengthened relationships, travelers forged new friendships, and the cares of home could be forgotten for a time. When the travelers reached their destination, they were certain to pick up a souvenir before they left—perhaps a shell, a feather, or a container of holy water—that they might never forget their experience. Those early Christian treks formed the basis for modern-day pleasure travel, and many of the ancient traditions survive today.

## How to Use This Book

If you would like to integrate your faith with your travel, then Christian travel is for you. In fact you may already be doing it without putting a label on it. The way in which your family makes its travels Christian will be as unique as you are. *The Christian Traveler's Companion: Western Europe* is designed to help you decide what's best for your family.

You may have tried to add Christian sites to your itinerary in the past and been discouraged by the lack of help in the standard guidebooks. That's why this book is special. Sites are included here that would be ignored or glossed over by other guidebooks. *The Christian Traveler's Companion* includes literally thousands of sites within Europe that offer special inspiration and, yes, fun for Christian families. (After all, most people travel for enjoyment, and Christian travel can and should be fun!) The listings of the countries of western Europe are by city, beginning with the country's primary metropolis and arranged alphabetically after that. Within each city are listings that are quite varied, just as families' interests and styles are varied.

Look within your desired destination for sites that are worth a special trip, as well as for bits of Christian trivia. You will find listings of historic churches as well as fine art exhibits that will be of special interest to Christians. You will find historic sites and sites that simply offer good, wholesome family fun.

Europe's Christian history is a long and rich one. In addition to each country's listings you'll find boxes that highlight special locations. We spotlight some of Christianity's most influential leaders and provide background information on the continent's most important works of Christian art, architecture, and music. We discuss the history of Christianity in each country and we also recommend some of the best places to enjoy God's creation.

Because our focus is on Christian sites, we assume that this guidebook will be used in conjunction with other books on the market that offer comprehensive maps and information about lodging and dining and general information about travel abroad.

## INTERNET RESOURCES

Visit our web site: www.christiantraveler.com for updated information on Christian travel. Because addresses can change over time and because more web sites are continually being created, we have compiled a complete and updated listing of Internet links on our web site. All of the web sites included in this book are available on our web site and are updated as needed. You will also find many more listings as they become available. This links page serves as a handy reference tool, a clearinghouse for all of the Christian travel sites you will ever need.

## QUESTIONS AND ANSWERS ABOUT CHRISTIAN TRAVEL IN EUROPE

*Q: It's so hectic when we travel. Is it possible to enhance my spiritual life when we're so busy?*

A: Consider packing a good Christian book to read along the way. Take along a tape or CD player and headphones and listen to Christian music, sermons, or a Christian book on tape as you travel. Identify a church for Sunday worship, no matter what city you're in. Take early morning walks alone and use the time for meditation and prayer.

*Q: I have young children. Is it possible to add a Christian emphasis to our vacation?*

A: Yes! Even very young children can see God's handiwork around them. Tell the story of Noah's ark before visiting a zoo and remind them to look for all the wonderfully unique designs that God parceled out to the animals.

Remind your family of the creation story as you make your way through the Alps to enjoy the area's natural beauty. And share with them your appreciation for a healthy and fit body when you set off on a hike through England's Lake District.

Older children will enjoy reading stories that tie into the day's activities. On your way to Assisi, read a brief biography of St. Francis and his love for animals. On your way through central Germany, listen to excerpts from Handel's *Messiah*. Or base your morning's devotions on Christ's commandment to love one another before visiting Anne Frank's house in Amsterdam.

This kind of travel will require a little planning before your trip, but the effort will be worth it.

*Q: Shouldn't we just skip church when we're away from home? We won't know anyone even if we do find a church to attend, and we might not speak the language either.*

A: It may be interesting and informative to visit a church of a different denomination, language, or worship style while you're away

## WHAT AMY'S KIDS LOVED IN EUROPE

1. Feeding the pigeons in St. Mark's Square, Venice
2. Chasing cats in the Roman Forum
3. Riding in a gondola, Venice
4. Riding in trains all over Europe
5. Rhine River Cruise
6. Turning somersaults in castle courtyards in Wales
7. Eating pizza in Italy
8. Attending a marionette play in Prague
9. Berlin Zoo
10. Street musicians and artists throughout Europe

from home. Many Christians seek out a historic cathedral or look for a church known for its wonderful art, architecture, or music. Perhaps you would enjoy worshiping in a church in the land from which your ancestors emigrated.

Some of the most deeply moving worship experiences Bill and Amy ever enjoyed were when they worshiped with the locals, taking time to reflect on the unity of God's family. It is inspiring to think that we are all part of the body of Christ, although we sing in different tongues and practice different traditions.

But many of Europe's biggest cities offer church services in English. *The Christian Traveler's Companion* lists some of those churches. You can learn of others from the local church staff or tourist office.

*Q: My husband never wants to go to church when we're away from home. What should I do?*

A: You don't have to be in a formal worship service to worship. The family can gather around a campfire, in a park, or even in your hotel room and read the Bible, sing favorite choruses or hymns, read a devotional, and pray together.

The important thing is for the family to decide what is best for them. You may choose to go to a church one Sunday and do it yourself the next.

*Q: Shouldn't a vacation be fun? Why should I expect my family to learn something while we're traveling?*

A: Learning about Europe's various ethnic groups and traditions will be enlightening and help you and your family better appreciate what you are seeing. A visit to Wittenburg, where Martin Luther tacked his 95 theses to the church door, will be more meaningful if you have a sense of the great danger that he risked in doing so. And Luther's success will seem all the more powerful if you understand the tragedy that befell Jan Hus who died a martyr's death after attempting many of the same reforms a century earlier.

Before going to an area, whet the family's appetite. Prior to a trip to France, learn a few words of French, listen to some French Christmas carols, and read the story of Joan of Arc or Bernard of Clairvaux. Try your hand at creating a few French meals before you leave so family members will have a sense of what to expect when they arrive. With a little prior preparation, your family will find their "educational" trip lots of fun. Children especially love discoveries. If you don't tell them it's educational, they'll never know!

*Q: All of the members of our family have different interests. How can we plan a family vacation that everyone will enjoy?*

A: You cannot please all of the people all of the time, but there are ways to ensure that everyone in your family is pleased some of the time. Sit down with your family (or other traveling companions) and compile a list of the kinds of things a person could do on vacation. These activities should be general rather than specific. For example, listing a visit to an amusement park is permissible, but listing Disneyland Paris is not.

Some of the things that end up on the list may be learning something new, visiting a national park, going to an amusement park, visiting cultural sites like museums and concerts, visiting historic sites, and shopping. Then ask all members of your family to rate

## WHAT BILL'S KIDS LOVED IN EUROPE

1. Running away from all the pigeons in front of Milan's Duomo

2. Chasing a kitty-cat at the Colosseum

3. Staring with wonder at the flowers at the Keukenhof Gardens, Lisse, Netherlands

4. Eating baked Alaska at the Eiffel Tower

5. Watching illuminated yo-yos at night in St. Mark's Square, Venice

6. Enjoying a paddleboat ride on Lake Lucerne

7. Visiting Anne Frank's house and hearing the chimes of the church next door

8. Tossing a lire in the Trevi Fountain in Rome

9. Singing hymns in English in Lamorlaye when everyone else was singing in French

10. Trying to buy a cheese-steak sandwich in Paris

those activities on their own sheet of paper in order of preference. The activity that sounds like the most fun will receive a #1, and the activity that sounds the most boring will receive a #10. When everyone is finished, compare the sheets. Then begin planning a trip that will incorporate everyone's #1, as many #2s as possible, and so on down the lists.

This works especially well in families where interests may be very diverse and compromising skills are limited. Children can be reminded that while they may have to endure a personal #10 at some time on the trip, they will have their own personal #1 to look forward to, as will everyone else.

This rating system ensures that everyone's interests are met on a vacation, but it does much more. It also teaches young people lessons in compromise and respect for others' interests. And you may all learn more about what other family members enjoy.

Q: I would love to travel, but with a young family, we just don't think we can afford it. What can we do?

A: The first key to affording a vacation is to decide that travel really is important. Over the years Amy has taken her family over half the globe on vacations that would sound pretty exotic to most people. But she and her husband decided early in their marriage that travel would be a priority for them. Beyond their personal excitement at the prospect of visiting new places, they recognized the educational value of seeing the world and they wanted to give that gift to their daughters as well.

You may have to sacrifice some things to afford overseas travel. Amy's family has given up cable television, movies, and eating dinner out and they carefully save a set dollar amount every payday to reach their travel goals. There may be other things that you can give up.

Remember that vacations don't have to be elaborate to be valuable. What is important is that you take time away from your daily environment to rejuvenate mind, body, and soul. Disconnect yourselves from the television, telephone, and fax and focus your attention on one another.

Q: But a trip to Europe would be so expensive! How did you manage such expensive vacations?

A: Travel to Europe can be expensive but it doesn't have to be. Restrict your travels within Europe to the rail system. Large European cities are known for their safe, clean subway systems, which run promptly, are easy to use, and cost the equivalent of 1 dollar or less to use. Once you leave the big cities, Europe's network of trains covers nearly every city and small town on the continent. Purchase point-to-point tickets or take advantage of Eurail or other regional rail passes like the Austrian Rail Pass or the France Rail Pass to travel longer distances. You might also consider occasionally buying seats in sleeper cars to combine the cost of lodging with transportation. When you wake up, you'll be in your new destination. (And children love to travel by train!) Visit the comprehensive European rail web site, www.railpass.com, for a listing of all the passes available to you, including point-to-point ticket options, price comparisons, and train schedules, or call 800-722-7151.

You should budget about 100 dollars per day for a family of four for entrance fees to attractions and for food. Since European inns and hotels include breakfast with the room, that's one meal you won't have to worry about. Europe's colorful outdoor markets make shopping for lunch and snacks easy. You can purchase everything you need inexpensively from these vendors and eat a

## AMY'S FAVORITE PLACES IN EUROPE

1. Heidelberg, Germany—Walking along the Philosopher's Way

2. Prague, Czech Republic—The incredible view overlooking Charles Bridge and the city from Hradcany Castle

3. Harlech, Wales—Exploring the ancient castle

4. Venice, Italy—Traveling along the canals

5. Malbun, Liechtenstein—Enjoying the spectacular scenery while hiking through the Alps

6. Salzburg, Austria—Shopping in the Getreidegasse

7. Ulm, Germany—Climbing the world's tallest cathedral spire

8. Amsterdam, Netherlands—Visiting Anne Frank's house

9. Enjoying the view nearly anywhere in Switzerland

10. Naples, Italy—Eating wood-fired pizza in the city that invented it

picnic lunch in the city square or park. Items like fresh produce, cheese, bread, and cold cuts are widely available, and they'll give your family a taste for the local culture. The rest of your food budget can be spent on a more expensive restaurant meal at night.

*Q: Do you have any advice for reducing expensive hotel costs?*

A: Visitors from North America will find that the familiar hotel chains from home and other full-service hotel options are abundant throughout Europe. However, they are often prohibitively expensive, especially for a family. The most economical lodging in Europe will be found in local bed and breakfast establishments or pensions. These are small, privately owned inns located throughout the continent. At the cheapest lodging you will probably be expected to share a community bathroom. Most inns offer private baths for those willing to pay a little more. A family of four should budget about 100 dollars per night for basic lodging in Europe.

You'll pay a little less if you consider staying in youth hostels. Contrary to their names, European hostels (with the notable exception of those in southern Germany) accept guests of all ages, from families with children to senior citizens. Hostels can vary a lot, but you'll find basic, safe surroundings, nearly always located near major train stations, for the equivalent of 10 to 15 dollars per person per night.

Some hostels insist on separating males from females, but most hostels provide family rooms where parents and children can all stay in the same room. While some hostels offer very basic accommodations, with dormitory-style lodging and shared baths down the hall, others are downright luxurious. Many of Germany's Rhine River castles have been converted into hostels. What a fun overnight experience! Visit Hostelling International's web site (www.iyhf.org/) to learn about membership (it will cost about 25 dollars), get a hostelling guide, or book a room on-line. Or call the American hostelling office in Washington at 202-783-6161.

Many of Europe's biggest cities have apartments available for visitors to rent by the week. This may be the cheapest way to stay in big cities if you're traveling with a family, since many hotels do not have rooms with beds for more than two people. An apartment will provide access to your own kitchen, a washer and dryer, and room for your kids to let off a little steam. For a listing of apartment or hotel options, contact your local travel agent or the tourist information number at the beginning of each country listing in this book.

And if you find yourself in need of lodging when you enter a new city, look for the little green *i* signs for local information. These services can help you find a room on short notice within your price range, make the reservation for you, and provide directions too.

*Q: Is it possible to stay in a convent while we're in Europe?*

A: Yes, some convents do offer overnight accommodations, although they are often rather sparsely furnished. Keep in mind that many convents offer rooms for only one gender, depending on whether the order is male or female, and some insist that men and women lodge in separate facilities.

Having said that, convents can offer a wonderfully relaxing atmosphere in which to stay, which can be particularly meaningful to Christians. Safety is almost never a concern, and you don't need to worry about finding yourself in an environment that might run counter to your values.

*Overnight or Short Stay at Religious Houses Around the World,* by James Hughes, is a directory listing over 2,000 religious guest houses operated in 65 countries throughout the world. The book is published by Hugen Press. *The Good Retreat Guide,* by Stafford Whiteaker, lists over 300 religious retreats in the United Kingdom, Ireland, France, and Spain and is published by Rider Books. (Not all of those retreats are Christian, however.) Try contacting your church's international mission board. There may be church members or missionaries overseas that could offer assistance. You can also ask your travel agent for help finding a convent to meet your requirements, or stop at the little green information signs when you arrive at your destination.

*Q: What about the language? Will we be able to get around using English?*

A: English-speaking travelers have a great advantage when they set off on a foreign trip. Nearly all of the rest of the world has made efforts to learn English, particularly young people.

You'll find this to be especially true in Europe. In any big city you will find that knowledge of the local tongue is not necessary.

You can ask to speak with someone who knows English, ask for an English menu, and sometimes even pay in American currency! If you're a North American, you may find that locals recognize you as such immediately and will address you in English before you have a chance to worry. As towns become smaller you'll find you have greater difficulty getting around with English alone.

But even where speaking the local tongue is not a necessity, take the time to learn a few words and phrases anyway. You'll find that you not only avoid communication problems, but your efforts will be appreciated. It takes so little to learn words like *hello, please,* and *thank-you* in a foreign language, and your attempts will go a long way toward breaking the stereotypes of laziness and arrogance that are often attached to English speakers. A trip to your local library for some language tapes will be well worth the effort.

*Q: Is it safe to travel through Europe?*

A: Yes! Most of the cities of western Europe have a considerably lower crime rate than comparable cities in North America. But wherever you go, if you are pegged as a tourist, you may become the target of a pickpocket attempt or a more serious crime. Travel wisely. Use traveler's checks or ATMs and don't carry large amounts of cash in obvious places. Be aware of your surroundings. Always carry your passport with you. And if you run into problems, call for help. You'll be amazed at how quickly locals will rush to your aid.

*Q: I sometimes feel that travel just for the sake of travel is an indulgence that I as a Christian shouldn't allow myself. What do you think?*

A: One of the most meaningful experiences a Christian can have is service travel. But many Christians, especially families, shy away from this type of travel. They don't want to give up valuable vacation time working, they're unsure of their abilities, and they see little opportunity to include children in such a venture.

The fact is that many missions are eager to take any help they can get, even if you are willing to donate just a day or two. And most mission boards have a variety of work opportunities available for a variety of skills, from medical and computer expertise to carpentry, gardening, and painting.

Some service organizations offer free or reduced accommodations and meals in exchange for your time. This can be a real asset to families on a tight budget. And those who live and work in the mission field can share inside information on out-of-the-way places to visit.

If you have an interest in a service trip, begin by determining the area you would like to visit. The more flexible you are the greater the likelihood that you will find a good match.

Next, assess your skills. Is your field of employment transferable to the mission field? How about your hobbies? Don't despair if your answer to these questions is no. Many work sites have a place for people who are willing to do odd jobs, and many offer basic on-site training.

Consider how much time you have available and how the entire family can be part of the experience. Some mission projects offer opportunities specifically designed for families, including young children. But you need to be sensitive to the amount and intensity of the work that you plan for younger family members. This

## BILL'S FAVORITE PLACES IN EUROPE

1. Venice, Italy—St. Mark's Square in the evening

2. Copenhagen, Denmark—Tivoli with the fireworks at night

3. Sognefjord in Bergen, Norway—A boat ride through the fjords is awesome, but so is a train ride

4. Vienna, Austria—In the Stadtpark, watching dancers waltz as peacocks fly to their nests

5. Seville, Spain—A carriage ride through the Old City

6. The Rhine River, Germany—Seeing the castles and the almost-vertical vineyards from aboard ship

7. Cotswold, England—The area is filled with beauty, but the little village of Castle Combe is extra special

8. Florence, Italy—Almost anywhere in the city, but especially the Ponte Vecchio

9. Lisse, Netherlands—The breathtaking 70-acre Keukenhof Gardens

10. Lucerne, Switzerland—The boat ride on the lake and the cog rail up Mt. Pilatus

is their vacation, too, and if you push them into a project that is too demanding or uninteresting, you may sour them on volunteerism for the rest of their lives.

Finally, contact your denomination's mission board. Ask them for a listing of work opportunities. You will probably receive a lengthy listing or booklet to browse through. If you don't find exactly what you're looking for, don't be shy about asking for additional contacts. Most mission boards want to encourage volunteerism in any capacity and are happy to recommend one another.

This is a good way to travel and at the same time feel that you are doing something worthwhile by helping others.

## VALUING TRAVEL

Wherever your journeys take you, whether to a modest bed and breakfast establishment in Wales or to a converted château hotel, learn to value travel as a means of spiritual renewal. Avid travelers already know that travel is fun. With a little preparation your vacation can be more than fun; it can be life changing.

Travel will allow you the time and opportunity to deepen existing relationships with family and friends, as well as to foster new friendships. It will also give you an opportunity to distance yourself from your ordinary life and to seek God's leading. A trip into nature can remind you of God's incredible creative powers. Service travel can change lives forever—including your own—through opportunities to witness and to show Christ's love in action. Travel can also enhance your understanding of other peoples and cultures, and it can remind you of your connections to distant brothers and sisters whom you have never met, who may speak in different tongues and worship in different styles, but who all share the same Father.

It is our hope that you will commit to making all of your travels Christian.

# Andorra

Andorra Tourism
  US 212-750-8064
  UK 020-8874-4806
Web site
  Entire country www.turisme.ad
For a complete list of updated links, visit www.christiantraveler.com

### Country in a Capsule

*Size:* About one-seventh the size of Rhode Island with about one-sixteenth its population.

*Religion:* Most are Roman Catholics (94 percent), but there are about 200 Protestants and 200 Jews in the country.

*Language:* Catalan (the language of Northern Spain) is most commonly used, but French and Castilian Spanish are also widely spoken.

*Money:* French francs and Spanish pesetas are accepted. Andorra has no coinage of its own.

*Food:* Restaurants serve a variety of foods, but Andorrans like trinchat, a mountain specialty mixing potatoes, cabbage, and bacon. Stewed mountain goat is also popular. For breakfast try an omelet with wild mushrooms, or some of the local cheeses like formatge de tupi.

*Shopping:* It's a good place to buy consumables like chocolates and cheese. Perfume is also a good buy, and if you know what you are doing, cameras and computers can be purchased inexpensively.

*Brief history:* Charlemagne is said to have granted Andorra a charter in A.D. 784, but it usually claims its birth date as 1278, when it became a coprincipality of France and Spain. Since then the bishop of Spain's Urgel diocese and a representative of France have both had a say in the government. Today the people of Andorra elect the prime minister.

Andorra welcomes about 12 million tourists a year, mostly skiers.

**Andorra la Vella** This old town of 20,000 is the nation's capital and is loaded with fast-food chains and duty-free shops. It also has department stores and three-story supermarkets. In the largest department store you will find an entire aisle dedicated to chocolates. The city's annual festival is the first Saturday, Sunday, and Monday of August. Andorra la Vella's big attraction, other than its shopping, is the Casa de la Vall (House of the Valley), which overlooks the town's main square. It dates back to 1580, is the seat of Andorra's government, and contains some outstanding religious frescoes.

**Canillo** The area around this town may offer the best skiing in the country. About 1.5 miles east is Sant Joan de Caselles, a Romanesque church that Andorrans are proud of. The bell tower, the highest in the country, is remarkable. Inside, the altarpiece painted by Canillo (1525) shows the life and visions of St. John, and a fresco, *Crucifixion,* depicts a scene from Calvary. In town is the Museu Nacional de l'Automobil, a museum with about 80 antique cars, motorcycles, and bicycles. The Sanctuari de Meritxell is not much to look at (it looks something like a factory), but it is the national sanctuary of Andorra and was built to honor Andorra's patron saint.

**Encamp** Only about four miles from the capital is this old town with a 12th-century church, Sant Roma de les Bons. The medieval buildings are fascinating, and the scenery is great. You may also enjoy riding the Funitel, which is a 20-passenger funicular car/gondola that goes to the ski slopes.

**Les Escaldes** Only a 15-minute walk away from downtown Andorra la Vella is this spa town that boasts Sant Miquel d'Engolasters, a Romanesque church. It's a steep climb up the hill, but once you get there, the view is sensational.

**Ordino** This tiny village is best known for its old church Sant Martide la Cortinado, which has 12th-century frescoes and some remarkable wooden furnishings. Mass is celebrated between 7:00 and 8:00 in the evening.

**Santa Coloma** About 2.5 miles south of the capital city is the very old church, Santa Coloma de les Bons, parts of which date to the 9th and 10th centuries. Frescoes inside date back to the 12th century. You will notice the church because of its round tower, the only one in the country like it.

# *Austria*

Austrian National Tourist Office
  US 212-944-6880
  Canada 416-967-3381
  UK 020-7629-0461
  Australia 02-9299-3621
*Web sites*
  Entire country www.austria-tourism.at
  Graz www.graztourism.at
  Innsbruck www.tiscover.com/innsbruck
  Linz www.tiscover.com/linz
  Salzburg www.salzburginfo.at
  Vienna www.info.wien.at
For a complete list of updated links, visit www.christiantraveler.com

### Country in a Capsule

*Size:* About the same area as South Carolina, but with more than twice as many people.

*Religion:* About 78 percent Roman Catholic and about 6 percent Protestant, split among several groups. Less than 40 percent of the people attend church once a month. The largest Protestant denomination here is the

Evangelical Church of the Augsburg and Helvetic Confessions (Lutheran) with about 400,000 members.

*Language:* German is the national language, but in major cities and in tourist areas, English is understood and spoken. When you are traveling to smaller towns, it is best to know a few German phrases.

*Money:* The Austrian unit of currency is the schilling, which is subdivided into 100 groschen. The schilling is worth about 6 cents.

*Food:* The most famous entrée is wiener schnitzel, which is veal fried in egg and bread crumbs served with potato salad. Dumplings (knodeln) made of liver or flour are sometimes served instead of vegetables. For dessert, the most famous is sachertorte, a chocolate cake with chocolate icing, above a thin layer of apricot jam. Linzertorte is an almond pastry filled with raspberry or apricot jam and covered with a pastry lattice. And then there are many different kinds of strudels.

*Shopping:* Glassware and crystal in Vienna, although prices are higher in major cities and resorts. You might do better price-wise in a smaller city like Linz, or at a showroom or factory outlet of a glassmaker like those near Schrems on the Czech border.

*Brief history:* For Charlemagne, it was his eastern frontier (Ostmark), and gradually that name made its way into the English word Austria. For nearly 300 years it was under the Babenberg dynasty, but when the last of the Babenbergs was killed in battle, the Habsburgs took the throne. For the next three centuries from about 1300 to 1600, the Habsburgs expanded their domain through war, diplomacy, and especially through judicious marriages. Then came the Thirty Years' War in the 1600s, three wars in the 1700s—the War of Spanish Succession, the War of Austrian Succession, and the Seven Years' War. Despite the remarkable reigns of Maria Theresa and her son Emperor Joseph II, Austria was on the decline.

In the 20th century Austria was defeated in World War I and then was a pawn of Hitler in World War II, further reducing its influence and its borders. However, in the last half century, Austria's rapid industrialization and economic advance have revitalized the country, and once again "the hills are alive with the sound of music."

**Vienna** The centerpiece of imperial Vienna is the Hofburg, or Imperial Palace, which is composed of an extensive complex of buildings and courtyards. The fabulous domed entry, St. Michael's Gate (Michaelertor) leads through courtyards into the large grassy plaza known as Hero's Square (Heldenplatz). The complex includes St. Augustine's Church (Augustinerkirche), the National Library (Nationalbibliothek), the Court Chapel (Hofburgkapelle), the Spanish Riding School (Spanische Reitschule), the New Palace Wing (Neue Burg), the Imperial Treasury (Schatzkammer), and the Butterfly House (Schmetterlinghaus). (See details on each of these below.) The various buildings date from the 13th through the 18th centuries. Main streets circling the complex are Opernring, Augustinerstr., Schauflerg., and Dr. Karl Renner-Ring.

St. Augustine's Church (Augustinerkirche), built in the 14th century, is actually part of the larger Hofburg palace complex. The interior of the church has undergone considerable restoration. During the Baroque period the church received the typical gilt and marble flourishes, but in 1780 much of that ornamentation was removed. The sole reminders of the church's one-time ostentation are its gilt organ decoration and the main altar. St. Augustine's Church, on Josefspl., was the court church, and as such the Habsburg rulers' hearts are preserved in a chamber within the church. On Sunday, the 11:00 A.M. mass is sung here in Latin.

The Butterfly House (Schmetterlinghaus) is always popular with children, but even adults can't resist the charms of these delicate and beautiful insects. Part of the larger Hofburg palace complex, the house is alive with hundreds of unusual butterflies. Entrance is in Hofburg's Burggarten.

The Court Chapel (Hofburgkapelle) is home to the world-renowned Vienna Boys Choir, who sing their hearts out in the Gothic chapel that was built in 1449. Visitors need tickets to hear the boys sing mass at 9:15 A.M. Sundays, mid-September through June. Tickets can be purchased through travel agencies (although they are usually much more expensive this way), at the chapel itself (open daily 11:30–1:00 and 3:00–5:00), or by writing at least two months in advance to the Hofmusikkapelle (Hofburg, Schweizerhof, A–1010 Vienna, Austria). General admission runs

AS60 while the prime seats cost AS340. The City Tourist Office (Kärntnerstr. 38, behind Staatsoper) or your hotel travel desk can sometimes help acquire tickets too. A few standing-room-only tickets are available for free. Arrive at the chapel no later than 8:30 A.M. on Sunday to see if there are any spots left.

*Lipizzan stallions.* Vienna's famous Lipizzan stallions appeal to young and old alike, and in a city packed with adult activities, visitors traveling with children are always looking for ways to entertain their youngsters. To see the stallions going through their paces, you'll need to visit the Spanish Riding School. To learn more about the extraordinary horses, visit the Lipizzaner Museum at Reitschulg. 2 in what was once the imperial pharmacy. Exhibits explain the history of the stallions from the 16th century to the present through paintings, videos, and photographs. Visitors can also visit the stables and see the horses up close through a window. You can purchase tickets separately or buy a combination ticket to the museum and a morning training session.

The Lipizzaner stallions are probably the only horses that perform in a building as ornate as the Spanish Riding School, (Spanische Reitschule), a part of the larger Hofburg palace complex. Its interior is gleaming white and is adorned with crystal chandeliers. The white Lipizzaner horses train and perform for thousands every year. When they are relaxing, you can find them stabled across the Reitschulgasse to the east side of the school. For performance schedules and tickets, write to the Spanische Reitschule (Michaelerpl. 1, Hofburg, A–1010 Vienna, Austria) AT LEAST three months in advance. These performances are extremely popular. Travel agents can also acquire the tickets for travelers before they leave. The American Express office sometimes has a few last-minute tickets (Kärntnerstr. 21–23) but expect a hefty surcharge.

Visitors can also watch the two-hour training sessions beginning at 10:00 A.M. Tuesday through Saturday during much of the performance season (tickets available only at the door). The performances are lovely but they aren't cheap. Expect to pay between AS250 and AS900 for regular performances. Training sessions are cheaper at AS100 and may be combined with a ticket to the Lipizzaner Museum for a discounted price. You can phone or fax ticket requests to 01/533-9031-0; fax 01/535-0186. Performances are held March through June and September through mid-December.

*The National Library (Nationalbibliothek).* Part of the larger Hofburg palace complex, the National Library is noted for its fabulous Baroque central hall. It is considered one of Europe's most spectacularly decorated showpieces. The collection of globes in the Globe Museum (on the library's third floor) is fascinating.

*New Palace Wing (Neue Burg).* The vast New Palace Wing, part of the larger Hofburg palace complex, is quite modern by Viennese standards—it was built in the 19th century. It was from this building that Hitler announced the annexation of Austria in 1938. Today the building houses a series of museums, including musical instruments (like Beethoven's piano) and weapons (lots of armor). Christians will be most interested in the Ephesus Museum. Austrian archaeologists did the digging that unearthed the biblical city of Ephesus, and many valuable artifacts from the excavation are on display here. These will enhance your understanding of Paul's Epistle to the Ephesian church.

The ticket that you use to get into the Ephesus Museum also entitles you to enter the Sammlung Alter Musikinstrumente (the musical instrument museum). In this unique collection you will see (and hear) pianos played by Hayden, Beethoven, Schubert, Schumann, Brahms, and Liszt. As you go from room to room, you put on headphones and hear the instruments.

*The Imperial Treasury (Schatzkammer).* In modern times the word *treasury* implies money. The Imperial Treasury, part of the larger Hofburg palace complex, houses items you'd hope to find in a treasure chest. The display is almost overwhelming, including magnificent crown jewels, imperial crowns, regal robes, and other treasures both secular and sacred. A highlight is the imperial crown of the Holy Roman Empire, which is over 1,000 years old.

*Other Vienna churches.* The most unusual aspect of the otherwise common Capuchin Church (Kapuzinerkirche) is its crypt. The Kaisergruft, or imperial vault, is located here and was the resting place of choice of the Habsburg royals. Many sarcophagi are located here, with the oldest tomb being that of Ferdinand II, dating from 1633. The newest tomb is that of the widow of the last kaiser, Empress Zita, who died in 1989. The church is located at Neuer Markt 1.

St. Charles' Church (Karlskirche) on Karlspl. is one of Vienna's best-known landmarks, identified by its classical Baroque facade and dome with two large twin columns. The church was built in the early 18th century by Fischer von Erlach. The interior is surprisingly small and oval in shape. Its ceiling has beautiful frescoes. The Baroque altar is embellished with a stunning sunburst of gilded rays.

St. Stephen's Cathedral (Stefansdom) on Stefanspl. is one of Vienna's most recognizable landmarks, its towering Gothic spires dominating the skyline. Its famous diamond-patterned tile roof is not authentic at all, having been added in the 19th century. The oldest parts of the church are the massive Great Entry (Riesentor), and the Heathens' Towers (Heidentürme), constructed in the 13th century. Inside, the church feels decidedly medieval, with its collection of monuments, sculptures, paintings, pulpits, and tombs, although a number of Baroque flourishes were added in the 17th century. Three hundred and forty-three stairs lead visitors to the top of the south tower, sometimes called Alte Steffl or Old Steve, offering a positively magnificent view of the city. The north tower is ascended by elevator, where visitors can visit the Pummerin, a 22-ton bell cast in part from cannons captured from the Turks in 1683.

St. Mary's on the Bank (Maria am Gestade) on Salvatorg. and Passauer Pl., was built around 1400 and was erected primarily for fishermen from the nearby canal. The church's most intriguing feature is the carved stone latticework "folded hands" spire.

St. Rupert's Church (Ruprechtskirche) is Vienna's oldest church, dating from the 11th century. While the building located on Ruprechtspl. is often closed, it is the location for many local art shows and summer evening classical concerts.

Despite its name, the monks who founded the Scottish Church (Schottenkirche) at Freyung 6 were not Scottish at all, but Irish. The church was originally established in 1177, but the present building dates from the mid–17th century. Don't let the building's plain exterior fool you. The church's interior positively bursts with angels, cherubs, and other flourishes. The Benedictines have established an interesting museum here, the Museum im Schottenstift, and while it is small, it is particularly interesting to Christians for its collection of mainly religious artwork. The museum entrance is in the courtyard.

*Schönbrunn Palace (Schloss Schönbrunn)* is the Versailles of Vienna, a fabulous Baroque residence with lovely formal gardens. The palace was built for the Habsburgs between 1696 and 1713, and has been a summer residence for such dignitaries as Maria Theresa, Napoleon, and Kaiser Franz Josef I. A budding musician, six-year-old Mozart performed in the Hall of Mirrors for Maria Theresa and her court.

The best way to see the palace is on the guided tour, which leads visitors through 40 of 1,441 rooms. Take time to wander the palace grounds as well. Children will especially enjoy the Schöner Brunnen (Beautiful Fountains) for which the palace was named.

On the grounds of the Schönbrunn Palace is a zoo (Tiergarten). This is Europe's oldest zoo, established in 1752 to amuse and educate members of the court. The original Baroque enclosures are used today as viewing pavilions, while the large assortment of animals are housed in more modern cages.

*Museums.* Mozart lived in a small apartment on a narrow street not far from St. Stephen's cathedral from 1784 to 1787. Today the little apartment has been transformed into a commemorative museum called the Mozart Memorial Rooms (Mozart Erinnerungsräume). The museum is at Domg. 5 and features fascinating Mozart memorabilia. It was here that the master is said to have lived the happiest years of his life, composing among other things *The Marriage of Figaro* (which is why the museum is sometimes called the Figaro House).

The Albertina is housed in an unassuming building in the heart of Vienna, but the simplicity of the edifice belies its contents, one of the greatest collections of old master drawings in the world. In fact it is the largest such collection including works by Dürer, Rembrandt, Correggio, and Michelangelo. A number of the works depict religious themes, including Dürer's famous *Praying Hands.* The museum is located at Augustinerstr. 1.

*Am Hof* is a lively square, the name of which translates simply to "At Court." On Thursdays and Fridays in the summer, the square is home to a colorful open-air antiques market, and at other times seasonal markets are held here selling a variety of goods. On the northeast corner of the square is probably the most ornate fire station in the world. And on the east side is the Kirche am Hof, a Baroque church dating from the 17th century. Am Hof is bounded by Tiefer Graben, Naglerg, and Seitzerg.

*The Upper Market (Hoher Markt)* is a square composed of ancient cobblestones. At the center of the square is a massive monument celebrating the betrothal of Mary and Joseph. This sits atop the remains of a 2d-century Roman encampment. Every hour visitors to the square enjoy the charming Anker-Uhr, an animated clock with figures that parade around and mark the hour. A plaque on the clock's lower left identifies the moving figures. The market is located at Judeng. and Fisch-hof Str.

*Music.* There's always plenty of music in Vienna. The city has four symphony orchestras and several major concert halls. The

Vienna Festival is held early May to mid-June. Outdoor symphony concerts are performed weekly in the courtyard of the Rathaus on Friedrich Schmidt-Platz, and many of the churches have outstanding musical events as well.

*The Prater.* Across the Danube Canal along the Praterstrasse, northeast of the city, is Vienna's most famous park, the Prater, and thanks to Emperor Joseph II in 1766, entrance to this amusement park is free, although the rides are not. The landmark attraction is its 200-foot Ferris wheel, which was seen in the 1949 film *The Third Man.* It takes ten minutes to make a complete circuit, and the views of the city are fantastic.

*Unusual Museums.* If your head isn't spinning after the Ferris wheel ride, go to the Clock Museum (Uhrenmuseum), at Schulhof 2 where there are more than 3,000 timepieces, some from the

> ### AUSTRIA
>
> On the Rock of Ages founded,
> What can shake thy sure repose?
> With salvation's walls surrounded,
> Thou may'st smile at all thy foes.
>
> JOHN NEWTON, SUNG TO THE TUNE "AUSTRIA"
> BY FRANZ JOSEPH HAYDN OF VIENNA, AUSTRIA

15th century. If you get there at noon, it's real bedlam. It's a little more peaceful next door at the Doll and Toy Museum (Puppen und Spielzeugmuseum) with teddy bears and trains, as well as dolls and doll houses.

And still another intriguing museum is the Museum of Court Silver and Tableware (Silberkammer) at Michalertrakt. If you want to see the full table settings for royalty, for festive occasions as well as their day-to-day silverware, you will see it here.

*Christmas Market (Christkindlmarkt).* If you pass through Vienna in December, be sure to check out the Christmas market on Rathausplatz. The glitzy street fair includes scores of craft and food booths where you can purchase last-minute Christmas ornaments and gifts.

**Baden** Twenty miles southwest of Vienna is this delightful town known for its Kurpark, where you can often hear outdoor concerts in the afternoon at the pavilion and operetta in its summer arena. Children will enjoy the Doll and Toy Museum (Erzherzog Rainer-Ring 23), and music lovers will spend some time at the

Beethoven House (Rathausgasse 10), where the composer often stayed.

**Christkindl** The name of this village, located two miles west of Steyr, means the Christ Child, so, as you can imagine, it is a popular place around Christmas. The Austrian Postal Service sets up a special post office here each December to send Christmas messages around the world. Nearly two million are sent each year. The only chapel in town, a Baroque chapel, was built in the early 18th century and dedicated to the baby Jesus.

**Ehrwald** Whether it's skiing season or not, you can enjoy the climb up the Zugspitze. You can drive up, you can walk up, or you can take the cable car up the mountain. The upper station of the cable car is at the summit, and the view is gorgeous. At least, it is on a clear day.

**Eisenstadt** This is the hometown of the great Austrian composer Joseph Haydn. The Haydn Haus on Haydngasse contains a small museum. In the Schloss Esterhazy is a Haydn Room (on the first floor) where a Haydn quartet plays in costume every Tuesday and Friday at 11:00 A.M.

**Gänserndorf** About two miles south of town is a combination Safari Park and Adventure Park. You can drive through the natural habitats of live wild animals. If you don't have a car, hop on a safari bus. A petting zoo and animal shows are also available.

**Gmünd** About six miles southwest of Gmünd on Rte. 30 is the fairy-tale castle Heidenreichstein, built in the 15th century, with walls dating back to the 13th century. It is the best preserved of all moated castles in the country, and it is open for tours. There is also a narrow-gauge railway that comes here from Schrems.

**Göttweig** Göttweig Abbey (Stift Göttweig) is one of three old abbeys in the area. The abbey sits high above the Danube across the river from Krems and about 20 miles northeast of Melk on Rte. 303, Furth bei Göttweig. The impressive 11th-century Benedictine abbey offers terrific views of the Wachau valley below. Visitors can stroll through the lovely grounds and visit the chapel. (See also Klosterneuburg and Melk.)

**Graz** With a quarter of a million population, Graz is Austria's second-largest city, but it is often overlooked by tourists. The Old Town of Graz is one of the best historic centers in the German-speaking world.

The Stadtpfarrkirche (on Herrengasse) has organ concerts in the church every Thursday night in the summer. It also has an unusual stained glass feature; in one of the panels there is a depiction of the flagellation of Jesus Christ. The depiction itself is not so unusual, but Hitler and Mussolini shown taking part in the flagellation is unusual.

**Gurk** This small town with a funny name has a great old cathedral in the heart of town, built between 1140 and 1200. Throughout the church, starting with the porch, are murals depicting scenes from the Old and New Testaments. The bishop's chapel behind the facade has a series of Romanesque murals with the inscription in Latin: "Here shines in splendor the throne of the great King and of the Lamb."

**Innsbruck** This city is a tourist haven and to get a good look at it, take a funicular (the Hungerburgbahn) up to the Hungerburg for a delightful overview. The city is rich in history and legends. In the heart of the Old Town is the Annasäule, a monumental column, put up in 1706, thanking the Virgin Mary and St. Anne for a victory in the War of the Spanish Succession. The Tiroler Volkskunstmuseum on Universitätsstr. is an intriguing museum filled with Tyrolean Christian crib scenes on the ground floor, and models of Tyrolean farmhouses on the floor above. One floor above that is a collection of religious folk art from the Tyrol.

The Alpenzoo (Alpine Zoo) at Weiherburgg. 37 offers a unique opportunity to see 150 species of Alpine animals in their native habitat. Many of the animals housed here are extinct in the wild.

Innsbruck's Cathedral (Domkirche) at Dompl. 6 was built in 1722 and dedicated to St. James. The church's interior is decorated with stunning painted ceilings and a high-altar portrait of the Virgin Mary by Lucas Cranach the Elder. The portrait is far older than the cathedral, dating back to about 1520.

The Court Church (Hofkirche) at Universitätsstr. 2 would be a stunning church in its own right. What it is most famous for is its mausoleum and tombs. Maximilian's mausoleum is surrounded by 24 marble reliefs depicting his life's accomplishments, and 28 oversized bronze statues portray his ancestors. Make sure to visit the heavily decorated altar in the Silver Chapel (Silberne Kapelle) dating from the 1500s.

**Klagenfurt** Do you and your kids need a break from museums and churches? Try visiting Klagenfurt's Minimundus, a popular amusement park. More than 150 scale models of the world's most famous buildings and monuments from every major continent make for an enjoyable experience. The United States is represented by the Statue of Liberty, Independence Hall, the White House, and a Mississippi steamboat. The tiny reproductions share space with miniature golf and other fun pastimes. Minimundus is located on Villacherstr. 241.

The Diozesanmuseum on Bahnhofstrasse has an excellent display of religious art from the 12th century to the 18th century. It's a combination of folk art and traditional great works of art.

**Klosterneuburg** There are three lovely old abbeys worth visiting between Vienna and Melk, perched on the banks of the most scenic stretch of the Danube River. Klosterneuburg (Stift Klosterneuburg) is located at Stiftspl. 1 about ten miles outside of Vienna, and its abbey dominates the small market town. Established in 1114, the abbey is a major agricultural landowner in the area and is known for its excellent wines. Daily guided tours are given every hour between 9:00 and 12:00 and 1:30 and 4:30. (See also Göttweig and Melk.)

**Linz** If you want to know what a rococo church looks like, go inside the Wilhering Abbey church, 5 miles southwest of Linz on the south bank of the Danube. Rococo seems to carry flourishes to an extreme. Besides the paintings on the high altar, the frescoes in the side chapels, and the 5,000 square feet of ceiling, there is the elaborate stucco work for which the rococo style is famous. It has been called "the most brilliant example of the rococo style to be found in any of the German-speaking countries."

**Matrei in Osttirol** This town is known as a holiday resort, especially for its skiing, but it is a great place for hiking into the Eastern Alps, and its St. Nikolauskirche is worth some time too. The Glocknerblick chairlift is just one of the options here. Regarding the church, St. Nikolauskirche, it was built before 1200 and has some fascinating 13th-century frescoes in its choir. One depicts creation with Adam and Eve; another focuses on the New Testament and church history. To reach the church, which sits on a hill overlooking the town, take the bridge from the town square to Linzerstr., continue to Bichlerstr., and bear right until you reach the church.

**Melk** The Benedictine Abbey of Melk (Benediktinerstift Melk) is one of the most impressive abbeys in Europe, perched high above the Danube and dominating the landscape. Many visitors also consider it one of the most impressive sights in all of Austria. Its library is renowned for fabulous art as well as books. Be sure to look up at the ceiling frescoes. The abbey is on Abt Berthold Dietmayr-Str. 1 and is one of three lovely abbeys in the area. (See also Göttweig and Klosterneuburg.)

**Murau** If you have a little time on your hands, take a ride on a steam train and see the Mur Valley. It is picturesque, to say the least, at any time of the year. The 46-mile ride to Tamsweg and the return will take you about five hours.

**Oberndorf** The little village of Oberndorf is just 13 miles north of Salzburg, and it has one claim to fame: It was here, on Christmas Eve, 1818, that Franz Gruber composed "Silent Night" to Josef Mohr's lyrics. A little memorial chapel on Oberndorferstr. marks the location where the church was originally located, and inside you'll find a replica of the composition (the original is in the Carolino Augusteum museum in Salzburg). Stained glass windows represent Gruber and Mohr, and there's also a nativity scene inside. The local Heimatsmuseum on Stille-Nacht-Platz also documents the history of the beloved Christmas carol.

**Rattenberg** This is a little frontier town of less than 1,000 people, but it makes the most of what it has. And what it has is the Augustinermuseum, founded in 1384, containing some Tyrolean art treasures; and the Pfarrkirche

> Silent night, holy night, Son of God, love's pure light,
> Radiant beams from Thy holy face,
> With the dawn of redeeming grace,
> Jesus, Lord, at Thy birth.
>
> JOSEF MOHR OF OBERNDORF, AUSTRIA

St. Virgil, alongside the castle bluff, with frescoes of the Last Supper in the main nave and of the transfiguration in the chancel.

**Salzburg** The films *Amadeus* and *The Sound of Music* are both set in Salzburg, and now everyone wants to see what this city is really like.

*Mozart.* Salzburg's connections with Mozart are legendary, and the city will remind you of those ties at every turn. Never mind that during Mozart's life he was little appreciated, that he died thinking himself a failure, and that he was buried in a pauper's grave. Today Salzburg loves the composer like no other. Mozart's birthplace (Mozart Geburtshaus) is located on the famous and lovely pedestrian street, the Getreidegasse. Located on the small Hagenauerplatz, and distinctly labeled as Mozart's Geburtshaus (the official address is Getreideg. 9), the small house is now a museum filled with memorabilia of the composer's life. Directly across the Salzach River at Makartpl. 8 is the Mozart Residence (Mozart Wohnhaus) where the composer's family lived for some years. Today the building includes a small recital hall and the Mozart Audio and Film Museum. If you plan to visit both places, buy a combination ticket that includes both locations. It's cheaper than buying tickets individually.

*Music and theater.* Ever since Mozart, Salzburg has been a city in love with music. Write or fax ahead for tickets to the world-famous Salzburg Festival (Salzburger Festspiele), which provides hours of listening pleasure in late July and August. You can also obtain tickets to the Easter Festival (in early April) and the Pentecost Concerts (late May) from the same source: Salzburger Festspiele, Postfach 140, A–5010 Salzburg, Austria; fax 0662/8045-760. Don't wait until you arrive, as it is very difficult to obtain tickets on short notice.

Then there is the famous Marionettentheater (at Schwarzstrasse 24) where some of the great operas like *The Magic Flute* and *Figaro* are staged and you forget that the actors are mere puppets.

*Salzburg's Dom* (cathedral) at Dompl. 1, is stunning. Visitors enter through huge bronze doors. Inside, a small museum houses a church treasury that is hundreds of years old.

*Salzburg Fortress (Festung Hohensalzburg)* was built in the 12th century, and it has dominated the city's skyline ever since. To reach the mighty castle, walk along the narrow Festungsgasse at the end of Kapitalplatz. You can either walk the footpath up the hill or take a five-minute ride on the funicular (Festungsbahn). The footpath is more work, but it offers the most breathtaking views of the city—views that will impress even the most hard-to-please visitors. Don't miss the fortress's main attraction, St. George's Chapel, which was built in 1501. The chapel acquired its 200 pipe organ in 1502. It is played daily in summer at 7:00 A.M., 11:00 A.M., and 6:00 P.M. Some of the best views of the city are from the Hohensalzburg.

*Franciscan Monastery.* You'll recognize the 13th-century Franciscan Monastery (Franziskanerkloster) at Franziskanerg. 5 by its tall graceful spire. Architecturally the church is a mix of Romanesque and Gothic styles, and the Baroque altar is note-

## GRÜSS' GOTT!

The standard Austrian greeting is Grüss' Gott, which means literally, "Greet God." Travelers in Austria quickly see how reasonable it was for the Austrians to have come up with this kind of greeting. God's handiwork abounds in the snowcapped mountain peaks, crystal-clear lakes, and fields of wildflowers.

Hohe Tauern National Park is Europe's largest national park, encompassing more than 200 glaciers and more than 300 mountains. The park takes its name from the Tauern, or ice-free footpaths, that traverse the landscape. The Glocknergruppe is the mountain range lying in the heart of the park, home of the Grossglockner, Austria's highest mountain peak. Travelers can enjoy the great natural beauty from their car window as they travel along the Grossglocknerstrasse, one of the world's most spectacular mountain roads.

The town of Krimml makes a nice base from which to explore the area by foot, including the 1,300-foot Krimml Waterfalls. Nearby Zell am See has no less than five cable cars that ascend surrounding snowcapped peaks for terrific views. Or pick up hiking information in the Wanderplan, available throughout town.

To enjoy the beauty of the Danube River, consider traveling by bicycle. A paved bike path stretches all the way from Salzburg to Vienna by way of Passau and Linz. The flat terrain and scenic beauty make for ideal biking conditions, even for youngsters. Numerous villages lie scattered along the way with castles to visit, parks to run around in, and plenty of shops and restaurants to explore. Bicycles can be rented locally. Contact the Austrian National Tourist Office for detailed information, or look for the green *i* sign located in nearly every city or town in Austria.

worthy. Consider attending mass on Sunday at 9:00. The music is frequently Mozart.

*The Collegiate or University Church (Kollegienkirche or Universitätskirche)* was established in 1707 and designed by Fischer von Erlach, the Baroque master. The church is one of the finest examples of Baroque architecture in Europe. The church is located on Universitätspl.

*Hellbrunn Castle (Schloss Hellbrunn)* lies south of Salzburg in the little burg of Hellbrunn. The castle was built in the 17th century for royalty and remains popular today, although most of its visitors can claim no royal lineage. When the castle was built, a unique system of Wasserspiele—hidden water jets that unexpectedly spit at passersby—was hidden in its gardens to entertain the resident royals. Don't be surprised if you get sprinkled on your visit. As you might imagine, this feature makes Hellbrunn Castle a hit with kids. Tours are available daily from 9:00 to 5:00, with additional evening hours in July and August.

In the park complex of the Hellbrunn Castle are two other attractions that may interest families. The Monatsschlössl is a historic hunting lodge, which presently houses a small folklore museum. And a sure hit with any family is the Tiergarten (zoo), which is considered outstanding for its natural animal enclosures. The zoo is open daily.

*The Bürgerspital* at Bürgerspitalg. 2 was built as a hospital centuries ago. Today its purpose is a little more entertaining; it is the home of a toy and musical instruments museum (Spielzeug Museum). Visitors may want to consider purchasing a combined ticket with the Carolino Augusteum Museum (the city art and archeology museum at Museumspl. 1), the cathedral's excavations, and the Folklore Museum at Schloss Hellbrunn to save money over buying the tickets separately. Take note of the 15th-century royal Pferdeschwemme, or horse watering trough, nearby on Herbert-von-Karajan-Platz.

*St. Peter's Cemetery*, its catacombs, and the adjacent St. Peter's Abbey, all clustered around St. Peter Bezirk, are must-sees for every Christian traveling to Salzburg. Two wrought iron gates lead into the small graveyard where several notable people were buried, including Mozart's sister Nannerl, Haydn's brother Michael, and the cathedral's architect.

The graves were placed as close as possible to Mönchsberg, Salzburg's mountain, and they adjoin monks' cells and catacombs carved into the cliffs. Two ancient tiny chapels are hewn out of the rock, dating from the 3d century when Christianity was outlawed by the Roman state. Converted Romans tunneled into the rock and worshiped here secretly until Constantine made Christianity the official religion of the empire. Tours of Salzburg's ancient catacombs leave from the cemetery. Tours are run daily at 10:30, 11:30, 1:30, 2:30, and 3:30, by guides who offer descriptions in a variety of languages, including English.

St. Peter's Abbey (Stift St. Peter) at St. Peter Bezirk just off Kapitalpl., is a late-Baroque masterpiece widely considered the most luxurious church in Salzburg. The church is the final resting place of St. Rupert, who founded a monastery on the city's mountain, Mönchsberg, or Monk's Mountain. Taken together, the catacombs, cemetery, and St. Peter's offer a moving history of Christianity in a nutshell, from secret worship under the fear of persecution to the most glorious and public religious art in the city. Those early Christians would have been pleased.

*Schloss Leopoldskron*, located about 2 miles south of town on Leopoldstr., was the castle made famous by *The Sound of Music*. It was built in 1744 as a summer residence for an archbishop and then was bought in 1918 for cultural and artistic purposes by one of the founders of the Salzburg Festival. Certainly it is a romantic setting for a movie. Maria von Trapp was indeed brought up by Benedictine nuns in Salzburg, but you have to allow the scriptwriter a bit of artistic latitude.

**St. Florian** The abbey here, at Kleinmünchen and Ebelsberg, the largest in Upper Austria, has been a learning center as well as a religious center for nearly 1,000 years. Florian had been the chief Roman administrator of the territory before he became a Christian. Because of his conversion, he was martyred. Near the site of his grave, the St. Florian monastery was built. The present abbey, which was rebuilt in the early 18th century, is 702 feet long, with three great towers on top of it. Inside is a library of more than 140,000 books, including many valuable early texts. The Altdorfer Galerie, which is the abbey collection of art, is a showcase for the paintings of Albrecht Altdorfer, a 16th-century painter. His scenes of the passion of Christ are particularly moving. Austria's greatest 19th-century composer of religious music, Anton Bruckner, attended choir school here, taught here, and became the organist here. According to his desires, he is buried beneath the organ, which had aided him in gaining international fame as a composer.

**St. Wolfgang** For hundreds of years the faithful have come here to pay homage to the city's namesake. St. Wolfgang is credited with constructing the first chapel in town during the 11th century on the location of the present-day 15th-century Pfarrkirche (parish church). The church is loaded with art masterpieces. The 1481 Michael-Pacher Altar and the 39-foot-high altarpiece show scenes from the life of the Virgin Mary. A second altarpiece, completed about 200 years later, depicts the holy family on their way to Jerusalem. St. Wolfgang's beautiful location has attracted thousands of visitors, religious or otherwise, in modern times. Since the church doesn't have a large parking lot, consider parking at the Schafberg train station about 1/2 mile from the Pfarrkirche and walking from there.

**Traunkirchen** The Pfarrkirche was rebuilt in its present form in 1632, but its predecessor was part of an abbey of the 11th century. Corpus Christi festivals are major celebrations in many parts of Austria and certainly in Traunkirchen. Located on the Traunsee, the church has a Fisherman's Pulpit, made in the form of the disciples' fishing boat, including the dripping nets. The decoration in the church carries the water motif further as it remembers the life of St. Francis Xavier, who introduced Christianity to Japan, but in the course of his voyage he was shipwrecked and lost his crucifix. According to the artist's rendition of the story, a lobster came to his rescue, found the crucifix, and returned it to him.

**Wels** If you are a bird watcher and you want some peace and quiet, travel about four miles north of Wels to the Vogelpark von Schmiding (bird reserve). About 200,000 visitors come here each year, so you won't have the huge reserve to yourself, but since 350 different species of birds live here, you will probably be able to spot a few of them. And you will also be able to spot a few antelopes, monkeys, kangaroos, and gazelles. How did they get into a bird reserve?

**Werfen** Not far from Salzburg near the town of Werfen is the World of the Ice Giants (Eisriesenwelt), on Rte. E14/A10 the largest complex of ice caves in Europe. The formations inside the caves look much like those you might see in earthen caves, but all of the stalactites and stalagmites are created from ice. Keep in mind that no matter what the temperature is outside, it will be well below freezing inside the cave. Dress appropriately and wear shoes with good treads. The tour is rather strenuous. The cable car on site climbs only about half the distance up, and once inside the cave you will encounter plenty of stairs. Tours are conducted in German, but the giant frozen waterfalls, domes, and halls are worth seeing and are popular with kids.

**Zell am Zee** This is a great starting point for a hike; in fact you have several options of what direction to go. The most famous way is the Pinzgau walk, which will take six hours. It's not difficult, but you need to be in decent shape to do it. The route is well marked and you can return by cable car and bus to Zell am Zee. A shorter trip is up the Schmittenhohe. Both walks provide you with sensational scenic views of the area.

# *Belgium*

Belgium Tourist Office
  US 212-758-8130
  Canada 514-484-3594
  UK 0891-887-799
*Web sites*
  Entire country www.belgium-tourism.com
  Antwerp www.dma.be
  Brugge www.brugge.be
  Brussels www.tib.be
  Gent www.gent.be
For a complete list of updated links, visit www.christiantraveler.com

### Country in a Capsule

*Size:* About the same size as the state of Maryland but with twice as many people. Its largest city, Brussels, has a population of a million, and its second largest, Antwerp, has a population of about a half million.

*Religion:* About 75 percent Roman Catholic; about 50,000 Protestants, with Belgian Evangelical Church, Assemblies of God, Southern Baptists, Plymouth Brethren, and Churches of Christ having the largest numbers.

*Language:* More than half speak Flemish-Dutch, about 38 percent speak French, and fewer than 5 percent speak German. Each region in Belgium has its own official language.

*Money:* The Belgian franc is the currency in all regions of Belgium, and it is also accepted in Luxembourg. At press time the franc is worth about 2 cents.

*Food:* Regional specialties include rabbit with prunes, Flemish braised beef, beer and onions, and boiled goose. Belgians also enjoy hops shoots in a mousseline sauce or Brussels chicory baked with cheese and ham. Naturally, brussels sprouts and Mechelen asparagus are on the menu. Belgian ice cream is also very good.

*Shopping:* Belgian chocolates are always a good and tasty buy. Brussels and Bruges have long been known for lace.

*Brief history:* In 51 B.C. Julius Caesar conquered a fierce Celtic tribe known as the Belgae, and that is the origin of the country's name. Christianized in the 7th century, Belgium was absorbed into the Frankish Empire in the 8th century. In the 16th century, the Low Countries (Netherlands and Belgium) were brought under Catholic Spanish rule, which Protestant Netherlands didn't like, but Catholic Belgium didn't mind. Netherlands broke away in 1581, but Belgium was passed around from country to country, one war after another, going from Spain to Austria to France and to the Netherlands, until 1839 when Belgium's independence was recognized. Today Belgium is a parliamentary, constitutional monarchy with a prime minister. The legislature is composed of a 212-member Chamber of Deputies.

**Brussels** You can describe Brussels in a variety of ways, and you'll be right. It's a dignified, button-down kind of city: It is the home of NATO and of the EU, and its World Trade Center and Manhattan Center are impressive tower blocks. It is a city of culture: Its Museum of Ancient Art, its annual Queen Elizabeth Festival each

*45*

spring, and its Europalia Festival are internationally regarded. It is a fun-loving city: The citizenry find every excuse they can to have a party, a parade, or a festival. It is also a religious city, although certainly not as religious as it used to be.

*Cathedrals.* If you have rationed yourself to just one church in Brussels, see the Cathédrale St-Michel et Ste-Gudule. This cathedral on Parvis Ste-Gudule is named for the archangel and a little-known local saint of the 7th century. This is the main cathedral in Brussels. Its construction was begun in 1226 and combines Romanesque and Gothic architectural styles. Against the nave are statues of the 12 apostles. Its real treasures include an elaborately carved pulpit, dating from 1699, that depicts Adam and Eve being banished from the Garden of Eden. The stained glass windows were designed by an early 16th-century court painter, Bernard van Orley. Visitors can see what's left of the original 11th-century Romanesque church in the crypt.

Free Sunday morning and lunchtime concerts take place at the Cathédrale St-Michel et Ste-Gudule, as well as at the Eglise des Minimes at rue des Minimes 62. For more information, as well as other churches throughout the city that offer concerts, visit the churches' information desks.

*Museums.* Not far from the Cathedral (to give you another side of Brussels) is the Museum of Comic Strip Art, at rue des Sables 20, known in Brussels as Centre Belge de la Bande Dessinée. Housed here are 3,000 original plates by the greatest comic strip writers, though only 300 are on display at any one time. In another section you can see how comic strips are made.

If you want to go from the ridiculous to the sublime, go next to the Museum of Ancient Art (Musée d'Art Ancien), at rue de la Régence 3, which is internationally known for its masterpieces by Bruegel the Elder and Rubens. Room 31 is where Bruegel shines, and here you see his *Fall of the Rebel Angels* and *Census at Bethlehem*. The works of Rubens are scattered throughout. Note especially his *Ascent to Calvary*.

Another fascinating museum, especially if any family members play musical instruments, is the Musée Instrumental, which houses a collection of 6,000 musical instruments. Adolphe Sax, inventor of the saxophone, was from Belgium, so wind instruments are given favored treatment on the ground floor. The next floor is devoted to keyboard instruments, and then you work your way up to stringed instruments.

If the only horn you toot is your automobile horn, you might try Autoworld, with 450 vehicles on display in the south hall of the Palais du Cinquantenaire at Parc du Cinquantenaire 11. The oldest car on display is the 1896 Léon Bollée minicar.

*The Grand-Place* is a row of ornate Baroque guild houses, completed in 1695. The tops of the buildings are manned by gilded statues of saints and heroes. The area is today one of Europe's most popular market squares, featuring a colorful flower market open daily from spring right through to the end of the growing season. On summer nights you can enjoy music in the well-lit square, and you can always find an interesting place to shop or dine. During the Christmas holiday the square is home to the European Christmas Market. Stalls sell wares from many different nations, and a life-size nativity scene is animated with real animals. The square is bounded by the rue du Beurre, rue du Chair et du Pain, rue des Harengs, rue de la Colline, rue de l'Etuve, and rue de la Tête d'Or.

The dominant structure in the Grand-Place is the Town Hall (Hôtel de Ville), which was constructed about 300 years prior to the guild houses, around 1400. Notice the central tower atop the building. It includes a statue of St. Michael (the creature that he's crushing under his feet is the devil).

*The Grand Sablon* is a fashionable square, filled with restaurants, cafes, art galleries, and antique shops. The elaborate Gothic church at the upper end of the square is the Notre-Dame du Sablon, built in 1304 by the crossbowmen who used to train here. Light glows from within the church at night, illuminating the beautiful stained glass windows and creating a lovely spectacle. Outside the church on weekend mornings a colorful antiques market is held. At the lower end of the Grand Sablon stands the 12th-century Eglise Notre-Dame de la Chapelle. Its Gothic exterior and unlikely Baroque belfry have recently been restored. The square is located at the junctions of rue des Minimes, rue des Pigeons, rue Stevens, rue de Rollebeek, rue Libeau, rue de la Paille, rue Sainte-Anne, rue Rodenbroek, rue des Sablons.

*Brussels' open-air markets* are fascinating. Enjoy some of the local color and do a little shopping at the antiques and book market on Place du Grand-Sablon, the flea market on Place du Jeu-de-Balle, or at the bird market on Grand-Place.

*Theaters and parks.* Young and old alike will love the Toone Marionette Theater (Théâtre de Marionettes Toone) at Impasse Schuddeveld off Petite Rue des Bouchers. The tiny family-run theater uses only puppet actors. Plays may include everything from Shakespeare classics to more modern stories. Most are performed in Flemish, but don't let that stop you. You'll be able to follow the action, and you may already know the story lines. Ask about occasional performances in English, or in French or Dutch if you like. The adjoining museum is free to those who have purchased a ticket to the show. Daily performances are at 8:30 P.M.

In Heysel, just north of downtown Brussels is Mini-Europe. Maybe you can save your money on traveling elsewhere on the continent and see it all here. This five-acre park is filled with miniature buildings from the 15 members of the European Union countries, including scale models of Athens' Acropolis, Madrid's El Escorial, the English city of Bath, Danish Viking longhouses, and others. The park is located at bd. du Centenaire 20.

Children between the ages of 2 and 12 will love the Children's Museum (Musée des Enfants) at rue du Bourgmestre 15. The hands-on museum's activities include dressing up in crazy costumes, playing with goo, finding your way through a hall of mirrors, and crawling through tunnel mazes.

In Anderlecht, just southwest of the city is the Maison d'Erasme (Erasmus's House), rue du Chapître 31, built in 1468. Actually it wasn't really Erasmus's house, but he was a frequent guest here, and you can see his study and where he probably slept. He paved the way for Luther's Protestant Reformation, although he refused to go along with Luther's revolutionary changes.

**Aarschot** Onze-Lieve-Vrouwekerk, a lovely sandstone church, dates from the 14th century and has a tower about 280 feet high. *Disciples of Emmaus*, a painting by P. J. Verhagen, is on the south side of the church.

**Aisne Valley** A scenic tramway follows the valley to the village of Forge. It's a worthwhile excursion.

**Antwerp** Antwerp may be number two in population, but it doesn't have to apologize for anything. There is plenty to see and do here.

*Cathedral of Our Lady.* The white 400-foot Gothic spire of the Cathedral of Our Lady (Onze-Lieve-Vrouwekathedraal) on Handschoenmarkt can be seen from far away. Begun in 1352, work continued for more than 200 years. Paintings and statues have been stolen from the church countless times by numerous armies, but you can still view four Rubens altarpieces. His *Descent from the Cross* is accompanied by paintings depicting Mary's visit to Elizabeth and Jesus' presentation in the temple. The masterpieces are commonly considered some of the most touching biblical paintings ever created. The cathedral is the largest in Belgium and it houses a carillon of 47 bells. On Monday nights you can enjoy beautiful carillon concerts. Consider listening from the Vlaeykensgang, a cobblestone alley in the downtown area where you can imagine yourself transported back in time to 16th-century Belgium.

Antwerp is sometimes known as the City of Madonnas. A statuette of the Virgin Mary is located on many streetcorners throughout the city.

*The Antwerp Zoo (Dierentuin)* at Koningin Astridplein 26 houses animals in settings reminiscent of their original habitats. For example, the giraffes and ostriches are in an Egyptian temple and the okapis are located near an Indian temple. There is also a winter garden, a dolphin area, an aquarium, and a planetarium, as well as a restaurant on site.

*Museums.* The Museum Plantin-Moretus at Vrijdagmarkt 22 will introduce you to Christophe Plantin. Plantin was a religious dissident as well as a well-known printer in the city of Antwerp. He founded a printing house here that flourished for no less than 300 years, and the presses still work today. He is best known for his Biblia Regis, a Bible printed in five languages (Hebrew, Syrian, Greek, Latin, and Aramaic). It is exhibited on the first floor along with a rare copy (one of only 13 in the world) of the Gutenberg Bible. All told there are 25,000 old books here, besides priceless paintings and engravings. In the museum you will see many portraits by Rubens.

Rubenshuis, at Wapper 9, the home of Rubens for most of his life, can be seen here including his large studio. The studio contains a gallery in which the artist could display his paintings to students and visitors.

St. Jacobskerk, a few blocks east of the Cathedral of Our Lady, is decorated in Baroque style and contains several outstanding paintings, including Jordaens's *The Calling of St. Peter*.

Just southwest of the city center is the Royal Museum of Fine Art (Koninklijk Museum voor Schone Kunsten), Leopold de Waelplaats 2, an unusually notable collection of paintings, with two rooms devoted to Rubens. In the corner of the first floor is a room full of Dutch paintings, where Rembrandt's *Portrait of a Preacher* is displayed.

The Museum Leonardo da Vinci, west of the city in the suburb of Tongerlo, contains a copy of the *Last Supper* that was painted only 20 years after the original that graces the wall of a convent in Milan, Italy. This copy came to Tongerlo in 1525. Music and commentary explain the biblical scene that the artist has depicted. Tongerlo is also home to a large abbey associated with the Premonstratensian order.

The Vleeshuis, once the guild hall for butchers, is now a fascinating museum of decorative arts, musical instruments, and archaeology. Panels of earthenware tiles depict the conversion of Paul, and here you will see some old harpsichords. Antwerp was famous for its harpsichords 300 years ago. The museum is located at Vleeshouwersstraat 38–40.

The Open-Air Sculpture Museum (Openluchtmuseum voor Beeldhouwkunst Middelheim) displays more than 400 sculptures on about 30 acres in Middelheim Park. Rodin is included as well as modern sculptors like Calder.

**Bastogne** On December 22, 1944, the American officer, General McAuliffe, was ambushed in Bastogne by German troops and asked to surrender. The weather was cold, snowy, and foggy, and his troops were virtually surrounded. His famous reply was, "Nuts." Thus began the Battle of the Bulge. But the next day the weather cleared, and supplies were airlifted in to McAuliffe's forces. A month later, the German front line was defeated. Remembering McAuliffe's reply, Belgians here have a walnut festival each December.

Commemorating the Allied victory, an Allied tank sits in the town center, accompanied by a bust of McAuliffe. A large monument 2 miles east of town on N84 is dedicated to the American soldiers who died in the Battle of the Bulge. But also note the Eglise St. Pierre, a 15th-century church with scenes from the Old and New Testaments.

**Bokrijk** Domein Bokrijk is an open-air museum, playground, nature preserve, and rose garden on a large provincial estate that once belonged to the Herkenrode Abbey. A narrow-gauge railway encircles the estate. The open-air museum has about 100 buildings on a 222-acre site. Divided into four sectors, the museum gives you a look at what Flemish provincial life was like in past centuries.

**Brugge (Bruges)** If you suddenly opened your eyes after you had entered this city, you would think you were in the Middle Ages. The buildings, the churches, the canals all transport you back to a time long past. If you can rent a bike, take a horse-drawn carriage ride, or loll in the back of a boat, those are the best ways to enjoy this city.

*Basilica of the Holy Blood.* Located on the corner of the Burg, next to the Town Hall, is the Basilica of the Holy Blood (Heilig-Bloed Basiliek). The Lower Chapel is the oldest portion of the building, built in a somber 12th-century Romanesque style. The Upper Chapel was rebuilt in the 15th century and again in the 19th century, when it received its elaborate Gothic stairway. The basilica has a vial of what is said to be a few drops of Christ's blood, which can be seen by the public here every Friday. (It was brought back from the Holy Land on the Second Crusade.) The Museum of the Holy Blood (Heilig-Bloed Museum) has a reliquary and some lovely paintings. The Procession of the Holy Blood takes place annually on Ascension Day, an elaborate combination of religious and historical pageantry.

*The Béguinage (Begijnhof)* off Wijngaardstraat has been considered an oasis of peace for over 750 years. The first Beguines consisted of widows of fallen crusaders. While they were not nuns, they lived a devout life of service to the community. The last Beguines left the small whitewashed houses in 1930, but a Benedictine community replaced them. You may join them, if you're quiet and discreet, for vespers in their small church.

*The Memling Museum* at Mariastraat 38 is dedicated to the fine art of local painter Hans Memling. While Memling is not a widely recognized name in America, he is considered the greatest and most spiritual of the early Flemish painters. There are six masterpieces in the museum, including the altarpiece, *St. John the Baptist and St. John the Evangelist.* There are also a number of Memling miniatures surrounding the St. Ursula shrine. The building itself has a connection to Christianity. It was at one time the St. John's Hospital (Sint-Janshospitaal), where the sick and invalid were treated for more than 700 years. The 17th-century pharmacy is open for visitors as well.

*The Groeninge Museum* at Dijver 12 enjoys a reputation much larger than its building's small size. Its terrific and varied collection includes a large number of paintings by Flemish masters, most with religious themes, including Van Eyck's *Virgin and Canon*

*Vander Paele,* Pieter Bruegel's *Preaching of John the Baptist,* Memling's *Moreel Triptych,* and Hieronymus Bosch's *Last Judgment.*

The *Church of Our Lady (Onze-Lieve-Vrouwekerk),* reaching 381 feet into the air, is the tallest brick structure in the world. Inside are a number of other noteworthy achievements. A collection of paintings and carvings are among its treasures, including the small *Madonna and Child* by Michelangelo. The elaborate tombs inside are those of Duke Charles the Bold of Burgundy, who died in battle in 1477, and his daughter Mary, who married into the Habsburg family and died at age 25. The church is on Gruuthusestraat.

*Canals.* One of the most endearing parts of Brugge is its maze of *reien,* or canals, and the old, arching stone bridges that cross them. Explore on foot, or take a boat ride for a different perspective of the city. You can get more information on boat tours at the Brugge Tourist Office (Toerism Brugge) at Burg 11.

*Flea market.* If you are there on a Saturday afternoon, you won't want to pass up the flea market on Dijver near the Kantmuseum (Lace Museum). Lace in the stores can be expensive, but sometimes it's available in the flea market for less.

**Charleroi** If you are interested in photography, visit the Musée de la Photographie at av. Paul Pastur 11. You can see how the art developed (as well as how photos develop), and you can see work by some of the world's finest photographers. There's also a Christian connection—the museum is housed in an old abbey.

**Diest** Averbode Abbey, 5 1/2 miles northwest of Diest, was founded by the Premonstratensian order in 1134 and 1135 and is one of the principal abbeys of the order. The Premonstratensian (sometimes called Norbertine) order is the largest Catholic order in Belgium. The abbey church is lovely with statues of St. Norbert on the right and John the Baptist on the left. Norbert was the founder of the order, which is based on the Rule of St. Augustine.

**Gent (Ghent)** St. Bavo's Cathedral (Sint-Baafskathedraal) on Sint-Baafsplein is worth visiting if only for its van Eyck masterpiece. In the De Villa Chapel is the extraordinary *Adoration of the Mystic Lamb,* a 24-panel painting completed in 1432. Thought to have been one of the first oil paintings ever created, the painting's central panel is based on Revelation 14:1: "And I looked, and, lo, a Lamb stood on Mount Sion, and with him an hundred forty and four thousand."

In medieval times, a time before literacy was commonplace, this painting was considered a theological summation of all things revealed about the relationship between God and the world. The painting has been stolen and recovered many times. During World War II, it was entrusted to the French; German authorities found it and sent it to Austria. But in 1945 U.S. troops found it in a salt mine and returned it to the cathedral here. The cathedral's other treasures include a Rubens masterpiece, *The Vocation of St. Bavo*. The convert cloaked in red is the artist himself. Notice also the altarpiece, *Jesus among the Doctors* by Pourbus the Elder. In the crypt below is a 9th-century gospel book and an interesting Calvary triptych by van Gent. You may attend on Sundays for worship, but you are not allowed to visit the chapel or explore during services.

The Museum voor Volksskunde (Folk Museum) at Kraanlei 65 shows you what life was like a hundred years ago in this city. There is also a theater here with traditional Gent puppets.

The Fine Arts Museum (Museum voor Schone Kunsten) at Nicolaas de Liemaeckereplein 3 displays a wide array of paintings and sculptures from the Middle Ages to the early 20th century. Included in the collection are a large number of works based on religious themes, including Hieronymus Bosch's *St. Jerome* and *The Bearing of the Cross*. The tapestries here are unusually fine as well.

**Han-Sur-Lesse** The Grottes de Han at rue J. Lamotte 2 is a limestone cave system that is almost ten miles long. The tour by tramway takes you about one-fifth of the way. The sound and light show is impressive. When you have emerged from your subterranean explorations, you can take a little train through a magnificent estate containing a variety of forest animals. This is the Reserve d'Animaux Sauvages.

**Huy** For years local residents have bragged about four things: their bridge, the rose window in their church, their fountain on the plaza, and their fortress. To get an overview of the town, take a boat trip on the Meuse River. Then take a cable car up to the fortress for a different look at the town. And don't forget to take a look at the rose window (30 feet across) in the church, the Eglise Collégiale de Notre-Dame (Collegiate Church of Our Lady), at rue de Cloître.

**Ieper (Ypres)** This town was completely destroyed in World War I. It is hard to imagine, but 300,000 Allied troops were killed here. Now there are more than 170 military cemeteries in the area. Three miles east of town, past several military cemeteries, is Belle-waerded Park, where you and your family can take a safari tram ride through an African landscape, see lions and tigers, and go under a waterfall.

**Leuven (Louvain)** The world-famous Louvain University, founded in 1425, is located here. The university's French-speaking students attend the campus in Louvain-la-Neuve, while its Flemish speakers study at the campus in the city proper. It became a model for universities throughout Europe. It now has about 25,000 students. The great philosopher Erasmus founded the Three Languages College, where Hebrew, Latin, and Greek were taught.

While you are in town, visit St. Pieterskerk on Grote Markt, a 15th-century Gothic church, and see van der Weyden's *Descent from the Cross,* a statue of the Madonna and Child, and a huge wooden statue of Christ.

If you enjoy religious art, visit the Museum of Religious Art (Museum voor Religieuze Kunst). Highlights include Dirck Bouts's *Last Supper* and a 13th-century wood carving head of Christ (Tête de la Croix Torturée).

**Liège** This city of about 150,000 people has several major churches, mostly on the west bank of the Meuse River. Eglise St-Barthélemy on pl. St-Barthélemy was consecrated in 1015 and contains Liège's greatest treasure, a half-ton brass baptismal font created by artist Art Mosan. Eglise St-Jacques on pl. St-Jacques is known for its magnificent architecture, its 15th-century Pietà, and its 17th-century organ. Eglise St-Jean, just off blvd. de la Souveniere on the west bank of the Meuse River, built around 1200, is known for its wooden statues of Mary and John as well as Madonna and Child.

The Museum of Religious Art and Mosan Art (Musée d'Art Religieux at d'Art Mosan) houses local religious art from the early Middle Ages. Of particular interest are the many statues of Mary in silver and gold.

**Mechelen (Mechlin)** This city of about 70,000 is the residence of the Roman Catholic primate of the country, and it is famous for its carillons, its lace-making, its furniture, its brewing, and its asparagus. Not many cities can boast of such variety.

Students from the carillon school here now play on carillons around the world. Concerts are given at the Hof van Busleyden, which also houses the bell ringing school and the municipal museum.

Regarding the tapestries, check out the Koninklijke Manufactuur Gaspard DeWit, Schoutetstraat 7, (you can just call it the tapestry works). A guided tour here will show you how old tapestries are restored and new ones made. Everything is done by hand. You will also learn about the history of tapestry making and of course you will see some lovely tapestries along the way.

The cathedral in town is called St-Romboustkathedraal on Grote Markt. The magnificent tower is nearly 320 feet high, and some have called it "the eighth wonder of the world." So it is worth seeing. In the south transept is van Eyck's *Crucifixion*.

**Mons** This city of 75,000 near the French border is worth seeing in its own right; its Collégiale Ste-Waudru Gothic church, pl. du Chapître, is quite impressive. Two miles south in the little community of Cuesmes is the Maison de Van Gogh, rue du Pavillon 3, where the famous artist came in 1879 to preach the gospel to the miners and farmers in the area. You can see the reconstruction of the room in which he lived and also a documents room.

**Nivelles** Collégiale Ste-Geretrude on Grand' Place goes back to 1046 when it was consecrated by the bishop of Liège. The archaeological basement takes you back further yet, as you see ruins of churches that go back to the 600s. Just south of town is the Parc de la Dodaine, a lovely flower-filled park around a pond and lake; it has a fine children's play area.

**Oostende (Ostend)** This is known as a transfer point, as travelers to or from England use the ferry or hydrofoil to cross the North Sea, but there is a bit more to see and do in this city than eat oysters (for which it is famous). You might be interested in seeing the Opleidingszeilschip Mercator, a three-master, which is now a floating museum (Vindictivelaan). It participated in many scientific missions and it brought back from Hawaii the remains of Father Damien, the great missionary to the lepers.

**Redu-Transinne** If you combine a village for book lovers with a village for aspiring astronauts, you get Redu. As unlikely as it seems, this is a bibliophile's heaven, with about 30 secondhand bookstores here. Near the E411 motorway is the Euro Space Center on rue Devant-les-Hêtres 1, with tours of space ships and films in the auditorium. Young people love it.

**Sougne-Remouchamps** On the last weekend in June the annual daisy festival is held here, but even if daisies don't get you too excited, this place with the unpronounceable name is still a pleasant place to visit. A cave (grotte) can be explored, allowing you to pass a frozen waterfall and some petrified rock pools before going down a flight of steps to the Rubicon River. One underground room is called the Cathedral, 328 feet long, and the crystal concretions here are in three colors. The tour ends with a boat trip beneath other multicolored rocks to the Precipice Chamber.

**Spa** Yes, there is a Belgian town named Spa, and its sparkling clear waters have been extolled for their curative powers since Roman times. There is much to be enjoyed here. In the winter many come here for skiing and tobogganing; in the summer there is the Spa Theatre Festival; in the fall it's the autumn music season; and in the spring there are pleasant signposted walks.

**St-Hubert** The first church here goes back to the 7th century. The present Gothic basilica at pl. de l'Abbaye dates from the 16th century. Pilgrims have been coming to this

## MAGNIFIQUE!

Belgium's cities offer some of Europe's finest art and architecture, much of which is rich in Christian history. But God's handiwork in the outlying natural areas shouldn't be missed. The castle-dotted hilly landscape around the area of the Ardennes offers great escapes for hikers, bikers, kayakers, and spelunkers.

The serene city of Namur makes a good home base for hiking, biking, caving, and kayaking. Tourist offices in town can provide maps, guided tours, and information on rental companies. Phone them at 081/222-859 or find them on the Internet at www.ville.namur.be.

The town of Dinant is also a good base for exploring God's creation, with caves, hiking, and kayaking possibilities, as well as a citadel (which is very imposing). Contact the town's tourist office at 082/222-870 or find them on the Internet at www.maison-du-tourisme.net.

church and its predecessors for more than a millennium. Each July the Juillet Musical sponsors concerts in town and in the surrounding area.

**Tournai** The Cathédrale Notre-Dame at pl. Paul-Emile Janson is a gigantic church, 440 feet long and 216 feet wide. Some parts of the church are from the 12th century. The Beffroi (belfry) is the oldest in Belgium. If you want to climb the 256 steps, you can get a great view of the city. The 44-chime carillon provides regular concerts.

Two museums here are outstanding—the Musée des Beaux-Arts at Enclos St-Martin and the Musée de la Tapisserie on pl. Reine Astrid. From the Grand-Place you can enjoy carriage rides and a small tourist train through town.

**Waterloo** Where did Napoléon meet his Waterloo? At Waterloo, of course, in 1815, when the Duke of Wellington defeated the French military genius. There is much to see here commemorating that battle. At the base of a 147-foot mound is a visitors center; a massive panoramic painting depicts the decisive moments of the fight.

**Wavre** Just southwest of town is a 123-acre amusement park, the most popular in the country. It has a variety of rides and entertainment, as well as a swimming pool complex.

# Czech Republic

Czech Tourist Authority
US 212-288-0830
UK 020-7291-9920
*Web sites*
Entire country www.czech.cz
Prague www.A-Zprague.cz
Ceský Krumlov www.ckrumlov.cz/uk/mesto/soucas/i_zakinf.htm
For a complete list of updated links, visit www.christiantraveler.com

### Country in a Capsule

*Size:* Slightly smaller than South Carolina, but with three times as many residents (10 million).

*Religion:* About 40 percent are Roman Catholic, 5 percent Protestant, 3 percent Eastern Orthodox, and 40 percent atheist.

*Language:* Czech and Slovak, although German and English are widely understood in the cities.

*Money:* The koruna is the equivalent of about 2.5 cents.

*Food:* If you want true Czech cuisine, learn how to say knedlíky, thick loaves of dough that we would refer to as dumplings in English and that are commonplace on the Czech table. Meat and potatoes are the mainstay of the Czech diet, and a favorite dinner entrée would be vepřo-knedlo-zelo, roast pork with sauerkraut and dumplings. Gulás is a local stew that's also popular. For dessert try kolác, a tart filled with poppyseed jam or sweet cheese.

*Shopping:* The Czech Republic is known for its beautiful Bohemian crystal and delicate Christmas ornaments. Other good buys include marionettes, porcelain, and ceramics.

*Brief history:* Czechoslovakia was first recognized as an independent nation after World War I. In 1939 Hitler marched in and annexed it to Germany, and after World War II it came under Soviet control. After Soviet authority collapsed in 1991, freedom came again. Two years later, the land was divided into the Czech Republic and Slovakia. Today the Czech Republic is governed as a parliamentary democracy.

**Prague** The Protestant reformer Jan Hus is a national hero in the Czech Republic, and evidence of his life permeates Prague. It was in the pulpit of the Bethlehem Chapel (Betlémská kaple) that Hus preached his message of reform in the early 15th century. Unfortunately much of the chapel was rebuilt in the 1950s, but the door through which Hus entered the pulpit remains original, as are most of the inscriptions on the wall. The church is located on Betlémské nám.

*Old Town.* A further reminder that this was Jan Hus's territory is located in the old commercial center of the Old Town, in Staroměstské náměstí, or Old Town Square. The square is a pleasant meeting place, surrounded by architectural beauty and graced by a larger-than-life sculptural group with Jan Hus as its centerpiece.

Hus's followers were responsible for building the Týn Church in the 15th century. Its more accurate name is the Church of the Virgin Mary before Týn (Kostel Panny Marie před Týnem), which is a mouthful even for a Czech speaker; hence the shortened Týn Church. The church has twin towers. Another interesting church is the Church of St. Nicholas (Kostel svatého Mikuláše), a white Baroque building tucked into the square's northwest corner. Both churches are on the Old Town Square (Staroměstské nám.).

Visitors to the Old Town Square are always enamored with the famous 15th-century Clock Tower of the Old Town Hall (Staroměstská radnice). The clock's ancient mechanism activates a parade of the 12 apostles every hour on the hour. The skeleton tolling the clock's bell is the figure of Death.

*Wenceslas Square,* or václavské náměstí, is the Times Square of Prague. It is not so much a square as it is a wide boulevard with a spacious median that offers plenty of park benches and grassy areas to relax. This is the favorite meeting place of young and old alike, and you can count on activity here no matter the time or day of the week. It's a great place to sit in the sun, enjoy lunch from a local food vendor, or shop for souvenirs.

Hundreds of thousands of Czechs voiced their disdain for the ruling Communist regime in this square in November 1989, and thus began the "Velvet Revolution." The large building at the top of the boulevard is the National Museum (Národní muzeum). The large character on horseback is St. Václav (Wenceslas), another Czech hero.

*Churches.* At Karmelitská 9 is the Church of Our Lady Victorious (Kostel Panny Marie Vítězná), built in 1613 by Lutherans but taken over by the Carmelites in 1620. This church is the home of the world-famous *Infant Jesus of Prague,* a wax figure of Spanish origin believed to have worked miracles. The little statue has a wardrobe of 39 costly robes and is always clothed in one of them, depending on the time of year.

The Church of St. Nicholas (Chrám svatého Mikuláše) at Malostranské nám. shares more than just a patron saint with its Baroque counterpart in the Old Town; both churches were designed by the same architect, Kilian Ignatz Dietzenhofer, although he worked in partnership with his son on this Bohemian Baroque masterpiece. You'll be hard-pressed to find a better example of this style of church, which is unique to Prague. On clear days take time to climb the

## JAN HUS (1374–1415)

A priest and a professor at the University of Prague, Jan Hus was influenced by John Wycliffe of England. Like Wycliffe he stressed the role of Scripture as an authority in the church. He defended the traditional authority of the clergy, but he taught that only God can forgive sin. Like Luther a hundred years later, he condemned the sale of indulgences.

Hus was called to the Council of Constance to defend his beliefs and traveled there under the emperor's promise of safe conduct. But before he had a chance to explain his views, he was arrested, condemned, and burned at the stake. In his native land, Hus became not only a martyr but a national hero.

Sites associated with Jan Hus's life and those of his followers can be seen throughout the city of Prague and in Tábor, as well as in Konstanz and Worms, Germany.

church tower for great views of this beautiful city. For some time the concertmaster at the Church of St. Nicholas was none other than Wolfgang Amadeus Mozart.

*Charles Bridge.* There are few sites more synonymous with Prague than the Charles Bridge (Karlův most) between Mostecká ul. and Karlova ul. This statue-lined bridge is undoubtedly one of the world's most beautiful, not only for its graceful style but for its gorgeous setting. The bridge was a gift to the city of Prague from the Holy Roman Emperor Charles IV and was constructed in the 14th century. Its 30 sculptures were added during the 17th century, although most of the statues today are reproductions of the originals, which have been moved indoors for protection from the elements. Since its creation, the bridge has been more than a means of crossing over the Vltava River; it is also a popular meeting place and a place of business for dozens of street musicians, artists, and souvenir vendors.

*Prague Castle.* If there is another site as synonymous with Prague as its famous bridge, it would have to be Prague Castle (Pražský hrad). Perched high atop a narrow hill, this castle complex has watched over Prague for more than 1,000 years. Christians will be pleased to learn that the heart of the castle, both physically and spiritually, is St. Vitus Cathedral (Chrám svatého Víta). The stunning cathedral was begun in 1344, but was not completed until nearly 600 years later, in 1929. The interior of the cathedral will leave visitors' necks stiff as they gaze up at the ceiling. "Good King" Wenceslas, who was actually only a prince, is buried in his own chapel in the south transept. The Christian ruler of Christmas carol fame was martyred for his faith and generosity; his brother, not too fond of Wenceslas' evangelistic zeal, became so angry with Wenceslas that he killed him. A painting within the ornately bejeweled chapel depicts the brother's fatal act.

To get a clear sense of the contrast between Gothic and Romanesque architectural styles, visit the older St. George's Basilica (Bazilika svatého Jiří) next door. The cool Romanesque building feels ancient and is very simple in its ornamentation. The ex-convent adjoining the church houses a great collection of Bohemian art, from medieval religious sculptures to Baroque paintings.

Approach the castle via Nerudova, Staré zámecké schody, or Keplerova. The main ticket office is in the Second Courtyard.

*The Loreta* in Loretánské nám. is a Baroque church and shrine located in the Castle District and dedicated to the Virgin Mary. Legend has it that angels transported the Madonna's house from Nazareth to the Italian town of Loreta—hence the church's name. The church is worth visiting if for no other reason than to view its fabulous treasury, which houses the Sun of Diamonds, studded with 6,222 precious jewels. Visitors who arrive on the hour will also be treated to the music of the Loreta's 27-bell carillon.

> Fairest Lord Jesus, ruler of all nature,
> O Thou of God and man the son.
> Thee will I cherish, Thee will I honor,
> Thou, my soul's glory, joy, and crown.
>
> AUTHOR UNKNOWN, BUT MAY HAVE FIRST BEEN SUNG BY FOLLOWERS OF JAN HUS, NEAR PRAGUE, CZECH REPUBLIC

*Mozart's music* was popular in Prague while the Viennese were still yawning over it. When Mozart got news that his opera *The Marriage of Figaro* was a hit in this city, he quickly headed to Prague. *Figaro* was so popular that Mozart received a commission to write another opera, *Don Giovanni,* which was composed in this city. There's a small Mozart museum on the outskirts of town (Villa Bertrámka, Mozartova 169), which is open daily. The Oscar-winning movie *Amadeus* was filmed almost entirely in Prague.

*Music and theater.* Tourists interested in fine arts and culture are in for a treat in Prague. The city has long loved the arts, as evidenced by its museums and theaters that dominate the city far more than any of its governmental buildings. Many of the city's largest palaces and cathedrals offer musical performances in surroundings that are sure to please. Check the entrances of these buildings as posters are frequently tacked up announcing the evening's program. Both of the Churches of St. Nicholas, in the Old Town and in the Lesser Quarter, are known for offering superb concerts. St. James' Church on Malá Stupartská (in the Old Town) features a variety of cantatas. And in the Prague Castle's Garden on the Ramparts, music is accompanied by a fabulous view.

If you have children (and even if you don't), don't miss the opportunity to visit a puppet show at the National Marionette Theater (Žatecká 1, phone 02/232-4565). Marionette performances are a traditional form of Czech entertainment. They are usually adaptations of operas set to recorded music. But it matters little what the program or the music is; this is an experience you will never forget. Information and tickets to all of Prague's cultural events can be obtained at the Prague Information Service (PIS) located at Na Příkopě 20 and at Staroměstské nám. 22 (Old Town Square).

**Brno** Peter and Paul Cathedral (Biskupská katedrála sv. Petra a Pavla) is on Petrov Hill, and like many churches has a bell tower that sounds the time. But these bells ring daily at 11:00 A.M. instead of noon. Legend has it that the bells confused Swedish soldiers who were trying to lay siege to the city in 1645. The general in charge declared that he would withdraw his troops if they hadn't captured the city by noon. The tricky townspeople rang the church bells at 11:00, the Swedes left, and the tradition of the early noon bell-ringing continues.

Brno is in the heart of Moravia. Large numbers of Hussite followers in the region organized a group known as the Unitas Fratrum in 1457. Centuries later the group sent colonist missionaries to the New World, the first of which settled in Bethlehem, Pennsylvania. They were consequently known as Moravians.

**Český Krumlov** The city of Český Krumlov is hailed as one of the most lovely towns in the world and is virtually unchanged since the 18th century. Cobblestone streets, medieval winding alleys, and Bohemia's second-largest castle have made this one of the most popular cities in central Europe.

Český Krumlov castle keeps sentinel high above the city—you can't miss it. The stone courtyards are free and open to the public. If you want to tour the lavish interior, you'll be charged a modest admission fee, but it's worth it. Highlights are the frescoed ballroom and a Baroque theater.

If you're content to stay in the countryside (and you may well be), there are plenty of hiking trails in the area. Rent a horse from Jezdecký klub Slupenec, on Slupenc 1 (phone 0337/711-053) for horseback riding in the area. Or you can rent bicycles from Globtour Vltava on Kájovská 62.

**Karlovy Vary** Karlovy Vary is the largest and oldest of the Czech Republic's many spas. The town is known as much for its beautiful setting as it is for its hot springs, and countless famous people have

63

## EUROPE'S OSSUARIES

Most North Americans aren't familiar with ossuaries. The word might be translated as "bone chapels."

These chapels are unique to European Christianity and are rare even in Europe. Simply put, ossuaries are chapels that have been decorated with human bones. One of the most elaborate of these bizarre churches is in Kutná Hora. Bones are used to create pillars, garlands, and even chandeliers, creations that might be beautiful if they weren't so grim.

But ossuaries didn't develop out of some dark artistic bent. They were most commonly constructed during the 17th century, when the Black Plague was raging through Europe, claiming as many as one out of four people. Death had become a part of life, and people simply couldn't afford to take a single day of life for granted. In an effort to impress their parishioners with their certain mortality and to urge them to make their peace with God, monks began creating these macabre chapels. Remember, they seem to be saying, your time is coming.

made their way here, including Beethoven, Brahms, Chopin, Liszt, Goethe, Bismarck, Schiller, Tolstoy, and Karl Marx. Ludvík Moser came to town in 1857 and began a glassmaking operation. Since then, Bohemian crystal has been prized all over the world.

If you'd like to take the cure yourself, head to the Sprundel Spring (Vrídlo) in the Vrídelní Colonnade. Every minute 2,000 liters of 72.2 degree mineral water shoot up from underground. You'll see lots of Czech tourists walking around with little cups in their hands. Bring your own cup and try some of the water. It may do you some good.

If you'd prefer to soak in the thermal water, go to the open-air pool at the Thermal Sanitorium. The other spas in town are reserved for patients undergoing prescribed treatments, but the sanitorium is public. It will cost you the equivalent of about 1 dollar per hour.

To enjoy views of the surrounding countryside, take the Diana Funicular Railway up the hillside off Stará Louka street. There are some nice hiking trails at the top. And if the hill isn't high enough for you, you can ride up the Diana Tower another 555 meters for a panorama that is second to none.

**Kutná Hora** Visitors to Europe have the opportunity to visit more Christian churches than anywhere else in the world. If the cathedrals begin to look all the same to you, consider visiting

Kutná Hora's ossuary (Kostnice) on Zámeckáy. In the 13th century a group of monks sprinkled soil from Golgotha Cemetery on the town's own cemetery, and soon the rich and superstitious angled for burial there. One thing led to another, and by the 15th century a monk began using the bones to create rather unusual ornamentation in the cemetery's chapel, including a chandelier that simply defies belief. The church is without a doubt unlike any other—and perhaps not for everyone.

If you need to lighten up a bit after the bone church, visit the Hrádek Mining Museum on nám. Národního odboje. Located in a 15th-century palace, the museum contains an exhibit that recounts how mining made Kutná Hora wealthy. The main attraction is the 45-minute guided tour of medieval mine shafts on one of the 20 underground levels. You'll get to wear a white coat and helmet and pick up a miner's lamp before you make the descent.

**Tábor** The Hussite reformist movement, which preceded Luther's Reformation by about 100 years, was begun in Tábor in the early 15th century. After Jan Hus's death at the stake in 1415 for preaching reforms similar to Luther's, his followers established a commune on a fortified hill above the Lužnice River. The Hussites became one of Europe's most feared armies under the command of Jan Žižka, whose statue graces Žižkovo náměstí, Tábor's town square. The town of Tábor itself became a defense. Its twisting streets were designed to confuse enemies. Beneath the city streets were a similar maze of tunnels and cellars, which served at times as living quarters and as links with the outside world. The story of the Hussites is told in the local Hussite Museum (Husitské muzeum) just off Žižkovo náměstí on Křivkoa 31. The museum is open only during the warm-weather months, from April to November, daily from 8:30 to 4:00.

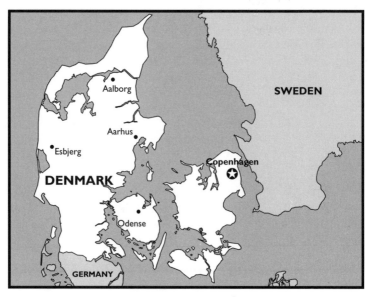

# Denmark

Danish Tourist Board
  US 212-885-9700
  UK 020-7259-5959
*Web sites*
  Entire country www.visitdenmark.com
  Copenhagen www.woco.dk
  Scandinavia www.goscandinavia.com
For a complete list of updated links, visit www.christiantraveler.com

### Country in a Capsule

*Size:* A little larger than Maryland and Delaware combined, but with about the same population. Copenhagen with 1.4 million people is the largest capital in Scandinavia.

*Religion:* About 90 percent are affiliated with the national church, which is Evangelical Lutheran. However, church attendance is estimated to be only 5 percent of the population. There are about 30,000 Catholics and about the same number in Protestant denominations other than the state church.

*Language:* The Danish language is related to but different from either Swedish or Norwegian. Fortunately, most Danes speak English.

*Money:* The krone is worth about 11 cents.

*Food:* For lunch make sure you try smorresbord (this is not smorgasbord). It's an open-face sandwich that features roast beef or pieces of baby shrimp on rye or wheat bread. For dessert, try wienerbrod, a sausage bread. Many hotels serve a limited version of det store kolde bord, the Danish equivalent of a smorgasbord.

*Shopping:* Royal Copenhagen Porcelain for porcelain, George Jensen for silver, Tin Centret for pewter ware, all located in Copenhagen.

*Brief history:* The first king was Gorm the Old in the 10th century. His son Harald Bluetooth (don't you love those names?) introduced Christianity and converted the whole country. Around 1400 Margareta I established a union with Sweden and Norway, and Norway stayed under Danish control until 1814. Denmark became Protestant in 1536, and its golden age came under Christian IV about 75 years later. Denmark remains a monarchy today.

Looking for an unusual way to get around Denmark? Consider bicycling. Some say the Danes have the greatest number of bikes per capita in the world. Whether that's true or not, few places are better suited to bicycling. The landscape is flat and the roads are uncrowded. Visitors can rent bikes at some train stations, at many tourist offices, and from private companies. For more information contact the Danish Cyclists' Association (Dansk Cyklist Forbund) at Rømersg. 7, DK 1362, Copenhagen. In the warm-weather months, look for Bycykler (City Bikes) parked at special bike stands around town. Deposit DKr20 and the bike is yours. You get the deposit back when you return the bike.

**Copenhagen** The founder of Copenhagen was its first bishop, Bishop Absalon. His statue sits on top of the main entrance of the City Hall (Rådhus), which is a good place to start your tour of the city. If you're feeling well rested, take a guided tour up to the top of the 350-foot tower to see the entire area.

*Shopping district.* Copenhagen's main shopping district is the Strøget, just northeast of City Hall Square. Strøget is the world's longest pedestrian mall, so a lot of tourists do some serious window-shopping here.

*The Church of Our Lady.* North of the Strøget on Nørregade, you will come to Vor Frue Kirken (The Church of Our Lady), which has been Copenhagen's cathedral since 1924. Bishop Absalon built a chapel here in the 13th century and ever since then this site has been a place of worship. Inside you will see marble statues of Christ and the apostles by Danish sculptor Bertel Thorvaldsen.

## SØREN KIERKEGAARD (1813–1855)

A philosopher and theologian, Kierkegaard's only joy in life seemed to be challenging the system. Poor health made him morbid, and the status of the state church in Denmark made him pessimistic. His target in his writings was not corruption in the church but rather the spiritual indifference engendered by a rationalistic approach to faith, which was supported by the state church.

Christendom, he said, had destroyed Christianity. The faith that counts is one that is willing to put all at risk for God, while leading a life of personal discipleship. Kierkegaard's philosophical writings influenced the thinking of later existential philosophers like Sartre and Heidegger.

Sites associated with Kierkegaard are located in Copenhagen.

*Christiansborg Castle.* A little further northeast across the Frediksholms Kanal is Christiansborg Slot (Christiansborg Castle). This is where Bishop Absalon built the city's first fortress in 1167. The current castle was built only a hundred years ago, but the excavated ruins of Absalon's fortress can be viewed underneath. The castle contains the Parliament House and the Royal Reception Chambers.

*Det Kongelige Bibliotek (Royal Library)* on Slotsholmen has Denmark's largest collection of books and manuscripts. It also has early records of the Viking journeys to America and Greenland. The statue in the garden is that of philosopher-theologian Søren Kierkegaard. Admission is free.

*Churches.* Across the drawbridge in Christianshavn is one of the oldest parts of Copenhagen, and here you will find Vor Frelsers Kirken (Our Savior's Church) at Skt. Annæg. 9. It was built in 1696. You will notice its green-and-gold spire from a distance. Inside is an elaborately carved pipe organ and a Baroque altar with cherubs and angels. If you're brave and want an unusual view of the city, climb the 400 steps of the church's spiral tower. According to a legend, the staircase surrounding the fantastic gold-and-green spire was built curling the wrong direction. When the architect reached the top and saw what had happened, he is said to have jumped.

At least two other large churches in Copenhagen are worth seeing. The Marble Church (Marmorkirken) is more properly known as the Frederikskirke. Begun in 1749, the Baroque church at Frederiksgade 4 got its popular nickname from the expensive Norwegian marble from which it was constructed. Budget constraints left it unfinished for over 100 years from 1770 to 1874, but it was finally completed in 1894. The 16 statues that stand around the exterior of the church portray various religious leaders, from Moses to Luther. Below them stand sculptures of prominent Danish ministers and bishops.

St. Nicolai's church, on Nikolaipl., is a 16th-century structure opposite Illum's department store. You'll recognize it by its tall green spire. The present structure is relatively modern, built in the 20th century. It replaced a previous 13th-century Nikolaj Kirken, which was destroyed by a fire in 1728. The building is not used as a church any longer but is an art gallery and exhibition center. A prized treasure is Karl Heinrich Bloch's *Christ Blessing the Children.*

The Church of the Holy Ghost (Helligåndskirken) at Niels Hemmingsensg. 5 is the oldest church in Copenhagen, founded early in the 15th century. Although parts of the church have been rebuilt over the centuries, most of the building is original. The 18th-century choir contains a marble font by the sculptor Bertel Thovaldsen. The church's 15th-century abbey, Helligåndshuset, stands beside the church.

*Andersen.* The Danes love their native son Hans Christian Andersen, and *The Little Mermaid* (Den Lille Havfrue) statue is proof. Located on the Langelinie, a little peninsula of land near Churchillparken jutting out into the Yderhavn, the statue was erected in 1913 and has attracted thousands ever since.

*Tivoli.* If you're in Copenhagen with children, you simply can't miss Tivoli, the city's premier amusement park. And even if you aren't an amusement park fan, you are sure to love Tivoli's cultural offerings. In the 1840s Danish architect Georg Carstensen persuaded King Christian VIII that an amusement park for the public was a great idea: "When people amuse themselves, they forget politics." About four million people forget politics for a while every season from May through September at Tivoli, a sophisticated theme park with pantomime, an open-air stage, elegant restaurants, inexpensive food stalls selling a wide variety of items, and frequent rock, classical, and jazz concerts. Make sure to visit at least once at night for the elaborate weekend fireworks shows and the beautifully illuminated trees and fountains. While the park is generally closed during the winter months, in recent years Tivoli has opened up a month before Christmas with a gift and decorations market and children's rides.

*Amalienborg Palace.* While you are in Copenhagen, you should visit Amalienborg Palace on Amalienborg Pl., which has been the main royal palace since 1784. When the royal family is in residence in the fall and winter, the Royal Guard and band march through the city at noon to change the palace guard. The museum here has an impressive royal collection of art, silver, and costumery.

*Parks.* At the entrance of Churchillparken is St. Alban's, an English church, and in the middle of the park is the Kastellet (the Citadel), surrounded by two rings of moats. During World War II this area was used by the Nazis as their headquarters in Denmark. Nearby is the Frihedsmuseet (Liberty Museum) commemorating the Danish Resistance movement, which saved 7,000 Jews by hiding them in hospitals and homes and then smuggling them to safety in Sweden.

Copenhagen's 25-acre botanical garden (Botanisk Have) is a wonderful way to spend time outdoors. Its indoor exhibitions aren't so bad, either. The Palm House contains tropical and subtropical plants, and there is an observatory and a geological museum on the grounds as well. The garden is located at Gothersg. 128, and admission is free. The Kunst (National Art Gallery), which is also located here, has a variety of outstanding paintings by Rubens, Dürer, Matisse, and the Impressionists.

**Århus** This is the largest city on the Jutland peninsula, and the second-largest city in Denmark. While it doesn't compete with Copenhagen in the number of things to see and do, it still offers plenty to the tourist. Den Gamle By (Old Town) is an open-air museum of 75 half-timbered houses brought here from all over

Denmark. The museum also has a functioning bakery, silversmith, and bookbinder.

Århus's Domkirke on Bispetorv is Denmark's longest cathedral with a nave about a football-field long. Built and adorned in the 12th century with frescoes to convey biblical parables to illiterate peasants, the walls were whitewashed after the Reformation because the paintings included many legendary Catholic stories as well as the biblical ones. Now much of the original artwork has been restored, including paintings of St. George slaying a dragon and paintings of hell.

The 13th-century Church of Our Lady (Vor Frue Kirken) on Frue Kirkepl. has an interesting crypt church that was rediscovered in 1955. Dating from 1060, this is one of the oldest preserved stone churches in Scandinavia.

Århus also boasts a Tivoli, not as exciting as that of Copenhagen, but it has rides, music, and gracious gardens.

The city is known for its lively 10-day Århus Festival held annually in August. Music of all types, clowning, exhibitions, sporting events, and theater work together to create a fun experience for all ages.

**Billund** If you are traveling with children, you simply must visit Legoland, a park filled with scaled-down versions of cities, towns, harbors and airports, Mt. Rushmore, a safari park, the Statue of Liberty, and a Pirate Land, all constructed of millions of Lego building blocks. There are also some exhibits that do not include the childhood favorites, like Titania's Palace, a fabulous dollhouse built in 1907. A highlight is Castleland, as big as two football fields. Guests arrive in a dragon ride, and view pirates, safari animals, and knights inside, all of which are made from 45 million Lego blocks (give or take a few thousand). Lego blocks are manufactured nearby. The park is open from May 1 to mid-September.

**Helsingør** About 30 miles north of Copenhagen is Kronberg Castle in Helsingør, the setting of Elsinore Castle in Shakespeare's Hamlet. It's well worth seeing, even though Shakespeare's version of it is certainly fictional. The gabled and turreted structure was built in 1585 and has a 200-foot-long dining hall, a luxurious chapel, and royal chambers. It also has 12-foot walls to provide some safety from a possible Swedish invasion. The town of Helsingør is also worth seeing for its picturesque streets and

16th-century houses. The old cathedral here (Sankt Olai's Kirke) and Karmeliterklostret, Scandinavia's best preserved medieval monastery, are also worth a visit. The cathedral and monastery are connected to one another and located on Sct. Annagade.

**Hillerød** Frederiksborg Castle, perched on a hill overlooking Hillerød, is often cited as one of the most beautiful of all of Scandinavian castles. Located about 20 miles northwest of Copenhagen, Frederiksborg is constructed of red brick with a copper roof, its oldest parts dating from 1560 and the reign of Frederik II. Today the castle houses a major national history museum. Of Frederiksborg's many sites, perphaps the most interesting is its sumptuously decorated chapel with the king's pew, where Danish kings were once crowned, and the 23 frescoes depicting the life of Christ by Karl Heinrich Bloch. Among them are *Christ among the Doctors* and *Come unto Me*. The latter is his best known. Free recitals on the chapel's 17th-century organ are held weekly.

About 3 miles west of Hillerød is Aebelholt Abbey, at Aebelholt 4. Founded in 1175 by Abbot Wilhelm, the abbey constituted one of Denmark's largest medieval religious communities and was home to some of the most medically knowledgeable monks in all of Europe. Although the complex was destroyed following the Reformation, excavations have uncovered much of Aebelholt's original construction.

**Hojby** On the Odsherred peninsula, north of Svenninge, off Rte. 21, is the little community of Hojby. If you're interested in ecclesiastical art, visit the Gothic Renaissance Hojby Kirke (Hojby Church) and see the great frescoes there.

**Humlebæk** The town of Humlebæk is 22 miles outside of Copenhagen and is part of the "Danish Riviera" on the North Sjaelland coast. The primary tourist attraction is Louisiana, a wonderful modern art collection housed in a spectacular building. Even if you don't care for art, Louisiana is located in a large park with terrific views of the sound and, weather permitting, Sweden. The children's wing in the museum has child-friendly computers, pyramid-shaped chalkboards, and weekend children's programs.

**Jelling** Outside of the Jelling church are two granite stones inscribed with runes, the ancient alphabetical system used by early Scandinavians. One of these was erected in the early 900s by King Gorm the Old, Denmark's first king, in honor of his wife Thyra. The larger one, raised by Harald Bluetooth, bears the oldest figure of Christ in Scandinavia. It is called "Denmark's baptismal certificate." The inscription on the stone reads: "Harald king bade this be ordained for Gorm his father and Thyra his mother, the Harald who won for himself all Denmark and Norway and made the Danes Christians." Inside the small whitewashed church are frescoes dating from the 12th century.

**Maribo** About 12 miles west of Falster Island, on the island of Lolland, is the Aaholm Automobile Museum, the largest in northern Europe. The Museum has more than 200 vehicles and is 15 miles southwest of Maribo near the Aaholm Castle. Also near Maribo is Knuthenborg Safari Park, housing a variety of tigers, rhinos, zebras, giraffes, and camels. The Safari Park is 5 miles north of town on Rtes. 9 and 283.

**Nykøbing** About 62 miles south of Copenhagen is this enjoyable town with excellent beaches on the island of Falster. At the Middelaldercentret here (Center for the Middle Ages) you will find a reconstructed medieval village that invites school classes to dress up in period costumes and experience life as it was a thousand years ago. Day guests can participate in activities that change weekly, from cooking to animal herding to folk dancing.

**Odense** Denmark's third-largest city, Odense, is the birthplace of Hans Christian Andersen, and it is appropriately enough a great place to visit with children. To see the Andersens' house, visit the H. C. Andersens Hus at Hans Jensenstr. 37–45. The house and the surrounding area have been exquisitely preserved, with cobbled pedestrian streets that invite exploration. Inside the museum child-friendly exhibits shed light on the man and the time in which he lived through letters, diaries, photos, and drawings. Attached to the museum is a large library with Andersen's works translated into 127 languages, and audiotape recordings of his fairy tales.

Just down the street is the Children's Culture House (Børnekulturehuset Fyretøjet), at Hans Jensenstr. 21. The museum includes walk-through fairy-tale exhibits and studios where children can draw and write their own tales and plays, then dress up and perform them.

The Fyn Village (Den Fynske Landsby) at Sejerskovvej #20 is an open-air museum village consisting of 20 farm buildings. You can visit workshops with skilled craftsmen, a water mill, a windmill, and a vicarage. There's also a theater with—what else?—summertime performances of Andersen's fairy tales. Consider taking a boat trip down the Odense River for an enjoyable trip.

**Osterlars** On this Baltic island south of Sweden, the Osterlars Kirke stands out in this little village. Built in 1150, it is the largest of the island's four round churches. It was built from boulders and slabs of limestone and served both as a sanctuary and as a fortification against enemy armies and pirates. Wall paintings of the annunciation and nativity are among several Gothic works of art that have survived since the 1300s. In neighboring Nylars, the village church dates from 1150. On its central pillar are chalk paintings of the Old Testament, perhaps dating back to about 1250. The runic stones on the church's porch are even older.

**Rebild National Park** If you are in the area around July 4, you won't want to miss it. Founded in 1942 by Danish-Americans, this Park features the largest Fourth of July celebration outside the United States. It also has a Lincoln log cabin and souvenir shops to make you feel at home. The park also features an unspoiled area of hills and heathland as well as a good walking trail.

**Roskilde** A trip to Roskilde, 19 miles west of Copenhagen, is a trip into the past. The busy market town was one of the most important of Viking cities and remained one of the largest European cities through the Middle Ages. The town's 1,000-year legacy can be appreciated in its spectacular cathedral. The Domkirke (cathedral) at Domkirkestraede 10 was built on the site of one of Denmark's first churches and has been the burial site of Danish royalty for over five centuries. You may also enjoy seeing the 16th-century clock above the entrance, where a small St. George on horseback slays a yelping dragon every hour on the hour.

For a look at Denmark's Viking past, don't miss the Viking Ship Museum (Vikingeskibshallen), a short walk south and through the park on Strandengen. Inside are five painstakingly restored Viking ships, discovered at the bottom of a Danish fjord in 1962. Explanatory signs and films on the excavation and reconstruction of the ships are in English.

**Vejle** Fifteen miles east of Billund is this village, beautifully situated on a fjord. In the town center is the St. Nicholas Church, which contains the skulls of 23 thieves, executed in the 17th century. More remarkable is what you will find in the left transept of the cross-shaped church. There, lying in a glass Empire-shaped coffin is the body of a woman that was found in the nearby peat bogs in 1835. Perfectly preserved, scientists have been able to date the body to 500 B.C.

**Viborg** About 40 miles northwest of Århus is this 8th-century city. In pagan times it was a place for sacrifice as well as a trading center. Later it became a Christian center with monasteries. Viborg's Domkirke (cathedral) on Mogensg., built in 1130, was once the largest granite church in the world. Only the crypt remains of that original church, but the building was restored in 1876. The biblical frescoes here were done by Danish painter Joakim Skovgaard in the early 20th century.

# Finland

Finnish Tourist Board
  US 212-885-9700
  UK 020-7930-5871
*Web sites*
  Entire country www.finland-tourism.com/
  Scandinavia www.goscandinavia.com
For a complete list of updated links, visit www.christiantraveler.com

### Country in a Capsule

*Size:* Finland is roughly the size of Michigan and Indiana together, but its population is only one-third of the two states. Its biggest city is the capital city of Helsinki with about a half million residents.

*Religion:* About 89 percent are members of the Lutheran National Church, and 1 percent belong to the Greek Orthodox Church. The largest Protestant church apart from the state church is the Evangelical Free

Church, but the number of Baptists, Methodists, and Brethren have been increasing recently.

*Language:* Finland has two official languages: Finnish and Swedish, and Finnish is spoken in a variety of dialects across the country. English is widely spoken in Helsinki, and if you need directions elsewhere, ask someone under 30 and he or she will probably understand English.

*Money:* The unit of currency in Finland is the Finnish mark or markka. Its value at press time is about 15 cents.

*Food:* Special Finnish dishes include reindeer casserole and lihapullat (meatballs with a creamy sauce). If you get to the northern part of Finland, make sure you enjoy some Arctic cloudberries for dessert. Of course, anywhere in Finland you will find a variety of fish; Finns enjoy rainbow trout and Baltic herring.

*Shopping:* Glassware, porcelain, and ceramics are good buys here. Finland is also known for its Arabia china and littala glass.

*Brief history:* The Lapps were the original settlers but were pushed north by the Finns who brought their language from what is now Russia. Vikings penetrated the area around A.D. 800, and the country was Christianized two centuries later. But during the last millennium Finland has been a pawn between Russia, Sweden, and Denmark. For 600 years Finland was a part of Sweden, but in the 1700s and 1800s Russia annexed it. It wasn't until 1917 that Finland achieved independence and even in the 20th century has had to fight to maintain it. Although missionaries had brought Christianity to the Aland islands in the 10th century, it wasn't until Bishop Henry of Uppsala, Sweden, came to Turku, Finland, in 1157 that Christianity was introduced to the entire country. The Reformation leader was Mikael Agricola, who translated the Bible into Finnish.

**Helsinki** Built on various peninsulas and islands of the Baltic shoreline, Helsinki is decidedly a city of the sea. On the western shore of the South Harbor near the huge ferry dock, visitors can have a look at Finland's fruit of the sea at the Old Market Hall (Vanha Kauppahalli). The brick market hall features amazing spreads of seafood, some of which you have never seen before, as well as meat and other products.

Also on the South Harbor and just north of the market hall is Market Square (Kauppatori). Bright orange tents mark the vendors' booths, displaying freshly cut flowers, fruits, and vegetables transported from the Finnish countryside, and crafts from small country villages. Customers love this colorful, bustling market held year-round Monday through Friday from early morning until early afternoon. Hours are extended to Sundays and evenings in July and August.

*Getting around.* Since this capital city sprawls over peninsulas and islands and since the sights are spread all over, you will probably use public transportation during your visit. Buses, trolleys, and a subway system are all available, and there is a flat rate of one ticket per ride, with free transfers. However, the best way to get a view of the city is by taking a boat trip around the offshore islands.

*Interesting places to visit.* Finland's Castle (Suomenlinna) is actually spread over six small islands. The fortress, begun in 1748 by Finnish units of the Swedish army, is home to a variety of small museums. The grounds are lovely too, filled with a generous scattering of parks and, in early summer, lilac bushes. Entrance to the castle is via ferry.

The Helsinki Zoo (Korkeasaari Eläintarha) houses a variety of animals that simply thrive in the area's cold arctic winters, including snow leopards and reindeer. There is also an outdoor play structure where kids can work off excess steam. Ferry service departs every 30 minutes from Market Square linking visitors to Helsinki Zoo and to Finland's Castle from May through September. Schedules and prices are listed on signboards at South Harbor.

Sibelius Park is a lovely green spot in the city of Helsinki, a great place to let your kids run around or eat a picnic lunch. The park has a monument to Jean Sibelius, famous for his composition *Finlandia,* and native of Finland. The design, constructed of steel tubes, is said to be reminiscent of organ pipes.

Because Helsinki is the northernmost capital in Europe, a winter visit will mean that you will view a frozen sea and Helsinkians braving the cold to ski and skate. If you visit in the summer, as most tourists do, you may be interested in one of the excellent beaches. Hietaranta is a beach near the city center, but the beaches on the islands, like Pihlajasaari and Seurasaari, are even more attractive.

The city's central square is Senaatintori (Senate Square), and its most prominent feature is Tuomiokirkko, the Lutheran cathedral with a green dome that dominates the skyline. When Hollywood producers want to make a film with a background that looks Russian, they do it here, because the square was modeled after St. Petersburg and even the stately cathedral has a Russian look to it. Inside the cathedral are statues of Martin Luther, his associate Philip Melanchthon, and Mikael Agricola. Agricola is called the father of Finnish literature, for he made the first rules for written Finnish.

*Churches.* There are several other churches in Helsinki worth going out of your way for. Temple Square Church (Temppeliaukion Kirkko) is located on Lutherininkatu 3 in a maze of streets. The modern church is striking, carved entirely out of rock and topped with a huge copper dome. The church is a favorite location for choral and chamber music concerts.

Not far from the Lutheran cathedral is the Orthodox Uspenski Cathedral (Uspenskin Katedraali). The red brick cathedral and its bulb-shaped domes stand guard over the east side of Market Square. The interior is decorated with icons.

If you are church-hopping, don't miss the little Holy Trinity church, directly behind the cathedral. Built in 1827, the Pyhan Koiminaisuuden Kirkko is probably more typical of the churches of the day than the big cathedral is.

*The National Museum.* In the early 20th century, three noted Finnish architects combined their genius to design the Kansailismuseo (the National Museum) at Mannerheimintie 34. Its architecture shows the influence of early Finnish churches and castles, but there are also elements of art nouveau in it. The exhibits in the museum trace the cultural history of the country from prehistoric times to the present.

*Olympic stadium.* Scandinavia is proud of its Olympic stadiums and Helsinki is no exception. At Etelainen Stadionintie 3, the stadium was designed for the Olympics of 1940, but then World War II broke out canceling the games. So Helsinki hosted the Olympics in 1952. Even if you aren't interested in the Olympics, you will be interested in the view of the city that you can get from the 225-foot tower. Sports buffs will find a museum just behind the tower.

*Museums.* On the outskirts of Helsinki in the community named Arabia is a porcelain factory that houses the Arabian Museum. Founded in 1873, the factory has a worldwide reputation for design, originality, and functionalism. In the factory tour you will see how the products are made and you can make purchases in the factory shop. The museum on the ninth floor details the 100-year history of the plant. In the summer there is free transportation from the city center.

Three miles west of Helsinki's city center is the Seurasaari Open-Air Museum (Seurasaaren Ulkomuseo) on Seurasaari Island, connected by bridge to the city proper. The museum transports the Finnish countryside to the city, highlighting traditional rural lifestyles and architecture on a small wooded island. Located here are about 100 buildings dating back to the 17th, 18th, and 19th centuries. The ornate Karuna Church (Karunan Kirkko), built in 1686, is one of the museum's highlights. Seurasaari also has a number of restaurants and beaches, including a secluded clothing-optional section. Ask directions before you find yourself unnecessarily embarrassed. The museum is open only from mid-May through mid-September. If you are here in midsummer, this is a good place to see the traditional Midsummer's Eve Celebrations.

A few miles north of the city on 1-45 is Ainola, the home of composer Jean Sibelius, who wrote his Third Symphony here. Sibelius is perhaps best known for *Finlandia,* part of which has been adapted as a tune for the hymn, "Be Still My Soul." The Steinway grand piano in the drawing room was given to him by friends on his 50th birthday in 1915.

About 20 miles southwest of the city (off road 51 and Keha Ring III in Luoma) is Hvitrask, an artist's studio home, where Sibelieus, Russian writer Maksim Gorky and Norwegian artist Edvard Munch frequently met as they sought to "return to nature." Eliel Saarinen was one of three famous architects who designed the castlelike building, and the Saarinen family lived here until Eliel won the competition to design the Tribune Tower in Chicago. Though Saarinen stayed in the United States for the remainder of his life, designing many outstanding buildings in America, he is buried in the forest of Hvitrask. The home is used today as a Finnish art and handicrafts center and is open daily.

You may want to take advantage of Helsinki's proximity to Russia and go by boat to St. Petersburg. It's only a few restful hours away.

**Åland** If you get to the Åland islands, and you should because they are breathtakingly beautiful, take note of two churches. In Jomala, Åland's oldest church, Sankt Olofs Kyrka is in the center of the village on the main road and dates from the early 1100s. It's a large church with interesting murals, four of which depict the parable of the prodigal son. Then about 12 miles farther north in Sund on the town's main road is the Johannes Doparens Kyrka with its 6-foot-thick walls. This church dates from the 13th century and commemorates one of Finland's earliest missionaries, Archbishop Wenni, who died here in 936. His body is buried in the graveyard.

**Espoo** Just west of Helsinki is this new city that is now the second largest in the country. Although Espoo dates only to 1972, when it was officially designated a city, it lies on an ancient road and so has a long history. Of special interest is the Espoon Kirkko, a 15th-century grey stone church with many mural paintings from the Middle Ages. The murals depict biblical scenes from creation to the last judgment.

> Be still, my soul: the Lord is on thy side;
> Bear patiently the cross of grief or pain.
> Leave to thy God to order and provide;
> In every change He faithful will remain.
> Be still, my soul: thy best, thy heavenly Friend
> Through thorny ways leads to a joyful end.
>
> WORDS BY KATHARINA VON SCHLEGEL OF COTHEN, GERMANY; USUALLY SUNG TO FINLANDIA BY JEAN SIBELIUS OF FINLAND

**Hämeenlinna** This old inland town boasts a medieval castle built at the end of the 13th century and the lovely Aulanko National Park, but most visitors come to see the birthplace of Composer Jean Sibelius (Sibeliuksen syntymäkoti) at Hallituskatu 11, the only remaining timber house in the town center. Here is where Sibelius spent his childhood and youth. The modest house, built in 1834, includes the harmonium Sibelius played as a youngster.

**Hamina** Near the Russian border stands this remarkable little town. During its history it has been ruled by Swedes and Russians as well as by Finns, as you can easily see from a quick look around town. In the octagonal center square of the town is the town hall built in 1798. Across from it is the Orthodox Church of St. Peter and Paul (1837) and behind the town hall is the Lutheran church (1843) in neoclassical style.

**Hanko (Hängo)** Whether you go for a swim or not, this town, which is Finland's southernmost community, is worth a stop.

The charming gingerbread houses were built in the late 19th century when Russia ruled the area. Many of the Russian nobility came to swim and some built summer residences. There are lots of good restaurants as well as large marinas where Finns dock their yachts. And Hanko is known for its sandy beaches, so enjoy!

**Hattula** The medieval Hattula Church (Hattulan Kirkko) is located five miles north of Hämeenlinna in the little town of Hattula. The interior is stunning, featuring frescoes of biblical scenes that were completed nearly 500 years ago, in 1510. The church is open daily from mid-May through mid-August.

**Hyvinkää** If you or your kids are fascinated by railroads, you should visit Suomen Rautatiemuseo, the Finnish Railway Museum in the center of town at Hyvinkäänkatu 9. Located about 25 miles north of Helsinki, the town was originally a health resort but then became a rail and industrial center. The big attraction at the museum is the imperial train, which was custom-built for Czar Alexander II of Russia in 1875.

**Imatra** The rapids here (Imatrankoski) were once Finland's preeminent tourist attraction; artists came here to find inspiration as they watched the 75-foot waterfall. Since the 1920s the waterfall has been harnessed to supply energy to the country, but during the summer the water is allowed to drop freely for 30 minutes each day and the sight is awesome. About six miles northeast of Imatra on the main road is Kolmen Ristin Kirkko, a modern church with 103 stained glass windows. Only two of the windows are identical.

**Ingå** The old 13th-century church in this village is dedicated to St. Nicholas. St. Nicholas was the patron saint of sailors, as you will discover as soon as you walk in the doors. An unusual mural on the north wall is called *The Dance of Death*.

**Jämsä** For some of the most fantastic scenery in Finland, take a 20-mile drive up to Korpilahti or, better yet, take a ferry ride viewing the beauty without worrying about the turns in the road.

**Jyväskylä** If you are a fan of automobile racing, you may want to visit this city, which is the home of the Thousand Lakes Rally, sometimes called the Finnish Grand Prix. The event draws between 200,000 and 300,000 spectators each August. The gravel roads and the dramatic bumps make the race unusual. About 20 miles west on road 23 is Petäjävesi, an unusual church built in 1763 and 1764, which is now on the UNESCO list of World Heritage Sites. The pulpit, which is older than the church, is supported by a primitive St. Christopher and decorated with angels.

**Kajaani** About six miles northwest of town is Paltaniemen Kirkka, a church built in 1726, adorned with a variety of frescoes by Emanuel Granberg. The frescoes depict scenes from the creation to the last judgment.

**Keuruu** If the church here doesn't interest you, maybe the church boat will. The church itself, Vanha Kirkka, is located at the junction of Rte. 23 and Keuruuntie Rd. and dates from 1758 and is an excellent example of a wooden church from that era. Its interior paintings illustrate several scenes from Scripture. The church boat, which is along the north churchyard wall, is about 65 feet long. It was used to bring worshipers from outlying villages. Today American churches sometimes have buses; in 18th-century Finland, churches had boats. And when you see the 15 pairs of oars, you'll realize that a boat like that is a lot cheaper to operate than a church bus.

**Kuopio** To really appreciate the beauty of the Lakelands, take the 11-1/2-hour boat trip from Savonlinna to Kuopio. Meals are available on board, and once you've arrived at Kuopio's passenger harbor, you can look forward to a small evening market located there daily from 3:00 to 10:00. If you want to shop earlier in the day, you can enjoy a larger marketplace in the city center, the Tori, weekdays from 7:00 to 3:00. The market is considered one of the most colorful in all of Finland.

There are two interesting sites of special interest to Christians in the town of Kuopio, both of which are related to the Orthodox Church, which dominates this area. The Orthodox Church Museum (Ortodoksinen Kirkkomuseo) at Karjalankatu 1 has an unusual collection of religious art from the monasteries of the eastern Finnish province of Karelia. But the real center of Russian Orthodox religious and cultural life in Finland is at the Valamo Monastery (Valamon Luostari) on Uusi Valamo. The main church and the icon conservation center display precious sacred objects and icons from the 18th century. Visitors can stay for meals or accommodations at a restaurant, hotel, and hostel located on the monastery grounds.

**Lahti** Located at the southern end of Finland's Lakeland, this resort city is known for its ski jumps in the winter and for its lake access in the summer. Its highest ski jump platform (about 450 feet) makes a good viewing platform in the summertime, if heights don't bother you. The lake district is so beautiful that you should see it by taking a cruise leaving from here.

**Lieksa** On the eastern shore of picturesque Lake Pielinen is this busy tourist center of 17,000 residents. But the big attraction is nearby Koli Hills. You can take a daily car ferry there to see the beauty, but 100 years ago painters, writers, and composers all climbed up the hill the hard way to be inspired. In fact if you want to believe the story, they say that Sibelius dragged a grand piano to the top to celebrate his honeymoon. In the little village of Vuon-isjarvi, about 20 miles south, is the Eva Ryynänen studio home, where the sculptor and wood-carver has her works displayed. Her masterpiece is called *Wilderness Church (Paateri),* and it is worth going a few miles out of your way to see.

**Naantali** This is a pleasant summer resort town with water on three sides, and you don't need another special reason to visit it. However, while you are here, stop in at the Luostearikirkko, a church in the center of Naantali's Old Town that was originally part of a Brigittine convent founded in 1443. The church clock shows 11:30, and according to the story, when it is 12 o'clock it will be the end of the world. It also has some remarkable works of art inside, including a painting by R. W. Ekman, *The Sinful Woman in the House of the Pharisee.* Also worth seeing in Naantali is the Old Town, which has been rebuilt to resemble a medieval burgh.

**Porvoo** When you wander down the narrow winding streets of Vanha Porvoo, you will think that you have gone back in time a couple centuries. On one side of town is the medieval section of wooden houses with the cathedral on the hill; on the other side is the Empire Town, which has its own charm.

**Rovaniemi** In case you had any doubts, Santa's Village does indeed lie within the Arctic Circle. In fact it's here, just north of Rovaniemi right on the Arctic Circle. Santa Claus Village at Arctic Circle Center offers plenty of opportunities to shop for gifts, and, if you like, you can have your purchases shipped back home with a special Santa Claus Land stamp. The Santa Train travels from the village past Reindeer Park, where visitors can size up Santa's sleigh team. Then it's on to Santa Park, a Christmas theme park located inside a rocky cave. Visitors can enjoy a magic sleigh ride, a Christmas carousel, a puppet circus, and much more.

**Savonlinna** The rough beauty of the Lakelands district forms the backdrop for the city of Savonlinna, the center of which is a series of islands linked by bridges. Visitors enjoy the open-air market that thrives alongside the main passenger quay. Just east of the city on a little island in the middle of the Kyronsalmi Straits is the castle Olavinlinna, one of Scandinavia's best-preserved historic monuments. Tours of the edifice are available in English every hour. Each July the castle's courtyard is the stage for the Savonlinna Opera Festival. If you're interested, be sure to make reservations for the popular event well in advance, both for the opera and for hotel rooms. More information can be obtained from the Savonlinna Tourist Office, ten minutes southeast from the quay, or by phone 015/517-510, or by fax 015/517-5123.

Enjoy the lifestyle and beauty of the Lakelands aboard a full-day boat excursion to the town of Kuopio.

**Snappertuna** About 40 miles west of Helsinki in Snappertuna, you will see the castle of Raseborg on a rocky outcrop overlooking the river. The original fortress was built here in the 14th century. The present building is a restoration from 1890. In the heart of the little village of Snappertuna is a wooden church from 1688. Inside are lovely paintings and other decorations.

**Tampere** There are two notable churches in the city of Tampere. On the east side of town is the modern Kaleva Church (Kalevan Kirkko) at Liisanpuisto 1, which was built by the famous husband-wife architectural team, Reima and Reili Pietilä. Tampere's cathedral, the Tuomiokirkko, located at Tuomiokirkonkatu 3, is also quite modern compared to the rest of Europe, having been constructed in 1907. The church is home to some of the best-known masterpieces of Finnish mural art.

If you're traveling with children, be sure to visit the nearby Särkänniemi peninsula. Of prime interest will be the Särkänniemi Amusement Center (Särkänniemi Huvikeskus), a large recreational area composed of an amusement park, a zoo, a planetarium, and an aquarium, complete with a dolphin tank.

**Turku** Founded early in the 13th century, Turku is the nation's oldest city and its original capital. Its cathedral (Turun Tuomiokirkko) is as old, having celebrated its 700th anniversary in 2000. The cathedral, the mother church of the Lutheran Church of Finland, is the seat of the archbishop of Finland. Its museum displays silver chalices, wooden sculptures, and a collection of medieval church vestments.

The Sibelius Museum here is a must for anyone involved in church music. It contains a variety of musical instruments from clavichords to organs. Then there's the castle built in 1280 and repaired almost every century after that.

If you're interested in local handicrafts, take time for the Luostarinmäki Handicrafts Museum (Luostarinmäen Kasityöläismuseo) at Vartiovuorenkatu 4. Open mid-April through mid-September, the museum features an authentic collection of wooden houses and buildings. Shops and workshops house traditional craft demonstrations, the results of which are available for purchase.

Just west of Turku in the little community of Nousiainen is a 13th-century church built as a memorial to Bishop Henry who brought Christianity to the area in 1156 and founded Finland's first church. A 15th-century marble tomb marks his burial place.

**Varkaus** This 20th-century town of 25,000 in the Lakelands area has a couple of things that will catch your attention, besides its scenic rapids and vast forests. You will want to see the Lutheran church here with its fascinating fresco *Thy Kingdom Come,* by Lennart Segerestrale. And someone in your family will no doubt want to stop at the museum of mechanical music here (Mekaanisen musiikin museo), which displays more than 200 instruments, including street organs, grammophones, and old phonographs.

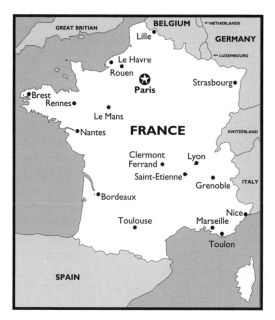

# *France*

French Government Tourist Office
  US 212-838-7800
  Canada 416-491-7622
  UK 0891-244-123
  Australia 02-9231-5244
*Web site*
  Entire country www.franceguide.com
For a complete list of updated links, visit www.christiantraveler.com

### Country in a Capsule

*Size:* The largest country in central Europe, France is larger than California but not as large as Texas, and its population exceeds that of both of those states combined.

*Religion:* Officially it's 80 percent Catholic, 5 percent Muslim, and 2 percent Protestant, but only about 20 percent of the Catholics go to church each week.

*Language:* French, and proud of it. If you are going outside of the big cities, take along a French phrase book or at least know the rudiments of the language. Make an attempt to speak the language and your efforts will be rewarded.

*Money:* The unit of currency is the French franc, abbreviated ff. The French franc is currently worth about 14 cents.

*Food:* Different sections of France have different favorite foods. In the southwest, a rich stew of white bean, tomatoes, sausage, and duck (cassoulet) is popular. In the Alps, you will enjoy fondue. Provence is known for its bouillabaisse fish soup. Burgundy is known for its escargot and its beef casserole. In Paris you might try some lamb cutlets or a veal stew enriched with egg and cream called blanquette de veau.

*Shopping:* Pottery, if you are near Marseille or Grasse; porcelain from Limoges; crystal from Baccarat; cheese, sausage, and olive oil in various parts of the country.

*Brief history:* Although the history of the area dates back to the Greek colonization in 600 B.C. and Caesar's conquering of Gaul in the 1st century B.C., it wasn't until Hugh Capet became king in 987 that various factions united into a kingdom. The Hundred Years' War (1137–1453) was renowned for the leadership of the Black Prince and Joan of Arc. The English won the war but lost the country and were eventually driven out.

From 1562 to 1598, Catholic and Protestant nobles fought the French Wars of Religion. The Protestant Huguenots were persecuted, notably at the St. Bartholomew's Day Massacre in 1572, when some 4,000 were murdered. The Edict of Nantes in 1589 finally granted freedom of worship and civil rights to religious minorities and the country came out of its civil war.

The 17th century saw France's power grow internationally under Louis XIII, Louis XIV, and Louis XV, but the absolutism of the monarchs also grew and became more inflexible. The storming of the Bastille during the reign of Louis XVI and the resulting Revolution of 1789 ended the absolute monarchy. Napoléon took over at the beginning of the 19th century, but his reign was short-lived, and instability followed. Since 1789 France has had five republics, two empires, and three brands of royal power as it has struggled with instability. The World Wars of the 20th century decimated the country, but it has shown resilience in reviving again after overwhelming difficulties.

**Paris** How do you describe Paris? It is indescribable. Paris has to be experienced, and once you have spent three or four days in the city, you will realize that you've only experienced a small part of it.

For a quick orientation, why not enjoy a tour of Paris via its waterways in the popular motorboats called bateaux mouches? The hour-long tours depart every half hour in summer from the pl. de l'Alma.

You cannot visit Paris without also visiting the Eiffel Tower, the city's most famous landmark. Built in 1889, the tower was created for the World Exhibition in Paris that year. Elevators take visitors 1,000 feet to the top for fabulous views of the city. The elevators are slow, and long lines are the rule unless you come in the evening.

*Churches.* Many churches throughout Paris offer inexpensive organ or chamber music concerts. Check the information board whenever you tour a church to see what might be playing during your stay.

Along with the Eiffel Tower, the white domes of Basilique du Sacré-Coeur delineate the Parisian skyline as the cathedral is perched on the top of Montmartre at 35 rue du Cheval de la Barre. Rather modern compared to most famous churches in France, it was built between 1876 and 1890. Inside you'll see a vast mosaic of Christ on the vaulted ceiling. The outside sure makes a great postcard! For a good view of the city, climb up to the dome.

Notre-Dame de Paris is located at Ile de la Cité, 4, on the Seine River. Notre Dame is another of those historic Parisian landmarks that you simply can't miss. It is one of the best known churches in the world. Its rose window, flying buttresses, and great bell— which was tolled by Quasimodo, Victor Hugo's fictional hunch- back—are world famous. Begun in 1163, it is considered one of the oldest Gothic cathedrals in the world, even though it wasn't completed until 1345. Although the church is dark and heavy, the beautiful stained glass windows filter colored light into the interior. Make the effort to climb all 387 stairs to the top of the towers. You'll be rewarded with a great view of the gargoyles and the city below. Visit in the early morning if you want to avoid large crowds. The treasury contains religious artifacts and clothing. If you find yourself in Paris on Christmas Eve, attend Notre-Dame's midnight mass for a very powerful service. All of Paris will be there. After visiting this cathedral, you may want to visit nearby Ste-Chapelle for comparison.

Located in the shadow of Notre-Dame, Ste-Chapelle (4 bd. du Palais, 1) is often overlooked among Paris's better known cathedrals. Don't make the same mistake. The walls of this chapel consist of narrow but dazzlingly beautiful 50-foot stained glass windows. Try to visit on a sunny day, and you'll think you've stepped into a kaleidoscope. Imagine how 13th-century worshipers, few of whom would have been literate, would have been reminded of important biblical events as they viewed the glass pictures. The chapel was built by Louis IX in the 1240s to house the Crown of Thorns he had just bought from Emperor Baldwin of Constantinople.

The American Cathedral of the Holy Trinity was built between 1885 and 1888. It holds services each morning at 9:00 and Sunday mornings at 9:00 and 11:00. It is located at 23 av. Georges V.

On the left bank of the Seine River, at 65 quai d'Orsay, the American Church not only conducts regular services but also provides help to English-speaking tourists.

St-Augustin is located on Pl. St-Augustin. This church was constructed around 1860 within an odd V-shaped piece of land. Built with metal pillars and girders—thus eliminating the need for exterior buttresses—the church was considered an architectural trendsetter when it was built.

Granted, Eglise de la Madeleine looks a bit like a Greek temple, but Catholic masses are said each morning at 7:30 and 8:00, and its location is great (on Place de la Madeleine) for the local residents as well as for tourists.

Eglise St. Germain-des-Prés, the oldest in Paris, traces its roots to the 6th century, although most of the present church comes from the 12th and 13th centuries. The frescoes in the nave depict scenes from the Old Testament. Organ concerts and recitals are frequently performed here. It is located at pl. St-Germain-des-Prés.

Eglise Saint Nicolas du Chardonnet is one of the few Catholic churches that still retain Latin in the mass, refusing to use French. The impressive 13-by-7 foot oil painting by Jean Baptiste-Camille Corot, *The Baptism of Christ,* is in the first chapel on the right.

The Hôtel des Invalides, or simply Les Invalides, on pl. des Invalides was founded in 1674 as a hostelry for wounded war veterans. Only a few old soldiers still live here today. The building complex is a lovely example of Baroque architecture. One of the local churches in Les Invalides, Soldiers' Church or St-Louis-des-Invalides, is a bit austere. The second church, the Eglise du Dôme, has a beautiful slender dome. Inside lay the remains of Napoléon.

The most striking feature of St-Sulpice, a colossal 17th-century church on Pl. St-Sulpice, is its beautiful 18th-century facade. A wall painting by Delacroix, *Jacob and the Angel,* in the first chapel on the right is worth viewing.

Many of the churches have concerts during the summer. Among them are Ste-Chapelle, Notre-Dame, St-Eustache (rue du Jour 1), St-Germain-des-Prés, St-Julien-Le-Pauvre (23 quai de Montebello 5), St-Louis-en-l'Ile (bis rue St-Louis-en-l'Ile), and St-Roch (rue St-Honoré 1).

*Museums.* The Louvre, on rue de Rivoli, is the world's largest and most famous museum. Begun as a fortress in 1200 and later transformed into a royal palace, the oldest parts still in use today date from about 1540. Modern architect I. M. Pei added the glass pyramid in front that forms the most recognizable and busiest entrance to the museum (there's another entrance at the Carousel du Louvre mall on rue de Rivoli that's less crowded). Everyone who visits the Louvre wants to see the museum's most popular attraction: Leonardo da Vinci's 1503 masterpiece, *Mona Lisa* (called *La Joconde* in French). Be prepared for heavy crowds.

Many of the museum's Renaissance and medieval works have sacred themes. Among the treasures are *The Wedding Feast of Cana* (1562–63), Paolo Veronese's oil on canvas work, which extends 32 feet long and 21 feet high; *Christ Blessing the Children* (1548) by the Master HB of the Griffin Head, a painting that children as well as adults will enjoy; *Christ Healing the Sick* (1650) by Nicolas Poussin; *Christ Driving the Merchants from the Temple* (1650) by Jacob Jardaens, an oil painting about 9 by 14 feet; and Rembrandt's *The Supper at Emmaus* (1648), which, though not large, is very powerful. To make your visit count, buy a pamphlet called "Visitor's Guide." It will maximize your time and save your aching feet.

The immense science and technology museum (Cité des Sciences et de l'Industrie), located on the northern end of Parc de la Villette, is housed in a five-story building that covers five acres. Highly interactive, it encourages visitors to play computer games and learn about space, the earth, and the ocean. A space station shows how astronauts live in space. Its cinema, La Géode, claims the largest projection screen in existence.

*Parks and Gardens.* Paris's Botanical Garden (Jardin des Plantes) has been around since the 17th century, but its name is a bit of a misnomer. There are botanical gardens here, including an alpine garden and several greenhouses, but there is much more than gardens. This is the home of a zoo, an aquarium, a maze, and several natural history museums. The Entomological Museum (Musée Entomologique) houses insects; the Mineralogical Museum (Musée Minéralogique) features minerals; and the Paleontological Museum (Musée Paléontologique) houses fossils and prehistoric animals. Don't let the name of the Great Hall of Evolution (Grande Galerie de l'Evolution) scare you off; the gallery features a huge assortment of stuffed and mounted animals, some of which are now extinct. The complex is located at 36 rue Geoffroy-St-Hilaire.

Not only can you get away from the hustle and bustle of Paris in the greenery of the Bois de Boulogne, but you can rent a bike to ride, you can go boating on Lac Inférieur, you can take a ferry to one of the islands, you can have your own picnic, or you can take your kids to a kiddie park/zoo/playground at the park's northside.

The lawns of the Jardin du Luxembourg are to be admired, not played or picnicked on. The special attraction here is the Théâtre des Marionnettes, with shows on Wednesday, Saturday, and Sunday at 3:00 and 4:00.

As you stroll through the Jardin des Tuileries, you can see all of Paris's great attractions: the Eiffel Tower, the Louvre, the Champs-Élysées, the Arc de Triomphe, the Seine. Rue de Rivoli borders the garden on the north and quai des Tuileries on the south.

Just southeast of Paris is Bois de Vincennes, a large park with several lakes, a zoo, a tribal art museum, a castle, a flower garden, an amusement park, and several cafes. The flower garden covers 70 acres, so that gives you an idea of how big the whole park is.

**Abbaye de Jumièges** Once an important Benedictine center, the Abbaye de Jumièges was founded in the 7th century but dismantled during the French Revolution. What is left of the abbey is largely ruins, but they are substantial and beautiful. Several chapels on site are worth visiting as well. The abbey is located at 24 rue Guillaume-le-Conquérant.

**Abbaye de St-Wandrille** The Abbaye de St-Wandrille, founded in A.D. 649, is still home to a Benedictine community. Arrive early in the morning so you can enjoy the Gregorian chants at Mass. Guided tours are available.

**Aigues-Mortes** Today Aigues-Mortes is a quiet Provençal village, its shores silted up so that you might not guess the town's history. But its historic city walls remain as a reminder that it was once a coastal fortress from which Louis IX launched his crusades to Jerusalem to reclaim the land for Christ. In the southeast corner of the walled city is the Tour de Constance, where religious prisoners were often kept. Catholic prisoners were the first inmates, then Calvinist inmates, and finally Huguenot women.

**Aix-en-Provence** Not all ancient cities are beautiful, but this one is. Founded in 103 B.C. by the Romans, it is sometimes called "the city of a thousand fountains." Its cathedral (Cathédrale St-Sauveur), rue Gaston de Saporta, dating from the 13th century, is known for Nicolas Froment's *Triptych of the Burning Bush*. The Tapestry Museum (place des Martyrs de la Résistance) displays gorgeous 17th- and 18th-century tapestries and is also the site of the annual Aix festival each summer. The artist Paul Cézanne lived here and his modest home is just north of town at 9 av. Paul Cézanne. The brochure *In the Footsteps of Paul Cézanne* can be picked up at the tourists office on pl. du Gen. de Gaulle. It will guide you along a walking tour of the city's Cézanne sites.

**Albi** A heretical sect called the Cathars (also known as the Albigensians) grew rapidly in southern France in the 12th and 13th centuries. It was headquartered here in Albi. It believed in two gods: a good god who created the spirit world, and an evil god who created the physical world, including the human body. They accepted the New Testament but rejected the incarnation of Christ. In 1208 Pope Innocent III waged an Inquisition Crusade against the Cathars, after which the Albi cathedral, Cathédrale Ste-Cécile on pl. Ste-Cécile, was built, looking somewhat like a fortress to show the townspeople that the church meant business. Inside is a huge fresco of the last judgment.

93

**Amiens** Here you will find the largest cathedral in France, Cathédrale de Notre-Dame, and that's saying a lot. It was started in 1220 to house the head of John the Baptist, which supposedly had just been brought back from the Crusades in 1206. The nave is 138 feet high. Richly adorned, its artwork features biblical scenes as well as scenes from the life of St. Firmin, who brought Christianity to the area, was the first bishop of the city, and was later martyred. Musée de Picardie, 48 rue de la République, features medieval religious sculptures and paintings. Incidentally, sci-fi author Jules Verne's home can also be visited in Amiens at 2 rue Charles Dubois.

**Angers** In this city's 15th-century chateau on pl. Kennedy, built by Louis IX, is one of France's finest medieval tapestries. Woven in the 14th century, it tells the story of the Book of Revelation, depicting battles between angels and dragons. Next to the castle is the St. Maurice Cathedral, with its outstanding 12th-century stained glass windows.

While imprisoned at the monastery of Angers in the 9th century, Bishop Theodulph of Orléans wrote "All Glory, Laud and Honor," a hymn often sung on Palm Sunday.

**Arles** In this old city, you can enjoy a little bit of everything. There are Roman remains, including a 20,000-seat Roman amphitheater, where bull fights are still staged in the summer. Among its churches are the Notre-Dame de la Major on pt. des Arènes, dedicated to St. George, who is the patron saint of cowboys, and 11th-century Eglise St-Trophime, with its 12th-century portal of the last judgment. The Eglise St-Trophime, an extraordinary Romanesque church, is classed as a world treasure by UNESCO. Right behind the church on pl. de la République is the St. Trophime Cloister (Cloître St-Trophime). The quiet Romanesque building is a jewel, one of the loveliest cloisters in Provence. There is also a Van Gogh museum in honor of the artist who spent 15 months here painting 300 canvases. The Van Gogh Foundation is located at 26 pt. des Arènes.

**Autun** Autun has been an important town since Roman times. You'll see well-preserved Roman archways, the Porte St-André, and the Porte d'Arroux, as well as a Roman theater, the Théâtre Romain, all located within the city. The town's principal feature is the Cathédrale St-Lazarus, a Gothic cathedral on pl. St-Louis that was reworked in the classical style in the 18th century by church leaders who were trying to keep up with the times.

**Auxerre** Auxerre is one of the most beautiful villages in France's Burgundy region. Three elegant churches are located on a large hill and are connected by steep meandering streets that are lined with half-timbered houses. The most interesting church is the Cathédrale St-Etienne on pl. St-Etienne, which was built between the 13th and 16th centuries.

The oldest above-ground section of the Abbaye de St-Germain on pl. St-Germain is the Romanesque bell tower, constructed in the 12th century. But if you visit the underground section inside you will find a much older crypt, begun in 859 by Charles the Bald. Its original Carolingian frescoes and Ionic capitals can still be seen. Guided tours of the crypt are available daily.

**Avallon** Avallon is a great place to enjoy the quiet French countryside. Its old streets make for pleasant strolling. Take the time to notice the St. Lazarus Church (Église St-Lazarus) on pl. St-Louis. Its exterior Romanesque stone carvings are striking.

**Avignon** Whether or not you're Catholic, you'll enjoy lovely Avignon and its Papal Palace (Palais des Papes) on pl. du Palais-des-Papes. Medieval alleys wind around the city's stone towers and walls. During the years 1309–1377 seven exiled Popes loved this place as well. Having fled the corruption in Rome, they set up headquarters here. The huge Papal Palace is actually two buildings. The Old Palace (Palais Vieux) was built between 1334 and 1342 by Pope Benedict XII, who frowned on frivolous decorations. It is, therefore, a rather austere building. The more decorative New Palace (Palais Nouveau) was built ten years later by Pope Clement VI, who enjoyed a more lavish existence.

Near the Papal Palace is the 12th-century Avignon Cathedral, Cathédrale Notre-Dame-des-Doms, on pl. du Palais, within which lie the remains of Pope John XXII. Behind the cathedral is the Bluff of the Dome (Rocher des Doms), a large park where you can get lovely views of the town and the river.

The Small Palace (Petit Palais) at 21 pl. du Palais was home to cardinals and archbishops in medieval times. Today it is an art museum with a terrific collection of old masters' paintings.

95

**Bayeux** You won't be able to miss the impressive Cathédrale de Notre-Dame in the heart of Bayeux on rue de Bienvenu. A mixture of Romanesque and Gothic architecture, its most interesting feature is over the portal on the south side, a depiction of the assassination of English Archbishop Thomas à Becket in Canterbury Cathedral in 1170.

**Beaune** Beaune's main church is the Collégiale Notre-Dame on av. de la République. The 12th-century building is known for its lovely tapestries that tell the story of the life of the Virgin Mary.

**Beauvais** Maybe you wouldn't go too far out of your way to see a clock, but this isn't an ordinary clock. It's part of the Cathédrale St-Pierre, a Gothic building begun in 1227 but never quite finished. It has collapsed a couple of times, but it is still safe to look at. Near the north door is a 90,000-part astronomical clock depicting Christ surrounded by his 12 apostles on the clock's face. Above the face of the clock are mechanical figures showing scenes from the last judgment. Below the face of the clock are indicators showing the age of the world and the time of the solstice.

**Besançon** Two missionaries from Greece came here in A.D. 180, set up shop in a cave in the middle of the woods, and began preaching to the people. For 30 years they preached, but because they refused to sacrifice to the pagan gods of the area, they were eventually beheaded in the amphitheatre. The 12th-century Cathédrale St-Jean on rue de la Convention is supposedly built on the site of the cave. The cathedral's bell tower with its astronomical clock (Horloge Astronomique) is a reminder of the fact that the city has a history of watchmaking. If you are here on the hour, you will see figures pop out of the clock, but there are also 62 dials, telling you the time in 16 places round the world, the tides in eight ports, and no doubt a few other things.

**Bourg-en-Bresse** The abbey church of Brou, just southeast of town on bd. de Brou, is no longer a church but is a remarkable site to visit anyway. There's a long story behind it, but basically the church was built by Margaret of Austria to fulfill a vow, and she spared no expense to do it. The sculptures, the tapestries, and the stained glass are all magnificent.

**Caen** There are two abbeys in the town of Caen, one for women and one for men. Both are masterpieces. The Women's Abbey (Abbaye aux Dames) on pl. de la Reine-Mathilde is now home to various government offices, but its lovely courtyard, reception rooms, and church can be visited during a free guided tour. The Men's Abbey (Abbaye aux Hommes) on pl. Louis-Guillouard was begun in 1066 but was later expanded during the 18th century. Its church is large and lovely. Both abbeys were commissioned by William the Conqueror and his queen Mathilda. William was also responsible for the massive fortress that sits on the hill in the city's center.

A World War II memorial is located on Esplanade Dwight-Eisenhower.

> Whence come these sores, whence this mortal anguish?
> It is my sins for which Thou, Lord, must languish;
> Yea, all the wrath, the woe, Thou dost inherit,
> This I do merit.
>
> JEAN DE FÉCAMP OF LE HAVRE, FRANCE

**Carcassonne** This restored medieval town recalls the Albigensian inquisition (see Albi) of 1209 with a siege stone at the Basilique St-Nazaire on pl. de l'Eglise. The crusaders stormed the city with orders to kill everyone they saw: "Kill them all. God will recognize his own!" Some 20,000 were killed. Some of the walls of the city date from Roman times.

**Chalon-Sur-Saône** Some of the first photographs ever taken were taken here (1816), and some of the earliest 19th-century submarines were built here. The photography museum is the Musée Nicephore-Niepce at 28 quai des Messageries. Both the St. Vincent's Cathedral on av. de la Poissonnerie and St. Peter's on pl. de l'Hôtel de Ville have much to offer, and so does the Denon Museum, also on pl. de l'Hôtel de Ville, with its important collection of 17th- to 19th-century paintings with Italian, French, and Dutch artists all represented.

**Chantilly** Located not far from Paris, this lovely area offers a chateau, a park, a forest, and an outstanding museum. In the Musée Conde, are several impressive works of art depicting the life of Christ. Start with *The Annunciation to the Shepherds* and

*The Nativity* by the Limbourg Brothers, and then see Raphael's *The Madonna di Loreto*, an oil on poplar work done in 1509. Also here is *The Resurrected Christ* by Salvatore Rosa, a 17th-century piece of art.

Not far from here in Lamorlaye is the home of the European Bible Institute, founded by the Greater Europe Mission (GEM).

**Chartres** You will see the Cathédrale de Notre-Dame looming over the city long before you actually arrive there. You couldn't ask for a better city in which to place such a grand cathedral, dating from before the Roman conquest. Chartres is lovely and still has its winding medieval streets. The Gothic Cathédrale de Notre-Dame is actually the sixth Christian church on this site and has remained basically unchanged since its construction in the 12th and 13th centuries. The life and triumph of Christ is depicted on the main facade and is considered one of France's best examples of Romanesque sculpture. Notice the beautiful deep blue in the cathedral's 12th- and 13th-century stained glass windows. The famous color is unique to Chartres stained glass, and its secret formula has never been divulged. Two unusual pieces of stained glass work are *The Tree of Jesse* from the 12th century, and *Madonna and Child,* often called *Our Lady of the Beautiful Stained Glass,* from the 13th century. The stained glass windows of the cathedral cover 26,900 square feet. Tours are conducted daily in English at noon and 2:45. Ask for information at the Maison des Clercs.

Alongside the cathedral is the Musée des Beaux Arts, with an outstanding collection of tapestries.

**Chinon** Located in a picturesque ancient town, the 12th-century Château de Chinon, perched on a hill overlooking the Vienne River, is mostly in ruins. Christians may be interested in visiting anyway, because the castle's Clock Tower (Tour de l'Horloge) contains the Joan of Arc Museum (Museé Jeanne d'Arc).

**Cluny** Although the Ancienne Abbaye St-Pierre et St-Paul is in ruins, you can still get a guided tour. Founded by William the Pious in 910, it became the most powerful monastic organization in Europe and was a major reforming force within the Roman Catholic Church. The church here was the largest in the world until the 16th century when St. Peter's Basilica was built in Rome. The remaining ruins in the old city will give you an idea of the abbey's original size and splendor. The Clocher de l'Eau-Bénite is a lovely bell tower that stands atop the only remaining section of the original abbey church. Visitors can visit the Musée Ochier, the abbey palace, where part of the resident monks' library is preserved.

A hymn sung in many Protestant churches, "Jerusalem the Golden," was written by Bernard of Cluny in the 12th century. Just southwest of town is the chapel in Berze-la-Ville with great 12th-century frescoes, no doubt similar to what were once in Cluny.

**Dijon** This city is noted for more than mustard and gingerbread. It is also famous for its architecture and its museum of fine arts. The museum (Musée des Beaux Arts) houses an outstanding collection of Flemish masters. Jacques de Baerze's triptych on Pentecost is notable, as is Veronese's *Moses in the Bulrushes,* and Robert Campin's *The Adoration of the Shepherds,* an oil on wood painting done in the first half of the 15th century. The collection is in the east wing of the Palais des Ducs de Bourgogne in pl. de la Libération.

## Très Beau!

Although France is best known for its culture, food, and romance, it has also been blessed with great natural beauty. The French Alps are among the country's chief outdoor attractions. While many associate the Alps with Switzerland, France is home to Europe's highest mountain peak, Mont Blanc. The city of Grenoble makes a nice home base for exploring the Alps, situated at the convergence of four mountain chains, each with its share of snowcapped peaks and sapphire-blue lakes. The tourist office, at 14 rue de la République, is located right in the middle of town and offers plenty of information about train and bus excursions into the surrounding mountains.

Skiing is a popular local sport. The Oisans region to the east claims the biggest and most impressive skiing, with the biggest ski-able glacier in Europe at Les Deux Alpes. Chamrousse is the biggest and most popular ski area in the Belledonne region, northeast of Grenoble, with plenty of good skiing even for beginners. In the summer these regions boast superb hiking and picnicking areas.

Enjoy the beautiful French countryside at the Morvan Regional Park (Parc Naturel Régionel du Morvan). Roads and trails meander through the hills and past picturesque lakes and forests. When Parisians decide to go to the country, they come here to hike the well-marked trails. You can find a number of gîtes (rustic bed-and-breakfast establishments) in the area, some of which have stables. Horseback riding in the area is popular.

There are several noteworthy churches in Dijon. One of the city's highlights is surely its Notre-Dame Cathedral on rue de la Préfecture. Thin towers, a lovely facade, and beautiful 13th-century stained glass are all among its features. One of Dijon's oldest churches is the Cathédrale St-Bénigne on pl. St-Bénigne. The interior itself is rather solemn, but its 11th-century crypt is worth visiting. The Eglise St-Michel on pl. St-Michel is a relatively new church. Its chief feature is a lovely Renaissance facade.

About 15 miles straight south of Dijon is the little community of Citeaux. Bernard, later known as Bernard of Clairvaux, joined the Order of Cistercians. He became the most popular preacher of the 12th century, practicing a rigid asceticism but emphasizing love and a deep devotional life. Among the hymns he wrote are, "Jesus, Thou Joy of Loving Hearts," "O Sacred Head Now Wounded," and "Jesus, the Very Thought of Thee."

**Dôle** Louis Pasteur, the great scientist, was born here in 1822. His birthplace is at rue Pasteur 43, and next door is the Pasteur Museum. The lovely church (Collégiale Notre Dame) dates from the 16th century and contains some of the first Renaissance works of art in polychrome marble.

**Douai** It was here that the Douai Version of the Bible was translated. It was also here that "O Come All Ye Faithful" was translated. The origin of the carol is still a mystery. Some say it was translated from an ancient Latin hymn, others say it was translated from a French poem, and still others think that the "translator" John Wade made it up himself.

**Fécamp** Fécamp is beautifully situated at the bottom of the highest cliffs on the Normandy coast. It was France's first place of pilgrimage. According to a legend, about A.D. 100 an abandoned boat washed ashore at this location. In the boat was a bottle containing Christ's blood. For centuries pilgrims came to see the miraculous find. The Church of the Trinity (Eglise de la Trinité) on rue Leroux was built nearby in the 11th century as a place for the visiting pilgrims to worship. Guided tours are available.

**Fontainebleau** About 50 minutes from downtown Paris is this historic chateau in a spectacular forest setting. The chapel, built in 1169, was consecrated by Thomas à Becket. Almost every French king from François I to Louis XIV had something to do with the building of Fontainebleau, but it was Napoléon who established its glory and made it his personal Versailles. By the way, it was here that Napoléon held Pope Pius VII prisoner until he signed the Church-State concordat of 1813.

**Fontenay** The Abbaye de Fontenay, which was founded in 1118 by St. Bernard, is the oldest extant Cistercian monastery. It was in active use until the French Revolution when it was sold and converted into a paper mill. In 1906 new ownership began restoring the abbey to its original appearance. The simplicity of the abbey church is striking. In the scriptorium manuscripts were copied, and an adjoining warming room was available for the monks to warm their cold hands.

**Fontevraud** The medieval abbey in Fontevraud (Fontevraud Abbaye) dominates the town. The English kings Henry II and Richard the Lionhearted are buried here. Guided tours of the church, cloisters, refectory, and octagonal kitchen are available, but only in French. Ask for an English brochure.

**Fréjus** Fréjus was founded by Julius Caesar in 49 B.C. and was originally called Forum Julii. There are still a number of Roman ruins around, including part of a theater, an arena, city walls, and part of an aqueduct. In the middle of town on pl. Formigé stands the Groupe Episcopal, which consists of an early Gothic cathedral, a Romanesque/Gothic cloister, and a baptistery dating from the 5th century.

**Honfleur** Honfleur was once an important port for maritime expeditions. It has more recently become a favorite for vacationers. Cobblestone streets, yachts, and lively restaurants and cafes make the town a memorable stop—as does the lovely 15th-century wooden church, Eglise Ste-Catherine on pl. Ste-Catherine.

**La Charité-Sur-Loire** This small town has a great history and a remarkable cathedral. The citizenry converted to Christianity early in the 8th century. The present church was built in the 11th century and the monks were so kind in helping the poor and the suffering that the town got the name la charité. The church, Notre Dame, which is almost 400 feet long and 90 feet high, could hold a congregation of 5,000. Incidentally the present population of the town is about 5,500.

**La Rochelle** It had been a Huguenot stronghold in the late 16th century, but after a long blockade and vicious fighting, it was finally laid waste by Cardinal Richelieu in 1628. As a result, much of the historic center dates from that time, but the cobbled streets, the scenic harbor, and the majestic tower, including the 15th century Tour de la Lanterne, make it a pleasant stop.

**Le Mans** This city is famous for its 24-hour automobile race each June, and its Automobile Museum is worth noting as well. The museum is 3 miles south of town on Circuit des 24 Heures. But even apart from cars, there is much to see. Its Gallo-Roman walls are the finest in France, and its old city area looks so much like a medieval city is supposed to look that it is frequently used as the set of Hollywood epics. But don't neglect looking at Cathédrale St-Julien, with its flying buttresses and its Romanesque portal that reminds you of Chartres.

**Le Puy-en-Velay** You don't find too many towns located in the bowl of a volcanic cone. Though it is a town of only 22,000, it has a medieval holy city complex. Its Notre Dame de France is a huge red statue constructed in 1860 out of 213 cannons captured in Russia during the Crimean War. But the city's finest structure is its Cathédrale de Notre-Dame with its famous Black Madonna statue. Since the cathedral sits on the volcanic hilltop in the city center, any road leading up will take you to the church, but the most stunning view is had by way of the stone steps of rue des Tables. The church also features Romanesque frescoes from the 11th and 12th centuries and the Bible of Theodulph, a 9th-century French bishop.

**Lille** Outside of Paris, you don't find many art museums better than Lille's Musée des Beaux Arts at pl. de la République. Its Flemish paintings are especially good.

**Limoges** Since 1770 Limoges and porcelain have almost been synonymous. Its old town has half-timbered houses and narrow streets that invite you to explore them. There are also two museums, one tracing the history of ceramics from early Greek and Chinese times, and the other displaying about 500 Limoges enamels. Consider visiting the Musée Adrien-Dubouché, pl. Winston Churchill; the Pavillion de la Porcelaine, rte. de Toulouse; or the Musée Haviland, also on rte. de Toulouse.

**L'Isle-sur-la-Sorgue** This lovely Provençal town is everything a visitor could hope for. On Sundays the quiet town becomes a lively crowded marketplace. Streets are filled with crowds of bargain hunters, looking for antiques and filling its cafes. Take the time to visit the town's 17th-century church, Collégiale Notre-Dame-des-Anges. Its treasures include extravagant gilt and marble decorations and frescoes.

**Lourdes** Ever since Bernadette Soubirous had a vision of the Virgin here in 1858, people have been making pilgrimages to Lourdes. Now about four million come here for healing each year. They come to the cave where the visions occurred, Grotte Massabielle. The Lourdes complex includes a large assemblage of shrines, churches, and hospices all clustered around the spring said to have miraculous healing power.

**Lyon** This was a major city in New Testament times, and one of the early church fathers, Irenaeus, was bishop of Lyon in the 2d century. Today you can see three excavated Roman amphitheaters (one holding 10,000 spectators). The Théâtre Romain and the Odéon are both on rue de l'Antiqualille and continue to host musical performances from opera to rock. A third, the Amphithéâtre des Trois Gaulles on rue des Tables Claudiennes is in ruins but remains open to the public daily. A number of Christians were martyred in this amphitheater.

Its churches include the Cathédrale St-Jean on pl. St-Jean, which was begun in the late 12th century and the Basilique Notre-Dame-de-Fourvière. Sitting atop Lyon's overhead cliff on pl. de Fourvière, the Basilique is the city's most striking symbol. Built in the 19th century, the basilica's interior contains a mishmash of styles. Some disdain it as overkill. But the climb is worthwhile if only for the stunning view of the city below. The Abbaye St-Martin d'Ainay on rue Vaubécour, dating back to 1107, has been impressively restored and is worth visiting.

Only the Louvre in Paris has a more important collection of art than the Musée des Beaux Arts at 20 pl. des Terreaux. Here are a few paintings you might want to look for: Albrecht Bouts's *Man of Sorrows* (ca. 1500), Lorenzo Costa's *The Nativity* (ca. 1490), Jacob Jordaens's *The Adoration of the Shepherds* (ca. 1644), Paolo Veronese's *The Adoration of the Magi* (ca. 1583), and *The Entry of Christ into Jerusalem* by Master of the Monogram AH (ca. 1500 or before).

In the 12th century a merchant named Peter Waldo (Valdez) was converted, sold all his property, and started a movement called "the poor men of Lyon," later known as the Waldenses. He tried to get permission to preach to the common people and to work for the reformation of the church, but permission was denied. Waldo and his followers were eventually excommunicated and at a Council in Toulouse it was decreed that they should be forcefully suppressed. The Inquisition came down hard on them, but the Waldensian denomination continues to exist today.

> What language shall I borrow to thank Thee, dearest Friend,
> For this Thy dying sorrow, Thy pity without end?
> O make me Thine forever, and should I fainting be,
> Lord, let me never, never outlive my love to Thee.
>
> ATTRIBUTED TO BERNARD OF CLAIRVAUX, FRANCE

**Marne-la-Vallée** If you or your kids get tired of French culture, get a dose of American pop culture at Disneyland Paris, located 20 miles east of Paris on 1,500 acres. The park is surrounded by a steam railroad. In the center of Disneyland (just as you hoped) is Sleeping Beauty Castle, surrounded by the various Disney "lands": Frontierland, Fantasyland, Discoveryland, and Adventureland. Main Street USA (not Main Street France) connects the castle to the entrance. You can also visit Disney Village, with restaurants, a theater, dancing, souvenir shops, a post office, and a tourist office.

**Marseille** You can describe this city just about any way you want and be correct: old, modern, a fishing town, corrupt, cosmopolitan, exotic, cultured, even religious. It dates back to Greek times. See the Jardin des Vestiges with its remains of the original port at the Vieux Port—it was a major port for the Romans. Dumas wrote about it in his *Count of Monte Cristo*. Among its lovely churches is the Basilique de Notre-Dame-de-la-Garde. Perched on a high hill overlooking Marseille, the basilica grounds offer a great view of the city. The Cathédral de la Major, on quai de la Tourette, was completed only in 1893, dwarfing the 11th-century Ancienne Cathédrale, which is alongside of it. There is an ancient legend that Lazarus, Mary, and Martha came here 2,000 years ago. Each February the Abbaye St-Victor (at Pl. St-Victor) celebrates the arrival of the "Boat of Bethany" by selling boat-shaped cakes.

**Moissac** The abbey of St. Pierre on Pierte Chabrie has gone through a lot since it was founded in the 7th century; in the 12th century it was the major monastery in southwestern France. The south portal of the monastery is what attracts many tourists; it is a masterpiece carved in the early 12th century, showing Christ sitting in judgment, holding the Book of Life in his left hand, with 24 elders wearing crowns of gold, following John's vision in the Book of Revelation.

**Montbéliard** A victim of the wars between Germany and France, this city has had a split personality. At times it has been part of Germany and at other times part of France, but it boasts the oldest Protestant church in France, Temple St-Martin, built early in the 17th century. The houses are colorfully painted in German style, and Christmas is celebrated in the square with its Lumières de Noel. Early in March the city hosts the Montbéliard Chocolate Carnival.

**Mont-Saint-Michel** A thousand years ago it was a Benedictine monastery, but Mont-Saint-Michel is much more than that today. The romantic and stunningly beautiful islet is one of the most spectacular sites in France and is the most visited destination out-side of Paris. The best views are from the road from Avranches, to the east. The best time to see Mont-Saint-Michel is during the high tides of spring and fall when the sea fully encircles the mount. A modern causeway links travelers to the mainland regardless of the tide.

The construction on the mount is remarkable as well. It was built during the 8th century, as tons of granite were brought in and hauled up the 260-foot peak to construct La Marveille (The Wonder), the name given to the group of buildings on the top. The fortress on top is not really a fortress at all, but rather a series of architectural layers that have been added since its beginning through the late Gothic period. Guided tours in English are available.

A small 15th-century chapel is dedicated to St. Aubert, who founded the monastery in A.D. 708. After the French Revolution, the abbey here was turned into a prison, but now once again it is a church manned by Benedictine monks.

**Nantes** In 1598 Henry IV signed the Edict of Nantes which allowed Protestants the freedom to practice their faith. However, persecution continued in the next century and in 1685 Louis XIV revoked the Edict of Nantes. Despite the temporary nature of the edict, it was a milestone for French Protestants. It was signed in the Château des Ducs de Bretagne (at pl. Marc Elder).

At Nantes's Musée des Beaux-Arts at 10 rue Georges Clemenceau is Gustave Doré's impressively moving *Christ Leaving the Praetorium*. This oil on canvas painting measures nearly 16 by 24 feet.

**Nice** Nice is known for its trendy shopping, nightlife, and Mediterranean beaches, but Christians will enjoy an unusual museum located here. The Chagall Museum of Biblical Themes (Musée National Message Biblique Chagall) is located on av. du Dr-Ménard. Marc Chagall's incredible *The Message of the Bible* is displayed in this museum. The collection is spread over 17 huge canvases and took him 13 years to create.

The prettiest parts of Nice include the Cours Saleya flower market and the streets of Old Nice (Vieux Nice). Also in the area is the lovely 18th-century Chapelle de la Miséricorde on cours Saleya, famous for its incredible Baroque interior and sculptured decorations.

**Nîmes** The old Roman amphitheater in Nîmes that once featured chariot racing and gladiators is now the site of concerts, operas, and bullfights. It is exceptionally well preserved. The main road from Rome to Spain (the Domitian Way) passed through the heart of the town, and if the apostle Paul ever went to Spain, he probably passed through Nîmes. The Cathédrale de Notre-Dame et St-Castor, which dates from the 11th century, was rebuilt in the 19th century. The west front of the church displays dramatic Old Testament scenes. Young people will be interested in learning that denim originated in Nîmes ("de Nîmes").

**Noyon** The Reformation theologian John Calvin was born in Noyon in 1509 and went to church in the Cathédral de Notre-Dame. A small museum (Musée Jean Calvin) is nearby. The cathedral dates from 1150, although there were four previous churches built on the same site. No doubt, Calvin knew well the library on the church's east end as well as the bishop's palace, which is now a local history museum. Calvin's father served as attorney and secretary for the bishop of Noyon.

**Orléans** This is Joan of Arc's city; there's no doubt about that. On May 8, 1429, the 17-year-old Maid of Orléans saved the city from the English, and that date is etched in the memory of the citizenry. A year later, however, she was captured by the English, and in 1431, at the age of 19, was burned at the stake in Rouen. In 1920 she was canonized by the Roman Catholic Church. The half-timbered Maison de Jeanne d'Arc

> All glory, laud, and honor to Thee, Redeemer, King.
> To whom the lips of children make sweet hosannas ring.
> Thou art the King of Israel, Thou, David's royal Son,
> Who in the Lord's name comest, the King and blessed One.
>
> THEODULPH OF ORLÉANS, FRANCE

at pl. de Gaulle 3 is a reconstruction of the home where she lived in 1429. East of her home on rue de l'Etape is Hôtel Groslot, where several kings of France stayed. It served as the town hall until 1982. Now it contains Joan of Arc memorabilia as well as some Renaissance paintings. Her story is retold in the windows of the stunning Holy Cross Cathedral (Cathédrale Ste-Croix) on pl. Ste-Croix.

Also associated with Orléans is Jeanne Guyon. Madam Guyon's deeply spiritual devotional writings are read by Catholics and Protestants alike. Her Scripture commentary drew attention from the church. Between 1694 and 1702 she was arrested, charged with being a Quietist, and imprisoned in the Bastille in Paris.

**Poitiers** Poitiers has literally been through the wars. It was here in 732 that Charles Martel stopped the Muslim invasion from the south. Some 850 years later Huguenots were strong here, and their eradication left deep scars on the town as well. The city features several historic churches—in fact, Poitiers is known in France as *La Ville des Eglises,* or the City of Churches. Perhaps its finest is Notre-Dame-la-Grande on pl. Charles de Gaulle, with 12th-century Poitevin sculpture and a Romanesque fresco, *Christ and the Virgin.* The Baptistère-St-Jean on rue Jaurès, dating from the 4th century, is the oldest Christian building in France. Early converts were baptized here. The 12th-century Palais de Justice on rue Gambeta is thought to be where Joan of Arc was examined by theologians in 1429.

About 4.5 miles north of town is Futuroscope, a theme park that includes the Magic Carpet cinema and the biggest screen in Europe. It emphasizes discoveries in visual communications. So Poitiers's architecture goes from the the 4th-century Baptistère to the 21st-century Futuroscope.

**Reims** This city is known for its cathedral, where kings of France since the 11th century came to be crowned. Joan of Arc came here in 1429 for the coronation of Charles X. Although a church has existed where the cathedral now stands since 401, and Clovis, king of the Franks, was baptized here in 496, the present Cathédrale de Notre-Dame was begun in 1211. Severely damaged in World War II, it has now been restored. The west facade is decorated with 2,300 statues, and Marc Chagall designed stained glass windows, one depicting the crucifixion, another the sacrifice of Isaac. Like Notre-Dame in Paris, it too has a fabulous rose window. Its nave is taller than the nave at Chartres.

**Rouen** If the facade of Cathédrale de Notre-Dame in Rouen looks familiar to you, it may be because Claude Monet featured it in 30 paintings. He was fascinated by the effect of the changing lights on its facades, and so he kept painting variations on the same theme. Incidentally the heart of Richard the Lionhearted is buried here (the rest of his remains were buried at Fontevraud). The church, located on the pl. de la Cathédrale, lost a little of its splendor in war, but its two towers, the Tour St-Romain and the Tour de Beurre, are recognizable and beautiful. The Tour St-Romain is the less detailed and the older of the two. It dates back to the 12th century.

At the Musée des Beaux Arts on pl. Verdrel are Pieter Aersten's *The Adoration of the Shepherds* (ca. 1550) and Caravaggio's *The Flagellation of Christ,* from the early 17th century.

The modern, fish-shaped Joan of Arc Church (Eglise Jeanne d'Arc) on the Pl. du Vieux-Marché was built in the old market square on the site where Joan of Arc was burned at the stake in 1431. A 20-foot cross marks the exact spot. Notice the church's stained glass. Much of it is much older than the church itself, dating back to the 16th century. It was salvaged from a church that was bombed in World War II.

The beautiful abbey church Abbaye St-Ouen on the pl. du Général-de-Gaulle was built in the 14th century and has stunning stained glass windows. The 19th-century organ's tonal quality is considered to be among the best in all of France.

**Saulieu** This tiny town is well-known for two things: good food and Christmas trees. The town harvests and sells a million trees every holiday season. The interesting abbey church is the Abbaye St-Andoche.

**Sens** Sens's Cathédrale St-Etienne, which utterly dominates the town, is one of the oldest in France, built in the 12th century. Its large interior has beautiful stained glass of various time periods. Next door is the Synodal Palace (Palais Synodal) built in the 13th century. Its most striking feature is its diamond-tile roof, which was added during a restoration in the 19th century. Apparently the restorer thought the building wasn't attractive enough as it was originally

## Joan of Arc (1412-1431)

At the age of 16, as the English were about to capture Orléans in the Hundred Years' War, Joan heard voices telling her to come to her nation's rescue. She convinced the French Dauphin to let her lead the troops into battle. Miraculously, the French troops drove the English out of Orléans. After winning four more battles, Joan prevailed on the Dauphin to march into Reims, where he was crowned king. However, a few days later, she was defeated in another battle with the English and captured. The English gave her over to an ecclesiastical court at Rouen where she was tried for heresy, sorcery, and for wearing men's clothing into battle. Condemned to death, she was burned at the stake as a witch and heretic at the age of 19. Nearly 500 years later, Joan of Arc was canonized, but she has always been a national heroine in France.

Sites associated with her life and death are located in Orléans, Chinon, Poitiers, Reims, and Rouen.

built. Inside the palace's annex is a museum with archeological artifacts from the Gallo-Roman period. On the museum's second floor you can see the cathedral's treasury, one of the finest in France.

**Stes-Maries-de-la-Mer** This town in the Camargue region of France has an interesting history. Legend has it that a boat washed ashore carrying the remains of the three biblical Marys—the Virgin Mary, Mary Magdalene, and Mary the sister of Martha. A church was built to house the caskets of the "Saintes Maries," and the town quickly grew up around it. Hence the name Stes-Maries-de-la-Mer, which means Saints Mary of the Sea. In addition to the famous church, visitors can enjoy the town's sandy beaches and the large flocks of migrating birds that are drawn to the area's marshes.

**Strasbourg** The best way to see this city is to take a boat ride along the waterways that encircle it. Then you will see the covered bridges, the medieval watchtowers, and the major historic structures. It was here that John Calvin wrote his commentary on Romans, preached to a congregation of French refugees, and found a wife.

The Cathédrale de Strasbourg dominates the city. The church is unusual in that it has been home to both Catholic and Protestant congregations. Its rose window and 16th-century astronomical clock are well worth seeing. Each day at 12:30 P.M. figures of the 12 apostles march around while the cock crows a greeting to St. Peter. While you wait for the clock, take notice of the 13th-century Pilier des Anges (Angels' Pillar), considered a Gothic masterpiece.

**Taize** Six miles north of Cluny is the little village of Taize, which has gained an international reputation since 1940 for its ecumenicity. Begun by Pastor Roger Schutz (Brother Roger), the community now numbers more than 80 brothers who come from about 20 different countries and from both Catholic and Protestant churches. Their mission is to work with young people and to achieve unity and reconciliation. The place of worship is the Eglise de la Réconciliation. There are three daily prayer services for the community. The church itself is simple and was consecrated in 1962.

**Tanlay** Six miles east of Tonnerre, the Château de Tanlay can be approached either by car on D 965 or by houseboat on the canal de Bourgogne. The circular room at the top of the Tour (Tower) de la Ligue was used for Huguenot meetings during the Wars of Religion. The builder of the chateau, François Coligny d'Andelot, was a Huguenot leader.

**Thoiry** Located 25 miles west of Paris, Thoiry makes a great field trip for families with kids, and for that matter even for families without kids. It has an exquisitely furnished 16th-century chateau, enhanced by some nicely manicured French gardens. It contains an Archives Museum with papal bulls and letters from Napoléon, Thomas Jefferson, and Benjamin Franklin, as well as a Gastronomy Museum, exhibiting the banquet showpieces used when the king of England or the emperors of Austria or Russia came to dine. There is a very creative play park for the children, as well as a safari park with giraffes, tigers, lions, and elephants. You are encouraged to view the animals from your car.

**Tours** This city, which goes back to Roman times, became a center of Christianity in the 4th century under St. Martin, who was the bishop of Tours at the time. For a while it was even the capital of France.

The Cathédrale St-Gatien on rue Lavoisier is one of France's most impressive. Begun in 1239, it took nearly 250 years to complete. Notice the beautiful stained glass in the choir, some of it dating back to 1320.

Hôtel Goüin, at 25 rue du Commerce, is the finest Renaissance building in the area, with an interesting archaeological museum. The Historial de Touraine at 25 quai d'Orléans in the Château Royale is a much better than the average wax museum with 165 wax figures, depicting 15 centuries of local history.

At the Municipal Museum is Andrea Mantegna's tempera on wood, *The Resurrection of Christ* (1459). Mantegna's *Christ in the Garden of Gethsemane* is also a classic.

**Ussé** Château d'Ussé is actually in the village of Rigny-Ussé and is one of many charming castles in the Loire Valley. Although it is not the most stunning, children may enjoy its storybook history. The castle claims to be the setting of the French fairy tale *Sleeping Beauty*. Its turrets and terraces make that claim believable. Romantic as it is, however, this is not the Sleeping Beauty castle that Walt

Disney made famous. His model was Neuschwanstein in Bavaria. Take time to visit the little Renaissance chapel in the park.

**Vendôme** Vendôme's largest church, the Eglise de la Trinité, exhibits a large array of architectural styles. Its highlights are the intricately carved choir stalls and the elaborate west front. The church was designed by Jean de Beauce, who was famous for the spire he created for the Chartres cathedral.

**Versailles** Château de Versailles is overwhelming. Sometimes the castle itself overwhelms you, and at other times, the crowds of tourists overwhelm you. But the visitors come because it is worth seeing. The gardens in the back of the chateau are spectacular, and they are free.

A pleasant little family excursion for you might be a boat ride down the Grand Canal here just beyond the Apollo Basin.

## BERNARD OF CLAIRVAUX (1090-1153)

Born near Dijon, France, Bernard of Clairvaux entered the monastery of Citeaux of the Cistercian order when he was 21, and four years later he led a group of his fellow monks to start a new monastery at Clairvaux. Inside the monastery, he practiced self-denial and asceticism, spending much time in prayer. Outside the monastery, he became a popular preacher, emphasizing God's love and saying that the way to know God was by loving God. His teaching affected the spiritual life of the medieval church, and his writings, particularly his hymns, have enriched all of Christendom ever since. Among his hymns are "Jesus, the Very Thought of Thee," "Jesus, Thou Joy of Loving Hearts," and "O Sacred Head Now Wounded." Sites associated with Bernard's life and ministry are located in Dijon, Fontenay, and Vézelay, France.

**Vézelay** This is a great little Burgundy town with a little bit of everything, which added together is a lot. Its history goes back to the middle of the 9th century. It was a pilgrimage city during the Second Crusade after St. Bernard preached here. St. Francis of Assisi chose it to be the first site in France for one of his monasteries. In the 16th century it was the birthplace of Theodore Beza, who preached the Reformation with John Calvin.

The Basilica of Ste-Madeleine on Pl. de la Basilique is richly adorned and is today considered one of the finest Romanesque buildings in the world. The tympanum over the central doorway shows Christ enthroned, surrounded by the apostles, with the Holy Spirit upon them, and extending the gospel to people around the world. The crypt inside is said to contain the tomb and relics of Mary Magdalene. For a while crowds came to see them, but when it was discovered that another church in France was claiming the same thing, the crowds dwindled. During the summer, concerts are given at the church on Tuesday and Friday evenings.

# Germany

German National Tourist Office
  US 212-661-7200
  Canada 416-968-1570
  UK 020-7495-0081
  Australia 02-9267-8148
*Web site*
  Entire country www.deutschland-tourismus.de
For a complete list of updated links, visit www.christiantraveler.com

### Country in a Capsule

*Size:* Put New York, Pennsylvania, and Ohio together and you have an area about the same size as Germany, but the population of Germany is about twice the population of the three states.

*Religion:* About one-third claim Protestant ties and most of the Protestants are Lutheran; and about one-third are Catholic. However, weekly church attendance is less than

5 percent of the population. Baptists, Methodists, Plymouth Brethren, Mennonites, and Eastern Orthodox make up most of the remainder of the Protestant contingent.

*Language:* Mostly German, of course, but there are a million Turks and a growing number of people from other Middle Eastern lands. In larger cities, in tourist areas, and among the younger generation of Germans, English is widely understood.

*Money:* The deutsche mark is worth about 50 cents.

*Food:* You can find a Wurst or a Schnitzel almost anywhere. But there are major regional differences. In Bavaria, try leberknodel (liver, bread, and chopped onion made into a dumpling); in the Rhine Valley, try reibekuchen (potato pancakes). Pork is a mainstay of almost every menu and schweinepfeffer (a spicy pork made into a ragout) is good. In the north, try labskaus (a combination of beef, pork, and salted herrings topped with cucumber and fried egg).

*Shopping:* Germany is known for its delicate wood carvings and crystal, but linens and Christmas ornaments are also good buys. Many tourists set their hearts on a Black Forest cuckoo clock—but be sure to check its manufacturer's tag. Some clocks are built in Asia.

*Brief history:* Although Germany didn't exist as a modern nation until the 19th century, its known history goes back to the time of Julius Caesar. In A.D. 314 the first Christian bishopric of the area was established in Trier. Early in the 6th century Clovis, king of the Franks, was converted and his people were brought into the church with him. In the early 700s Boniface, known as the Apostle to the Germans, became archbishop of Mainz and did much to bring order and stability as well as education to the area. In 800 Charlemagne became emperor of the Empire of the West, consolidating all of western Europe, but in a time of political unrest and religious conflict in the 13th and 14th centuries, regional princes grabbed more power, weakening the Holy Roman Empire.

Martin Luther and the Reformation came after 1517, and the country was further divided. A series of wars in the following centuries was climaxed as Napoléon entered Berlin in 1806. The German Holy Roman Empire was dissolved, but interest in German unity began shortly afterward and Bismarck established modern Germany in 1871.

Germany's participation in World War I under Kaiser Wilhelm II and in World War II under the Nazi-led Adolf Hitler are well-known. After World War II, Germany was a divided nation with East Germany under the rule of the USSR. In 1989 the Berlin Wall came down, and the following year Germany was reunited.

**Berlin** Berlin's oldest historic quarter is known as the Nikolaiviertel or Nicholas Quarter. The area is filled with colorful shops, restaurants, and cafes. Berlin's oldest building, St. Nicholas Church (Nikolaikirche), is located in the nearby Nikolaikirchplatz. In this church the Reformation was introduced to the city in 1530. The church was started in 1230 and a new nave constructed in 1470. Though it was completely demolished by bombs in World War II, it was rebuilt in the 1980s. Today it is a concert hall and conference facility. A display of sacred objects is inside.

*Churches.* Kaiser Wilhelm Memorial Church (Kaiser-Wilhelm-Gedächtniskirche) on Breitscheidpl. once symbolized West Berlin and is today a dramatic memorial of the destructiveness of war. The original church tower was left in its postwar condition, a blackened bombed-out shell, as a daily reminder of the country's dark past, and is referred to by Germans as the Höhlene Zahn, the Hollow Tooth. The 19th-century church was dedicated to Kaiser Wilhelm and is now adjoined to a modern active church and bell tower. The stained glass for the new building was made in Chartres. Over the altar in the new chapel is a chased-metal piece called *The Risen Christ.* The organ with 5,100 pipes and 63 registers soars 28 feet high.

The medieval St. Mary's Church (St. Marienkirche) on Karl-Liebknecht-Str. is one of the finest in Berlin. Inside is the sullen but interesting late-Gothic fresco *Der Totentanz* (Dance of Death), which had been obscured by pollution and grime until its restoration in 1950. The cross on top of St. Mary's Church was an eternal thorn in the collective sides of the city's leaders when this section of Berlin was under Communist rule. Reflections from the golden cross were easily visible in the windows of the Fernsehturm TV tower, the pride of East German Communist architects. Free tours are available Monday through Thursday at 1:00 and Sundays at 11:45.

The impressive Berlin Cathedral (Berliner Dom) on Am Lustgarten is one of the great churches in Germany. Built in the 19th century, its enormous green copper dome is visible from quite a distance. Severely damaged in World War II, the building was restored and reopened in June 1993. More than 80 tombs of Prussian royals are on display in the cathedral's catacombs.

The Kirche Maria Regina Martyrum at Heckerdamm 230 is a Catholic memorial church "to those who shed their blood for freedom of religion between 1933 and 1945." The building, completed in 1963, has a lower church with a Pietà in front of which are graves of two Catholic leaders who were martyred by the Nazis, and an upper church with a large mural depicting the New Jerusalem and the Lamb from the Book of Revelation.

St. Hedwig's Cathedral (St. Hedwigskathedrale) is notable not only for its lovely architecture. When it was constructed in 1747, it was the first Catholic church since the Reformation to be built in Berlin—a city that was very firmly Protestant. Today St. Hedwig's, located at Hinter der Katholischen Kirche 3, is considered Berlin's premier Catholic church.

*Museums and other sites of interest.* Museumsinsel (Museum Island) is an island containing five major museums. They are all outstanding, and two will be especially appreciated by anyone interested in biblical artifacts. The Pergamonmuseum is sensational. It has one section devoted to materials from Asia Minor and Greece, including a market gate from Miletus (a city which the apostle Paul visited) and the altar to Zeus at Pergamon (one of the seven churches of Revelation). In another section on ancient Babylon and Sumeria, the entire Ishtar gate of Nebuchadnezzar is on display. The Bodemuseum has a world-famous collection of works from Egypt—dating from the times of Abraham, Joseph, and Moses—as well as early Christian art. A highlight of the Ägyptisches (Egyptian) Museum at Schlosstr. 70 is a 3,300-year-old bust of queen Nefertiti, recognized around the world. The museum also includes some of the best preserved mummies outside Cairo.

The Tiergarten district, which has Berlin's oldest park, is home to several great museums itself. The Painting Gallery (Gemäldegalerie) is one of Germany's most famous art museums with a large collection of Dutch, Flemish, German, and Italian artists. And the

Philharmonic Hall in Tiergarten is a superb concert hall, home of the Berlin Philharmonic Orchestra. In an annex, the Musical Instruments Museum (Musikinstrumenten-Museum) now displays more than 2,500 instruments from the 16th to the 20th centuries.

Also in the Tiergarten district is Berlin's fantastic zoo (Zoologischer Garten), one of the largest in the world. Located right in the heart of one of Europe's biggest cities, the zoo has the world's largest variety of individual types of plant life as well as a fabulous aquarium. But it is the zoo that you will enjoy, from the elephants, to the wild cats, to the orangutans (watch out—they spit). The zoo is just a stone's throw from the Kaiser Wilhelm Memorial Church—you'll see it from the zoo entrance. The zoo is located at Hardenbergpl. 8 and Budapester Str. 34.

The Berlin Museum (on Lindenstrasse) shows the city's history from the 16th century to the present. In a new extension the history of Jewish people in Berlin is chronicled. Before Hitler 170,000 Jews lived in the city, and there were 100 synagogues. The collection here traces the history, shows religious artifacts, and serves as a reminder of the atrocities that were committed in the not-so-distant past.

*Christmas Bazaar.* Berlin's annual Christmas Bazaar is an outdoor market held on the Kurfürstendamm Breitscheidplatz near the Kaiser Wilhelm Memorial Church. Visitors can purchase food and drinks, handcrafted jewelry, and clothing, as well as Christmas gifts and ornaments.

**Aachen** It was in this most westerly of all German towns that Charlemagne authorized the construction of a basilica, shortly before A.D. 800. It would be a domed octagonal building similar to those in the Eastern Roman Empire. The circumference would be 144 Carolingian feet to resemble the New Jerusalem. A 9th-century monk said that it was "built by human hands but with the inspiration of God." The Aachen Cathedral is now a UNESCO World Heritage Site. The gold altar is decorated with 11th-century scenes from the Passion of Christ and Christ in Majesty. The Schatzkammer (the cathedral treasury) is the richest treasury in northern Europe. The cathedral is located right in the center of Aachen, on Münsterpl.

**Augsburg** This ancient city founded in 15 B.C. by two stepsons of Augustus Caesar became an important city to Lutherans—and to all Protestants—in the 16th century. German princes were divided on what to do with Protestants. Luther was summoned to Augsburg and told to recant. He refused. A dozen years later at a second Diet of Augsburg, Luther was banned from attendance but his lieutenant Philipp Melanchthon presented the Augsburg Confession on behalf of the Protestant princes. That confession has been a basic creed for Lutherans ever since. But it wasn't until 25 years later with the Peace of Augsburg in 1555 that Protestantism was legally recognized.

In Augsburg Lutheran churches frequently appear next to Catholic churches. There are two Münster St. Ulrichs and two Heilig-Kreuz-Kirches, one Catholic and one Protestant, side by side. The Cathedral (Dom) on Hoher Weg dates from the 11th century but was added onto several times. Its stained glass windows are the oldest in Europe. The Augsburg Confession was first presented in the Fronhof, facing the facade of the cathedral.

St. Anna Kirche (St. Ann's Church) on Annstr. is the most significant Protestant church in Augsburg. This was the church where Martin Luther found a refuge when he first arrived in the city in

---

## Martin Luther (1483-1546)

When he nailed his 95 theses to the church door in Wittenberg, Luther ignited the Protestant Reformation. Born in Eisleben, he studied law in Leipzig, then entered an Augustinian monastery in Erfurt when he was 22. In 1510 he was sent to Rome, but was disillusioned by what he saw. Luther then became a professor of theology at Wittenberg, a position he held for the rest of his life.

After long struggles, he came to accept three basic principles, keys to the Reformation: that man is justified by faith alone, that every believer has direct access to God, and that the Bible is the sole source of authority for faith and life. He nailed up his 95 theses, however, to debate the excesses of indulgences.

Summoned to the Diet of Worms in 1521, he refused to recant. He was excommunicated, but after a ten-month refuge at the Wartburg Castle in Eisenach where he translated the New Testament into German in just 10 weeks, he continued his public teaching and his writing of commentaries, hymns, catechisms, tracts, and letters. He stressed preaching of the Word, and congregational singing in church services, and sought to exemplify what a Christian marriage and Christian family should be.

Sites associated with Luther's life and ministry are common throughout Germany, but the primary sites are located in Augsburg, Coburg, Eisenach, Eisleben, Erfurt, Speyer, Stolberg, Wittenberg, and Worms, Germany, as well as in Rome, Italy.

---

1518. Today part of the Carmelite monastery has been turned into a Lutheran museum. You can also see the room in which Luther stayed in 1518 and the excommunication bull that resulted from his refusal to recant. An extension to the nave of the church is a chapel called Fuggerskapelle because it was funded by two wealthy brothers named Fugger in 1509. Usually chapels are off to the side of the nave, but the brothers didn't want anyone to miss this one, and it is lavish beyond question. In the church itself, don't miss the painting *Jesus, the Friend of Little Children* at the high altar.

**Baden-Baden** Five miles west of town (leaving by the Langestrasse) is the Autobahnkirche, which as you might guess, is a church for travelers. Under the patronage of St. Christopher, who is the patron saint of travelers, this church was built in the 1970s with a contemporary flair. Sculptures and stained glass follow biblical and symbolic themes.

**Bamberg** Because of its isolation (about 40 miles north of Nürnberg), this beautiful small city escaped the ravages of war and remains one of Europe's loveliest. If you happen to be visiting in December, you are in for a special treat. The Advent season is celebrated with the Bamberger Krippenweg or the Bamberg Christmas Crib Circuit. Some 30 churches and museums prepare decorated crib scenes. The variety is amazing.

The Domplatz (Cathedral plaza) is lovely, and the cathedral itself dates back a millennium.

**Bautzen** Forty miles east of Dresden, Bautzen has a cathedral, St. Petri Dom on Fleischmarkt, used by both Catholics and Protestants, with Catholic Masses in the chancel and Protestant services in the main nave. This division has continued since the Reformation. Balthasar Permoser's masterpiece *Crucifixion* hangs in the Catholic section.

About 15 miles out of town on B 178 is the little town of Herrnhut, where Count Nikolaus von Zinzendorf brought Moravian refugees in 1722. He wrote many of his hymns here, including "Jesus Thy Blood and Righteousness." The witness of the Moravians was instrumental in the conversion of John Wesley.

**Bergen** At Bergen-Belsen, four miles southwest of Bergen, is a monument in 13 languages honoring the memory of those who died in the Nazi concentration camp here. The mass graves remain, but the buildings were destroyed after the war for fear of a typhoid outbreak. One of the victims was Anne Frank, the Jewish girl who wrote the famous diary.

It is difficult to put the grim reality of a concentration camp aside, but Heide-Park Soltau is an excellent leisure park laid out on different themes and with a variety of rides.

**Bonn** Bonn is noted for two things: It was the capital of West Germany during the Cold War, and it was Ludwig van Beethoven's birthplace. So now's the time to sing, "Joyful, Joyful We Adore Thee," the hymn set to Beethoven's "Ode to Joy." The house in which Beethoven was born (Bonngasse 20) is now a simple museum. On display are some of the instruments that he played as well as ear trumpets, which a friend made for him because of his advancing deafness. Although the composer

> Lord, I believe Thy precious blood,
> Which, at the mercy seat of God,
> Forever doth for sinners plead,
> For me, e'en for my soul was shed.
>
> NIKOLAUS VON ZINZENDORF
> OF HERRNHUT, GERMANY

was indeed born here, he lived most of his life elsewhere. The tour and most exhibits are in German, but there is some English material available and you will gain insight into the intensity with which the great composer lived his life.

One of Bonn's most impressive structures is its 900-year-old Münster, or cathedral, on Münsterpl. The church has an enormous octagonal tower and an ornate rococo pulpit that shouldn't be missed.

Just north of the city in the little village of Schwarzrheindorf is a 12th-century Doppelkirche, which had been built for the lord of the local manor. The rare Romanesque frescoes here are unique. Notice *The Vision of Ezekiel, The Transfiguration,* and *The Apocalypse.*

**Boppard** South of Koblenz is the lovely town of Boppard, once an important city in the Holy Roman Empire. Located on a bend in the Rhine River, the town is home to the remains of a Roman fort and castle, which, appropriately enough, house Roman artifacts. There are several interesting churches in Boppard, including the Carmelite Church (Karmeliterkirche) on Karmeliterpl. and the Romanesque Church of St. Severus on Marktpl. From Boppard you can enjoy a view of two ruined Rhine castles, Liebenstein and Sterrenberg. Boppard is a common stop on Rhine River cruises.

**Brühl** It used to be that Schloss Augustusburg at Schlossstr. 6 was the reason that people came to this town south of Cologne. After all, this sumptuous rococo castle seems to have come straight out of a fairy tale. It was the creation of an 18th-century archbishop, who frankly didn't live very piously, but that didn't stop him from being successful.

Today people come to Brühl to go to Phantasialand, the first amusement park in Europe to rival Disneyland. Famous for its rides, it has four themed areas.

**Bückeburg** The Stadtkirche on the top of the Langestrasse was one of the first Protestant churches ever built. The emphasis was on preaching to the congregation, so the pulpit had a center position. The base of the pulpit is adorned with scenes from the life of Christ, and on either side are figures of Moses and Paul. The massive organ here was played for 45 years by the son of Johann Sebastian Bach. Over the facade of the church is the inscription, "An Example of Piety, not of Architecture," but the architecture isn't bad either.

At the edge of the town center is the Schloss (castle), parts of which go back to the 14th century. The Schlosskapelle, designed for Lutheran worship, is covered with frescoes and filled with gilded and carved furniture.

To bring you back into the 21st century, there is the Helicopter Museum (Hubschraubermuseum) with about 40 helicopters. It also traces the evolution of flight from da Vinci to the present.

**Coburg** It was probably at Veste Coburg (Coburg Fortress) that Martin Luther wrote his great hymn "A Mighty Fortress Is Our God" (*Ein Feste Burg*) in 1530. He had been forbidden to go to the Diet at Augsburg, but his friend Melanchthon was permitted to go in his place and read the Protestant Confession known thereafter as the Augsburg Confession. Luther was not sure what the outcome would be; he thought it likely that he and his followers would be hunted down as heretics. In this fortress of Coburg, which remains one of the largest medieval fortresses in Germany, Luther found refuge. But as he wrote the hymn based on Psalm 46, he acknowledged that his refuge wasn't in Coburg but in Almighty

God. The castle, which dates back to the 12th century, towers high above the valley and has a triple ring of fortified walls. Inside, the Hohes Haus has outstanding art and armor collections. Luther stayed in the Furstenbau, where his room is preserved as a museum.

**Cologne** Long before you reach the city of Cologne, you will see its massive and famous cathedral soaring over the Rhine River. The Cologne Cathedral (Kölner Dom) is one of the world's most famous cathedrals, and you really can't visit it without saying, "Wow." Begun in 1248 and completed in 1880, it is one of the largest Gothic structures ever built. Its twin towers, at 515 feet, were by far the tallest structures in the world at the time. The extraordinary cathedral, dedicated to St. Peter and the Virgin Mary, was built to house what were believed to be the relics of the three Magi. The original gold-and-silver reliquary is still on display today. Take note of the Gero Cross, a huge oak crucifix that dates from 971, which is in the last chapel on the left as you face the high altar. Notice also the *Adoration of the Kings* triptych, painted in 1440 by Cologne's most famous medieval painter, Stephan Lochner. If you want to climb 509 steps, you can have a wonderful view of the city from the South Tower. In the belfry is the largest swinging church bell in the world. It weighs 24 tons.

*Churches.* Although not the most outstanding of Cologne's churches (this award goes to the glorious Cologne Cathedral), Great St. Martin (Gross St. Martin) on Lintg. is the best of the city's 12 Romanesque churches. It has a massive 13th-century tower, unusual turrets, and an impressive spire. The colorful old section of town near the church is known as the Martinsviertel (St. Martin's Quarter). It is home to a number of attractive, medieval gabled buildings and twisting alleyways. The place becomes lively with diners and people-watchers at sunset.

Not far from Great St. Martin and St. Martin's Quarter is the 12th-century St. Cecilia's Church (Cäcilienkirche). Located at Cäcilienstr. 29, the church no longer serves as a house of worship but it is nonetheless an interesting sight for Christians. It houses one of the world's finest museums of medieval Christian art, the Schnütgen Museum. While the museum focuses primarily on early and medieval sacred art, it also has an impressive collection of Renaissance and Baroque pieces.

St. Gereon's Church (St. Gereonskirche) is one of the most impressive medieval buildings still in existence. The lovely

Romanesque church at Gereonshof 4 stands on the location of a Roman burial ground. Its massive dome is supported by walls that were once covered with gold mosaics. Part of the structure is composed of original Roman masonry, which is believed to have been built on top of the grave of the church's namesake, the 4th-century martyr and patron saint of Cologne, St. Gereon.

Other intriguing churches include the sailors' church of St. Maria in Lyskirchen with several outstanding 13th-century frescoes of Old and New Testament stories; St. Georg, which is an 11th-century pillared basilica on Severinstr.; and the Protestant parish church of Antoniterkirche, at Schilderg. and Nord-Süd Fahrt, which sponsors a Bach cantata one Sunday night a month.

*Museums.* The city is filled with fascinating museums, ranging from the Romisch-Germanisches Museum at Roncallipl. 4, showing life in Cologne during the Roman period, to the Schokoladenmuseum on Rheinauhafen, dedicated completely to chocolate.

*Rhine River cruises* are always a favorite way to enjoy the beautiful landscape and ruins scattered along the Rhine valley. (See also under Frankfurt.)

**Dachau** This picturesque town 12 miles north of Munich, was at one time known for the painters and artists who lived here. But since World War II, it has become notorious as the site of Germany's first concentration camp and will surely never be able to live down that history. From its opening in 1933 to the Allied liberation in 1945, the camp at Dachau held more than 206,000 prisoners, including Jews, political dissidents, clergy, and other enemies of the Nazis. More than 32,000 of those prisoners died here. At first, only political prisoners were imprisoned, one of whom was Pastor Martin Niemoller; then Jews of various nationalities were brought here. A Jewish memorial, a Protestant commemorative sanctuary, and a Catholic expiatory chapel have been built near the old camp. The Dachau Concentration Camp Memorial Site (KZ-Gedenkstätte Dachau) preserves the memory of the prisoners through photographs, contemporary documents, a few remaining cell blocks, and the crematorium. Notice the memorial's sculpture, which incorporates human forms in shapes reminiscent of barbed wire. The documentary film is shown in English at 11:30 and 3:30. This is an important historical site, but it is haunting and disturbing, and you may not want to take young children. Admission is free.

**Darmstadt** The Hessisches Landesmuseum is an excellent art museum, one of the best in the country, and its picture gallery, with Lochner's *Presentation in the Temple* and works by Rubens, Bruegel, and Cranach, is outstanding. The museum is located at Friedensplatz l.

**Dresden** One of the most severely damaged German cities in World War II, Dresden is rapidly coming back to its earlier glory. Its pleasure palace, called the Zwinger, contains several museums, and some say it rivals the Louvre of Paris. The 18th-century palace is among the finest examples of Baroque architecture in all of Europe. Six connected pavilions entirely enclose a central courtyard of manicured lawns and pools. The complex is covered with sandstone nymphs, cherubs, garlands, and other Baroque sculpture. The Zwinger is also home to the world-renowned Semper Gallery (Sempergalerie), where works by such artists as Dürer, Holbein the Younger, Vermeer, Rembrandt, Raphael, and Correggio are displayed in the Gallery of Old Masters (Gemäldegalerie Alte Meister). Two classics with New Testament themes are Titian's *Christ and the Pharisees* and Maratta's *Holy Night*. The palace's Porcelain Collection (Porzellansammlung) is also interesting; it's famous for its Meissen pieces. The palace is located at Theaterpl. and Sophienstr.

In spite of its name, the New Market (Neumarkt) comprises the heart of the historic center of old Dresden. Located on the square is the Church of Our Lady (Frauenkirche), once a mighty Baroque masterpiece, and Germany's greatest Protestant church. Until recently the church has been severely neglected and allowed to deteriorate. Reconstruction is slowly bringing the lovely church back to life. The New Market is bordered by Schlosstr., Landhausstr., Tzschirnerpl., and Brühlsche G.

The Catholic Court Church (Katholische Hofkirche), also known as the Cathedral of St. Trinitas, is the largest church in the German state of Saxony. Located on Schlosspl., the building was consecrated in 1754. Saturday afternoons at 4:00 during the summer, you can hear recitals on the 18th-century organ. In the crypt lie the remains of 49 Saxon rulers, as well as a precious vessel containing an unusual relic—the heart of August the Strong.

The Kreuzkirche, which is the city's oldest, is a lush Baroque masterpiece known for its choir. Check out its Sunday evening concert schedule. The church is located on the Altmarkt.

**Düsseldorf** This city of a half million people is not only a key financial and corporate center for the nation but also a city of the arts. The musicians Mendelssohn and Schumann called it home. The Kunstmuseum at Ehrenhof 5 has an extensive display of religious paintings, and it was here that Count Nikolaus von Zinzendorf saw the painting *Ecce Homo* with Christ wearing a crown of thorns. Underneath it was the inscription, "All this I did for you. What are you doing for me?" That changed the direction of Zinzendorf's life.

Nine miles east of the city is a valley named after Joachim Neander, who spent time in meditation and writing hymns there. One of the hymns he wrote was "Praise to the Lord, the Almighty, the King of Creation." Incidentally, it was in a cave in the same valley named after the hymn writer that the famous Neanderthal Man skeleton was found.

## COUNT NIKOLAUS VON ZINZENDORF (1700–1760)

Zinzendorf was a gifted German count, who became a pastor, teacher, theologian, missionary, hymn writer, and denominational administrator. The son of a Saxon cabinet minister, he was educated in law and entered civil service. But, after being deeply moved by a painting of Christ wearing a crown of thorns, he offered himself for Christ's service, wherever. When Moravian religious refugees asked him for asylum, he opened his estate, and that began an exciting new life for Zinzendorf. He soon became the leader of the movement, promoting worldwide evangelism and holy living. Moravian missionaries were quite influential in the conversions of both John and Charles Wesley.

Sites associated with Zinzendorf can be found in Bautzen and Düsseldorf, Germany, and in Moravia, Czech Republic.

**Eisenach** The city of Eisenach doesn't generally make it on most tourists' itineraries—maybe because it is still in recovery from its years under Communism—but it is worth visiting to see the two houses associated with two men who changed the world. Johann Sebastian Bach was born and baptized here; Martin Luther's mother was born here, and Martin went to Latin school here.

The Bachhaus on Frauenplan 21 is a must for Bach music lovers. Although the composer himself probably never lived here, the 16th-century house has re-created his life and times in excruciating detail. Period furniture shares space with original handwritten musical scores and old instruments, many of which were used by Bach during his residence in the city. Every half hour there is a live 15-minute concert featuring a musician who makes beautiful music on one of the museum's 18th-century instruments. Pfarrkirche St. Georg on Karlstr. is the church in which Bach was baptized. Luther preached here once in 1521; earlier he had sung here as a choirboy.

The Lutherhaus at Lutherpl. 8 is where Martin Luther actually lived in his teens from 1498 to 1501, so it may be a bit more interesting in that respect. Although there are period-decorated rooms and some of Luther's personal effects, the museum is small. If you want deeper insight into the great reformer's life, you're better off visiting the permanent display in Wartburg Castle nearby.

Wartburg Castle is ancient. No one knows for sure when it was built, but it was surely before the 12th century. The castle is considered a textbook example of German castle architecture, the cream of the crop. But the Wartburg's best exhibits are those associated with its former famous resident, Martin Luther. It was here that Luther was taken after the Diet of Worms. He was presumed to have been kidnapped; instead he voluntarily holed up here in 1521 to hide from the Pope and the German emperor, neither of whom held much love for him after he had tacked his 95 theses onto a church door in Wittenberg.

He stayed here ten months, translating the New Testament from Greek to vernacular German in only 10 weeks, thus creating the foundations of modern written German. A museum here is filled with paintings, sculptures, and tapestries and the Lutherstube is probably the room where Luther translated the New Testament. In the Lutherstube, the reformer claimed to have done battle with Satan on a regular basis. Luther once wrote that he was "fighting the devil with ink." Many believe an unsightly stain on the wall was where Luther hurled his inkwell at Satan, and over the years the faithful have chiseled away at the wall for souvenirs, leaving a large hole. Also in the room is Luther's footstool, sculpted from a fossilized whale vertebrae. To reach the castle, follow Wartburger Allee to its base and ascend one of the steep footpaths up to the Wartburg.

**Eisleben** About 14 miles west of Halle in this small mining town Martin Luther was born. His birthplace is at Lutherstrasse 16. The house in which he died is also here, at Andreaskirchplatz 7. There are small museums at both locations that are well worth visiting.

**Erfurt** You can tell that this city has been strongly influenced by Christianity in the past when you notice all the steeples and spires in the skyline. Boniface started a church here in 742. Meister Eckhart, the mystic and pietist who may have been the most powerful force in Germany's spiritual life before the Reformation, lived here as a Dominican monk. Martin Luther went to the university and later entered the Augustinian monastery here, against his father's wishes.

The cathedral, Mariendom on Domhügel, built in 1154, is a mammoth Gothic structure. It is renowned for its bell, one of the world's largest, and for its stained glass windows. East of the Gera River on Kircheng. is the Augustinerkloster, the monastery where Luther lived from 1505 to 1511 as a novice, monk, and priest. The monastery now serves as a Protestant college. The school's library houses some of Germany's most prized possessions—several early Bibles with handwritten notations made by Luther himself. You can see Luther's room on the tour. The stained glass windows in the monastery depict the life of St. Augustine. The city's main Protestant church is the Predigerkirche, located at Predigerstr. 4, built in the 13th century when Eckhart was a Catholic monk here.

> The Lord is never far away,
> But, though all grief distressing,
> An ever-present help and stay,
> Our peace and joy and blessing.
>
> JOHANN JAKOB SCHUTZ
> OF FRANKFURT, GERMANY

Ten miles south of Erfurt is the small town of Arnstadt, where Johann Sebastian Bach served as organist for five years. He was organist at the parish church that bears his name. A local history museum has exhibits on the noted composer.

**Frankfurt** This is Germany's central city, cosmopolitan, commercial, brimful of activity, and in some ways the most Americanized city in the country.

The Carmelite Church and Monastery (Karmeliterkloster) was secularized in 1803 and fully renovated in the 1980s. The building now houses the Museum of Prehistory and Early History (Museum für Vor- und Frühgeschichte) at Karmeliterg. 1. While the museum is itself interesting, Christians will especially enjoy the main cloister at Münzg. 9, with its art exhibitions. Don't miss the largest religious fresco north of the Alps, a huge 16th-century representation of Christ's birth and death.

*Churches.* There are several interesting churches that you may want to visit or worship in while in Frankfurt. St. Catherine's Church (Katharinenkirche) was originally built around 1680 and was the first Protestant church built in the Gothic style. The first Protestant sermon delivered in Frankfurt was also given here. The church is at the junction of An der Hauptwache and Katherinenpfad.

St. Leonard's Church (Leonhardskirche) is a beautifully preserved 13th-century church. Its five naves display lovely old stained glass. The hanging, elaborately carved piece in the ceiling vault was already a major tourist attraction as early as the 17th century. The church is located at the junction of Leonhardstr. and Untermainkai.

St. Nicholas's Church (Nikolaikirche) on the south side of Römerberg is a small red sandstone church dating from the 13th century. Its wonderful Glockenspiel chimes three times daily, at 9:00, noon, and 5:00.

St. Paul's Church (Paulskirche) on Paulspl. is known less for its religious function than for its secular one. The first all-German parliament meeting took place in Paulskirche in 1848. The parliament lasted only about one year, but the secular nature of the church remains intact. Today the church is used mainly for formal ceremonial events, but the building is open for tours and is worth visiting.

The Church of St. Bartholomew (St. Bartholomäus) has always been referred to as a church (its alternate name is Kaiserdom or Imperial Cathedral), but this building on Domstr. isn't actually a cathedral at all. It is, however, a very impressive structure, built between the 13th and 15th centuries. Most of its original treasures survived the bombings of World War II, including the tall red sandstone tower, which was constructed between 1415 and 1515. In front of the main entrance you can see the excavated remains of an early Roman settlement and the foundations of a Carolingian imperial palace.

The Städelsches Kunstinstitut (on the south bank of the Main at Schaumainkai 63) is the outstanding art gallery here with a broad collection of works, but with particular strength among the Netherlandish artists.

If you're in the area in August, head out to Aschaffenburg, a suburb of Frankfurt. The local fortress, Johannisburg Castle (Schloss Johannisburg) at Schlosspl. 4, is not a terrific destination in itself, but it does offer a great Carillon Fest late in the summer. The east tower's 48 bells are put to good use by a variety of international carillonneurs at a number of performances throughout the month.

*Rhine cruise.* The preferred way of enjoying the scenic Rhine River and its fairy-tale castles is aboard a cruise down the Rhine River. The granddaddy of all Rhine cruises is the Köln-Düsseldorfer Rheinschiffahrt, commonly called the KD Rhine Line in English. Cruises are available in a variety of lengths, from several days to a few hours. The ships run generally from Frankfurt north to Cologne, but you can get on and off at a variety of locations along the way. Food and drinks are available on board but tend to be a little pricey. You might consider buying some fresh produce, bread, and cheese from a local market beforehand and eating a picnic lunch as you enjoy the view. The KD Rhine Line also runs cruises on the Mosel, Saar, Neckar, Danube, Elbe, and Main Rivers. Reservations may be made in Germany at Frankenwerft 15, D–50667 Cologne, phone 0221/208-8288. The company's U.S. representative is JFO CruiseShip Corp. at 2500 Westchester Ave., Purchase, NY 10577, phone 914-696-3600; or 323 Geary St., Suite 603, San Francisco, CA 94102, phone 415-392-8817.

**Freiburg** Freiburg is a lovely Black Forest (Schwarzwald) locale, located only a little distance from the French border. Although Freiburg is more a city than a town—it is one of the region's largest—it has retained its romantic medieval look, having been founded in the 12th century. Adding to the city's appeal is its most famous landmark, the Cathedral (Münster) on Münsterpl. It was started as a parish church around 1200, but it ended up looking like a great cathedral. By the time you have made your way around the church viewing the artwork, you have gone through much of the New Testament. You can't help but admire the church's spire, one of the loveliest in the world. Tours of the Münster are available Mondays and Fridays at 2:30 P.M., Wednesdays, Thursdays, and weekends at 10:30 A.M.

On weekdays the square in front of the cathedral, the Münsterplatz, becomes a lively and colorful town market where you can buy produce, sausage, and cheeses for lunch. West of the city is the Augustinermuseum with its excellent Medieval Art section.

**Freudenstadt** The little town of Freudenstadt lies in the middle of the Black Forest (Schwarzwald). Most of the town is not original—it was flattened during World War II—but it's been beautifully restored. The main square, one of Germany's largest, is surrounded by arcaded houses with plenty of shops and a little fountain in the center. Visit the Protestant Parish Church just outside the square. Its L-shape is a bit unusual and is even more so when you consider the church was built in the 17th century. Located inside is a much older lectern, dating from the 12th century, which depicts Saints Matthew, Mark, Luke, and John.

**Fulda** Back in the 8th century Boniface founded an abbey here, and after his martyrdom, pilgrims began coming to the monastery where he lies buried. The Dom (cathedral) was rebuilt in 1704 in an Italian Baroque style. At the western end of the town's center is the Landesbibliothek at Heinrich von Bibra pl. 12 with a Gutenberg Bible, some illuminated manuscripts, and a number of other fascinating drawings and manuscripts from medieval times. Some members of the family, however, might be more interested in seeing the Deutsches Feuerwehrmuseum on Stadtschloss, a museum in which you can see two centuries of fire-fighting equipment.

**Füssen** Bavaria's royal castles, Hohenschwangau and Neuschwanstein, lie just outside of Füssen. The epitome of German fairytale castles, these fortresses were two of Mad King Ludwig II's residences. The king earned the name "mad" in part because the castles were built in the 19th century, when kings just didn't embark on such projects anymore for fear of bankrupting the kingdom and overburdening the citizenry. Hohenschwangau is extravagant enough, especially Ludwig's bedroom with its ceiling painted to resemble heaven and covered with stars that actually light up. But the king outdid himself with Neuschwanstein, studding his fortress with pinnacles, gold, elaborate hand-carved wood, and a grotto complete with stalactites. The castle served as a model for Walt Disney's Cinderella Castle in Walt Disney World, Florida. Ludwig lived here only 170 days before his mysterious death.

Take time to walk the footpath on the grounds of Neuschwanstein to Mary's Bridge (Marienbrücke). The alpine scenery and views of the castle are simply stunning. When it came to choosing building sites, Ludwig wasn't so crazy.

**Gotha** This market town, 15 miles from Erfurt, is dominated by the Friedenstein Palace, which doesn't look like much on the outside but is positively lavish on the inside. The picture gallery has some unique pieces. There is a magnificent altarpiece with 157 panels depicting the life of Christ, a diptych of *The Fall and Salvation of Man,* which is an illustrated tract of Philipp Melanchthon's teachings, as well as some excellent sketches by Rubens. While you are there, take a walk in the delightful Schlosspark.

**Halle** Ever since the Brotherhood of Musicians and Fife Players was created in the 13th century, this city has been involved with music. The best-known Halle musician is George Frideric Handel, born here in 1685. In the middle of the Marktplatz is a statue honoring him. His birthplace, the Handel House (Händelhaus), just east of the Domplatz, at Nikolaistrasse 5, has been transformed into a museum. Inside the house is a piano that was used by the composer himself as well as a number of original musical scores. Next door in the Markt-Schlösschen is Handel House's instrument collection. The composer of the *Messiah,* who had become the church organist here when he was 17, left the city when he was 25 and made his mark in London, where he became a British citizen. The cathedral where he served and the organ he played can also be seen. Incidentally, a few years after Handel left Halle, Johann Sebastian Bach tried to get the organist's position but was unsuccessful.

> Praise to the Lord! O let all that is in me adore Him!
> All that hath life and breath, come now with praises before Him!
> Let the amen sound from His people again;
> Gladly forever adore Him.
>
> JOACHIM NEANDER OF DÜSSELDORF, GERMANY

Another Christian leader who went from Halle to England was George Müller, who is known for the orphanages he operated on faith.

**Hamburg** Though it was bombed heavily in World War II and its city center was completely razed, there is still much to see and do in this second-largest city in Germany. St. Jakobikirche on Mönckebergstr. with its famous 1693 organ is worth a look, and so is St. Michaeliskirche with its famous tower built in 1786. St. Michael's Church, often cited as northern Germany's finest Baroque church, is Hamburg's principal Protestant house of worship. Its distinctive 433-foot brick and iron tower supports the largest tower clock in Germany, at 26 feet in diameter. Above the clock is a viewing platform that offers a magnificent view of the city and the Elbe River below. The church is located at Krayenkamp 10.

From the end of November until Christmas Eve, Hamburg celebrates the holiday season with the Christmas Market (Weihnachtsmarkt) that centers on the Rathausmarkt. Locals dress warmly and head out to shop for Christmas ornaments and gifts, food, hot cider, and the popular German holiday drink, warm mulled wine (Glühwein).

The city's Fine Arts Museum (Hamburger Kunsthalle) on Glockengieserwall Str. has one of the country's largest art collections, ranging from medieval to modern.

While you are here, take a boat trip around the port. It's one of the best ways to see the activity of the busy city.

**Hannover** Perhaps the best way to enjoy this city that was demolished during the war is to go to the Herrenhausen Royal Gardens in the northwestern part of the city in Herrenhausen Park on Nienburger Str. The Grosser Garden here is a showpiece. Music by Handel is often presented at its theater during the summer. Hannover's zoological garden with its gorilla mountain and its elephant and sea lion performances provides good family entertainment as well. The zoo is located at Adenauer Allee 3.

**Heidelberg** The natural beauty of Heidelberg has made it popular with everyone who visits the town. Surrounded by mountains, forests, vineyards, and the Neckar River, the town has been visited and praised by writers as diverse as Goethe and Mark Twain. Hordes of tourists still come through, but don't let that stop you.

Sitting on a ridge overlooking the city is the Heidelberg Castle (Heidelberger Schloss). The castle's oldest remains date from the 15th century. If you want to tour the interior of the castle, you'll have to join a tour, but there's plenty to enjoy just wandering around the grounds. The hike up is strenuous. If you're not up for it, consider buying a ticket on the funicular (Bergbahn), which runs every ten minutes.

The Church of the Holy Ghost (Heiliggeistkirche), on Hauptstr. and Marktpl., is a highlight in the city, begun in the early 15th century. You may find the souvenir stands scattered around the exterior of the church a bit commercial, but the tradition is not new. The stalls have been here as long as the church. You can see where the old canopies used to be attached.

Enjoy the natural beauty of the city by taking a stroll along Philosopher's Way (Philosophenweg), so named because of the university students and faculty who enjoyed thinking their deep thoughts from this lovely vantage point. You can enjoy beautiful public gardens, walk past the ruins of St. Michael's Basilica and St. Stephen's Cloister, view the Neckar, the city, the castle—and question whether you really want to go home.

Many Protestants are familiar with the Heidelberg Catechism. It was written here at the Heidelberg University in 1562 by a 28-year-old professor Zacharias Ursinus and a 26-year-old preacher Caspar Olevianus.

Christmas is always fun in Heidelberg. Like many German cities, Heidelberg celebrates the event with a Christmas Market (Weihnachtsmarkt), where locals and tourists purchase Christmas tree ornaments, finish up their shopping, and fill up on potato pancakes, cookies, and sausages.

**Hildesheim** Some 18 miles south of Hannover, Hildesheim, though damaged by the war, still retains much of its former charm. St. Michael's church on Michaelistr. outshines the cathedral as the church to visit. A thousand years old, its painted wooden ceilings were removed during the war, and as a result about 900 of the original oak panels have been saved. Though the church became Protestant during the Reformation, Catholics were allowed to retain the crypt where the body of the founder, St. Bernward, was interred. Summer concerts are held regularly in the Protestant churches of the city.

If you're interested in Egyptian antiquities, visit the Römer-Pelizaeus Museum at Am Stein 1–2, which is one of the best in Europe.

**Hinterzarten** Hinterzarten is one of many lovely Black Forest towns, but this 800-year-old town is the most popular for cross-country skiing and hiking in the region. It's also a quaint place to visit, with some of its buildings dating from the 12th century, including St. Oswald's Church, built in 1146.

**Karlsruhe** When you look at a map of this city, it looks like a wheel with spokes coming out from the center. At the center is the castle, which isn't what it used to be, but its museum has some fascinating objects, including a relief of two horsemen from Nineveh (from Jonah's time) and a carving of a gift bringer to Xerxes (from Esther's time). In the Renaissance gallery upstairs are some gorgeous stained glass monastery windows and some excellent artwork by Riemenschneider.

The Fine Arts Museum (Kunsthalle) at Hans Thomas Str. 2–6 has a fine display of German primitives as well as paintings by Rubens, Jordaens, and Rembrandt.

**Kassel** This industrial city of 200,000 people is known as the home of the Brothers Grimm of fairy-tale fame. The Brothers Grimm lived, studied, and worked as librarians in Kassel for most of their lives, and you can get a taste of all of that at the Brothers Grimm Museum on Schöne Aussicht 2. Housed within the Bellvue Schlösschen Palace, the museum documents the lives of Wilhelm and Jacob Grimm with furniture and other items from their family home, drawings and paintings of Kassel at the time they lived here, and, of course, copies of the brothers' famous fairy tales in many different languages. There are even some pop-up Grimm books.

A block away is the Deutsches Tapetenmuseum (German Wallpaper Museum), the only museum in the world devoted to wallpaper, and it's a lot more intriguing than it might seem.

The Wilhelmshöhe Castle, located in a 600-acre park of the same name, is certainly worth a visit. Nearly 800 different kinds of trees grow in this, the largest city park in Europe. The park's highlight is the Water Staircase, down which water falls 656 feet in a sequence of steps. The National Art Collection is housed in the palace, with a strong emphasis on the Dutch painters like Rembrandt, but also works by Titian and Murillo.

In the late 17th century and on into the 18th century, Huguenots found refuge in Kassel, after being expelled from France. Some of them found a home in nearby Bad Karlshafen, where they developed the harbor town. The role of the Huguenots in this town is remembered in the Hugenotten-Museum at Hafenplatz 9a.

**Koblenz** The ancient city of Koblenz began as a Roman encampment more than 2,000 years ago at the Deutsches Eck (German

Corner), a sharp peninsula where the rivers Mosel and Lahn flow into the Rhine. On summer evenings the nearby Blumenhof Garden is the place to enjoy outdoor concerts. Most of the city's historic churches are within walking distance of the German Corner, including the Church of Our Lady (Liebfrauenkirche). Completed in the 13th century, the church was later modified and consequently features Romanesque, Gothic, and Baroque elements. The church is located on An der Liebfrauenkirche.

St. Castor's Church (St. Kastor Kirche) on Kastorhof is Koblenz's most important church, combining Romanesque and Gothic elements. Its altar tombs are quite unusual. Notice also its rare Gothic wall paintings.

St. Florin's Church (St. Florin Kirche) was built in the Romanesque style around 1100 but was remodeled in the Gothic style in the 14th century. In the 17th century the church was again remodeled and received Gothic windows and a vaulted ceiling. The vaults under St. Florin's house some interesting Roman remains. The church is located on St. Florins Markt at Auf der Danne Str.

**Konstanz** This beautiful old city on the Swiss border took its place in church history as the site of an ecumenical Roman Catholic Council in 1414. Three Popes were vying for power at the time, and the primary purpose of the council was to reunite the church, which they eventually did with the election of Pope Martin V. However, they also dealt with Jan Hus of the University of Prague, a religious reformer who contested papal primacy and certain church practices. Though he had been guaranteed safe passage to and from Konstanz, he was condemned as a heretic and burned at the stake. Hus was such a popular figure that his martyrdom did nothing to stop the growing sentiment that resulted in Protestantism a century later.

All of the action took place in the cathedral, or Münster, the highest point in the old city. The spot on which Hus is said to have stood during his trial is marked on the central aisle by the 24th row. Next door in the Sylvesterkapelle is a cycle of frescoes depicting the life of Christ. When you have looked around inside, climb up the tower to get a great view of the city.

**Köthen** The little town of Köthen was home to J. S. Bach for six years, and it was here that the composer created some of his most famous works, including the Brandenburg Concertos. To honor the famous former resident, the town hosts an annual Bach festival every November. Concert halls throughout the city ring out with his Baroque masterpieces. Contact the local tourist information center on Markt 9A, phone 03496/23-78, for detailed information.

**Leipzig** The countryside around this city of a half million is not too exciting, but Leipzig itself has always generated excitement. In Leipzig in 1989 a peaceful revolution was waged that toppled the East German government. The city has long been known for its trade fairs and has been called the "City of Books." But for those who love music, and in particular church music, it is the city of Johann Sebastian Bach.

*Bach.* The site to visit is St. Thomas' Church (Thomaskirche) on Thomaskirchhof (just off Grimmaischestr.), since Johann Sebastian Bach, one of the world's greatest sacred music composers, called this church home for 27 years. Bach did much more than worship here. The church was also his workplace. Most of his cantatas were composed for the church's boys' choir. Check with the church or the local tourist office to see whether a concert is scheduled while you're in town. Quite often the choir, which Bach once directed, can be heard on Fridays at 6:00 P.M., Saturdays at 1:30 P.M., and at the Sunday services at 9:30 A.M. Incidentally, the choir originally had only 12 singers, but now it has 90 members. Outside of the church is a monument to Bach.

> Jesus lives, I know full well
> Naught from Him my heart can sever,
> Life nor death nor powers of hell,
> Joy nor grief, henceforth forever.
>
> CHRISTIAN GELLERT OF LEIPZIG, GERMANY

Although Bach is buried in the vault of the church, he wasn't fully appreciated here during his lifetime and didn't arrive in his final resting place until 1945. In fact Bach's music was somewhat forgotten until Felix Mendelssohn came to Leipzig as the director of the city's concert orchestra. Mendelssohn not only transformed the city into an internationally recognized musical center, he also revived Bach's music, especially *St. Matthew's Passion.*

Across the street from St. Thomas' Church is the Bosehaus, the home of one of Bach's friends during his lifetime. The house has been converted into a Bach museum, with exhibits about the composer's life as well as a display of period musical instruments.

*St. Nicholas' Church.* The exterior of St. Nicholas' Church (Nikolaikirche) on Nikolaikirchhof won't impress you nearly as much as its interior. The church's treasures include an elaborate 16th-century pulpit and an unusual ceiling, decorated in a diamond pattern. The support pillars are topped with carvings resembling palm fronds. Prayer vigils held in this church for 10 years until 1989 are credited with helping to topple East Germany's Communist leadership.

*The Augustusplatz,* just south of the Nikolaikirche, is the city's concert hall—where the concert orchestra performs—an excellent Egyptian Museum—the Germans love their Egyptian museums—and a fine arts and crafts museum.

*Martin Rinckart.* About 15 miles northeast of Leipzig in the little town of Eilenberg, Pastor Martin Rinckart made his church a refuge for the homeless during the Thirty Years' War. The war was followed by pestilence and famine. During the height of the disaster, Rinckart conducted up to 50 funerals a day. In spite of the devastating sorrow and anguish, Rinckart found time to write the hymn "Now Thank We All Our God."

**Lemgo** If you want to find a delightful town that isn't overrun by tourists, stop by Lemgo, southwest of Hannover. The Marienkirche on Breitestr. in the Old Town is noted for its swallows-nest organ, one of the oldest in Germany. If you have a chance to hear it played, take the opportunity. This town is noted for its music.

**Lübeck** This busy seaport city on the Baltic has a lovely historic area from medieval times. Since the early 17th century, the city churches have performed organ recitals. The Marienkirche, perched on a hill overlooking the city on Marktpl., has two modern organs that can be heard at Saturday evening recitals at 6:30; one of these organs is the biggest in the world. Jakobkirche's organs, which are older and smaller, are featured in concerts at 5:00 on Saturdays. The church is located on Breitestr.

At Klein Petersgrube 4–5, is the Museum für Figurentheater, which reputedly has the world's largest collection of puppet theater material. The adjoining marionette theater has matinees for kids every day at 3:30.

**Mainz** A must-see for Christians in Mainz is the Gutenberg Museum. The museum honors the printing pioneer Johannes Gutenberg, whose experiment with movable type in 1450 changed the world—and Christianity—forever. The museum houses woodcuts, lithographs, early presses, and a replica of Gutenberg's early workshop. Don't leave without seeing his famous Gutenberg Bibles, 550 years old, and the first book printed using movable type. For a more hands-on printing experience, check out the schedule of demonstrations at the museum's Print Shop (Druckladen) across the street. The museum is located at Liebfrauenpl. 5.

One of the finest Romanesque cathedrals in all of Germany is located in Mainz. The Mainz Dom at Domstr. 3 is the focal point of the old city, dating from the 11th through the 13th centuries. Its impressive spire was a Baroque addition, added in the 18th century.

Standing on a hilltop in the middle of town, St. Stephan's Church (St. Stephan Kirche) at Kleine Weissg. 12 is a lovely Gothic place of worship. Its most notable feature, however, is a more modern addition—the six stained glass windows in the choir created by Marc Chagall. Chagall was Jewish and designed the windows in part to encourage Jewish-Christian unity. Unfortunately, the artist died before the last of the windows were officially unveiled.

**Munich (München)** Munich is Germany's third-largest city and the capital of Bavaria. It is known for its Oktoberfest, its beer, and its love of arts and culture.

*The Square of Our Lady (Marienplatz)* is the center of the activity in Munich's Altstadt, or Old Town. Surrounded by shops, restaurants, and outdoor cafes, the square is named for the gilt statue of the Virgin Mary that has watched over it since 1638, looking a bit out of place during the more raucous city festivals. This is the place to enjoy the famous New Town Hall (Neues Rathaus). Built between 1867 and 1908 in the neo-Gothic style, this is Munich's current city hall. It is beloved for its famous Glockenspiel, or chiming clock. Swarms of tourists stand in the square to watch two levels of dancing and jousting figures spin around at 11:00 A.M. and noon daily in time to ringing bells. From May to October you can also catch the show at 5:00 P.M. and 9:00 P.M. daily. You can enjoy a view from higher up on the elevator that serves as an observation point near the top of one of the town hall's towers. Marienplatz is bordered by Kaufingerstr., Rosenstr., Weinstr., and Dienerstr.

The Old Town Hall (Altes Rathaus) also on Marienplatz, is smaller. It was built in 1474, and has a charming medieval appearance. The building is rarely open to the general public, but its tower provides a lovely setting for a little toy museum.

Churches. The major old city churches include Michaelskirche, a Jesuit sanctuary built between 1583 and 1597 in honor of the victory of Catholicism over Protestantism in the region; the Frauenkirche with its twin onion-domed towers both more than 300 feet high; and the Peterkirche, just off Marienpl. on Rindermarkt, a 13th-century Gothic structure with a statue of St. Peter in front of the high altar. If you climb to the top of "Old Pete," as they call the latter church, you get a great view of the city.

St. Michael's Church (Michaelskirche) at Neuhauserstr. 6 is one of the most magnificent Renaissance churches in Germany. Simple and beautiful, with its white stucco interior, the Jesuit church was built in the late 16th century and modeled after Il Gesù, the Jesuit church in Rome. Guided tours are available Wednesdays at 2:00.

The lovely red brick Church of Our Lady (Frauenkirche) on Frauenpl. is almost synonymous with Munich itself. The Gothic masterpiece was built between 1474 and 1494, and its slightly mismatched towers were added in 1524 and 1525. The interior of the cathedral is rather stark. Notice the footprint in the concrete just inside the entrance. Legend has it that shortly after the church's construction, the devil himself snuck into the church to check it out. Standing in this spot, he determined that there was no light in the church at all and stomped his foot in triumph, leaving the footprint. Had he stepped only a few feet farther in, he would have seen the sunlight streaming through glorious stained glass windows. You can step in the footprint, known as der Schwarze Tritt or the Black Footprint, and then see for yourself what the devil missed. The elaborate tombs located within the Frauenkirche contain the remains of the Wittelsbachs, the family that ruled Bavaria for seven centuries until 1918.

The beautiful yellow stucco Theatine Church (Theatinerkirche) at Theatinerstr. 22 takes its name from the Theatine monks for whom it was built in the mid–17th century. The lovely facade and the church's two towers were added about 100 years later.

There are those who consider the Asam Church (Asamkirche) so ostentatious that it is ugly. Others find it one of the most beautiful late-Baroque churches in Europe, if a bit overdone. Either way, if you're in Munich you really should visit this church, located on Sendlingerstr. and built in 1730 by the Asam brothers. Its style might be described as sculpt-'til-you-drop. Every square inch of the interior is covered with gold, marble statuary, and billowy clouds. The church was dedicated to St. John Nepomuk, a 14th-century monk.

*English Garden.* If you tire of the big city, head to the English Garden (Englischer Garten) on the eastern side of Munich's Schwabing district. Designed by Count Rumford, a refugee of the American War of Independence, the park is 3 miles long and more than 1/4 mile wide and follows the informal style preferred by English aristocrats of the 18th century. Enjoy a stroll through shady paths, rent a boat, relax in one of several beer gardens (try the one near the Chinese Pagoda), or ride a bike. You may want to steer clear of the large section behind the Haus der Kunst—it's been designated a nudist area.

*The Alte Pinakothek* at Barestr. 27 is Munich's great art gallery, and it is a great one. Among the works it holds are Rogier van der Weyden's *Adoration of the Magi,* Botticelli's *Pietà,* and Rembrandt's *The Resurrection of Christ.* Dürer's *The Four Apostles,* his last work and perhaps his greatest, is also here.

*Science museum.* One of the finest science museums in the world is the Deutsches Museum located on the Museuminsel. It's huge, covering about 500,000 square feet with about 18,000 exhibits, featuring submarines, aeronautics, and everything in between.

*Open-air market.* Munich's open-air food market, the Viktualienmarkt, is popular with locals and visitors alike. Southeast of Marienpl. via Tal or Rindermarkt, the market offers a wide range of traditional German food items, including heaps of fresh produce, crusty breads, meats, cheeses, beers, and wines. There are also lots of picnic tables where you can rest your feet and enjoy lunch and some great people watching. The market is open daily, except Sundays, from 7:00 to 6:30.

*Nymphenburg Palace (Schloss Nymphenburg),* northwest of Munich's city center on Amalienburgstr., was the summer palace of the Wittelsbach family. The oldest parts of the palace date from 1664, but construction continued for some 100 years, with most of it completed between 1680 and 1730. The interior of the castle is everything you might wish for, with plenty of whorled adornments and gilt statuary. The Banquet Hall (Festsaal) is especially lovely, decorated in greens and golds. Visitors will also enjoy a stroll through the palace's elaborate gardens.

*Olympic Park.* From a distance, the white stadium roofs over Munich's Olympic Park or Olympiapark look more like circus tents. This was the site of the Olympic games of 1972. Visitors can tour the complex via trains that run throughout the day from March through November. For a fabulous view of the city and the Alps nearby, take the elevator 960 feet up to the top of Olympia Tower. There's a revolving restaurant at the summit as well. The former Olympic cycling stadium was converted into an Olympic Spirit exhibition and fun-park, where visitors of all ages can enjoy participating in virtual-reality Olympic sports.

**Münster** In Münster, after the bloody Thirty Years' War was ended, the Peace of Westphalia was signed, recognizing the independence of Switzerland and the Netherlands and also recognizing three religious faiths, Catholicism, Lutheranism, and Calvinism. The room at the Rathaus, located on Prinzipalmarkt, where the treaty was signed is called Peace Hall (Friedensaal).

The city itself has always been Roman Catholic except for two years when Anabaptists took over. Then the Anabaptist leaders were overthrown, hanged, and their bodies put in iron cages for all to see. High up on the tower of the St. Lamberti church on Prinzipalmarkt, the three wrought-iron cages can still be seen.

**Nuremberg (Nürnberg)** Nuremberg's central open-air market (Hauptmarkt) is a colorful meeting place. Vendors sell fruit, flowers, and souvenirs, and street artists and musicians pass time here as well. In the winter months the market fairly teems with activity around the Christkindlmarkt, the huge pre-Christmas festival that lasts from late November through Christmas Eve. In the center of the square is the Beautiful Fountain (Schöner Brunnen), 66 feet high and elaborately carved around 1400. Forty figures grace the fountain, including Moses, the prophets, Julius Caesar, and Alexander the Great.

On the eastern side of the square is the Church of Our Lady (Frauenkirche), which replaced the Jewish quarter here in the 14th century. People flock to the church every day at noon to enjoy the large clock, the Männleinlaufen, on the church's facade. A procession of Holy Roman electors dance, spin, and bow to Kaiser Karl IV.

Though this city was badly damaged in World War II, it has come back (thanks to some exquisite restoration) to be a gorgeous tourist destination once again. St. Sebaldus on Hauptmarktpl. is the city's oldest and most important church with works of art dating to the 14th and 15th centuries.

If you have children with you, don't miss the Toy Museum (Spielzeugmuseum) at Karlstrasse 13–15, with all sorts of miniatures, toy soldiers, and dolls displayed in a 17th-century burgher's house.

During the summer, Nuremburg comes alive with music. In late May there is Musica Franconia, a weeklong series of concerts played on period instruments. An international theater festival is held for ten days in June, followed by an international organ recital using the facilities of the various city churches, and so on through the summer.

Albrecht Dürer's house is located on Albrecht-Dürer-Str. 39. The artist lived in this medieval gem from 1509 until his death in 1528. His home is open to the public and displays a large collection of his woodcut prints. Many of Dürer's works followed religious themes, including the famous *Praying Hands*.

Ten miles north in the town of Erlangen is a community where French Huguenots settled. A Protestant church on Hugenottenpl. was their house of worship.

**Oberammergau** During the 17th century the black plague decimated much of Europe's population. Oberammergau faced its share of deaths as well, until in 1633 the epidemic was inexplicably cut short. In thanks to God for the miracle, the citizenry vowed to produce the now world-famous Oberammergau Passion Play every ten years. The next performance will be in 2010, but in the meantime you can visit the Passion Play Theater (Passionspielhaus) on Passionweise. Open daily, the museum allows a backstage look at the making of the famous play. To order tickets, contact a local travel agent or the Oberammergau tourist office at Eugen-Papst-Str. 9A, phone 08822/10-21.

Oberammergau is also famous for its Lüftlmalerei—literally, air paintings. These elaborate frescoes, first appearing in the 18th century, adorn the exteriors of many of the city's buildings. Themes range from simple dressed-up windows to fairy-tale characters, like Little Red Riding Hood, and religious themes. The Pilatushaus, on Ludwigthomstr., is the most renowned and depicts Christ with

## WUNDERBAR

Southern Germany's Bavarian Alps rank among the most beautiful natural sights in Europe. The magnificent mountains' snow-capped peaks are the source of countless waterfalls. Viewing picturesque villages and medieval castles and churches, visitors can't help but keep a lookout for strapping Bavarians in lederhosen.

One of the loveliest ways to enjoy the alpine scenery is along the German Alpine Road (Alpenstrasse). Stretching from Lindau in the west to Berchtesgaden in the east, the route passes through Füssen with its magnificent castles; wraps around the Zugspitze, Germany's tallest mountain; through Oberammergau, home of the world-renowned Passion Play; to Berchtesgaden, famous for having been chosen by Hitler as his mountain retreat. Who could blame him? Numerous opportunities to stop and hike or picnic abound, and each bend in the road exposes visitors to some of God's loveliest landscapes.

Don't miss the opportunity to scale the Zugspitze for a tremendous view of the Bavarian Alps. There are several ways to reach the top, including an incline railway, cable cars, or hiking. In the winter months skiing is widely available. All of these options begin in Garmisch-Partenkirchen. You can obtain detailed information from the city's tourist office on Richard Strauss Platz.

Pontius Pilate. Inside you can watch Bavaria's best wood carvers chipping away in the workshop.

**Ravensbrück** In Brandenburg province east of Berlin, Ravensbrück was the concentration camp where Corrie ten Boom and her sister were imprisoned. Her sister, Betsie, died there. The camp had the highest mortality rate of any in Europe. Not far away near Oranienburg was the notorious Sachsenhausen camp.

**Regensburg** This medieval town doesn't seem to have changed much in the past 500 years, and thus it has retained its charm. There are 1,300 buildings of historical interest listed here. St. Peter's Cathedral on Dompl. took 300 years to build. It would have been finished sooner if the laity hadn't become Lutheran, much to the bishop's dismay. Just east of the cathedral is the Nidermünster, built atop previous churches. You can see the remains of the other churches and also some Roman buildings underneath. One of the most famous choirs in western Europe comes from this church. It's called the Domspatzen (meaning "Cathedral Sparrows"). Hear them, if you have a chance.

The town's smallest chapel is the Maria-Laeng-Kapelle on the corner of the Pfauengasse by the Domplatz. The custom here is to write out your prayers ahead of time and leave them in the church. While the Catholic hierarchy has never sanctioned the practice, it hasn't stopped the parishioners from doing it. The idea is that if your prayer is about the same length as the Virgin Mary's, it has a good chance of being answered.

The main Protestant church in town is the Neupfarrkirche, about two blocks southwest of the cathedral on Neupfarrpl. During the summer, concerts and plays are frequently held in the courtyard of the Thon Dittmer Palais at Haidpl. 8.

**Rothenburg ob der Tauber** There are many picturesque towns on the famous "Romantic Road"—a line of about 30 of Germany's most scenic medieval towns, stretching from Würzburg to Füssen. None is more lovely than Rothenburg. It is the only walled city in Germany without a single modern building. It suffered greatly during the Thirty Years' War, mostly because it was a Protestant city in the wrong location. After the war, the citizens had no money to build new buildings so they just fixed up the old ones.

St. Jakobskirche, at Klosterg. 15, dating in part from the 14th century, displays some great work by Tilman Riemenschneider. Note particularly the left wing of the altar showing *Christ's Entry into Jerusalem,* as well as his centerpiece *The Last Supper.*

Why not start your Christmas shopping in Rothenburg? The city is home to two stores devoted exclusively to the holiday: Käthe Wohlfahrt's Christkindlmarkt and Weihnachtsdorf are located right next to each other at Herrng. 1 and 2.

**Soest** Though it is near Germany's most industrial area, this city of about 45,000 has retained its medieval charm. Its churches are all unique. For example, the stained glass windows of St. Maria zur Wiese (St. Mary in the Fields), on Wiesenstr., portray the Last Supper, and there are local favorites on the table: pumpernickel bread and pitchers of beer. Other works of art in the church are a bit more conventional.

**Speyer** Protestants got their name in Speyer. After Luther's teachings had been condemned at the Diet of Worms in 1521, Lutheran states formally "protested" the ruling, and so a council was convened at Speyer in 1529 to hear the "protest." The Diet of Speyer confirmed the earlier decision at Worms. But the protesting action earned the Lutherans the title "Protestants." The Gedächtniskirche on the Bartholomaus-Weltz-Platz is a Protestant church with a statue of Luther on the front porch, recalling that protest.

The Romanesque Speyer Cathedral, nearly a thousand years old, dominates the city and has the largest Romanesque crypt in Germany. Four emperors of the Holy Roman Empire and four German kings are buried there.

**Steingaden** In the middle of meadows and peat bogs south of Steingaden stands the Wieskirche, or Meadow Church, a gorgeous small church that people come from miles to see. Its exterior is plain enough, but the white and gold inside are breathtaking, and your eyes are drawn to the silver lamb above the altar. The artist intended to show the glories of heaven contrasted with the plainness of earth, and the central fresco of the second coming is designed to represent God's love and forgiveness spreading over all the earth.

**Stolberg** In the Harz mountains, this town was the birthplace of Thomas Münzer, an Anabaptist leader who embraced the doctrines of the Reformation and preached them at Zwickau. But he got carried away to such extremes that Luther denounced him. He became an anarchist leading the Peasants' Revolt and bringing the Anabaptist name into disrepute. Because he had advocated a communal society, he became a hero in East Germany in the 20th century when the Communists took over after World War II. Just before the Communist regime fell, it had honored the 500th anniversary of the birth of Münzer. On the top floor of the Alte Münze along the Niedergasse is a memorial to Münzer.

In the middle of the Peasants' Revolt, Martin Luther dared to come to St. Martini Church here and preach against the teachings of Stolberg's favorite son. Incidentally, the best place to see the whole town is from an outlook known as Lutherbuche, just off Niedergasse and up the hill behind Münzer's birthplace.

**Stuttgart** Along with Leipzig, Stuttgart is a city where you can hear a lot of Bach. If you get a chance to hear a concert by Helmut Rilling's Bach Collegium, by all means, do so. Free concerts are frequently held in churches, and during the winter months the Stiftskirche on Schillerpl. has a series of evening concerts.

Stuttgart's Christmas fair is Germany's oldest and largest, begun in the 7th century. The Christmas Market (Weihnachtsmarkt), common in many German cities, is a commercial extravaganza, where you can purchase ornaments, gifts, and lots of potato pancakes and cookies.

**Triberg** Triberg, one of the loveliest towns in the Black Forest (Schwarzwald), is the home of Germany's highest waterfalls, more than 500 feet high. In this area you will find the best the Black Forest has to offer, including pom-pom hats, straw-roofed farmhouses, and cuckoo clocks. A great way to see the area is via the Black Forest Railway (Schwarzwaldbahn), on the Offenburg-Villingen line. Another good option is the Black Forest Museum (Schwarzwaldmuseum) at Wallfahrtstr. 4, which has lots of exhibits relating to Black Forest culture, including a cuckoo clock dating back to 1640.

**Trier** German cities don't get much older than this one. It was founded by Augustus Caesar in 16 B.C.; Constantine established it as the premier bishopric north of the Alps in A.D. 314. The Dom (cathedral) on Hauptmarkt dates from A.D. 1030, although some of the masonry may go back to the 4th century. The most impressive structure may be the Konstantinbasilika, just south of the Dom on Konstantinstr., dating from A.D. 310. It was once Constantine's throne hall. Today it is the church of the local Protestant community. Below it are the catacombs and there are tours at 3:00 most afternoons. An unusual church is St. Paullin (via Thebaerstrasse). The designer was Balthasar Neumann in 1757, who believed that entering church should be like entering heaven. It is a rococo extravaganza.

**Tübingen** This is a university town, something like Oxford or Cambridge in England, where the school is larger than the town. Both Protestants and Catholics have major seminaries here. Evangelisches Stift, on Kronenstr., the Protestant seminary, was established as an Augustinian monastery but was converted into a Protestant school. Many German theologians attended here, including Dietrich Bonhoeffer. Wilhelmstift, on the other hand, located on Holzmarktstr., was formerly a school for Protestants but was converted into a Catholic seminary. The noted Catholic theologian Hans Kung taught here.

**Ulm** This city of 110,000 people is best known as the birthplace of Albert Einstein and as the site of the tallest church steeple in the world. You will have a hard time finding much relating to Einstein here, but you won't have trouble spotting the church spire. It's 528 feet high. Though the cathedral was begun in 1377, it wasn't until 1890 that the twin towers and the spire were erected. For a good look at the spire as well as getting a panorama of Ulm, you can climb 768 steps to a tower platform. The art in the cathedral was not done by well-known artists, but it is visually powerful nonetheless. Every other Saturday during the summer, choral music is performed here. Besides that, you can hear the five-manual organ every day from 11:00 until noon.

If you are checking the unusual museums of Germany, you might look in on the Deutsches Brotmuseum. Yes, it's a bread museum. Realizing that there was no museum in the entire world devoted to one of the most necessary ingredients of life, an Ulm businessman decided to show the 8,000-year history of bread and bread making in a museum. Why not? The museum is located at Salzstadelg. 10.

**Weimar** This city of about 60,000 symbolizes the highs and lows of the German nation. Many of the great names of Germany passed through here. Goethe, Bach, Liszt, Strauss, Nietzsche, Cranach, and Schiller all lived here. It has been the intellectual and art center of the country. After World War I, a new constitution establishing the Weimar Republic was approved here, but soon the Nazis came to power in Germany and before long set up the notorious Buchenwald concentration camp just north of the city.

The Stadtkirche on Herderplatz is also known as Herderkirche, honoring the brilliant pastor who served here for three decades. The famous Cranach triptych is there with scenes from the Old and New Testaments flanking a depiction of the crucifixion.

## DIETRICH BONHOEFFER (1906-1945)

Dietrich Bonhoeffer, the German theologian who wrote *The Cost of Discipleship,* practiced what he preached and paid the price. A lecturer at the University of Berlin when Hitler came to power, he vigorously opposed Naziism. During World War II he was forbidden to preach or to publish. He turned down a job in America where he would have been safe, choosing to stay in his homeland, where he was arrested in 1943 for his involvement in smuggling 14 Jews into Switzerland. Bonhoeffer was hanged by the Nazis in April 1945 for plotting against Hitler.

Sites associated with Bonhoeffer's life are located in Tübingen.

**Wittenberg** Wittenberg has one claim to fame, albeit a large one: His name is Martin Luther. Travelers will find nearly all of the sites associated with the reformer clumped around the city's Old Town. The central market, or markt, at the end of Collegienstr., is adorned with the statues of Martin Luther and Philipp Melanchthon, his friend and supporter. Visitors can tour Melanchthon's house on Collegienstr. 60, which has been converted into a museum.

At the opposite end of the Old Town on Collegienstr. is the Castle Church (Schlosskirche), the church to the door of which Luther nailed his famous 95 theses. A replica of the door is now cast in bronze—the originals were destroyed during the Seven Years' War. Inside the church are the tombs of both Luther and Melanchthon. Incidentally, it was in this church in

> If thou but suffer God to guide thee
> And hope in Him through all thy ways,
> He'll give thee strength, whate'er betide thee,
> And bear thee through the evil days.
>
> GEORG NEUMARK OF WEIMAR, GERMANY

Luther's absence, on Christmas Day 1521, that the first Protestant service was conducted.

Wittenberg's oldest building is Stadtkirche St. Marien, located on Marktpl., a twin-towered Gothic church with parts dating back to 1470. Luther often preached here, he was married here, and his six children were all baptized in the church's baptismal font.

On the far eastern end of the Old Town is the Lutherhalle on Collegienstr. 54, where Martin Luther lived and worked until his death in 1546. Today the building is a museum with many of Luther's papers, including drafts of his famous theses. An English-language guidebook is available at the front desk to help you understand the exhibits. It is nearly impossible to exaggerate the influence that Luther had on the church and on Germany, and this museum will help to make that point.

**Worms** Remember, it's pronounced "vorms," not "worms." However you say it, the city of Worms is worth taking time for, particularly if you're Protestant. In the Lutherplatz you'll see the Luther Monument (Lutherdenkmal), erected in 1868. The great reformer is depicted standing boldly with his documents in hand, much as he must have looked when he stood in front of the Imperial Diet in 1521 to make his case for church reform. Surrounding the monument are fountains, small flower gardens, and statues of others who were helpful in bringing about the Reformation. Included are Petrus Waldo, founder of the Waldensian Church of Italy, John Wycliffe of England, Jan Hus of the Czech Republic, and Savonarola of Italy.

> Thou canst be merciful while just,
> In thy redeeming grace I trust,
> Upheld by Thee I stand secure
> Thy word is firm, Thy promise sure.
>
> MARTIN LUTHER OF WITTENBERG, GERMANY

The City Museum of Worms (Museum der Stadt Worms) is located in the old Romanesque church and cloister of Andreasstift at Weckerlingpl 7. The building itself is beautiful, and the exhibits offer a detailed historical look at the city. Martin Luther is honored as well, although the exhibits are brief.

The Heylshof Art Museum (Kunsthaus Heylshof) at Im Heylshofgarten houses Gothic and Renaissance art, much of which has sacred themes. A highlight is Rubens's *Madonna with Child*. The building itself has even deeper Christian significance than is obvious from the art. It was at this site that Martin Luther stood before the Imperial Diet after nailing his theses on the door of the Wittenberg church. "Here I stand. I can not do otherwise. God help me. Amen," he is credited with declaring.

The 11th-century Cathedral of St. Peter (Dom St. Peter) on Domplatz is a huge solid-looking church. Although categorized as Gothic because of its high arches, the church contains many Baroque elements like the gilded columns and gold crowns above the altar. A short distance away on Andreasstr. is the Magnuskirche, which resembles a New England church. It has the distinction of being one of the oldest Protestant churches in Germany.

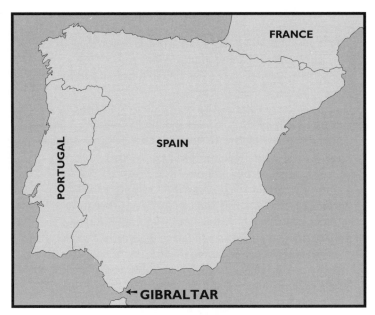

# Gibraltar

Gibraltar Tourist Board
  US 202-452-1108
  UK 020-7836-0777
*Web site*
  Entire colony: www.gibraltar.gi
For a complete list of updated links, visit www.christiantraveler.com

### Country in a Capsule

*Size:* About 2.5 square miles, which means that it is 15 times the size of Vatican City, but that it is only one twenty-fifth the size of Washington, D.C. Its population is about 38,000.

*Religion:* Most of the population (75 percent) is Roman Catholic; 8 percent is Anglican; 8 percent Muslim.

*Language:* The official language is English, but Spanish is common here as well.

*Money:* The official currency is the Gibraltar pound, which is tied to the British pound, but you can use your Spanish money here too. See United Kingdom and Spain for approximate exchange rates.

*Food:* Restaurants in Gibraltar tend to split into two camps: those offering Spanish and Mediterranean cuisine, and those offering English specialties. International cuisines are available, but restaurants are expensive.

*Shopping:* Gibraltar is a duty-free shopping area.

*Brief history:* In 1462, when Spain recaptured Gibraltar from the Moors, it was annexed to Spain. Then in the War of the Spanish Succession (1704), the British captured it and the land was ceded to Britain. In 1969 the people of Gibraltar indicated their desire to stay with Britain, rather than go with Spain, and Britain granted it full self-government. Since that time it has been governed by a locally elected House of Assembly with a governor appointed by Britain.

*The Rock.* When you look at a map, it is difficult to think of Gibraltar as anything other than a part of Spain, but nevertheless the tiny promontory is a British colony. Gibraltar is really a large rock, albeit an impressive one, just 3-3/5 miles long and 1/2 mile wide. The Rock, as it is often called, has been battled over for centuries, claimed first by Spain, later by the Moors, captured by an Anglo-Dutch fleet in 1704, and finally ceded to the British in 1713. English speakers will no doubt enjoy the opportunity to relax a bit and converse in their native tongue. Whether you fly or drive into Gibraltar, you will nonetheless cross a runway. The Gibraltar Airport stretches across the narrow neck of land that connects it to Spain, and farther out into the Bay of Gibraltar.

*The Barbary Apes* are said to be Gibraltar's oldest residents; they are certainly its most famous. The cinnamon-colored monkeys were introduced by the British, and legend has it that as long as the apes remain, the British will maintain control of the Rock. Although the United Kingdom officially holds title to the land in perpetuity, the British are taking no chances; they're feeding the monkeys. Winston Churchill himself ordered the maintenance of the Barbary ape colony when its numbers began to dwindle during World War II. Now British soldiers feed the apes twice daily. Visitors can easily access the apes' den via cable car, which has a stop halfway up its ascent to the Top of the Rock for just that purpose. Be careful of the little apes; although they look cute and cuddly, they can be aggressive.

The view from the Top of the Rock offers fabulous views of the ocean and surrounding landscape of Europe and northern Africa. To board the cable car that will transport you, go to the southern end of Main St., near the Gibraltar Botanic Gardens. A round-trip ticket includes entrance to the apes' den and St. Michael's Cave. For a more active, less expensive option, consider buying a one-way ticket to the top and enjoy the view as you hike down. Cable cars depart every ten minutes from morning until supper time.

*The Great Siege Tunnels* were carved out to provide defense during the Great Siege of 1779 to 1783, when the Spanish and French attacked. One of the tunnels in the network was named the Holyland Tunnel because it faces due east, the precise direction of Mecca.

*Europa Point (Punte Grande de Europa)* is the Rock's southernmost point, and from this location you can get a great view across the Strait of Gibraltar to Morocco. In ancient times the Rock of Gibraltar was known as one of the two Pillars of Hercules; the other was across the strait, a mountain between the cities of Ceuta and Tangier in Morocco.

*St. Michael's Cave.* The natural grotto called St. Michael's Cave has been popular for centuries. The underground labyrinth is beautifully adorned with stalactites and stalagmites and is a popular location for concerts, ballet, and drama.

*Churches.* Once the site of a mosque, the Shrine of Our Lady of Europe in Europa Flats was converted into a Catholic chapel in 1462, after the capture of Gibraltar by the Spanish. The shrine has been venerated ever since. It is located at the southern end of the Rock. The light that was kept burning in a tower above the chapel was the original Gibraltar lighthouse; its light was kept burning for centuries thanks to the provision of oil that was brought by sailors who made a point of stopping to visit the shrine as they passed by. Much of the shrine was plundered by the pirate Red Beard, but the 15th-century statue *Virgin and Child* remains.

The Cathedral of the Holy Trinity on Cathedral Sq. was founded in 1825 by Governor of Gibraltar General Sir George Don, who was later buried there. The beautiful cathedral was consecrated in 1838.

The Cathedral of St. Mary the Crowned sits on the site of what was once the chief mosque in the center of town. During the Great

Siege, between 1779 and 1783, most of the old Spanish and Moorish buildings in Gibraltar were reduced to rubble, but this cathedral is one early structure that can still be seen and enjoyed.

*The Convent.* As its name suggests, The Convent, bordered by Main St. and Line Wall Rd., was once home to an order of Franciscan Friars. Since 1782 the building has served as the official residence of Gibraltar's governors. While visitors are not welcome inside the private residence, the exterior is attractive and worth seeing. It is the site several times a day on weekdays of the Changing of the Guard by soldiers of the Royal Gibraltar Regiment.

*The Gibraltar Botanic Gardens* were first planted and opened in 1816. Today the gardens contain about 600 species of trees, shrubs, cacti, and flowering plants. After you've enjoyed the plants, you can take your trip to the Top of the Rock, as the cable car entrance is nearly surrounded by the garden.

*Cruises.* For interesting natural sights of another sort, consider booking a dolphin cruise. The Bay of Gilbraltar is home to three species of dolphins, and it is not uncommon to see the lovable creatures in the waters offshore. On a dolphin cruise you will see the creatures up close. Dolphin Safari claims to be the original dolphin cruise company in the area and can be reached by phone at 350/71-914, on the Internet at www.dolphinsafari.gi, or at the Marina Bay Complex. Tours last between 2 and 2-1/2 hours.

*Nimo,* Gilbraltar's only research vessel, also offers tours that focus on dolphin preservation. Reach them by phone at 350/73-719, on the Internet at www.gibraltar.gi/helpinghand, or find them at the Queensway Quay Marina on Queensway. The trip runs between 2 and 2–1/2 hours.

*Parson's Lodge.* With a name like Parson's Lodge visitors might expect to find the historic home of a kindly preacher. It is actually the site of numerous battles, first between the Moors and the Spaniards, later between the British and their French and Spanish attackers. Throughout history the small rock, sometimes called a mini-Gibraltar, has been appreciated for its strategic military importance. It seems the name Parson's Lodge was an irreverent reference to the small hermitage and chapel of St. John the Green, situated immediately landward of Parson's Lodge Rock.

# *Iceland*

Icelandic Tourist Board
  US 212-885-9700
  UK 020-7388-7550
*Web sites*
  Scandinavia www.goscandinavia.com
  Entire country www.goiceland.org
For a complete list of updated links, visit www.christiantraveler.com

### Country in a Capsule

*Size:* About 20 percent larger than the state of Maine, but with only one-fifth the population. However, the capital of Iceland, Reykjavík, with 110,000 people, is larger than Portland, the capital of Maine, with about 65,000 people.

*Religion:* 95 percent of the population officially belongs to the Evangelical Lutheran Church. Free Lutherans, Seventh-day Adventists, Roman Catholics, and native religionists compose most of the remainder.

*Language:* Officially, the language is Icelandic, which is related to the old Norwegian language. But your English will be understood by most everyone, especially the younger generation in the larger communities.

*Money:* The monetary unit is the krone, and you can exchange a U.S. dollar for about 75 kronur.

*Food:* Fish is prominent on the menu with catfish, haddock, halibut, and cod leading the way. During the summer, you can get trout and salmon. Lamb is the preferred meat, although if you're up for it, you might sample broiled lundi (puffin), which tastes a little like liver. For dessert, try skyr, which is something like yogurt.

*Shopping:* A warm and wooly Icelandic jumper, lopapeysa, is the common tourist purchase, but woolen scarves, socks, hats, and gloves are also popular. Crafts, leatherwork, and costume jewelry are worth buying here as well.

*Brief history:* The first European settlers were probably Irish monks, who came to evangelize the island around A.D. 700. It is doubtful that they found any natives to evangelize, but in the late 9th century the Vikings came and began to colonize the area. In the next 50 years the island was settled with 30,000 to 40,000 people, and a code of law was established for the area. Christianity came to Iceland about 1000 and unified the entire island. By 1400 Iceland was brought under Danish control, and when the Reformation came to Denmark, Iceland was forced to convert to Protestantism as well.

For several centuries Iceland suffered from oppression under foreign rule, crop failures, invasion by pirates, volcanic eruption, epidemic, and unusually harsh winters. In 1874 a new constitution brought self-rule to Iceland under the Kingdom of Denmark, but it wasn't until 1944 that Iceland became an independent republic.

**Reykjavík** There is a lot going on in this capital city with its shops, cafes, galleries, museums, and artistic events. If you ever get lost, look up and see the 210-foot grey tower of Hallgrim's Church (Hallgrímskirkja). You can see it from almost anywhere in the city. The locals appreciate it, because they know it took nearly 40 years to build, but they may not like it, because it resembles a mountain of basaltic lava. The church was named in honor of Hallgrimur Petersson, who was the author of a hymnal called *50 Passion Hymns*. The church is now open to the public, and you can get a good look at the area from the vantage point of the church tower. An elevator will take you up, but there is a fee. Also there are organ concerts at 8:30 Sunday nights in the summer, but once again there is a charge.

The gentleman standing in front of the church is Leif Eriksson, the first European to set foot in the New World. The statue of Eriksson was given to Iceland by the United States to celebrate the 1,000th anniversary of Iceland's Parliament.

About 20 minutes from downtown is an open-air folk museum (Árbæjarsafn) that exhibits a village of relocated 18th- and 19th-century homes. The turf church here dates from 1842. The museum is located in the district of Arbær.

Reykjavík traces its history to the time in 874 when the Viking explorer Ingolfur Arnarson settled here. A statue of the intrepid Viking is on Arnarholl, overlooking the city.

*The Lutheran Cathedral (Dómkirkjan)* on Austurvöllur is an 18th-century stone church a block north of Tjörnin Lake. Inside, the congregation treasures its baptismal font carved in the early 19th century by sculptor Bertel Thorvaldsen. It is open daily from 10:00 to 4:00, except Wednesdays and Saturdays, but on Wednesdays you can hear an organ recital at 12:10.

*Hofoi house.* If you want to see where President Ronald Reagan met Mikhail Gorbachev in 1986, go to the Hofoi house, near the junction of Borgartun and Notun. It is open to the public in the summer. It is still used for official receptions and social functions.

*The Kolaportio Flea Market* is Iceland's largest. It has become increasingly popular and is open on Saturdays and Sundays one block from the National Bank of Iceland building on Geirsgata.

*The National Gallery of Iceland,* located behind the Frikirkjan church near Tjorn, is open daily except Mondays. Admission is free. The exhibits are not extensive, but if you want to see Icelandic art, this is the place.

*Fun-park.* You probably won't be able to pronounce its name, but if you have children, they will want to go there anyway. It is a family fun-park and zoo in Laugardular. The family fun-park is designed around Nordic and Viking themes. The zoo specializes in animals native to Iceland, like Icelandic horses, Arctic fox, seals, and reindeer. Oh yes, the name? It's Fjolskyldugarourinn and Husdyragarourinn. It is open daily in June, July, and August.

*The Perlan restaurant.* For a unique, though expensive, restaurant experience, try the Perlan (Pearl) on Öskjuhlíd Hill. It is a revolving restaurant standing on top of tanks that hold hot water pumped from deep underground. Alongside the restaurant are exhibitions and a mechanical geyser that erupts at regular intervals beside the central staircase. The surrounding grounds provide wooded slopes that are popular with walkers and runners.

At *Tjarnarbio,* Iceland's longest-running theater production, *Light Nights,* goes on every day except Sunday, all summer long. It is performed in English and staged for tourists, and it gives you a history of Iceland, condensed into two hours.

*Swimming.* Iceland's ample supply of geothermal water allows for the luxury of no less than seven public swimming pools within Reykjavík. The natural temperature of the water is a warm 84 degrees Fahrenheit year-round. Most tourists head to Laugardalur swimming pool, the largest, in Laugardalur Park (phone 553-4039). The facility offers an outdoor pool, four "hot-pots," whirlpool, wading pool, curved waterslide, steambath, and a professional massage service.

Southwest of Reykjavík is the Blue Lagoon, a large geothermal pool of hot water in the middle of a lava field. The lagoon's water is actually runoff from Perlan, Reykjavík's power plant. Don't worry—the water is perfectly safe. In fact some claim that the naturally occurring minerals in the water are healthy for your skin and can actually cure psoriasis. Whether you are in need of healing or not, you'll enjoy the relaxation of a pastime that is uniquely Icelandic.

**Akureyri** It's a town of only 14,000 but it is full of churches and museums. On the north coast of Iceland, a few miles south of the Arctic Circle, Akureyri has a great climate, and the residents make the most of it with flowers, trees, and gardens. The main church (Akureyrarkirkja) was built in 1940 and has a 3,200 pipe organ, a center window from the Coventry Cathedral in England, and some unusual reliefs of the life of Christ. The Botanic Gardens (Lystigardurinn) on Eyrarlandsvegur exhibits every plant that grows in the country plus many from elsewhere around the world.

**Bláfjöll** The top ski area in the country is the Blafjöllafolkvangur reserve, just southeast of the capital. It is open from mid-November to early May. During the summer there are plenty of good hiking trails here.

**Egilsstadir** South of the town of Egilsstadir is Iceland's largest forest, Hallormsstadarskógur. Birch, aspen, and spruce grow here, and the area is considered ideal for hiking and horseback riding. Horseback riding tours are available from Hekluhestar, at Austvadsholt, IS–851 Hella, phone 453-8383; Polar Horses, at Grý tubakki 2, IS–601 Akureyri, phone 463-3179; and Eldhestar-Volcano Horses, at Vellir, Ölfus, P.O. Box 90, IS–810 Hveragerdi, phone 483-4884.

**Geysir** We get our word geyser from the name of these hot springs (which incidentally is pronounced gay-zeer). The world's largest geyser, known as Geysir, erupted from the 14th century to early in the 20th century and then stopped when tourists started putting rocks on it. But, not to worry, nearby is Strokkur, another geyser that spouts and sprays every three minutes. If you look around a little, you will also find blue and rust-colored boiling mud pots.

**Grimsey** If you want to cross into the Arctic Circle, you have to go to this island north of the mainland. Grimsey is a place where you can see the midnight sun, it's the home of 60 different kinds of birds, and it's a famous colony for chess players. American journalist Daniel Fiske, hearing that Grimsey residents were avid chess players, financed a library and left part of his estate to the community. A picture of Fiske hangs in the community center. Oh, by the way, Fiske never set foot on the island.

**Gullfoss** The two falls of the Hvita River here are worth seeing. Not only are the 100-foot falls breathtaking, but the canyon below is 200 feet deep and worth capturing with your camera. If you are there when the sun in shining, you will probably see a rainbow through the mist.

*159*

**Hafnarfjördur** This lovely suburb of Reykjavík is a good place to rent a bike. From the bus terminals, you can rent bikes and go on the Blue Biking Tour for the day. A shorter tour leaves at 7:30 in the evening. If you want to see elves, leprechauns, fairies, and other wee people, you will have to sign up for the Hidden Worlds Tour. In early July during odd numbered years, this town hosts an International Viking Festival with parades and horse shows.

## GOD'S CREATION

There are many places throughout Europe that can claim evidence of God's creative powers. There are few that can argue God hasn't finished yet. But that is clearly true of Iceland. Located right over one of the most geologically active areas on the planet, Iceland has an extraordinary amount of volcanic activity. Visitors can see landscapes here unlike any others in the world, encompassing mountains, active volcanoes, hot springs, glaciers, fjords, lakes, waterfalls, and rugged coastlines. And it is all bathed in an eerie 24-hour light in the summer months, when the sun never sets.

Consider visiting Thingvellir National Park, which straddles two tectonic plates causing the park to spread by 2 centimeters every year. A boat trip on the glacial lake Jökulsárlón is a great way to enjoy the stark contrast of long black sandy beaches and gigantic iridescent blue and black icebergs. Take a snowmobile ride on Vatnajökull, Europe's largest glacier, covering over 3,200 square miles. Visit Geysir, strewn with broken rock, steaming pools of hot water, and a geyser that erupts like clockwork. And when you're all worn out, you can relax in the steaming mineral waters of the Blue Lagoon.

**Húsavík** Húsavík is a charming port village on Iceland's north coast. It's a bustling harbor with a quaint century-old timber church, but its greatest attraction to travelers is its proximity to natural areas. In the winter, visitors can ski or explore glaciers by snowmobile. In the summer, consider hiking, horseback riding (see also under Egilsstadir), or whale watching. Nordur Sigling (Box 122, IS–640 Húsavík, phone 464-2350) is a good option for viewing the giants of the deep. Cruises take place aboard three classic oak ships.

The real gem of the Húsavík area is Mývatn, a lake about 35 miles southeast of town. Its false craters and birdlife, found nowhere else in Europe, attract many visitors every year. The countryside surrounding the lake consists of lava barrens and black sand, an otherworldly place—or perhaps a "new worldly" place. Icelanders like to remind visitors that their homeland is the most geologically active country in the world, and is still being created.

A popular and stunningly beautiful waterfall in the area is named Godafoss (Waterfall of the Gods). The name is supposed to have come from the last Viking follower of the pagan Norse faith, who tossed his icons into the waterfall after converting to Christianity.

**Hverageroi** This is called Iceland's flower town because it rests against the mountains in a valley bubbling and steaming with hot springs. You will probably note a tiny geyser spouting every few seconds. Much of the resulting power is harnessed for heat. A place called Eden is where the tour buses stop, and if you get beyond the gift shop, you will see a variety of tropical plants (bananas and pawpaws, for instance) that you don't expect to see in Iceland.

This is great hiking country, and the hike usually begins by getting your feet wet as you cross a small stream. For kids, there is a puppet museum, Grundersafnio, which features puppets in old Icelandic clothing. It is open on Tuesday, Thursday, Saturday, and Sunday afternoons.

**Kirkjubæjarklaustur** The word Kirkjubæjarklaustur, which is quite a mouthful for English speakers, translates literally to "church farmstead cloister." This town was once the site of a medieval convent, but in 1783 disaster threatened the community when the volcano Laki erupted, producing the greatest amount of lava from a single eruption in recorded history. The fervent prayers of a priest living here is credited with having stopped the lava before it reached any inhabited areas. A tiny chapel commemorates his devotion. There are also two waterfalls in the town, and in August a chamber music festival is a popular attraction.

**Laugarvatn** It's now an educational center, a camping center, and a place to start your hiking. Historically, however, Laugarvatn was the place where most baptisms were performed. Why here? Because of the hot spring. It's better than chopping through ice to be baptized.

**Pingeyrar** In north central Iceland, this was the site of Iceland's first monastery in 1112. In a few years the monastery had become the country's greatest library, where monks wrote and studied. Though the monastery no longer stands, a delightful 19th-century stone church is here and worth a stop. In it is a 17th-century pulpit from Holland, a 15th-century altarpiece from England, some 16th-century oak statuettes from Germany, and some alabaster reliefs from the original monastery. If you decide to visit the church, wear sturdy walking shoes. From the intersection of Ring Rd. and Rte. 721, it's a 4-mile walk north along the footpath. First, check in with the Blöduós Tourist Office at 452-4770 to make sure the church is open, or the 8-mile round-trip will be for naught.

**Reykholt** If you stay in Iceland for a day or two, you will certainly hear the name Snorri Sturluson and wonder if he ever existed or if he is one of Iceland's trolls. Sturluson certainly existed and he is one of the most famous people in Icelandic literature. Born in 1179, he lived in Reykholt and wrote his greatest works here. This is also where he was assassinated by a political enemy. A statue of Snorri stands outside the school, and a new church displays some of his writings. There is also a pool nearby called Snorri's pool, and a passage behind the pool leads to the cellar where Snorri was murdered.

**Skalholt** For about 700 years this town was one of the two major theological centers of Iceland and it was known for its displays of religious drama. Now it hosts a classical music festival during the summer featuring musicians from continental Europe as well as Iceland.

**Skaftafell National Park** Visitors pass over lowland sands into lush foothills from the foot of the Skaftafellsjökull. Svartifoss has polygonal lava sides, and in the upper regions you can visit hidden glacial canyons and stunning mountaintops. Just outside the park's borders is Iceland's highest summit, Mt. Hvannadalshnjúkur.

**Thingvellir National Park** The nation of Iceland was founded at this site in 930 by a democratic assembly, the Althingi, the world's first and oldest parliament. Seventy years later, in the year 1000, another historic event took place at Thingvellir. Iceland's chieftain, Thorgeir Ljósvetninggagodi, announced that the nation should universally reject its pagan religion and adopt

Christianity. With fairly little argument, the switch was made, and all Icelanders were baptized.

The park's church (Thingvallakirkja) was one of the first in Iceland, probably consecrated in about 1020. When the first church collapsed in 1118, a local farmer donated a building, which has since been enlarged and moved to the site of the present church. The new church built in 1859 has one of the original church bells, a pulpit dating to 1683, and an interesting painting of Christ healing a blind man as an altarpiece. If the church is locked, go to the national park warden's house nearby.

Beyond the religious importance of Thingvellir, the park offers plenty of opportunities to enjoy fantastic natural beauties. Lake Thingvallavatn is the largest lake in Iceland. The park straddles both the European and North American tectonic plates, causing the park to spread by 2 centimeters every year (watch your step!), and the river Öxará slices its way through those jagged fissures and lava fields. In 1928 Thingvellir was made Iceland's first national park.

# *Ireland*

Irish Tourist Board
  US 212-418-0800 or 800-223-6470
  Canada 416-487-3335
  UK 020-7493-3201
  Australia 02-9299-6177
*Web site*
  Entire country www.ireland.travel.ie
For a complete list of updated links, visit www.christiantraveler.com

### Country in a Capsule

*Size:* The Republic of Ireland is a little smaller than the state of South Carolina, but it has a few more people. Its major city, Dublin, has a population of nearly a million, but no other city has more than 200,000.

*Religion:* Nearly 94 percent are Roman Catholic, about 2 percent are members of the Anglican Church of Ireland, and about 1.5 percent are Presbyterian. Methodists and Baptists have smaller representations.

*Language:* According to the Constitution, Irish is the first official language and English the second. Irish Gaelic is spoken primarily in the western districts of Ireland.

*Money:* The currency is the Irish poung (punt), which is currently worth about $1.10.

*Food:* Irish stew is the first thing that comes to your mind, but you might try collar and cabbage, which is made up of a collar of boiled bacon, coated with breadcrumbs and brown sugar and served with cabbage cooked in a bacon stock. Colcannon is another favorite. This is a mix of potatoes, onions, parsnips, and white cabbage, mixed with butter and cream.

*Shopping:* The craft stores are often a good place to start. Donegal is a good place for tweeds, but anywhere in the country you may find good buys on glassware, linens, and ceramics.

*Brief history:* The Irish culture flourished after the introduction of Christianity by St. Patrick in 432. Viking raiders encroached on the land from about 800 to 1000, perhaps founding Dublin in 840. Then Brian Boru united Ireland and ended Norse power around 1014, but about a hundred years later Henry II of England tried to subjugate Ireland. It wasn't until Henry VIII broke the power of the feudal lords and took the title of King of Ireland in 1541, however, that England really gained control. Under James I about 100,000 Scottish Presbyterians moved into Ulster in the northeast, beginning in 1607. In 1782, after the American Revolution, the Irish Parliament was given more freedom. The devastating potato famine in the late 1840s killed more than one million Irish with two million more emigrating across the Atlantic. In 1920 and 1921 Ulster was given its own home rule parliament. The Dublin government remained neutral during World War II and left the British Commonwealth in 1949, choosing the name Republic of Ireland. There is a continued conflict over the status of Northern Ireland. Although located on the island of Ireland, it remains a principality of the United Kingdom.

*165*

**Dublin** There are two must-see churches in Dublin, whether you are ordinarily a cathedral-hopper or not. St. Patrick's on Patrick St. has the most interesting history. According to legend, St. Patrick baptized many converts at a well on the site of the cathedral during the 5th century. The existing building dates from 1190. It is the longest church in Ireland, measuring 305 feet, and houses Ireland's largest and most beautiful organ. Oliver Cromwell, ruler of England in the 17th century and no great fan of the Irish people, used the cathedral as a horse stable at one time. It wasn't until the 19th century that the damage left by years of misuse was repaired. Memorials to many famous figures from Ireland's past cover the cathedral's walls, including that of Jonathan Swift, author of *Gulliver's Travels,* who was dean of St. Patrick's from 1713 to 1745. His tomb as well as his pulpit and writing table can be seen here.

St. Patrick's is Ireland's grandest house of worship, but Christ Church Cathedral, located at Christ Church Pl. and Winetavern St., is Dublin's oldest. Construction of the church began in 1172 by Strongbow, a conqueror for England, but it was the 1875 renovation of the building that gave the exterior its familiar appearance. Surrounded by old housing and factories and with an interior of faded murals and tapestries, it is not the most inviting place, and yet there is a charm to it. The crypt is nearly as large as the church. You will see some 17th-century punishment stocks there. The crypt is the oldest surviving structure in Dublin. Its vaults were constructed during the 12th and 13th centuries.

> Praise the Savior, ye who know Him!
> Who can tell how much we owe Him?
> Gladly let us render to Him
> All we are and have.
>
> THOMAS KELLY OF DUBLIN, IRELAND

*Museums.* The National Gallery of Ireland is on the west side of Merrion Square and houses what is considered the country's finest collection of old masters paintings. Many of the medieval paintings have sacred themes, including Caravaggio's *The Arrest of Christ.* Free guided tours are available Saturdays at 3:00 and Sundays at 2:15, 3:00, and 4:00. Admission is free. If you arrive at lunchtime, head to the gallery's restaurant. It is widely recognized as one of the best spots in town for a first-rate budget lunch.

The National Museum on Kildare St. is most famous for its massive collection of ancient Irish artifacts. Some of the items date back to 6000 B.C., but the collection spans up to the present. Christians may be especially interested in the Chalice of Ardagh and the Cross of Cong. Admission is free.

*Grafton Street.* If you are interested in shopping, eating, or people watching, Grafton Street is the place to be. The pedestrian mall leads from Trinity College to Stephen's Green, and constitutes the premier shopping district in Dublin. On side streets leading off the main route, you'll find trendy shops, pubs, flower vendors, and street musicians.

*Public library.* Just west of Stephen's Green on St. Patrick's Close is Marsh's Library, Ireland's first public library. The building was opened in 1701 and announced itself open to "All Graduates and Gentlemen." If you're traveling with students, take them through the lovely cottage garden into the library's entrance. They'll enjoy seeing the interior, virtually unchanged since it was built, especially the "cages" erected around the room. Students interested in reading old or rare books were locked inside the cages until they were finished in an apparent attempt to discourage students from taking the books with them.

*Trinity College.* The oldest university in Ireland is Trinity College, bordered by College, Pearse, and Nassau Sts. It was established in 1592 with a grant from England's Queen Elizabeth I. The college's official name is Dublin University, but it will probably always be known as Trinity. Queen Elizabeth offered a free university education to all Catholics—provided they converted to Protestantism. One hundred years ago the last stipulation was dropped, and the school has had an open admissions policy, but until 1966, any Catholic who wished to study at the university had to obtain a dispensation from his or her bishop or face excommunication. That rule no longer exists and now 70 percent of Trinity's students are unapologetic Catholics.

Ireland's largest collection of books and manuscripts is housed in Trinity College Library; since 1801 a copy of every book published in Ireland has been sent to the library. The library's most precious manuscripts are kept in the Treasury, including the Book of Kells, considered the most striking manuscript ever created in the Western world. The book is a 9th-century gospel that was painstakingly penned and illustrated by monks. Much larger than modern gospels, the Book of Kells is 682 pages long, but only a few pages are displayed at a time, although an exhibit has reproductions of many of the other pages. But while the Book of Kells is the most famous text on display here, it is by no means the only one, nor is it the oldest. Productions of Irish religious texts from the 7th and 8th centuries from various Irish monasteries are also housed in the Treasury. Among them are the 7th-century Book of Durrow and the Book of Armagh from 807. It's best to visit early in the day if you can. At midday you may have to wait in long lines.

*Chester Beatty Library.* Speaking of libraries, the Chester Beatty Library, 20 Shrewsbury Rd., contains some of the earliest papyri manuscripts of the New Testament, going back to the 3d century, as well as a 13th-century manuscript of Omar Khayyam.

*The Royal Hospital Kilmainham* is considered the most important 17th-century building in Ireland and is just a short ride from Dublin's city center. Located on Kilmainham La., the building was originally constructed in 1684 as a hospice for soldiers. The building now houses the Irish Museum of Modern Art, exhibiting works by Picasso and Miró, but concentrating largely on native artists. Make a point of looking at the ceiling of the Baroque chapel while you're here. It's stunning.

*Phoenix Park* is a great place to relax after a busy day of sightseeing. Laid out in the 1740s by Lord Chesterfield, this is Europe's largest public park, covering over 1,700 acres of lawns, playing fields, lakes, woods, a flower garden, and including the Dublin Zoo, a 17th-century castle, and two residences: that of the president of Ireland and that of the American ambassador. Joggers love this park. If you visit on Sunday, you're likely to find a variety of games in progress. The cross in the center of the park marks the spot where the Pope celebrated mass in front of one million people in 1979.

*Museum of Childhood.* In Palmerston Park, just south of the city, is the Museum of Childhood, which was originally a private hobby but grew to an extensive collection of doll houses, teddy bears, trains, and dolls. Some of the toy furniture here was made by Duncan Phyffe.

**Adare** The Church of the Most Holy Trinity (on Main Street) dates back to 1230 but it lay in ruins until it was restored and enlarged in 1852. The Adare Parish Church (Anglican) also has a long history, going back to 1315.

About 7.5 miles west of Adare on the N21 is the Irish Palatine Heritage Centre. The Irish Palatines were Protestants from southern Germany (the Rhineland Palatinate section) who settled here in Rathkeale in 1709 after religious wars and severe weather forced them out of their homelands. John Wesley preached here and the Palatines responded warmly to the Methodist approach to Christianity. The Heritage Centre serves as a museum of their contribution to Ireland.

**Aran Islands** Three little islands stretching across the mouth of Galway Bay are the locale of seven ancient churches, now all in ruins. During early and medieval times, the monasteries here were important cultural centers. Gaelic is still spoken on the islands, and the culture has been described in plays, like J. M. Synge's *Riders to the Sea* and *The Playboy of the Western World*. If you're interested, check out the Aran Heritage Centre on the largest of the islands, Inishmore.

> All things bright and beautiful,
> All creatures great and small,
> And all things wise and wonderful
> The Lord God made them all.
>
> CECIL FRANCES ALEXANDER
> OF LONDONDERRY, IRELAND

**Blarney** Five miles northwest of Cork is the legendary Blarney Castle, where people come to kiss the Blarney Stone. Not much is left of the famous castle built in 1446, but people come to see it anyway, or maybe they simply come to see the stone. The stone, which is said to have been brought to Ireland during the Crusades (although that may be a bit of blarney too) is set inside the parapet at the top of the castle and can be reached only by laying upside-down with a guide holding onto your legs. Tradition has it that those who kiss the stone will be blessed with a gift of gab. No one knows where or why the odd tradition originated, but there is never a shortage of people waiting to pucker up.

**Cahir** On Old Church St. there is a ruined church that had an interior wall, separating Catholics and Protestants, thus allowing them to worship simultaneously.

In Ballyporeen, 11 miles southwest of Cahir, is the Ronald Reagan Centre, showing videos and souvenirs of the president's visit in 1984 to his ancestral home here.

**Cashel** The Rock of Cashel is one of Ireland's most visited sites, located a short walk north of town, its huge circular bulk rising 200 feet above the surrounding plains. The Rock was the seat of the Kings of Munster for centuries, but St. Patrick made it famous. It was on this rock that the patron saint of Ireland is said to have picked a shamrock from the ground, using it as an analogy for the Trinity. He gave Ireland its national symbol in the process. Atop the Rock is a cluster of old monastic remains, a good portion of which are still standing. Visitors can tour the remains, including a 13th-century cathedral, several High Crosses, a 92-foot round tower, and Cormac's Chapel with some of Ireland's earliest frescoes. The old dormitory block forms the entrance to the Rock, and also houses a museum. The Rock has an eerie quality at night when illuminated by floodlights.

**Clifden** Kylemore Abbey is about 15 minutes from Clifden, and is one of the most photographed castles in all of Ireland. The Gothic, turreted stone castle is not really as old as it looks. It was built as a private residence in the 1860s. When the owner's wife and daughter died unexpectedly, the castle was abandoned and sold. It became home to a group of Benedictine nuns during World War I and is now a girls' boarding school. Visitors may visit the restaurant, grounds, and craft shop, where you can watch the abbey's cream-colored pottery being hand-decorated with its hallmark fuchsia motif, and then fired. The grounds encompass some lovely lakeside walks, planted with rhododendrons and fuchsia. The abbey is located on N59.

**The Cliffs of Moher** One of Ireland's most breathtaking natural sites is the Cliffs of Moher. Rising straight up out of the sea, the cliffs form a wall more than five miles long. The visitors center is located at the base of the cliffs. From the center it's about a one-hour walk to the well-known point called Hag's Head. If you're up for a longer walk, it's three hours north from the visitors center to O'Brien's Tower, a landmark visitor observation point built during the Victorian era at the cliffs' highest point, about 710 feet.

**Clonfert** Clonfert Cathedral, a tiny cathedral that occupies the site of a monastery founded by St. Brendan in 563, is situated on a stretch of the River Shannon in the village of Clonfert. St. Brendan is believed to have been buried here. A great scholar, the saint founded many monasteries, but he is best known as a traveling missionary and a great navigator. His journeys are said to have taken him to Wales, Iceland, and North America in a little leather boat, a reproduction of which can be seen at Craggaunowen in Kilmurry. The highlight of the church is its large number of intricate stone carvings throughout.

**Clonmacnoise** The medieval monastery of Clonmacnoise was founded by St. Ciaran between 543 and 549. Lying in a remote spot by the River Shannon, and at the crossroads of several medieval routes, Clonmacnoise thrived from the 7th to the 12th century and was highly regarded for its piety and scholarship. Today the monastery is largely in ruins, with a group of stone churches, a cathedral, two round towers, and three High Crosses remaining. The craftsmanship and artistry that can still be seen make the site well worth visiting. A visitors center and museum are also located here. Pilgrims traditionally made Clonmacnoise the destination of an annual pilgrimage, and the walk is still carried out by some every year on September 9, St. Ciaran's Day. Clonmacnoise is on Rte. R357, 13 miles south of Athlone and 58 miles east of Galway.

## BRENDAN OF CLONFERT (484–578)

Sometimes known as Brendan the Navigator because of his legendary exploits on the Atlantic, Brendan was for about 20 years the abbot of a monastery he founded in western Ireland. He wrote an account of his travels in a book called *Navigatio,* written in medieval Latin. It tells of his trip from Brandon Mountain on the Dingle Peninsula across the Atlantic to "the Promised Land of the Saints." He returned eight years later. Until recently, it was thought that his trip was a figment of his imagination. But a 20th-century seaman successfully crossed the Atlantic using a reproduction of Brendan's boat and following the Irishman's likely course. And Brendan lived at a time when many missionaries were going out from Ireland to countries in Europe. Was Brendan a missionary to America?

Sites associated with Brendan of Clonfert are located in Clonfert, the Dingle Peninsula, and Kilmurry.

**Cobh** If you're an American of Irish descent, chances are good that your ancestors set sail from Cobh. Thousands of emigrants did, and their story is re-created at the Cobh railway station just off N25. Dubbed the Queenstown Project, the museum recounts the experiences of the emigrants who left this port between 1750 and 1950. The project also includes the history of the great transatlantic ocean liners, including the Lusitania, which was sunk just off this coast by a German submarine in 1915, and the Titanic, its last port of call being Cobh.

**Cork** St. Fin Barre's Cathedral (Bishop St., off S. Main St.)—
exuberant is the word for it. With a cannonball hanging south of
the altar, with a 3,000 pipe organ sunk 15 feet into the floor, with
gargoyles all over the place including one under the bookrest of
the pulpit, with three spires including one 240 feet high, with 18
stained glass windows in the nave, and with a woman buried
underneath the floor, it probably qualifies as exuberant.

St. Anne's Anglican Church (between Grand Parade and South
Main St.) may be Cork's most famous attraction, but people don't
come to attend church; they come to ring the Shandon Bells. In
1752 eight bells were hung in the 120-foot Shandon Steeple bell
tower. For a small fee, you can climb (or maybe it would be better to say, you may climb if you can) to the top of the 120-foot
tower and ring the bells. The bells were immortalized in the song,
"The Bells of Shandon." The bells play several different tunes,
one of which is Cork's anthem, "On the Banks of My Own Lovely
Lee." It is thought that the Elizabethan poet Spenser was married
in this church. Inside the church's library are several rare books
including a copy of *Letters of John Donne,* from 1651, and a Bible
printed in Geneva in 1648.

Christ the King Church at Turner's Cross was built in 1937 by
a Chicago architect, Barry Byrne. Another American, John Storrs,
sculpted a cubist-style representation of Christ for the facade of
the church. The interior is quite plain, and the exterior is strik-
ingly modern. From the front of the church you can get a great
view of the entire city.

**Dingle Peninsula** The Dingle Peninsula offers great scenic
beauty, but Christian travelers will also find a lot of great history
on the R559, the road that encircles the area. Near here is Mt.
Brandon, second highest in Ireland, which is named after St. Brendan, the 6th-century monk who reportedly sailed from Dingle
Bay to cross the Atlantic. In the town of Dingle (population
1,272), the Presentation Convent Chapel has a fine stained glass
collection featuring biblical scenes. Five miles west of town in
Kilmakedar is a ruined Romanesque church dating from the 12th
century. The walls are still intact. Kilmakedar was once a pagan
center of worship, but all of that changed with the advent of Christianity. The church here has some interesting stone carvings. The
graveyard still holds primitive pagan stones as well as a few crosses
and a sundial.

On the southern edge of the peninsula, the Dunberg Fort dates from the Iron Age, one of the best preserved forts of its kind in Ireland. Just behind the fort are the Fahan beehive huts, early Christian dwellings that are thought to have been built for visiting pilgrims. Continuing along the road to the Slea Head promontory, you'll see a sculpture of the crucifixion near the roadside. It is known locally as the Cross or An Cros.

On the northern edge of the peninsula is Riasc, an excavated monastic settlement dating from the 7th century. The enclosed area contains the remains of an oratory, an unusual carved pillar stone, and several crosses.

The Gallarus Oratory looks more like a brick oven than a church, but it is indeed a church. The little church was built some time between the 6th and 9th centuries and is charming in its simplicity. It was constructed using the dry stone method, which involves laying stones at a slight angle to allow water to run off and the elimination of mortar. After more than a thousand years, the Oratory is still watertight.

The town of Dingle also has an Oceanworld, where you can get close to sea rays and take a good look at sharks through an underwater tube. The harbor is home to a bottle-nosed dolphin nicknamed Fungi; local entrepreneurs offer boat trips to see Fungi.

### THE GREEN ISLAND

Even those who have never been to Ireland know of its stunning natural beauty, an island that is forever green and ringed by a stunning coastline. The scenic drive on the Iveragh Peninsula's Ring of Kerry gives you beautiful views of the coastal perimeter. There are lovely beaches along the way, particularly Ballinskelligs, and little creeks make their way to the ocean. Visitors can spend the day enjoying the views, stopping for walks or a picnic lunch, or continue to the Dingle Peninsula to the north, with similarly beautiful views and healthy doses of Christian heritage throughout.

The Giant's Causeway in Northern Ireland is an otherworldly sight. A prehistoric volcanic eruption forced flows of lava through fissures in the surrounding rock, resulting in about 40,000 hard basalt columns. The majority of the rock formations are hexagonal in shape, but some have four, five, seven, eight, or even nine sides. The effect is simply stunning.

**Drogheda** Not much remains of the ancient monasteries that dotted the area in and around Drogheda. Eight miles north of town is Monasterboice, the site of a monastery found by Boethius, who died in 521. Three crosses mark the site. Six miles west of town was the site of the Millifont Old Abbey, founded by St. Malachy in 1142. The modern Millifont Abbey is at Colton, three miles north.

The Hill of Slane (about seven miles west of Drogheda off N 51) has been a famous Christian site since the 5th century. It was in 433 that St. Patrick lit a fire on the top of the hill on Easter Eve to challenge the Druids who were holding a pagan festival at Tara. Because Patrick lighted a fire within sight of Tara, an act that was strictly prohibited under penalty of death, he was brought before the pagan High King. While there, he preached the gospel to him. The king wasn't converted but he allowed Patrick to build a church in the area.

> Come, ye disconsolate, where'er ye languish;
> Come to the mercy seat, fervently kneel;
> Here bring your wounded hearts, here tell your anguish;
> Earth has no sorrow that heaven cannot heal.
>
> THOMAS MOORE OF DUBLIN, IRELAND

**Galway** The Collegiate Church of St. Nicholas and the Roman Catholic Cathedral (known formally as the Cathedral of Our Lady Assumed into Heaven and St. Nicholas) are the two large Catholic churches here, the fourth largest city in Ireland. St. Nicholas's Church, on Lombard St., dating back to 1320, is perhaps the best preserved of Ireland's medieval churches. According to one tradition, Christopher Columbus worshiped here before setting off for the New World. The cathedral on Gaol Rd., on the other hand, is a newer church, built in 1965, but with some stone plaques that go back to the early 17th century.

In Eyre Square is a small park named after U.S. President John F. Kennedy, who visited Galway in 1963.

**Glendalough** The monastic ruins of Glendalough are among the most scenic in all of Ireland. Established by St. Kevin in the 6th century, Glendalough lies in a green valley nestled between two lakes. The monastery thrived for over 600 years, but was finally dissolved in 1539. Since that time it has been a place of pilgrimage and tourism. The old monastic site is mostly ruins, but it continues to draw pilgrims. In medieval times it was said that seven pilgrimages to Glendalough equaled one to Rome. The ruins are divided into two areas, one lying primarily near the Lower Lake and one lying alongside the Upper Lake. The chief attractions include St. Kevin's Kitchen (which was not a kitchen, but rather an oratory), one of the finest round towers in the country (110 feet high), a roofless 12th-century cathedral, and St. Kevin's Cross, one of the best preserved of Glendalough's various High Crosses. A footpath of nearly one mile connects the lower and upper sections. A visitors center explains the history of the monastery.

**Kells** Forty miles north of Dublin is this 8th-century abbey, where the famous Book of Kells was created. The original book lies in

## IRELAND'S HIGH CROSSES

The distinctive ringed cross has become a symbol of Irish Christianity. Its lovely design is still imitated and used in everything from T-shirts and coffee mugs to religious jewelry. Visitors to Europe will find the unique design carved in stone throughout the countryside in Celtic parts of the British Isles, but the quantity and quality are highest in Ireland.

The beautiful High Crosses associated with medieval Irish monasteries were carved between the 8th and 12th centuries. Early crosses generally bore strictly geometrical figures, with the distinctive ring not only serving a decorative purpose but also adding support for the head and arms of the crosses. The High Cross at Ahenny is typical of the early 8th-century design. Its interwoven patterns are reminiscent of Celtic metalwork and jewelry, designs that are frequently imitated today.

In the 9th and 10th centuries biblical motifs were introduced. Scenes from familiar Bible stories of both the Old and New Testaments have caused people to refer to High Crosses of this time period as "sermons in stone," which have further raised speculation that the crosses may have served as religious educational tools for the masses. However, the High Cross also served as a status symbol for a local patron or monastery. One of Ireland's finest examples of the High Cross is at Monasterboice. Muiredach's Cross was carved in the 10th century. Towering 18 feet high, the cross is actually three separate pieces of stone fitted together by a socket and tenon method. The cross is intricately carved with biblical scenes, the Old Testament on one side and the life of Christ depicted on the other side. Also at Monasterboice is the West Cross, also known as the Tall Cross. Although the carving has suffered from the elements, it remains one of the tallest crosses in Ireland, at 21 feet high.

In the late phase of High Cross art, the objects were often dominated by larger figures of Christ, saints, or religious leaders carved in the crosses in relief. The Doorty Cross, located in the cemetery of Kilfenora, dates from this period and prominently features the figures of a bishop and two clerics carved in relief.

Dublin's Trinity College Library, but visitors can view a facsimile in St. Columba's Church. The monastery was founded by St. Columba in the 6th century. Today on Market Street, in the churchyard of St. Columba's Anglican Church, you can see remains of the early monastery. They include the 9th-century South Cross, depicting Daniel in the lion's den, the three Hebrew children in the fiery furnace, Cain and Abel, and several other Bible stories. The remains of the abbey are worth exploring as well, including an ancient well-preserved round tower and a rare stone-roof church. Dating from the 9th century, this unusual church's roof is composed entirely of stones, with no mortar holding the pieces together. Try as they might, modern builders have been unable to learn the secret to this ancient building technique, nor have they been able to reproduce it.

**Kerry** If you're looking for a scenic drive, you'll be hard-pressed to find one better than the Ring of Kerry. Stunning mountains and coastal views run along the perimeter of the Iveragh Peninsula southwest of Killarney. The trip takes most of a day, and begins at Killarney by way of N71 and N70.

**Kildare** Kildare's economy is based largely on horse breeding, and the center of Irish horse breeding is the National Stud Farm about 1-1/2 miles south of town, clearly signposted off M7. If you enjoy horses, you'll enjoy the opportunity to visit the farm as well as its museum. But centuries before Kildare became known as a center for Irish horse racing, the town was known as a religious center. St. Brigid founded a Christian settlement in Kildare in the 5th century. St. Brigid's Cathedral, just off Market Square, is a lovely restoration of the previous 13th-century building.

> Riches I heed not, nor man's empty praise,
> Thou mine inheritance, now and always;
> Thou and Thou only, first in my heart
> High King of heaven, my Treasure Thou art.
>
> 8TH-CENTURY IRISH HYMN, SOMETIMES ATTRIBUTED TO COLUMBA OF DONEGAL

**Kilkenny** If you want to see an Irish medieval city, go to Kilkenny. Granted, it may be a bit difficult to feel truly medieval amid the swarm of tourists, but it is still a great experience. The two big attractions here are the Kilkenny Castle, built between 1192 and 1207, and St. Canice's Cathedral, on Dean St., built in the 13th century. The castle dominates the southern end of town and is located on The Parade. Not far from the cathedral is the Black Abbey on Abbey St., which the Dominicans built shortly after 1226. It is one of the few medieval churches in Ireland that is still in use for religious services.

**Killarney** This is a young town as far as Ireland goes. It goes back only to the 17th century. St. Mary's Cathedral (Catholic) at Post Rd. and Cathedral Pl. is the local landmark with its 185-foot spire. The Anglican St. Mary's on Main St. has a stained glass window that is a reproduction of Holman Hunt's *Light of the World* painting, and that is worth seeing too.

The 39-square-mile Killarney National Park can be explored on foot, by car, by a pony ride, or by boat. Take your choice.

**Kilmurry** Craggaunowen is an open-air historic center designed to bring the Bronze Age and Celtic culture to life, a culture that became increasingly Christian. The center was created on the grounds of Craggaunowen Castle in the 1960s, and while many of the displays are re-creations, a large number of the artifacts are authentic. Costumed interpreters demonstrate various trades of the past, including spinning and pottery. A French slave recounts how communities lived in the ring forts that were typically early Christian residences. One of the most interesting sights is the crannog, a man-made island enclosing wattle and daub houses. The building style was developed for defensive purposes and survived until early in the 17th century. Another interesting exhibit is the leather-hulled boat recreated in the 1970s after designs that were reportedly used by St. Brendan. If legend is correct, St. Brendan used the little boat on missionary journeys in the 6th century to places as far away as Wales, the Orkneys, Iceland, and perhaps the eastern coast of North America, predating Columbus by about 900 years. Craggaunowen is clearly signposted off the road Sixmilebridge.

**Knock** This little town of 2,500 people has a huge Catholic church (Basilica of Our Lady, Queen of Ireland) that can hold 12,000 people. It's all because in 1879 two village women had an apparition of Mary, Joseph, and St. John in the church. When miraculous cures happened, visitors swarmed into the city.

**Limerick** The Hunt Museum on Rutland St. has quite an outstanding collection, and since the Hunts had a special interest in medieval and religious art, you will find plenty of it. The second floor is devoted to their archaeological collection but the ground floor is where the religious art is on display.

**New Ross** Four miles to the south of this small town in Dunganstown is the ancestral home of John F. Kennedy. A privately owned whitewashed cottage is the birthplace of President Kennedy's great grandfather. And Kennedy relatives still live there. About 7.5 miles south is the Kennedy Arboretum, on the R733, which was opened in 1968 in memory of America's first Catholic president.

**Tara** Located about 20 miles northwest of Dublin is the Hill of Tara, closely associated with St. Patrick's Christianization of Ireland. Prior to the 5th century, Tara was considered the pagan religious center of the Emerald Isle. Pagan high kings made it their seat; even after Christianity had come, the Irish High King was associated with this place for many years. However, its stature was greatly reduced once St. Patrick arrived and began spreading the gospel of Christ. Not too much remains, but you can get an audiovisual presentation at St. Patrick's Church, located on the grounds. In the churchyard is a stone pillar, known as St. Adamnan's Cross. On it is a carved figure that may represent the Celtic god Cernunnos. A statue of St. Patrick stands at the top of the hill, a reminder of the influence that the saint had on this island and the world.

**Tralee** This town of 20,000, trying to lure tourists, now has a number of enticements. The Kerry County Museum in Ashe Memorial Hall on Denny St. gives you the sights and sounds of Ireland from 8000 B.C. to the present. You are carried through a partially reconstructed Tralee in time cars or streetcars. The AquaDome on Dingle Rd. has a wave pool and water slides, and even an adults-only section if you don't want children around. The National Folk Theatre of Ireland (Siamsa Tire) on Godfrey Pl. puts on shows six nights a week featuring dances and plays based on Irish folklore. If you are looking for the Rose of Tralee, you might find her at the Rose of Tralee International Festival, a beauty pageant held at the end of August. Just outside the town (two miles south) is the five-story Blennerville Windmill on the R560. A visitors center is next door where you can trace relatives who emigrated from County

Kerry during the Potato Famine. If that isn't enough, take a ride on the Tralee-Biennerville Light Railway. It was reopened to passengers in its centennial year, 1991.

**Westport** This quiet 18th-century town overlooks Clew Bay and its roughly 400 islands. But the dominating feature of Westport is not its bay but its mountain: Croagh Patrick. The mountain is 2,540 feet high and has been considered holy for millenia. From 3000 B.C. until the time of Patrick, it was a center of pagan worship. Now it is considered holy by Irish Christians, since this is said to have been the location where the Irish saint spent 40 days fasting and praying for his countrymen in A.D. 441. Whether there is any truth to the legend, the mountain is a popular draw for tourists, some 25,000 of whom climb it on the last Sunday in July to honor St. Patrick. The climb is exhilarating and takes about three hours. At the foot of Croagh Patrick is a statue of St. Patrick gazing out to sea.

## ST. PATRICK (CA. 389–461)

Born probably in Roman Britain, Patrick was seized by raiders as a teenager and sold as a slave to Ireland. After six years as a shepherd, he escaped and reached home again. Then, in a dream he heard an Irish voice calling, "We beseech you to come and walk among us once more." So he set out for Ireland, probably in about 430. He gathered people around him in open fields and preached Christ to them. Peasants and nobles alike were converted. He started scores of churches and baptized more than 100,000 converts. In Armagh he founded a monastery and encouraged monks to go out as missionaries to evangelize all of England and western Europe.

Sites associated with St. Patrick are common throughout Ireland, but the primary sites are located in Dublin, Cashel, Drogheda, Tara, and Westport, Ireland; and in Antrim, Armagh, and Downpatrick, Northern Ireland.

# *Italy*

Italian Government Tourist Board
  US 212-245-4822
  Canada 514-866-7667
  UK 020-7408-1254
*Web site*
  Entire country www.italiantourism.com
For a complete list of updated links, visit www.christiantraveler.com

### Country in a Capsule

*Size:* About two-thirds the size of California but with almost twice as many people. It has four cities with populations of more than a million: Rome, Milan, Naples, and Turin.

*Religion:* About 82 percent Roman Catholic, 15 percent no religion, and between 500,000 and a million Protestants. Pentecostals and Waldensians are by far the largest Protestant groups.

*Language:* Italian. In the major cities, English is understood by many.

*Money:* The Italian lire. An American dollar is worth about 2,000 lire.

*Food:* Americans are familiar with many of the Italian specialties, although they may look a bit different when served in Italian restaurants. A dinner usually begins with antipasto, followed by minestrone or other thick soup, then a rice or pasta course, followed by fish, cheese, fruit, and dessert. Take your time. After the meal, try some espresso coffee.

*Shopping:* You can usually do well with leather goods, silk ties, and ceramics. Venice is known for glassware and lace, Naples for cameos, Florence for leather goods, and Milan for silks.

*Brief history:* According to tradition, Rome was founded in 753 B.C. It became a power when Julius Caesar became dictator in 48 B.C. After two decades of civil war, Augustus Caesar restored order in 27 B.C. and ruled until A.D. 14. He was followed by such rulers as Caligula and Nero. The decline of the Roman Empire began at the end of the second century. In A.D. 325 Constantine moved the capital to Constantinople and made Christianity the official religion of the Empire. In A.D. 381 the bishop of Rome took the title of Pope and led the western half of the empire. But in 476 the barbarians from the North took over and the Western Empire was ended. Italy was not united again until 1870.

During the 14th century Italian city-states battled among themselves for prominence and dominance. After Napoléon's defeat in the early 1800s, the Italians struggled for independence. In 1860 Garibaldi led Italian patriots against French and Austrian forces. The patriots finally captured Rome in 1870, Victor Emmanuel assumed the title of king of all Italy, and Italian unity was complete.

In 1922 Mussolini became prime minister and then entered World War II against the Allies. After the war the country struggled with high unemployment and frequent changes of government, but in recent years it has gained more stability.

**Rome** The Arco di Costantino (Arch of Constantine), just off the Piazza del Colosseo near the Roman Forum, is one of Rome's best preserved triumphal arches. The 4th-century monument is as old as European Christianity itself, and not coincidentally so. Just before his battle with the Roman Maxentius in A.D. 312, Constantine experienced his famous vision of a cross in the heavens and heard the words, "In this sign thou shalt conquer." The victory led not only to the construction of this majestic marble arch but also to a grateful Constantine's decree that Christianity was a lawful religion and should be tolerated throughout the empire.

*The Colosseum.* Just across the street is the massive Colosseum (Colosseo), ancient Rome's most famous monument. The Colosseum took its name from a colossal 118-foot statue of Nero that once stood nearby. Inaugurated in A.D. 80, the Colosseum's beauty belies its cruel history, one that was especially cruel to Christians. "Games" that included offering Christians as sparring partners for vicious, hungry beasts led to the deaths of many early believers. A large cross erected in the center of the Colosseum stands as a reminder to those martyrs. Much of the large floor of the Colosseum has collapsed, offering a glimpse of underground tunnels where animals and contestants waited their turn before crowds of over 50,000 spectators.

> O Christ, our King, Creator, Lord,
> Savior of all who trust Thy Word,
> To them who seek Thee ever near,
> Now to our praises bend Thine ear.
>
> POPE GREGORY THE GREAT OF ROME, ITALY

*The Roman Forum* or *Foro Romano,* bordered on the north by the Via dei Fori Imperiali, was the political, social, and commercial center of ancient Rome, with public meeting halls, shops, and temples. What remains of the Forum is little more than rubble, but this was certainly the center of the known world 2,000 years ago. The apostle Paul was surely familiar with the Roman Forum; if he had a formal trial in Rome, it was probably here that he would have been tried before being taken outside the city limits and executed. And it is also quite likely that he may have been imprisoned (during his second imprisonment) in the Carcere Mamertino (Mamertine Prison) on Via San Pietro in Carcere. According to ancient tradition, both Paul and Peter were imprisoned here. Scripture doesn't give us any information about Peter in Rome, but we know that Paul was imprisoned twice in Rome, and the Mamertine Prison fits his second imprisonment. Whether this was the exact location of their imprisonment or not, the Mamertine prison certainly gives you a feel of what the early church leaders faced.

*Arch of Titus.* Another arch worth noticing is the Arch of Titus. Titus was the Roman general who stormed Jerusalem in A.D. 66 and after a four-year siege in which hundreds of thousands of Jews perished, the city was reduced to rubble and taken in A.D. 70. Titus returned triumphantly to Rome with the sacred objects of the temple in Jerusalem. The Torah was placed in the palace of the emperor. On the triumphal arch of Titus you can see reliefs of the candlesticks and the holy vessels of the temple.

*Circus Maximus.* In the giant arena called Circus Maximus, located on Via dei Circo Massimo, between 200,000 and 300,000 spectators watched chariot races in ancient Rome. Early Christians faced martyrdom here and in other Roman circuses.

*Domus Aurea.* After the devastating fire that burned Rome in A.D. 64, the city lay in ruins, but Emperor Nero built himself a grand palace in the center of the city. It was called the Domus Aurea, the Golden House. The entire complex covered 125 acres and was sort of a 1st-century Versailles. On the Colle Oppio, you can see traces of Nero's palace. Underground rooms will show you more.

*Santa Maria d'Aracoeli* is a 13th-century church on the Campidoglio at the end of the Roman Forum, built on the top of the old Roman Capitol. The ancient church can be reached by a long flight of steep stairs or, for an easier climb, via the stairs on the far side of the Museo Capitolino. Highlights include the Renaissance gilded ceiling and the frescoes by Pinturicchio, dating from the late 15th century.

*San Luigi dei Francesi* (on Piazza San Luigi dei Francesi) is the French national church in Rome, known for its outstanding works by Caraveggio. Note his *Calling of St Matthew, Matthew and the Angel,* and *Matthew's Martyrdom.*

*Churches.* Santa Maria sopra Minerva (Piazza della Minerva) gets attention for several reasons. First, it's just about the only Gothic church in Rome; second, it has outstanding artwork (Michelangelo's *Risen Christ,* for example); third, it is where the artist Fra Angelico is buried; and fourth, the Roman goddess Minerva is mentioned in the name. That's because there used to be a temple to Minerva, the Roman goddess of wisdom, here. So the builders put Mary over Minerva. Outside is a famous and charming Bernini statue, an elephant with an obelisk on its back.

The Church of Jesus or Chiesa del Gesù, is a huge 16th-century church, a model of Baroque style. Built by the Jesuits, its interior is ablaze with gold and marble. The fabulous painted ceiling extends down, joining with painted stucco figures to create a three-dimensional illusion. The church is located on the Piazza del Gesù not far from the Roman Forum.

Not St. Peter's in Vatican City, but San Giovanni in Laterano (St. John Lateran) on Via Vittorio Emanuele Filiberto is the official cathedral of Rome. Next to it is the Lateran Palace, which had been the papal residence until the 13th century. Behind the Palace is St. John's Baptistery, and across from it is the Scala Santa (the Sacred Stairs). According to Catholic tradition, this staircase came from the house of Pontius Pilate in Jerusalem, and so it is thought that Jesus walked up these steps prior to his crucifixion. Catholic faithful climb the stairs on their knees. When he was 27, Martin Luther climbed these steps, but as he did so, some of his first doubts about traditional church teaching crossed his mind.

At Via San Giovanni in Laterano, is St. Clement's Church (San Clemente), which is really three churches on top of each other. The upper church, dating from the 12th century, is interesting enough, but the middle church dates back to the 5th century. Below that in the subterranean rooms, you will see the remains of ancient Roman dwellings, for the bottom level reveals a Mithraic shrine, dating to the time of Nero.

San Pietro in Vincoli (St. Peter in Chains, off Via Cavour) displays the chains that, according to tradition, held St. Peter prior to his martyrdom. They are in a case under the altar, but most people come here to see Michelangelo's *Moses,* a gigantic sculpture alongside unfinished statues of Leah and Rachel. The present church dates to the 15th century, but it replaced a 5th-century church on this site.

Santa Maria Maggiore (St. Mary Major) on Piazza di Santa Maria Maggiore has an interesting relic on display in its sanctuary—the manger in which Christ is said to have been placed after his birth in the stable. The church was built in the 5th century and rebuilt in the 13th century. That's old, but if you are looking for unique (and probably a church you wouldn't want to take your whole family to), try the Santa Maria della Concezione (on Via Veeto 27).

The crypt of this Capuchin church contains the skeletons of 4,000 monks, artistically arranged in four chapels. Incidentally, Rome is home to 80 churches dedicated to the Virgin Mary.

San Pietro in Montorio (on Via Garibaldi) was built in 1481 on orders from Ferdinand and Isabella of Spain over the spot where it is thought St. Peter was crucified.

*Sant'Angelo Castle* (Castel Sant'Angelo), at the intersection of Lung. Vaticano and Lung. Castello, is an impressive sight, originally built as the tomb of the Emperor Hadrian in the 2d century and later transformed into a fortress. According to legend, the castle got its name in the 6th century. Pope Gregory the Great, passing nearby, saw an angel with a sword appear above the ramparts as a sign of the coming end of the plague that was sweeping the country. The ancient bridge spanning the Tiber River in front of the castle is simply beautiful. Called the Ponte Sant'Angelo, the bridge is adorned with two rows of beautiful Baroque angels that were designed by Bernini.

*Fountains.* Children on a visit to Rome can quickly tire of visiting churches, historic sites, and museums. Fortunately, the city's many piazzas are generously adorned with amusing fountains. One of the most popular is Trevi Fountain or Fontana di Trevi on Via Sabini. Mythical sea creatures surround Neptune in a Baroque fantasy of splashing water that children just love to watch. Legend has it that visitors must toss a coin into the fountain to ensure their return to Rome.

*Jewish synagogue.* Of course, the Jewish community in Rome predates the coming of Peter and Paul to the city, and so the Jewish synagogue (Sinagoga at Lungotevere Cenci), which contains a Hebrew museum, is worth seeing. However, most of the collection in the museum dates only from the 17th century.

*Via Appia Antica* (Appian Way), the road that the apostle Paul walked on his way to Rome, is still visible. It was built in 312 B.C., 18 feet wide, so that two wagons could pass abreast. It was the principal road from Rome to southern Italy. A few miles south along the Appian Way are the catacombs. The St. Callisto catacombs are the best preserved. The San Sebastiano catacomb burrows underground on four levels. The catacomb of Domitilla has a wonderful wall painting of the Good Shepherd.

*Villas.* Not quite 20 miles east of Rome in the town of Tivoli are two attractive villas: the Villa Adriana, or Hadrian's Villa, built by the Roman emperor in A.D. 117, and the Villa d'Este, built by a cardinal in the mid–16th century. Neither is as nicely tended as it used to be, but you can get the idea of the splendor of the past.

## BELLA ITALIA

The beauty of the Amalfi Coast can scarcely be put into words. Sheer rocky cliffs drop dramatically into the bright blue Tyrrhenian Sea. Tiny ancient villages literally cling to the rocks, and travelers often have the sense of climbing through some of the towns rather than strolling through them. Huge rocks jut out of the sea forming small islands, the largest of which is known as Capri.

The best way to view the overwhelming beauty of the area is along the coastal road N145. But only those with large amounts of either courage or foolishness would dare drive it themselves. The road is narrow and twisting, and the drivers are . . . well . . . Italians. A better option is to take a ride on a SITA bus, which leaves either Sorrento or Salerno every two hours. Try to sit on the right side when you head south, and on the left when you head north.

If you want to enjoy the coast from the sea, there are several ferry services that are well worth the trip. Travelmar (phone 089/87-31-90) operates ferries from Salerno to Amalfi via Positano. If you want to travel to Capri, ferry service also runs from Sorrento and from Positano.

**Amalfi Coast** There are any number of beautiful vistas and coastal towns along this, perhaps the most photographed, stretch in Italy. Positano, one of the prettiest towns, is a mishmash of pastel houses clinging to the mountainside above the sea. And that description—clinging to the mountainside—is no exaggeration. This town is exhaustingly vertical, and most of the streets are stairways. Still, nearly everyone who visits finds that the relaxed and friendly atmosphere more than compensates for the extra effort.

Amalfi, the namesake of this coastline, is a resort town. The drive to the town offers some of the most dramatic scenery in the country. Amalfi's piazza forms the center of town, with an assortment of shops and cafes clustered around an old fountain. The piazza's most impressive feature is its cathedral, with a lovely exterior and both cloisters and a museum that are open to visitors.

North of Amalfi is the town of Ravello, not really on the coast but on a high mountain bluff that overlooks the sea and the coast below. A series of switchbacks takes you up to the beautiful town, which is quite tranquil compared to the more heavily touristed towns below. The town center is the Piazza del Duomo. Its cathedral was founded late in the 11th century. Lovely 12th-century bronze doors lead inside, where two pulpits are decorated with mosaics. One depicts the story of Jonah and the whale, and the other is carved with fantastic animals. Composer Richard Wagner once stayed in Ravello, and as a consequence there is a Wagner festival every summer on the garden terrace of the 11th-century Villa Rufolo. The villa has a Moorish cloister, an 11th-century tower, beautiful gardens, and a great view.

**Arezzo** Located about 50 miles southeast of Florence is this old Etruscan city with its marvelous San Francesco church on Via Cavour. Built in the 14th century for the Franciscans, it has memorable frescoes that were painted a century later. These frescoes, *The Legend of the True Cross,* depict on the south, central, and north walls a delightful story of how Adam's son Seth plants a tree from the Garden of Eden on Adam's grave, how the Queen of Sheba has a vision of a tree on which the Messiah would be crucified and tells the vision to Solomon, how the cross of Christ was made from that tree, how the Emperor Constantine had a vision of the cross made from that tree, and then of the Empress Helen finding wood from the tree and bringing it back to Rome with her. Among the other art treasures worth seeing in this town are Francesca's *Magdalene* in the town's cathedral (Duomo) on Via Ricasoli.

**Assisi** It's just a little town of 3,000 residents but thousands of visitors, pilgrims, and lovers of Francis of Assisi come here each year. The Basilica of San Francesco on Via Portica honors him, and his coffin lies in a crypt below the Lower Basilica. Francis loved nature and simplicity, but the magnificent basilica is huge and ornate with Giotto's 28 frescoes of the life of St. Francis decorating the Upper Basilica. Most memorable is *St. Francis Preaching to the Birds.* Less than three miles east of Assisi is the Eremo Dele Carceri monastery where Francis and his followers often came to pray. This is a tranquil setting more in keeping with St. Francis' lifestyle.

**Bologna** This city of a half million people is known for science, art, macaroni, and sausage. Its noteworthy churches include St. Petronius' Basilica on Piazza Maggiore, which was started in 1390 and isn't finished yet. The frescoes of Giovanni di Modena are among the fine artistic pieces here. On Via Santo Stefano is St. Stephen's Church, which actually is a half dozen churches under

## FRANCIS OF ASSISI (1182-1226)

He wanted to become a knight, but after an illness, a vision, and the words of Christ to live humbly and simply, he experienced a spiritual awakening. Francis left home in a ragged cloak and a rope belt taken from a scarecrow. In 1219 he drafted a set of rules and got approval from the Pope to start a monastic order. He and his followers went out two by two preaching repentance, singing, aiding the poor, and caring for the sick and outcast. To encourage missionary work, he traveled to the Muslim lands of Morocco, Syria, and Egypt, but while he was traveling, problems arose in the order, and leadership and direction were given to another. Brokenhearted, Francis yielded, and retired to write his *Canticle to the Sun* and his *Testament.*

Sites associated with the life and ministry of Francis can be seen in Assisi.

one roof. Among them are the church of Sts. Vitalis and Agricola, which contains a 14th-century nativity scene, and the Church of the Holy Sepulchre, which contains a Pontius Pilate Courtyard. In the middle of the courtyard is a basin where it is said that Pilate washed his hands before the crucifixion.

**Cassino** Senior citizens remember the Battle of Cassino fought here by the Allies in 1943 and 1944, but Catholics know it as the location of the mother house of the Benedictines, and thus one of the holy places of Roman Catholicism. In 529 the Monastery of Monte Cassino was founded by St. Benedict, who is known for the rules that he drew up stressing study, labor, chastity, obedience, and poverty. The abbey, which was destroyed during World War II, has been rebuilt according to the original plans and is located just off Via Cassilina.

**Como** This city on the shores of Lake Como in northern Italy is not what it was before it became so industrialized, but the cathedral in the city's center and the Church of San Fedele just two blocks away have much to offer. The Latin writers, Pliny the Elder and Pliny the Younger, came from Como, and their busts are in the facade of the cathedral.

**Cortona** Less than 75 miles southeast of Florence is this delightful, seldom visited medieval city. It actually goes back before medieval time, but it looks as if it belongs to the 14th or 15th centuries. The Duomo (cathedral) on Piazza del Duomo, the Diocesan Museum right across the street, the Gesù Church, and the Praetorian Palace on Via Dardano are all rewarding stops.

**Cremona** Anyone who plays a violin should make a pilgrimage to Cremona at least once in his or her lifetime as if he or she were going to Mecca or Jerusalem. Located 60 miles south of Milan, it is known as the home of Amati, Stradivarius, and Guarnerius. At Via Palestro 17 is the Stradivarius Museum, and the City Hall (Palazzo del Comune) on the Piazza del Comune displays some of the original Stradivarius instruments on the second floor. In the cathedral (Duomo) directly across the street are numerous frescoes by several outstanding local artists. The adjoining campanile is 387 feet tall and that makes it the tallest bell tower in Italy.

**Fiesole** Just five miles north of Florence is this pleasant place where you can catch your breath after an exhausting time in Florence. In the Roman amphitheater at Via Portigianni 1, which seats 2,000 and dates from the 1st century B.C., concerts and classical plays are still presented in the summer. And if you are up for archaeology, the adjacent archaeological museum will take you into the ruins and back 4,000 years.

**Florence (Firenze)** Once you have visited Florence, you will want to return and spend much more time here. It is the city of Savonarola, Dante, and Machiavelli, and in the art world it is associated with names like da Vinci, Michelangelo, Botticelli, and Fra Angelico. Florence's cathedral (Duomo), more formally known as the Cattedrale di Santa Maria del Fiore, is one of the most famous churches in the world, in large part due to its dome, which was an architectural landmark when it was constructed by Brunelleschi in the early 15th century. The dome was the inspiration behind such later domes as the one Michelangelo designed for St. Peter's Basilica, and even the dome on the Capitol building in Washington, D.C. If you want to see the dome up close, you can climb up to the gallery on 463 steps that wind their way between the dome's double layers. The cathedral itself was begun much earlier, in 1296, but it took 140 years to complete.

In front of the Duomo is the Battistero, or baptistery, an octagonal structure that is one of the city's oldest. Excavations indicate its foundations were laid in the 4th or 5th centuries. Since the 11th century, Florentines have brought their children here to be baptized. The interior dome mosaics are fabulous but are eclipsed by the baptistery's famous gilded bronze east doors, which face the Duomo. The doors were created by Lorenzo Ghiberti, and Michelangelo nicknamed them, "The Gates of Paradise." The doors are actually elaborate re-creations of the originals, carefully preserved in the Cathedral Museum.

Also near the Duomo is the Bell Tower (campanile), designed by Giotto in the early 14th century. The tower is elaborately decorated with colored marbles and sculpture reproductions (the originals are in the Cathedral Museum). A 414-step stairway to the top is open for a commanding view of the city.

The Cathedral Museum (Museo dell'Opera del Duomo) includes many of the original works of art that at one time graced the Duomo, the Baptistery, and the Bell Tower. Protected from the elements are a number of sculptures by Donatello from the early 15th century, Ghiberti's "Gates of Paradise" bronze doors, and an unfinished Pietà, which Michelangelo intended for his own tomb. The Duomo, Baptistery, Bell Tower, and Museum are all located on the Piazza del Duomo.

*Piazza Della Signoria.* A few blocks south is the Piazza Della Signoria, which was the political center of Florence. A bronze plaque marks the spot where the heroic preacher Savonarola was martyred.

*Art galleries and museums.* Florence is an art lover's paradise. Two must-see galleries include the Uffizi Gallery (Galleria degli Uffizi) at Loggiato Uffizi 6, and the Accademia Gallery (Galleria dell'Accademia) at Via Ricasoli 60. The Uffizi was owned and furnished by the famous Medici family, who made it the world's first modern public gallery when they opened it to the public in the 17th century. The gallery's collection is thought to be Italy's most important collection of paintings, including Botticelli's *Birth of Venus*, Michelangelo's *Holy Family*, and works by

## GIROLAMO SAVONAROLA (1452–1498)

A Dominican priest and a popular preacher in Florence, Savonarola rose to a position of power (as city manager) when the Medici rulers of the city were forced to flee. Crowds came to hear him preach as he denounced the evils of the day and even the sins of the clergy. He initiated tax reform, helped the poor, and reformed the courts of Florence, but when he denounced the corruption of the papal court, he was excommunicated. The turning point came when the Pope placed the city of Florence under an interdict. The people turned against Savonarola and he was executed for heresy.

Sites associated with Savonarola's life are located in Florence.

Giotto and Raphael. The Accademia's claim to fame is Michelangelo's world-renowned *David*. The larger-than-life masterpiece was carved out of a piece of stone that had already been worked on and rejected by two other sculptors. Try to visit the Accademia right after opening at 8:30 A.M. to avoid crowds and to get the full impact of the statue.

You can see more beautiful artwork at the Museum of St. Mark (Museo di San Marco) at Piazza San Marco 1. This former Dominican monastery houses many priceless works by Fra Angelico, who lived from 1400 to 1455. While other monks contemplated in prayer, Angelico appears to have contemplated while he painted. He went quietly about his business, decorating many of the monastery's austere cells and corridors with brilliantly colored frescoes on religious themes. *Annunciation* is considered his masterpiece. You will also see Savonarola's cell here. The museum is closed the first, third, and fifth Sundays and the second and fourth Mondays of each month.

*Churches.* The massive church of Santa Croce, on Piazza Santa Croce, was begun in 1294. Its colossal size is appropriate when you consider the great thinkers buried here, including Michelangelo, Galileo, and Machiavelli. Inside you'll find art by other Florentine greats: two chapels frescoed by Giotto, a chapel painted by Taddeo Gaddi, and an annunciation and crucifix by Donatello.

The Santa Maria Novella church, on Piazza Santa Maria Novella, is another Florentine beauty. Inside are some famous paintings by Masaccio, a Giotto crucifix, and frescoes by Ghirlandaio. Adjacent to the church is a museum, the Museo di Santa Maria Novella, that is worth visiting for its Paolo Uccello frescoes from Genesis.

*The Old Bridge (Ponte Vecchio)* is Florence's oldest bridge, and certainly its most beautiful. You may find yourself walking over it before you realize you're on the bridge—at first glance it appears to be just another street lined with quaint old shops. Once you get to the middle, a break in the shops allows a view of the Arno River below. The Germans, with a reputation for blowing up every other bridge they crossed during World War II, spared this one. The bridge stretches between Via Por Santa Maria and Via de Guicciardini.

*Other sites worth visiting.* There is much more to see in Florence. Here are some suggestions: (1) The Laurentian Library (Piazza San Lorenzo 9), a library of 10,000 rare manuscripts, designed by Michelangelo; (2) the Medici Palace (Via Cavour 1) with Gozzoli's great *Procession of the Magi* and its delightful chapel on the first floor; (3) the Church of Santa Maria del Carmine (Piazza del Carmine) with its famous *Expulsion of Adam and Eve* by Masaccio and the fine frescoes on the life of the apostle Peter; (4) the Church of the Holy Cross (Santa Croce, at Piazza Santa Croce 16) with the finest collection of art of any of the Florentine churches; and last but not least (5) Michelangelo Lookout Point (Piazzale Michelangelo) with its copy of his *David* sculpture and the Iris Gardens and Rose Gardens nearby.

**Genoa** Genoa isn't what it used to be in the days of Christopher Columbus who was born here, but, industrial as it is, its medieval and Renaissance sections have a charm that make a visit worthwhile. Via Garibaldi is lined with a string of palaces, including Palazzo Tursi, where Paganini's violin is on display and played once a year on Columbus Day.

St. Lawrence's Cathedral (San Lorenzo on Piazza San Lorenzo) is about 900 years old and shows scenes from the life of Christ in the central doorways.

For children the Aquarium (on Ponte Spinola), which is Europe's biggest and second largest in the world, is both creative and educational. Children will also enjoy the many funiculars and elevators in the city. The Zecco-Righi funicular, for instance, is a seven-stop commuter ending up on the fortified gates of 17th-century walls.

> Lead, kindly Light! amid the encircling gloom,
> Lead thou me on.
> The night is dark, and I am far from home
> Lead thou me on.
>
> WRITTEN BY JOHN HENRY NEWMAN, STRICKEN
> WITH SICILIAN FEVER RETURNING FROM SICILY

**Herculaneum** Visiting this city, six miles south of Naples, is like being in a time warp and being transported back 2,000 years. In A.D. 79, Vesuvius erupted and Herculaneum was buried in volcanic mud. Systematic digs were started in 1920; today almost half of the city has been excavated. The private homes are remarkably well preserved. The oldest evidence of a Christian family in the Roman Empire is in a house called Casa del Bicentenario, where you see a small cross incorporated in a stucco panel. It may have been owned by Christians or rented out to a Christian craftsman. A 2,000-seat theater is now being restored.

**Lucca** This city of 90,000 just north of Pisa was the first city in the province to embrace Christianity. It is a fortress town that provides many photo-ops. It claims the composer Puccini as a native son and Napoléon's sister as a former ruler.

St. Frigidian's Church, on Piazza Scalpellini, is perhaps the oldest in the city. It was founded by an Irish missionary in the 6th century. St. Michael's, on the Piazza San Michele, a 12th-century church, features the Archangel Michael on the facade. The cathedral, Duomo San Martino on the Piazza San Martino, dates back to 1210. The cathedral is celebrated because it displays the Volto Santo (the Holy Face), which according to the legend was a piece of wood that was said to have come from Nicodemus who carved the features of Jesus on it.

## AMBROSE OF MILAN (340–397)

Born into a noble Roman family, Ambrose became civil governor of a large territory with Milan as his headquarters. When the bishop of Milan died, strife broke out between rival factions over who should become the next bishop. Suddenly people began shouting the name of their highly respected governor, and Ambrose, not a priest and not even baptized, was pressed into the position. He was baptized, began to study the Bible, and preached regularly on Sundays. As a public official turned ecclesiastic, he became an advisor to the Roman emperor, Theodosius. His preaching resulted in the conversion of St. Augustine. He is known for his hymns and for his introduction of hymn singing in the 4th-century church.

Sites associated with Ambrose's life and ministry are located in Milan.

**Milan** Its population of nearly two million makes Milan the second largest city in Italy, but economically the country revolves around Milan, not Rome. The city of Milan is truly ancient, dating back more than 2,500 years, and yet it is Italy's trendsetter. You might think that tourists would avoid such a busy, commercial city, but they don't. Why not? At least three reasons: da Vinci's *The Last Supper,* the La Scala opera house, and the majestic cathedral (Duomo).

The Madonna of Grace (Santa Maria delle Grazie) church on Piazza Santa Maria delle Grazie is a must-see site in Milan. The church itself is interesting, but the real gem is its rectory next door, where Leonardo da Vinci painted his world-famous fresco *The Last Supper.* The fresco has withstood considerable damage since its creation, but has now been painstakingly restored, and so the lines of viewers are longer than ever. But it's worth the wait.

The world-famous opera house (on Piazza della Scalla) is renowned for its acoustics. The opera season runs for six months beginning early in December.

No visit to Milan is complete without a stop at its famous Duomo, or cathedral, on Piazza del Duomo. The massive church is a colossal Gothic masterpiece, a mountain of marble carved into statuary, flying buttresses, and 135 spires. The Madonnina, a sparkling golden statue of the Virgin Mary, perched on the cathedral's highest spire, is a Milanese landmark. The Cathedral is Italy's largest Gothic structure, with a capacity of 40,000 worshipers, and the third-largest church in the world. Take the time to walk up the 158 steps (or take the elevator) to the rooftop where you'll enjoy an unsurpassed view of the city, the Lombard Plain, and the Alps.

> Holy God, we praise Thy name;
> Lord of all, we bow before Thee;
> All on earth Thy scepter claim,
> All in heaven above adore Thee.
>
> DERIVED FROM THE 4TH-CENTURY TE DEUM
> OF BISHOP AMBROSE OF MILAN, ITALY

*St. Ambrose's Basilica* (Sant'Ambrogio) on Piazza Sant'Ambrogio can be traced back to the 4th century, although the present building is mostly from the 11th and 12th centuries. The doorway actually has some bas-reliefs that go back to St. Ambrose's time. Ambrose is remembered for his role in the conversion of Augustine of Hippo and for his love of music. His hymns are still sung in both Catholic and Protestant churches. Another church famous for its ancient artwork is the Older San Lorenzo (San Lorenzo Maggiore) on Corsodi Porta Ticinese. Sixteen ancient Roman columns grace the front of the sanctuary. Inside, the Chapel of St. Aquilinus houses 4th-century mosaics.

*Family fun.* When you tire of visiting historic old churches, consider visiting another historic masterpiece. The Galleria Vittorio Emanuele is an extravagant late 19th-century glass-topped mall where you can shop, stroll, or sip cappuccino and read the paper at a trendy cafe.

About 22 miles northeast of Milan is Minitalia Park in Capriate San Gervasio just north of the A4, a theme park that shows you Italy in miniature. Some 200 replicas of the country's monuments are on display, and kids as well as grown-ups enjoy it. Another place that children enjoy is the Parco della Preistoria, about 16 miles east of Milan. The park, which has a picnic area and restaurants, features more than 20 full-size replicas of dinosaurs as you make your way around the grounds.

**Modena** It is better known as the hometown of opera star Luciano Pavarotti and the automobile city where Ferraris and Maseratis are made, but its cathedral (Duomo) on Piazza Grande and its library (Biblioteca Estense) deserve some attention too. The library has 600,000 volumes and 15,000 manuscripts on display, including the Bible of Borso d'Este, a 15th-century illuminated Bible with about 1,200 illustrated pages. The library is located inside the Palazzo dei Musei, in Largo Sant'Agostino on the west side of Via Emilia.

**Naples** Italy's third largest city isn't loaded with art masterpieces and fantastic churches as the cities of the north are, but it has a great balance of things for family fun along with things for spiritual stimulation. The cathedral (Duomo) on Via Duomo dates from the 14th century. Though originally built in a Gothic style, it has been redone in a Baroque. To the left of the church is the 4th-century Santa Restituta church with some old mosaics that go back to its founding. The chapel will also take you into an archaeological area with rooms dating from Roman times.

Two other churches in Naples are worth visiting, and they happen to lie across the street from one another in the Piazza Gesù Nuovo. The Santa Chiara church, built during the early 14th century, is constructed in Provençal Gothic style. A popular Neapolitan song celebrates the church's cloister, with its beautiful floral tiles. The church Gesù Nuovo has an unusual faceted stone facade and an elaborate Baroque interior.

> Thou rushing wind that art so strong,
> Ye clouds that sail in heaven along
> Thou rising morn, in praise rejoice,
> Ye lights of evening, find a voice
> O praise Him! Alleluia!
>
> FRANCIS OF ASSISI, ITALY

Speaking of underground antiquities, at the Catacombe di San Gennaro (on Via Capodimonte, next to the Madre di-Beon Consiglio Church), you will go into vast galleries and see pre–3d-century Christian paintings as well as a baptismal pool where new converts were immersed.

The Castel Nuovo (New Castle) on Piazza Municipio is a good stop for two reasons. First, you get to see a real castle. It isn't exactly new; it was built in the 13th century. It has a great triumphal arch and it is surrounded by deep moats. Besides that, the castle has a great display of religious art. More religious art in an equally fine setting can be seen at the Capodimonte Palace and Park north of town on Corso Amedeo. The Palace is a bit newer, but much of the art on display is much older.

For family fun try the Edenlandia in the Mostra d'Oltremare section, southwest of the city center. This is the largest amusement park in the area. After enjoying the park, you may want to take an evening boat tour of the Naples waterfront.

Naples claims to be the birthplace of the pizza, a fact that will particularly delight youngsters traveling with you. Celebrate one of the world's favorite foods here in Naples, where pizza is not quite like you buy at home, but without a doubt delicious.

**Pisa** This is the city of Galileo and the famous Leaning Tower. Galileo used both the Duomo (cathedral) and the Tower in his scientific studies. You can climb the 294 steps in the Leaning Tower to get a good view of the town. (Don't worry; you won't make it fall over.)

Work began on the nearby baptistery (Battistero) on Piazza dei Miracoli in 1153. Another typical example of Romanesque Pisan style, its most famous feature is its pulpit, sculpted by Nicola Pisano in 1260.

The largest building in the square is the Duomo on Piazza del Duomo. The oldest of the three buildings, it was begun in 1063. Its graceful facade is decorated with geometric and animal shapes, while the massive interior is supported by 68 columns. On the transept door facing the Leaning Tower, notice the Romanesque bronze panels telling the story of the life of Christ. The pulpit was carved by Giovanni Pisano, Nicola's son. Notice the suspended lamp that hangs across from the pulpit. It is known as Galileo's Lamp and is supposed to have inspired his theories on pendular motion.

The cemetery (Camposanto), said to be full of earth brought back from the Holy Land by Crusaders, is surrounded by Gothic arcades. Some of the small bays retain important ancient frescoes, including the *Drunkenness of Noah* and a 14th-century *Triumph of Death,* inspired by a great plague that raged through the area in the artist's day.

**Pompeii** Like Herculaneum, Pompeii was buried by the eruption of Vesuvius in A.D. 79. Two-thirds of the city have now been excavated and it is a remarkable history lesson to walk through the excavated area. During July and August, classical plays are presented in Pompeii's festival of the performing arts.

**Ravenna** For a short time, Ravenna was the capital of the Roman Empire, and it has always been known for its glorious mosaics, the finest in all of Europe. You'll find excellent examples in the Basilica di San Vitale on Via San Vitale; in the Museo Arcivescovile in p. Arcivescovado; the Church of Sant'Appollinare Nuovo on Via di Roma Sud; and at many other churches and museums throughout Ravenna.

Two tombs are of special interest. One is that of Dante next to the church of St. Francis at the end of Via Dante Alighieri; but more notable is the tomb of someone you may have never heard of: Galla Placidia. The sister of the last emperor of Rome, she helped her brother govern his crumbling empire. A strong Christian, she endowed churches throughout the country. Notice the deep blue mosaics adorning the mausoleum. These mosaics are considered the oldest and most interesting in the city. Notice too the touching mosaic of the Good Shepherd, the open bookcase containing the Gospels, and the stags (representing souls) drinking from the Fountain of Life. The mausoleum is next to the Basilica di San Vitale, at Via San Vitale 17.

**Siena** Just as Francis has made Assisi famous, so Catherine has favored Siena. Both are patron saints of Italy. Catherine was a mystic and a healer who worked for the unification of Italy and hence became a diplomat. She was involved in everything, seeking to purify the papacy, visiting the sick and imprisoned, writing a classic on her experiences with God, and working for peace throughout Italy.

Today Siena is perhaps the loveliest, most enchanting medieval city in Italy. Its cathedral (Duomo) on Piazza del Duomo may be the most outstanding Gothic cathedral in Italy. Its inlaid marble floors show biblical scenes and symbols. However, the church most associated with Catherine of Siena is San Domenico on Via della Sapienza with its Cappella di Santa Caterina. It was here where she had many of her ecstatic experiences. Frescoes depict scenes from her life. The Sanctuary of St. Catherine on Via del Tiratoio pays homage to the saint in a lovely garden setting.

In late July and August the Settimana Musicale Senese is held each year with a series of concerts in local churches and courtyards.

**Turin** This major city of over a million people in northwestern Italy is known for its famous Shroud of Turin. Though the authentic Shroud is housed in the Duomo di San Giovanni on Piazza San Giovanni, it is seldom on display. A canvas reproduction will have to suffice.

The Academy of Science (Palazza dell'Accademia delle Scienze) on the via of the same name contains both one of the finest Egyptian museums outside Cairo and an unusually fine art gallery with Dutch and Flemish as well as Italian masterpieces. The Egyptian museum within the Academy of Science has a 13th-century B.C. statue of Ramses II, considered by some to be the Pharaoh of the Exodus.

The Borgo Medioevale, created in 1884, is sort of a 19th-century theme park, located on the southern edge of the Parco del Valentino. The village is a reproduction of a small medieval village with houses, shops, churches, and stores clustered on narrow streets. In the middle is a medieval castle. What more could you want?

> Come down, O Love divine, seek Thou this soul of mine,
> And visit it with Thine own ardor glowing.
> O Comforter, draw near, within my heart appear,
> And kindle it, Thy holy flame bestowing.
>
> BIANCO OF SIENA

**Venice** The Piazza San Marco is the most famous piazza in Venice, and the ideal place to begin an exploration of the city. The beautiful city square is usually filled with crowds of people and pigeons. If you have children, look for the wandering vendors selling cracked corn to feed to the birds. The experience of having the gentle creatures flock to them and perch on their arms and shoulders looking for food is one your kids will never forget.

On the eastern side of the piazza is St. Mark's Basilica (Basilica di San Marco), one of the most beautiful Christian churches in the world. The church's onion domes give the building a slight resemblance to a Middle Eastern mosque. Begun during the 11th century, St. Mark's was constructed to hold the relics of St. Mark the Evangelist, the city's patron saint. Its richly decorated exterior is surpassed by a stunning interior of brilliant gold mosaics. Take time to see the Pala d'Oro, a 10th-century altarpiece in gold and silver studded with precious gems. St. Mark's remains lie buried under this altarpiece. Visitors can climb the steep stairway in the atrium to visit the church's museum and step out onto a balcony overlooking the piazza below.

Across the piazza from St. Mark's Basilica is St. Mark's Bell Tower (Campanile di San Marco). The existing bell tower is a reconstruction of the 1,000-year-old tower that previously occupied this spot until its sudden collapse in 1912. Visitors can take the elevator up for a grand view of Venice that is ordinarily only enjoyed by the local pigeons.

*Churches.* In the Campo dei Frari, in the San Polo district, is an interesting church whose style contrasts starkly with the beauty of St. Mark's Basilica. The Santa Maria Gloriosa dei Frari is a soaring Gothic brick church sometimes known simply as I Frari. In spite of the church's austerity, which reflects the Franciscans' vow of poverty, some of the most important paintings in all of Venice reside in this building. The most stunning is Titian's *Assumption of the Virgin,* over the main altar. Titian was buried here at the age of 88, the only one of 70,000 local plague victims to be given a personal church burial.

It isn't difficult to find interesting churches in Venice, nor in the rest of Italy. Just north of San Marco are several interesting ones. The Santa Maria dei Miracoli (on Campo dei Miracoli) is a beautifully proportioned marble Renaissance building constructed in the 15th century. The interior is decorated with marble reliefs by the church's architect, Pietro Lombardo. Southeast of the church, on Campo Santa Maria Formosa, is the Santa Maria Formosa church, a graceful white marble building constructed in 1492 on 11th-century foundations. Inside is a nice collection of Renaissance and Baroque artworks. Outside, on weekday mornings, visitors will find a small vegetable market in the square. To the north is the massive Dominican church of Santi Giovanni e Paolo (Campo SS. Giovanni e Paolo), sometimes called San Zanipolo. Twenty-five of Venice's doges (chief magistrates) are buried here, and a wealth of artwork keeps them company.

*The Rialto Bridge (Ponte di Rialto)* is one of the world's most famous and most photographed bridges. Stalls along the bridge are hung with scarves, gondolier's hats, Venetian glass, and carnival masks. This is the heart of Venice's shopping district. Once you cross over the bridge, you'll find Rialto's famous market, which is open Tuesday through Saturday, and is best visited in the mornings when business is in full swing. Fruit and vegetable vendors hawk their colorful wares, and nearby is the fish market, selling creatures that you might never guess were edible.

*Gondolas.* Visitors to Venice are always impressed by the romantic gondolas plying the canals of this beautiful city. If you can't resist the urge, wait until evening to treat yourself to a ride, when traffic is at a minimum and the only sound you can hear are your gondolier's oars. Gondola rides can be very expensive— a minimum of 120,000 lire for 50 minutes. Get a firm price before stepping into a boat.

If you simply want to get around in Venice, remember that the canals function as streets. Two-man gondolas called traghetto ferry people across the Grand Canal at fixed points, and are not only cheap—700 lire—they can save you a lot of walking. Look for the TRAGHETTO signs. You can also get around the city cheaply and easily by vaporetto, ACTV water buses that run the length of the Grand Canal and circle the city. There are several lines, some of which connect the city to the outlying islands. The fare is 6,000 lire on all lines, but you can also buy 24-hour, 3-day, or 7-day tourist tickets at the Piazzale Roma next to the city's main train station. Many (but not all) of the vaporetto landing stages also have ticket booths and all have timetables.

**Verona** This city of a quarter million people is best known as the city of Romeo and Juliet. The cathedral (Duomo) on Via Duomo is the official church here, but two other churches might be more interesting: St. Zeno Major (on Piazza del Zeno) has biblical scenes on its doors and a great 13th-century rose window; the city's largest church is the Church of St. Anastasia, on Corso Sant'Anastasia, which has elaborate carvings of Old Testament scenes in its doorway and inside, 17 terra cottas, from 1435, on the life of Christ.

The Museo Archeologico (Archaeological Museum) on Via San Alessio is a combination of monastery, Roman theater, and museum. It also provides a great vantage point from which to see the city. The theater dates from the time of Augustus Caesar; plays are still performed here.

The Arena di Verona in Piazza Brà, still pretty much intact, hosts Verona's summer opera. While you are sitting on the 2,000-year-old marble seats, remember that in the early centuries, people were watching Christians being thrown to the lions in the same arena.

Juliet's House (Casa di Giulietta on Via Cappello 23) is not really where Juliet lived, but it has a balcony and a small courtyard, so you can imagine it was. For that matter, historians aren't really sure Juliet ever existed, but if you wish, you can visit Juliet's Tomb, the Tomba Di Guiuletta (Via del Pontiere 35) anyway, and leave a note there along with thousands of others.

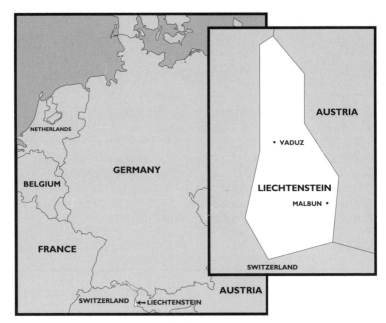

# *Liechtenstein*

*Phone numbers*
  Contact Switzerland Tourism (see page 290)
*Web site*
  Entire country www.news.li/touri
For a complete list of updated links, visit www.christiantraveler.com

### Country in a Capsule

*Size:* This little country has about the same area as the District of Columbia, with a total population of fewer than 30,000 people. Its largest city and its capital, Vaduz, has fewer than 5,000 people.

*Religion:* About 87 percent of the people are Roman Catholic, and about 9 percent are Protestant.

*Language:* Since the people are surrounded by German-speaking Swiss on one side and German-speaking Austrians on the other, German is the official language of the country, but since tourism is its major industry, English is widely understood.

*Money:* The standard currency is the Swiss franc, equivalent to about 57 cents.

*Food:* Try rosti (boiled potatoes, diced, fried, and finally baked with fried onion rings and bacon bits) or kalbsbratwurst (veal sausage).

*Shopping:* Buy a few postage stamps and mail some letters. After all, postage stamps account for 10 percent of the nation's economy. If you get away from the heart of Vaduz and into some of the other towns, you will find many possibilities, especially in ceramics.

*Brief history:* Liechtenstein was declared an independent principality in 1719 and has kept its independence despite Napoléon and the German Confederation. It declared its "permanent neutrality" in 1868, and neither of the World Wars of the 20th century caused it to change its position. Since 1919 it has been linked to Switzerland in currency, customs, and postal unions. It now has one of the highest per capita incomes in the world. It is a constitutional monarchy with a Parliament (Landtag). Prince Johannes Adam Pius is now the head of state, following a 50-year rule by his father, Prince Franz Josef.

**Vaduz** Fairy-tale castles are not unusual in Europe. Fairy-tale castles with princes still inhabiting them are far less common. Prince Johannes Adam Pius still rules from Liechtenstein's castle, the Vaduz Castle, and locals say he frequently eats dinner in local restaurants and chats with his citizens. Although his castle is a private residence and is open only to invited guests, travelers can drive or walk up to his 16th-century fortress and enjoy the extraordinary view from the cliff top that overlooks the city.

Tourist buses usually stop close to the post office, where stamp collectors can collect stamps. Other stops in town are the Kunstsammlungen, the State Art Collection at Städtle 37, which includes the Prince's Art Collection. The Landesmuseum at Städtle 43, is a historical museum that exhibits 16th-century paintings and religious sculpture as well as costumes, weapons, coins, and other articles that relate to the history of Liechtenstein.

**Maienfeld** About nine miles south of Vaduz near Maienfeld is the Heidi Fountain (Heidibrunnen), a memorial to Johanna Spyri, the popular Swiss writer of children's books, including *Heidi*. Technically, the memorial is in Switzerland, not Liechtenstein, but the best way to get to the Heidi Fountain is from Vaduz.

**Malbun** Perched up in Liechtenstein's Alps, the views from Malbun are simply heavenly. In the summer, miles of footpaths make their way through meadows and up, always up. Notice the little crosses perched at the tops of each mountain peak. You'll see plenty of the requisite dairy cows throughout the mountains, and if you miss them, you will surely hear their tell-tale Alpine cowbells. In the winter there are several ski resorts in town. Contact the Liechtenstein Tourist Office for ski information at Städtle 37, Box 139, Vaduz FL–9490, Liechtenstein; phone 075/232-1443.

# *Luxembourg*

Luxembourg National Tourist Office
  US 212-935-8888
  UK 020-7434-2800
*Web site*
  Entire country www.visitluxembourg.com
For a complete list of updated links, visit www.christiantraveler.com

### *Country in a Capsule*

*Size:* Slightly smaller than Rhode Island with about half as many people.

*Religion:* About 95 percent Roman Catholic; fewer than 5,000 Protestants.

*Language:* The official language of the people is Letzeburgesch, which is a form of German that sounds like Dutch. But most people here speak German and French as well, which are used in most official business.

English, however, is widely understood, so don't try to take a quick course in Letzeburgesch!

*Money:* There is a Luxembourg franc, but Belgian francs are also used, and the exchange rates are tied to one another. Currently the franc is worth about 2 cents.

*Food:* Along the street you will probably find waffle (gaufres) stands. The waffles are served piping hot with jam and honey. Some Luxembourg specialties are smoked Ardennes ham, smoked neck of pork with broad beans, and kachkeis, which is a salted handmade cheese. If you go there in September, try the local plum tarts.

*Shopping:* Luxembourg is known for its tableware, but try to find bargains outside of the capital city.

*Brief history:* In 963 Luxembourg became an autonomous country within the Holy Roman Empire. It passed under French rule in 1443, under Spanish rule in 1555, under the Austrian Habsburgs in 1714, and under revolutionary France in 1795. The 1815 Congress of Vienna made it a Grand Duchy tied to the Netherlands. But in 1890 the tie was broken, and except for its occupation by Germany in the World Wars, it has remained independent. It was a founding member of NATO. Now a constitutional monarchy under a grand duke, Luxembourg has no air force or navy, but it has an army of 800.

**Luxembourg** This capital city of 75,000 people has an unusual charm. It combines a magnificent setting with its business and financial environment, and if that seems too stodgy, there is the annual fair and market (Schuerberfouer) held each September since 1340 and the folk festival of l'Emaischen for young lovers in the Place du Musée.

The headquarters of one of the largest broadcasting companies in Europe is here, and many evangelical outreaches have been beamed across the continent from Luxembourg.

The Musée National d'Histoire et d'Art is housed in several mansions on the main square of Old Town. Its fine art collection features a range of religious sculptures from the 11th to the 18th centuries. The third floor has paintings by Dutch painters, many of which also have religious themes.

You won't miss the Cathédrale de Notre-Dame, which dominates the city's skyline. Built in 1613 to 1618, it represents mostly a Gothic style, but its beautifully carved portal and its organ gallery are a Baroque-lover's dream. The cathedral, located on rue Notre-Dame, is the site of a national pilgrimage every year during the two weeks beginning on the third Sunday after Easter.

Perched on the shores of the Alzette River, the Baroque Church of St. John the Baptist (Eglise de St-Jean Baptiste) on Rue Münster was once part of a Benedictine abbey. Of special interest is the Black Madonna, which was once thought to protect the citizenry from the plague, and the Stations of the Cross made of Limoges enamel. Take the time to explore the passageway outside the church. The view from the river is unforgettable.

When you are visiting Luxembourg, take advantage of its national network of walking paths. The main path, GR 5, crosses the country, and, in fact, crosses all of Europe, going from Holland to the Mediterranean. But Luxembourg has 447 miles of yellow-marked footpaths in all, and that's quite a bit for a country that is barely 50 miles wide.

**Diekirch** Located in the historic Ardennes, Diekirch has a beautiful little Romanesque church, the Eglise St-Laurent on pl. Bech. Of special interest are the Merovingian tombs.

**Echternach** This town is located on the German boarder in the part of Luxembourg called Mini-Switzerland (Petite Suisse), and you can guess why. Medieval town houses and cobbled streets make Echternach a pleasantly quaint visit.

In 698 Willibrord, a remarkable Anglo-Saxon Christian missionary, came and founded the abbey on Parvis de la Basilique, which became a Benedictine monastery during the Middle Ages. The abbey complex now spreads to a set of formal gardens by the river. The enormous basilica, named after St. Willibrord, was built in the 11th century on the site of an earlier church. It was destroyed during World War II, but the reconstruction after the war was extremely well done.

On the Tuesday after Pentecost every year, 15,000 pilgrims participate in a dancing procession that ends at the St. Willibrord Basilica (Basilique St-Willibrord). The basilica's namesake lies buried in the church's crypt, which is open daily. Highly detailed reproductions of the illuminated manuscripts created by the Echternach

School are displayed in the nearby Abbey Museum (Musée de l'Abbaye) at Parvis de la Basilique 11. At the museum you will see how the monks created the beautiful illuminated manuscripts a thousand years ago. The most famous of these is the Codex Aureus, a gold gospel book, from the 11th century. It was created here but is now in the German National Museum in Nuremburg.

**Rindschleiden** In northwestern Luxembourg, this little community has a church to admire. Dating from the early 15th century, the church is lined with frescoes depicting a variety of religious scenes. It also has a well of St. Willibrord, which is said to be miraculous and is hence the object of an annual pilgrimage. It's located in a little garden near the church.

**Rodange** Hop aboard the tourist train (about 1.25 miles south of the church on Le Sauvage Rd.) and enjoy a short trip (less than four miles) through the Fond du Gras valley. It won't be the speediest train trip you have ever had, because the train is pulled by steam engines that are 100 years old, but it will get you there and back amid great natural beauty.

**Vianden** The medieval castle Château de Vianden on Grand'Rue is surely the most romantic sight in all of Luxembourg. Perched on a hill overlooking the tiny village, supplied with a generous quantity of towers and spires, it's easy to remember that this country is a Grand Duchy. The castle, built in the 11th century, is what an old castle should be, complete with a Gothic dungeon, a banqueting hall, and another hall decorated with 17th-century tapestries. Then you can take a cable car even higher to a mountaintop where there's a restaurant with a terrace.

**Wasserbillig** There is not much here, but you can go to a lot of scenic places *from* here, both by road and by boat. If you want a leisurely cruise, take a boat ride up the Moselle River and go to Schengen about 25 miles away.

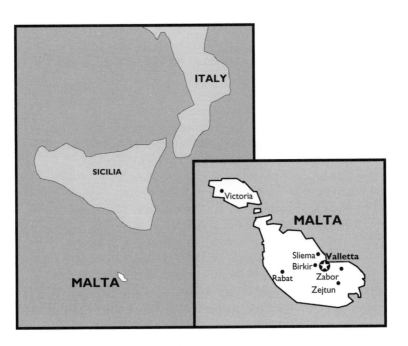

# Malta

Malta National Tourist Office
 US 212-695-9520
 UK 020-7292-4900
 Australia 02-9321-9514
*Web site*
 Entire country www.visitmalta.com
For a complete list of updated links, visit www.christiantraveler.com

### Country in a Capsule

*Size:* This island nation is about one-tenth the size of the state of Rhode Island, and about one-third the population.

*Religion:* 90 percent of the people are Roman Catholic, and about 2 percent are Protestant.

*Language:* The official languages are English and Maltese. Maltese is a semitic tongue related to Arabic dialects spoken in Algeria and Tunisia. However, the Maltese language uses the Latin alphabet, not the Arabic.

*Money:* The currency unit is the Maltese lira, currently equal to about $2.40.

*Food:* Maltese food is Sicilian and Moorish in origin, but Italian food is widely available. The Maltese national dish is fenek (rabbit), but local seafood is popular as well. Minestra, a local version of minestrone soup, and aljotta, or fish soup, are common. You'll also find many dishes cooked with capers, the buds of the *Caperis specicum* shrub that is local to the islands.

*Shopping:* The main streets of Valletta are filled with touristy souvenir shops. To find traditional handcrafted goods, veer off onto the side streets. Feel free to bargain with vendors in open-air markets.

*Brief history:* Malta's history goes back to Phoenician times, and it is mentioned in Scripture relating to the apostle Paul. In more recent times it passed through the hands of several European powers. Napoléon gained it in 1798; and then the British took it in 1800. With the opening of the Suez Canal in 1869, it became a major British base. In 1974 Malta became a republic within the British Commonwealth and is now governed by a 65-member House of Representatives and a prime minister.

## ▲ ISLAND OF MALTA

**Valletta** In the early 16th century the island of Malta was presented to the Knights of the Order of St. John as a gift from Charles V of Spain. The Knights' influence on the country is still felt in Valletta, particularly in St. John's Co-Cathedral (Konkatidral ta' San Gwann) on Pjazza San Gwann. (St. John's shares diocesan responsibilities with Mdina Cathedral, hence the title Co-Cathedral.) The lavishly decorated church, dating from 1578, is considered Malta's most valued treasure. Colored marble tombstones marking the Knights' burial places in the floor are gorgeous, and each of the side chapels is unique, having been decorated by separate national hostels of the Knights. Much of the church's ornamentation and paintings are by the island's own 17th-century painter Mattia Preti. The cathedral's museum is also worth visiting for its rich Flemish tapestries and illuminated manuscripts.

But the religious importance of Malta goes back much farther than the Knights. This island is the place on which the apostle Paul was shipwrecked. When you see the extravagant work poured into the Baroque St. Paul's Shipwreck Church (San Pawl Nawfragu), you'll recognize the importance of the saint to the people of the island. Highlights of the church include a large oval dome, a beautiful gated chapel to the left of the entrance, a wooden sculpture of the apostle, and, in the chapel to the right, the os brachii (arm bone) relic of St. Paul. The church is located on Triq San Pawl just north of Triq Santa Lucija.

**Birgu** Just below Birgu's main square on Triq San Lawrenz is the Church of St. Lawrence (Knisja ta' San Lawrenz), considered the city's finest church. The popular 17th-century painter Mattia Preti created the painting inside, *Martyrdom of San Lawrenz*.

**Ghajn Tuffieha Bay, Gnejna Bay, and Golden Bay** These three bays, located on the northwest shore of the island of Malta, offer good opportunities for swimming on the island. Of the three, Golden Bay tends to be the most crowded, but all offer secluded sandy beaches. The ride out will be enjoyable too, as you pass through rolling countryside, occasionally split up by ancient stone walls.

**Mdina** The ancient walled city of Mdina was once the home of the island's nobility. Thick golden stone is the rule, and since traffic is limited to residents' cars, the streets are pretty quiet. The church to visit here is the Baroque Cathedral of St. Peter and St. Paul (Il-Katidral Ta' l-Imdina) on Archbishop Square. Mattia Preti's 17th-century painting *The Shipwreck of St. Paul* is only one of a number of artistic treasures in the cathedral. Others are located in the cathedral museum, including Dürer woodcuts and illuminated manuscripts.

**Mosta** The Church of St. Mary, known as the Rotunda, is a stunning architectural achievement for a country as small as Malta. It has one of the largest unsupported domes in Europe, following behind St. Peter's Basilica in Rome and Hagia Sophia in Istanbul. A German bomb fell through the roof in World War II. Fortunately, it never detonated. The church is located on Rotunda Square.

**Rabat** The town of Rabat is actually a suburb of Mdina and is reputedly the location of the grotto where Paul took refuge after his shipwreck on Malta. Standing over the grotto is, understandably enough, St. Paul's Church (Knysja San Pawl) on Parish Square.

Running underneath much of Rabat is a series of catacombs, both St. Paul's Catacombs and St. Agatha's Catacombs. The underground passages no longer contain any remains, but the carved-out burial troughs can be visited and a number of Christian relics are still housed here. Be careful not to lose your way as you wander through the mazelike tunnels. St. Agatha's Catacombs were beautifully frescoed between 1200 and 1480. Unfortunately, invading Turks defaced the tombs in 1551. The catacombs are located on St. Agatha Street.

**Zurrieq** The Blue Grotto is popular with tourists, which will mean two things: The crowds can get a little thick, and the area is worth visiting. Phosphorescent blue water is the backdrop for not one but many grottoes in the rocky inlet, which can best be seen by boat (a variety of options are available in the area). If the water is warm and the boats aren't in your way, this is also a nice place to swim.

## ▲ ISLAND OF GOZO

**Ramla Bay** If you're interested in swimming while you're on the island of Gozo, head to Ramla Bay. The beach makes for the best swimming on the island, and it is also Gozo's largest and most popular.

**San Lawrenz** The cliffs of San Lawrenz and Dwejra are nothing short of spectacular. To see them best, arrive at sunset, or take a boat ride from the Inland Sea out into the Mediterranean. The trip makes its way through a natural tunnel under the cliffs. Be sure to ask the captain to swing past the Azure Window and Fungus Rock. The huge limestone arch juts out from the cliffs and is dotted with unusual rock formations. If you prefer, you can also reach the rock by foot.

**Victoria** The capital city of Gozo, Victoria, is a charmingly beautiful city with plenty of narrow winding streets. The hilltop

Cittadella comprises the Old City, with steep walled streets and fabulous views. There are two churches in Victoria worth visiting as well. St. George's Basilica (Bazilika San Gorg) on Triq San Guzepp is said to have the most beautiful interior on Gozo. The town's cathedral (Katidral) lost its dome in a 1693 earthquake. It has been replaced by a trompe l'oeil painting.

**Xaghra** The local church in the town of Xaghra, the Church of Our Lady of Victories, might not be notable were it not for its clock towers. The church has two, one of which has the correct time. The other clock is deliberately wrong to fool the devil. Apparently Satan is interested in the correct time.

# *Monaco*

Monaco Government Tourist Office
  US 212-286-3330
  UK 020-7352-9962
*Web site*
  Entire country www.monaco-tourism.com
For a complete list of updated links, visit www.christiantraveler.com

### *Country in a Capsule*

*Size:* Monaco is the second smallest independent state in the world; only Vatican City is smaller. Its area is less than a square mile. Its population is 28,000.

*Religion:* Monaco is 90 percent Roman Catholic, but the Church of England is also represented, and there is a synagogue here.

*Language:* French is the official language, but Italian and English are spoken here, as well as Monegaxque, which is a hybrid of French and Italian Ligurian.

*Money:* The French franc is the unit of currency. See France for an approximate exchange rate.

*Food:* Monaco's cuisine generally resembles that of France, but with a heavy emphasis on seafood and various Mediterranean spices.

*Shopping:* Most of Monaco's economy revolves around catering to the rich and famous who head to the country's elaborate casinos and lovely seacoast. Goods tend to be priced accordingly high.

*Brief history:* The Genoese built a fortress here in 1215 and the house of Grimaldi took it over later in the century. Monaco has retained its independence for much of the time since then, although it has depended alternately on France and Spain for protection. Prince Rainier took the throne in 1949 and captured headlines when he married the U.S. film star Grace Kelly in 1956. The country is governed by a minister of state who is nominated by the ruling monarch from a list of three submitted by the French government. A legislature is chosen by the local citizenry for five-year terms.

Monaco's cathedral is relatively modern, built in the late 19th century. It's located at 4 rue Colonel Bellando de Castro and is built in a lovely neo-Romanesque style. The cathedral's most famous tomb contains the remains of Philadelphia-born Princess Grace.

The Oceanography Museum and Aquarium (Musée Océanographique) on av. St-Martin is an internationally recognized research institute that was founded by Monaco's Prince Albert. For many years the famous underwater explorer Jacques Cousteau ran the facility. The aquarium is a highlight.

The Exotic Plants Garden (Jardin Exotique) on bd. du Jardin Exotique is home to 600 varieties of cacti and succulents. When you buy a ticket to the garden, you are also allowed admittance to the adjacent caves and the Museum of Prehistoric Anthropology (Musée d'Anthropologie Préhistorique).

# *Netherlands*

Netherlands Board of Tourism
  US 312-819-1500 or 888-464-6552
  Canada 888-464-6552
  UK 0891-717-777
*Web sites*
  Entire country www.goholland.com
  Amsterdam www.visitamsterdam.nl
  The Hague www.denhaag.com
  Rotterdam www.gorotterdam.com
For a complete list of updated links, visit www.christiantraveler.com

### Country in a Capsule

*Size:* If you combine Massachusetts, Connecticut, and Rhode Island, you have a land area close to that of the Netherlands. However, the Netherlands has about 50 percent more people than those three states combined, having four cities with populations of more than 200,000, compared to only one (Boston) in the New England states.

*Religion:* About 34 percent are Roman Catholic, 25 percent are Protestant, and 36 percent are unaffiliated. The Netherlands Reformed Church is the largest Protestant denominaton, followed by two other Reformed groups (the Reformed Churches in the Netherlands and the Christian Reformed Churches.)

*Language:* Dutch is the official language, but English is widely understood.

*Money:* The Dutch currency is based on the guilder, which was worth about 40 cents at press time.

*Food:* In Amsterdam, lunches are often eaten on the move, so snacks are popular, and patat frites (potato chips or fries with mayonnaise, ketchup, or peanut sauce) is a favorite. You can also get mackerel in a roll (broodje makreel) or salted raw herring from a sidewalk vendor. When eating out, many Amsterdammers choose Indonesian cooking; another favorite is the rijstaffel, which is sort of a Dutch version of a Scandinavian smorgasbord. The Dutch also enjoy split pea soup and boerenkool (kale and potatoes, served with sausage).

*Shopping:* Tulips and bulbs are naturals, and so are chocolates and cheeses. If you go to Delft, you will probably want to investigate the prices of the famous blue Delft porcelain. In antique stores you may find a good buy in Dutch tiles, clocks, or dolls.

*Brief history:* The known history of the area starts when Julius Caesar conquered Gaul in about 50 B.C. But it wasn't until King Clovis was converted to Christianity late in the 5th century, and missionaries like Willibrord and Boniface in the 700s spread the gospel northward throughout the entire region, that the Lowlands were united in one faith and as one country. In the 800s came a flurry of church building, and towns sprang up around the churches. For centuries, the Netherlands was fought over by the French, Spanish, and Austrians, but it wasn't until the printing press came, and Bibles were printed, and people like Erasmus of Rotterdam and Luther of Wittenberg, Germany, presented their ideas that radical change came internally. Faced with the Spanish Inquisition and the determination of Philip II to fight Protestant heresy with a sword, the northern provinces under William the Silent waged the Eighty Years' War, declaring their independence from Spain in 1581.

The Golden Age for the Netherlands began early in the 17th century, as refugees from other European countries found haven here. Banking, business, exploration, and the arts all blossomed, and suddenly little Netherlands was a major power and Amsterdam a world trade center. In 1848 the Netherlands adopted a new constitution that ushered in a new era of economic progress. Its policy of neutrality provided the country with the opportunity to host peace conferences and eventually the International Court of Justice at The Hague.

## DUTCH TREAT

The Hoge Veluwe National Park in the Netherlands is 30,000 acres of dense woods, moorlands, and meadows. Located within a triangular area between Apeldoorn, Amersfoort, and Arnhem, the park offers a natural oasis to enjoy God's creation only a short distance from the bustling city of Amsterdam. There are plenty of footpaths and quiet picnicking spots, but if you want to see the park the way the Dutch do, hop on a bike. At the entrance to the park are white bicycles, free for use by anyone visiting the park, to better enjoy the park's scenery. Yet even in a national park, you won't be far from a little culture. The park is home to one of the world's best modern art museums, the Rijksmuseum Kröller-Müller with works by Van Gogh, Seurat, and Picasso. For information about bike rentals anywhere in the Netherlands, visit the following web site: www.visitholland.com/find/rental/bike.html.

**Amsterdam** Shortly after Amsterdam was founded, its citizens organized themselves to defend the city. These citizen-militias continued when Amsterdam became Protestant during the Reformation. One of these militias is immortalized in Rembrandt's famous painting *The Night Watch,* which is on display at the Rijksmuseum. The museum displays more than 20 other Rembrandt works and is one of three major art galleries on the Museumplein. Rembrandt's paintings *The Prophet Jeremiah* and *The Prophetess Hannah* are two of his biblical paintings. Many of the other early works on display at the Rijksmuseum also depict biblical scenes. Note the brilliance of Lucas van Leyden's *Adoration of the Golden Calf,* for example. The other two art museums in the area are the Van Gogh Museum and the Stedelijk Museum.

*Boat tours.* One of the most pleasant ways to get acquainted with Amsterdam is on a boat trip along the city's canals. Departures are frequent from points near the Centraal Station (central train station), along the Damrak, and along the Rokin and Stadhouderskade near the Rijksmuseum. Tours lasting about an hour are available, as are candlelight dinner cruises. Tours and cruises can be booked through the tourist office in front of the central train station in Old Dutch Coffee House. A day card, which you can use to hop on and off the boat as often as you like, is available as well. Or take the Museum Boat, which has seven stops near 20 of the city's major museums.

*Vondelpark* on Stadhouderskade is Amsterdam's central park, a rectangle of shady green paths and lakes. A monument within the park honors its namesake, the 17th-century poet Joost van den Vondel. Special children's areas within the park offer paddling pools and sandboxes. In the summer months the park is frequently the site of free outdoor concerts and plays Wednesday through Sunday.

*Churches.* Oude Lutherse Kerk (the Old Lutheran Church at Singel and Spui) was built in 1632 to 1633 on the site of an old warehouse that Lutherans had converted into a church. In 1631 the city council said they could replace the old warehouse-church, providing that the new building looked like a warehouse on the outside. On Sundays Lutheran services are still held here; during the week the University of Amsterdam uses it for classrooms.

Contrary to its name, the New Church (Nieuwe Kerk) on the Dam isn't so new—at least not by North American standards. The huge Gothic building was expanded until 1540, when it reached its present size. In 1645 the interior was destroyed by fire, and it was reconstructed in the Renaissance style by strict Calvinists. Of special interest are the great oak pulpit, the stained glass windows, the 14th-century nave, and the 17th-century organ. On national holidays the church is generously decorated with flowers. The Nieuwe Kerk is the site of all coronations, including that of the current monarch, Queen Beatrix, in 1980. The church is also used as a meeting place, and it has a colorful cafe. Occasionally temporary exhibitions or concerts are held here as well.

Between the New Church and the Town Hall runs a street with the interesting name, Mozes en Aaronstraat (Moses and Aaron Street), demonstrating how the temporal and spiritual power were separate and yet working together. When the Germans took over the city in World War II, they did not like the Jewish biblical names of the street, so they called it Poststraat.

Amsterdam's Old Church (Oude Kerk) at Oudekerksplein 23 is indeed older than the New Church, just as you'd expect. In fact it's the oldest house of worship in the city, dating from the early 14th century. The church was badly damaged by iconoclasts after the Reformation, but it retains some lovely stained glass windows and its original bell tower from which you can enjoy a nice view of Old Amsterdam. The great 17th-century organ is still used for frequent concerts. Carillon chimes can be heard every day.

## ABRAHAM KUYPER (1837-1920)

This Dutch theologian and statesman began as a pastor in a small country church, then took pastorates in Utrecht and Amsterdam. Abraham Kuyper became famous as editor of *De Standard,* making it a strong voice for evangelical Christianity and urging Christians to work for a purer public national life. Kuyper became active politically and rose to the position of prime minister of Holland in 1901. He founded the Free Reformed University at Amsterdam and wrote several influential books.

The facade of the Museum Amstelkring at Oudezijds Voorburgwal 40 bears the words, "Ons Lieve Heer Op Solder," or "Our Lord in the Attic." This cryptic inscription is a testament to the religious tolerance of the Dutch. In 1578 Amsterdam embraced Protestantism and outlawed what it termed the Church of Rome. But municipal authorities were reluctant to arrest Catholic worshipers, and so turned a blind eye toward the secret Catholic chapels that sprung up. (At one time there were as many as 62 secret chapels in Amsterdam alone.) One of these chapels was held in the attics of three adjoining houses, built around 1660. While the buildings' lower floors were used as residences, services were held in the attics until 1888, when St. Nicolaaskerk was consecrated for Catholic worship. Inside the attic chapel, notice the swinging pulpit that can be hidden away, the Baroque altar, and the religious artifacts in the upstairs gallery.

Today Sint Nicolaas Kerk (St. Nicholas Church on Prins Hendrikkade) is an imposing neo-Renaissance church and is now the dominant Catholic church in the city.

In the early 17th century the English Church (Engelse Kerk) on Begijnhof was given to Amsterdam's English and Scottish Presbyterians. On the church wall and in the chancel are tributes to the Pilgrim Fathers who sailed to the New World in 1620 from Delftshaven (modern-day Delfshaven in Rotterdam). Across the street from the English Church is another secret Catholic chapel, dating from 1671, the exterior of which appears to be two adjoining houses.

Westerkerk (West Church) at Prinsengracht and Westermarkt was completed in 1631 and features the city's highest church tower, at 279 feet. Its nave is the largest nave among Dutch Protestant churches. The organ, decorated with pictures of musical instruments as well as biblical themes, was commissioned in 1682. It also has a beautiful carillon. Rembrandt, who died in 1669, and his son Titus are buried in the church. His wife Saskia is buried in the Old Church (Oude Kerk). In the summer you can enjoy a lovely view of the city from the top of the church's tower.

Most church services are of course in Dutch. Here are some in English: English Reformed Church (Begijnhof 48), Anglican Church (Groenburgwal 42), and St. John and St. Ursula Catholic Church (Begijnhof 30).

*The Beguine Court (Begijnhof)* at Begijnhof 29 is a little enclosed group of almshouses founded in 1346 offering a peaceful and quiet break from the city. The Beguines were originally the widows of Crusaders who chose to lead a convent life, although they were not nuns. In later years the lay sisterhood was opened to other women. The last Beguine died in 1974 and her house, Number 26, is preserved as she left it for visitors to tour. The oldest house in the Beguine Court and in all of Amsterdam, Number 34, dates from the 15th century and is the only one that retains its original wooden Gothic facade. The Engelse Kerk (English Church) in the Square is 600 years old. The American Pilgrim Fathers worshiped here during a brief stay in Amsterdam in the early 17th century.

*The Rembrandthuis* (Rembrandt's house at 4 Jodenbreestraat) in the Jewish quarter has been a museum since 1911. About 245 Rembrandt etchings can be viewed here.

*The House of the Rising Sun* at 118 Singel was a Mennonite sanctuary, built in the 17th century and sold to Mennonites of the "Sun" congregation.

*Anne Frank's House.* Anne Frank's touching story is familiar to nearly everyone, including children. The young Jewish girl, who hid with her family in an Amsterdam annex from 1942 to 1944, put a charming face on the often faceless victims of the Nazi Holocaust. Visitors can tour Anne Frank's House (Anne Frankhuis) at Prinsengracht 263, which has been left largely untouched since the Nazi's invasion. The museum is stark, with little left but a few personal effects, some furniture, and translations of Anne's diary in a variety of languages. Readers of the diary will be especially touched by Anne's Hollywood collage and the pencil marks on the wall, reminders of the child's growth while holed up in the annex. This is an especially good way to introduce the cruel history of the Holocaust to children who may be too young or sensitive to visit the more gruesome displays in Europe's concentration camp museums.

*Flower markets.* Holland is known for its flowers and flower markets have done business on its canals for centuries. One, the Bloemenmarkt (Flower Market on Singel near the Mint Tower), occupies about 15 barges on the Singel Canal and has been in operation since the 18th century or before.

*The Bible Museum* (366 Herengracht) is housed in a little museum attractively painted by the first Catholic painter in Holland to receive such a commission after the Reformation. The museum exhibits manuscripts and various Bible editions, including the Delft Bible, which was the first Bible printed in the Netherlands (1477).

*The Metropolis Science and Technology Center* is a wonderful modern interactive museum that will appeal especially to children, although it is designed to be of interest to all ages. The building is covered in copper and lurks over the harbor waters looking like the hull of a ship. Hands-on exhibits range from physics to new technologies. You can enjoy a great view of the city from the building's rooftop. The museum is located at Oosterdok 2, Prins Hendrikkade.

*Concerts.* Music lovers should know that most of the major churches host chamber and Baroque concerts. The Engelse Kerk at Begijnhof 48 is known for its lunchtime, afternoon, and evening concerts, with an emphasis on period instruments. In addition, the Muziektheater on Waterlooplein, where the Netherlands Opera resides, has free lunchtime concerts September to May.

Amsterdam's Concert Hall (Concertgebouw) at Concertgebouwplein 2–6 is home to one of Europe's finest orchestras. When international orchestras visit, ticket prices are rather high but are very reasonably priced at other times. If you really want a bargain, consider a Wednesday midday concert—they're free.

*Biking.* Before you are in Amsterdam very long, you will notice that half of the population seems to be riding bicycles. For visitors too it's a good way to see the city. And guess what? Instead of Yellow Cabs, they have Yellow Bikes you can rent. Rental bikes are widely available throughout Amsterdam at cheap prices, although most places will require a deposit and proof of identity. You can find several rental companies near the city's central train station, or ask at tourist offices for details. From April through October you might consider a guided bike tour as an interesting way to explore the city. There are also a number of guided tours to the countryside and neighboring villages. For city tours or country excursions, contact Yellow Bike Guided Tours at Nieuwezijds Kolk 29, phone 020/620-6940.

*Red-light district.* Most visitors to Amsterdam have heard of its notorious red-light district. Until you've been to the city, you may not be aware of how difficult it is to avoid. Located in the heart of downtown Amsterdam, and near many sites of interest to tourists, visitors frequently find themselves in the midst of some pretty tawdry sights and wonder how they could have made such a mistake. The red-light district is not clearly marked, but it lies between the Oudezijds Voorburgwal and Oudezijds Achterburgwal, two of the city's oldest canals. Although the area is generally pretty safe, it can be shocking, including pornographic photos in even the most wholesome-looking shops.

**Aalsmeer** What would the Netherlands be without tulips? Flowers are much more than decoration to the Dutch; they're big business. The world's largest complex of flower auction houses is in the Netherlands, and the biggest of these facilities is the flower auction (Bloemenveiling) in Aalsmeer at Legmeerdijk 313, close to Schiphol International Airport and Amsterdam. A building the size of three football fields (the largest in the world) has three auction rooms that sell their wares simultaneously weekday mornings. But if you want to enjoy the sights, get there early. The bidding is all over by 10:00.

**Alkmaar** This town, an hour away from Amsterdam, has been selling cheese on its main square since the 1300s; crowds still come to the cheese market here. It's held every Friday morning from mid-April to mid-September. If you're into cheese, you can tour the Kaasmuseum on Waagplein to learn more about the history of cheese and cheese making. If you've had enough of cheese, why not visit both the Stedelijk Museum on Doelenstraat and the St. Laurenskerk on Koorstraat, a 15th-century Gothic church with a large organ.

**Amersfoort** The beautiful 335-foot tower in town is the Onze Lieve Vrouwetoren, the Tower of Our Lady, on Breestraat. Part of a Gothic church, the tower's musical chimes ring every Friday between 10:00 A.M. and 11:00 A.M.

**Arnhem** Decisive battles of World War II took place in this area, and many visitors who come here recall those days. But other things are here too.

If you are traveling with children, take a detour to Arnhem's Open-Air Museum (Nederlands Openlucht Museum) at Schelmseweg 89. The 44-acre park includes original buildings and furnishings from throughout the Netherlands, brought here to create a comprehensive overview of Dutch rural architectural styles. Visitors will also learn some of the traditional Dutch ways of living. There are workshops, farmhouses and barns, animals, and those beloved windmills.

Just north of the Open-Air Museum is the large Hoge-Veluwe Park, which houses the Rijksmuseum-Kröller-Müller, an art museum with one of the best collections of Van Gogh anywhere.

**Delft** Delft is popular because (a) it is a pretty little city that looks like a Dutch city is supposed to look, (b) the Delft ceramic ware is made here, or (c) it was the hometown of artist Jan Vermeer. Probably all of the above.

Delft is one of the most attractive and traditional towns in the Netherlands, its streets lined with Gothic and Renaissance houses and intersected by canals. Delft's compact size makes it ideal for exploration by foot, although canal boat excursions are available from April through October. Horse-drawn trams offer another unique sightseeing option; they leave regularly from the marketplace. The town's blue and white ceramics, known as Delftware, are popular throughout the world.

Probably the finest building in town is the Old Church (Oude Kerk), a huge Gothic monument on Heilige Geest Kerkhof built in the 13th century. The church overlooks the city's oldest waterway, the Oude Delft canal. Don't be alarmed; the beautiful tower leans quite markedly but doesn't appear to be going anywhere soon.

Delft not only has an Old Church; it has a New Church. Delft's New Church (Nieuwe Kerk) is located in the marketplace, a lively spot in an otherwise tranquil town. The church was built during the 14th century and has a lovely Gothic tower and a 48-bell carillon. The remains of all of the members of the royal family have been buried in the church's crypt since King William I, who ascended the throne in the mid–16th century.

**Den Bosch** This city's official name is 's-Hertogenbosch, which means, "The Duke's Woods." The name you will more often hear is the abbreviated Den Bosch, simply "The Woods." If you want to get a good overview of this town, take a boat trip along the city moat. Then start walking. Enjoy a carillon concert played every Wednesday morning at 10:00 from the Stadthuis on Schopenmarkt, and visit St. Jan's Cathedral on Parade, which many say is the finest Gothic cathedral in the country. Built between 1330 and 1530, it has two paintings by Hieronymus Bosch, who lived in this town all of his life. Across the street at Hinthamerstraat 94 in the Zwanenbroedershuis is a collection associated with the Brotherhood of Our Lady, to which Bosch belonged. The aim of the Brotherhood was to promote religious art and music.

**Deventer** In the late 1400s, a street preacher named Gerhard Groote formed the Brotherhood of the Common Life here. He called people back to God and to the Bible. "Turn away from sin, live like Jesus, read God's Word," he told them. One of them that joined with Groote was Thomas à Kempis, who later wrote the classic, *Of the Imitation of Christ*. Its Lebuinuskerk (on Grote Pont) is one of the finest Gothic buildings in eastern Holland. The church has two great Baroque organs and the remains of some medieval murals.

**Dokkum** This town, which is one of the oldest in the state of Friesland, is where the English missionary, St. Boniface, and 52 of his companions were martyred while trying to bring the gospel to the pagan Frisians. The town is still part walled and moated, and lots of things are named in memory of Boniface. Besides that, you can look at a couple of windmills, go to a museum, and even buy a pizza.

**Edam** The town is famous for its cheese that the Dutch export around the world. After checking out the cheese, tourists usually visit the Grote Kerk, which is open every afternoon from April through October. Its stained glass windows are quite remarkable, which is more than you can say for its stubby spire. But its excuse is that the previous spires were twice hit by lightning, causing fires that threatened the entire town.

**Enschede** The Rijksmuseum Twente (at Lasondersingel 129) is one of the finest art museums in eastern Holland. A great variety of art is on display here, but the Dutch and Flemish religious paintings are of the most interest.

**Gouda** About 15 miles northeast of Amsterdam is another town known for its cheese and its Thursday-morning cheese market. You can enjoy the city's famous commodity at the cheese market (Kaasmarkt). Colorful farm wagons arrive at the market on summer Thursdays loaded with cheeses for sale. In the ornate Baroque Waag (weigh house) nearby, the Kaasexposeum (Cheese Exhibition) explains the history of cheese and other dairy products. The market is located at Markt 35–36 in July and August on Thursdays from 10:00 to noon.

The Church of St. John (Sint Janskerk) on the market square at Achter de Kerk was built during the 16th century. Its nave is the longest in the country, and its 64 stained glass windows are lovely. The oldest dates from 1555. The church holds carillon concerts in the summer. Next door is the Catharina Gasthuis with its Stedelijk Museum, containing some early religious art.

**Groningen** Most of the city was destroyed during World War II, but its Martinikerk survived quite well. Parts of the church go back to 1180; frescoes on the left side of the church tell of Christ's birth; frescoes on the right tell of his death.

**Haarlem** This was the city of Corrie ten Boom, the brave Dutch woman whose family sheltered Jews in "the Hiding Place" in their home at Barteljorisstraat 19 during the Nazi occupation. Her house and the street-level family clock shop are open to the public. Visitors can see the ten Booms' memorabilia and photographs, as well as the family's secret hiding closet.

The church Corrie attended was the Grote Kerk, on Grote Markt, a huge and beautiful church. Take note of the unusual Dog Whippers' chapel in the north transept. The chapel honors the men who succeeded in ridding the church of a pack of vicious dogs many years ago. The Christian Muller organ dates from 1738 and is one of the biggest in the world with 5,000 pipes and Baroque embellishment. Two of Europe's finest composers have played this organ: Mozart and Handel. An annual organ festival is held here every July. During the summers organ recitals are given on Tuesday evenings.

## CORRIE TEN BOOM (1892–1983)

Her best-selling book, *The Hiding Place,* made her name known around the world. During World War II Corrie, along with her sister Betsie and her father, hid Jews in a secret place in their home. Eventually they were discovered, and the ten Booms were taken to German concentration camps. Her father and her sister died, but Corrie survived three different concentration camps, ending up in Ravensbruck. On her release, she began an international ministry of speaking and writing, talking about her experiences, the need to forgive, and the importance of accepting God's love.

Sites associated with Corrie ten Boom are located in Haarlem, the Netherlands, and Ravensbruck, Germany.

**The Hague** As the de facto capital of the country, The Hague is expected to look prim and proper and it does. But don't pass it up. Its Royal Picture Gallery Mauritshuis (at Korte Vijverberg 8) is one of the best galleries in Europe. All the major Dutch masters are here. Rogier van der Weyden's *The Lamentation of Christ* is powerful, and Quentin Matsys' *Descent from the Cross* contrasts the suffering of Christ with the taunting crowd. *The Adoration by the Magi* by Jordaens is another excellent painting on a biblical theme.

Another museum, the Meermanno-Westreenianum Museum (Prinsessegracht 30), has a fascinating collection of medieval illuminated manuscripts and Bibles.

The Cloister Church (Kloosterkerk) is The Hague's oldest church, built in 1400. In addition to enjoying the church's beauty, you will be treated to the sight of hundreds of crocuses in the church square if you visit in the spring. On Thursdays in the summer visitors can shop at the colorful antiques market located here at Lange Voorhout 4 and Parkstraat.

Located between The Hague and Scheveningen is Madurodam, a sort of Netherlands theme park, with all of the country's most important buildings reproduced in miniature. The tiny buildings and train tracks are built on a scale of 1:25 with great attention to detail, including the 3-mile train track and the hand-carved furniture. Kids love it. It was built by a man whose son died in the Dachau concentration camp. The park is at George Maduroplein 1 and is open daily in summer.

**Kampen** One of the most important Dutch medieval churches is the Bovenkerk on the Oudestraat. It was built by the family of masons that worked on Cologne's cathedral. Concerts are held here on Saturday afternoons in July and August.

**Kinderdijk** If it's windmills you want, come to the Kinderdijk, about eight miles north of Dordrecht. There are 18 windmills lined up along a drainage channel. They were built around 1740.

**Leiden** This university city is memorable in many ways. Its Rijksmuseum Van Oudheden (Rapenburg 28) is the country's main archaeological museum. In a courtyard in front of the entrance is one of its major exhibits, which is free of charge. It is the 1st-century Temple of Taffeh, a temple to the worship of Isis. About 400 years later it became a Christian church in Egypt. The Egyptian government gave the structure to the Dutch, who helped the Egyptians unearth lost civilizations. The one proviso of the gift was that no one should have to pay to see it.

For many Americans the highlight of a visit to Leiden is a visit to the Pieterskerk and the Jan Pesijn Hofje (on Kloksteeg, right by the church). Buried in the churchyard is John Robinson, leader of the Pilgrim Fathers. He lived in what is now the Jan Pesijn Hofje. He had been a pastor in the Church of England, but because of his Puritan leanings he had been suspended. Chosen to be pastor of a group of separatists in Gainsborough, he and the congregation went to Amsterdam in 1608 and then to Leiden in 1609, where the congregation grew to 300. He encouraged his members to sail via Plymouth to America, and 100 of them did. He stayed behind with the rest of the congregation. For more information on Robinson and his congregation, go down to the Leiden Pilgrim Collection at Vliet 45.

This is only one of the sites in Leiden related to America's Pilgrim forefathers. The Pilgrim Fathers stayed a short while in Leiden before setting out for Delftshaven (modern-day Delfshaven, in Rotterdam) where they would undertake their difficult journey to the New World. The original documents related to their stay are kept in the archives of the Stedelijk Museum De Lakenhal (Oude Singel 28–32). But the Public Reading Room of the City Record Office (Stadsarchief) at Dolhuissteeg 7 has reproductions of the documents as well as other historical materials.

The Leiden American Pilgrim Museum (Beschuitsteeg 9) is a new establishment, opened in 1997. On display are a historic furniture collection in a 16th-century house as well as copies of documents relating to the Pilgrim Fathers.

The Windmill Museum (Molenmuseum de Valk) is housed, not surprisingly, in a windmill. The mill at 2e Binnenvestgracht 1 was built in 1747 and had been worked by ten generations of millers up until 1964. The museum has seven floors, which contain the original milling machinery, living quarters, and an old forge.

**Lisse** For a good look at the Dutch flower industry visit the Keukenhof Gardens, the largest flower gardens in the world (absolutely gorgeous). Keukenhof is a flower-lover's delight. The 70-acre park and greenhouse complex on N208 is planted every spring with thousands of flowering bulbs. Huge crowds come to enjoy row after row of the Netherlands' favorite bloom, the tulip, as well as hyacinths and daffodils, at this, the world's largest flower show. Visit in late March to late May daily from 8:00 to 7:30.

**Naarden** One of the highlights in a visit to this town is the Grote Kerk on Marktstraat, a Gothic church, open afternoons during the summer. Its 20 wooden panels painted between 1510 and 1518 give you Old Testament history on one side and New Testament history on the other. The panels are based on drawings by Dürer. Because of the great acoustics in the church, there are several performances of Bach's *St. Matthew's Passion* before Easter each year.

The Comenius Museum (Kloosterstraat 33) is interesting as well. Comenius was a 17th-century religious exile from Moravia (today the Czech Republic). An outstanding Christian leader, he was also an outstanding philosopher and did groundbreaking work in the field of education.

> Beside us to guide us, our God with us joining,
> Ordaining, maintaining, His kingdom divine;
> So from the beginning, the fight we were winning;
> Thou, Lord, wast at our side, all glory be Thine!
>
> 17TH-CENTURY NETHERLANDS FOLK HYMN

**Nijmegen** Southeast of the city is the Biblical Open-Air Museum (Profetenlaan 2), which contains reconstructions of Holy Land villages, including a Galilean village, a Palestinian hamlet, and even "Bedouin goats' hair tents as inhabited by the patriarchs."

**Rotterdam** A large commercial city like this is not easy for a casual tourist to visit. Its big attraction is the Boymans-Van Beuningen Museum (Mathenesserlaan 18–20) with a staggering collection of paintings. On the first floor is the Flemish and Dutch religious art section with paintings by Bosch, Aertsen, Bruegel, and others. For kids, the Toy-Toy Museum (at Greene Wetgering 1) may be a fun stop.

Rotterdam's Delfshaven area was known as Delftshaven when the Pilgrims set sail from here. It is the last remaining bit of old Rotterdam, complete with rows of gabled buildings and a windmill. Today Delfshaven is known for its hip galleries, restaurants, and cafes.

**Scheveningen** Just a couple miles from its dignified neighbor, The Hague, is this fun-loving coastal resort on the North Sea. Besides the swimming, which is iffy, the city boasts a Sea Life Center with an excellent aquarium that has gone out of its way to be kid-friendly. An unusual transparent underwater tunnel allows visitors to walk through and see sharks, fish, eels, and octopuses overhead, as if they were walking on the ocean floor. Located at Strandweg 13, the aquarium is open daily, but only in the months of July and August.

**Spaarndam** Do you remember the story of the little boy who saved the country of the Netherlands by sticking his finger in the hole in the dike? Of course, it is all fiction; the story never happened.

But recently, to remember the boy, they put up a monument in Spaarndam 8 miles northeast of Haarlem.

**Tilburg** A few miles north of town is the De Efteling theme park, Holland's answer to Disneyland. The park is just outside Kunstheuval, north of Tilburg. It has a little bit of everything for everyone and is generally very crowded on summer weekends, which makes it even more like Disneyland.

**Utrecht** This city's past was a lot more exciting than its present. Utrecht was at one time the academic and religious center of the Netherlands. Lovely gabled houses and canals still share space with a large number of Gothic churches. The main cathedral square is home to the Domkerk on Domplein, a late-Gothic cathedral with a series of beautiful stained glass windows. Classical and carillon concerts are regularly played here. The Domtoren (cathedral tower) is across the street. It was connected to the cathedral until a hurricane in 1674 separated the two. The bell tower is the tallest in the country, its 465 steep steps leading to a great view. From a vantage point near the top you can see Amsterdam and Rotterdam if the weather is good. Guided tours are available on the hour. Don't try to navigate the tower's maze of passageways and steps without one.

At the Central Museum (Agnietenstraat 1) notice the realistic drawing by van Scorel, *Christ's Entry into Jerusalem,* and the painting by Terbrugghen, *The Calling of St. Matthew.*

The National Museum of Mechanical Musical Instruments (Rijksmuseum van Speelkok tot Pierement) at Buurkerhof 10 is home to a wide variety of musical machines, including street organs, music boxes, and even musical chairs. During the tour visitors can see performances on some of the instruments.

Catherine's Convent Museum (Museum Catharijneconvent) at Nieuwegracht 63 includes the Netherlands' largest collection of medieval art, much of which has religious themes. Also on display are holy relics and vestments.

**Zaanstad** If you've come to Holland looking for windmills, you may have to look for a few days before you find one. However, when you come to Zaandam and the re-created Dutch village of Zaanse Schans, you have come to the right place. Some of the windmills here grind mustard and produce oil. But you can also see a clock museum, see how wooden shoes are made, and take a boat trip on the Zaan River.

**Zutphen** About ten miles south of Deventer, this rather ordinary town has a large Gothic church, St. Walburgskerk at Kerkhof 3, with a spectacular library, the Librije, in a side chapel. Established in 1560, it was one of the first libraries built for the general public and symbolized the Protestant desire to bring education to the masses. It contains early illuminated manuscripts and one manuscript attributed to Thomas à Kempis.

**Zwolle** Thomas à Kempis, author of the classic, *Of the Imitation of Christ,* moved to an Augustinian monastery near here in about 1400 and spent most of the rest of his life here. The old city in the shape of a star fortress is moated, and the old Grote Kerk on Grote Kerkplein has been recently restored.

# *Norway*

Norwegian Information Service
  US 212-885-9700
  UK 020-7839-2650
*Web sites*
  Entire country www.norway.org/travel
  Scandinavia www.goscandinavia.com
For a complete list of updated links, visit www.christian-traveler.com

### *Country in a Capsule*

*Size:* Norway is about 50 percent larger than Minnesota, but with about the same population. Oslo has about the same population as Minneapolis; Bergen has about the same population as St. Paul.

*Religion:* More than 90 percent of the people are on the membership rolls of the Evangelical Lutheran Norwegian State Church, but the percentage of those who attend regularly is small. The largest Protestant groups, besides the Lutherans, are Baptists, Pentecostals, and Methodists. There are about 25,000 Roman Catholics in the country. Historically the country has seen many religious revivals, both within the state church and outside of it, and the church has traditionally been quite missionary-minded.

*Language:* Norwegian is the national language, but English is the main foreign language taught in schools, so you will have no trouble unless you go to Lapland.

*Money:* The official currency is the krone, which is equal to about 11 cents.

*Food:* Norwegians like breakfast, so be ready for a large buffet of smoked fish, cheese, sausage, cold meats, and whole grain breads to start your day. Cod, salmon, and herring may be part of your evening meal, and if you are a bit daring, you might ask for reindeer or whale meat. A national specialty is brown goat cheese.

*Shopping:* Oslo has the best selection and is known for pewter, silver, glass, and sheepskin. You will also be attracted to the brightly colored and patterned knitware.

*Brief history:* Norway was unified under Harald I Fairhair around A.D. 900, Christianized under St. Olaf about a hundred years later, and internationalized by the Vikings around the turn of the millennium when they conquered Normandy, Iceland, Greenland, and parts of the British Isles. The Black Death decimated the country in the 14th century, killing about two-thirds of the population, and Norway passed under Danish rule. Norway became Lutheran with the Reformation in the 16th century, but remained under Danish control until the early 1800s, when Sweden took over. It wasn't until 1905 that Norway became an autonomous constitutional monarchy.

**Oslo** With a half million residents, Oslo is the largest city in Norway as well as its capital.

*The Oslo Cathedral (Domkirke)* on Stortorvet 1 was consecrated in 1697 and has gone through a number of renovations since that time. You may find the church modest in comparison with cathedrals of other European capitals, but take the time to visit the interior with its rich collection of Baroque treasures, including a carved wooden pulpit and altarpiece. The ceiling frescoes are downright modern, crafted after World War II by Hugo Lous Mohr. Behind the cathedral you'll find a nice variety of restaurants, shopping arcades, and, frequently, street musicians.

*Parks and museums.* Vigeland Park is a unique park featuring nearly 200 life-sized statues by Gustav Vigeland. The park's most famous statue is that of a baby boy stamping his foot and furiously scrunching his face. It is known as *Sinnatgaggen* (The Really Angry One). The park is free and always open and there is plenty of room for a picnic or a leisurely stroll. Across from the park is the Vigeland Museum, open daily with a small admission charge. It displays many of the plaster models for the Vigeland Park sculptures. The museum was built by the city in exchange for the artist's work.

Bornekunstkmuseet (Children's Art Museum), Lille Forensun 4, was started by a Russian immigrant who collected children's drawings from more than 150 countries to display here.

There are two historical museums that are always a hit with families. The Norwegian Folk Museum (Norsk Folkemuseum) on Bygdøy peninsula houses more than 150 centuries-old historic farmhouses taken from all over the country and reassembled in this large park. An entire section of 19th-century Oslo was moved here. You'll want to pay special attention to the 12th-century wooden stave church, a style of church unique to Norway. To reach the Folk Museum, take the ferry from Rådhusbryggen (City Hall Wharf) and walk along the well-marked road to Museumsvn. 10.

Norway is practically synonymous with Vikings, and you can whet your appetite for the ancient people at the Viking Ship Museum (Vikingskiphuset) at Huk Av. 35. The museum's chief attractions are three wonderfully preserved 9th-century ships that were last used by the Vikings as royal burial chambers off Oslofjord. Visitors are also able to view the treasures that were buried with the bodies. The beautiful workmanship visible in the ships and jewelry will convince you that the Vikings were more than just warriors.

Also on Bygdøy Peninsula are several maritime museums. The *Kon-Tiki* Museum at Bygdøynesveien 36 features the world-famous log raft *Kon-Tiki* and other artifacts associated with native scientist Thor Heyerdahl's voyage in 1947. Heyerdahl and his crew sailed an incredible 4,300 miles from Peru to Polynesia. The Norwegian Maritime Museum (Norsk Sjøfartsmuseum) next door at

Bygdøynesveien 37 features the maritime history and culture of Norway. The museum's Boat Hall is a highlight, including several small vessels, the polar ship *Gjoa* used by Roald Amundsen, and a three-masted schooner. The polar ship *Fram,* housed at the Frammuseet is on display at Bygdønes. Fridtjof Nansen sailed the ship across the Arctic late in the 19th century, and about 15 years later, in 1911, Roald Amundsen made history in the *Fram* as the first man to reach the South Pole.

*Boat excursions.* Norway's stunning natural beauty is a chief draw to the visitors that arrive here every year. Although the area around Oslo isn't considered fjord country, you can enjoy the lovely coastal towns nearby by boat. A round-trip one-day excursion leaves Oslo for Kragerø, the island of Jomfruland, and Risør. Refreshments are served on board. For more information contact the Norway Information Center at Vestbanepl. 1, at the Central Station east of Strandgt., or phone them at 22-83-00-50.

*Sleigh rides.* If you should find yourself in Norway in the winter, consider enjoying the area by horse-drawn sleigh. Rides are offered through Vangen Skistue. For more information, contact Laila and Jon Hamre, Fjell, 1410 Siggerud, or phone them at 64-86-54-81.

*The Holmenkollen ski jump* on a hillside outside Oslo will provide you with a panoramic view of the city and its fjord. It was used in the 1952 Winter Olympics. An elevator will take you part of the way up, but you will have to manage the last 114 steps yourself. There is also a ski museum here exhibiting skis and sleds going back to A.D. 600.

**Ålesund** At the turn of the 20th century what became known as the Great Fire destroyed much of the city of Ålesund. As a result, much of the old town was rebuilt with a unique collection of art nouveau buildings constructed between 1904 and 1907. Besides putting Ålesund on the map for its internationally recognized architecture, the new old town gave the city a romantic and colorful flavor.

To enjoy the marine life native to this area, consider visiting the Atlantic Sea Park two miles west of town. It is the largest aquarium in Scandinavia and is open year-round.

**Bergen** The city of Bergen is the second largest in Norway and is considered the capital of the fjords. Hardangerfjorden, Sognefjord, and Nordfjord are three of the deepest and most popular of the area's fjords. To see them best, take a guided boat tour. A wide variety of excursions are available, in varying lengths and distances. Contact the Visitor Information Center at Bryggen 7, or by phone at 55-32-14-80 to see what's available when you're there.

*Old harbor area.* In spite of numerous fires in past years, much of medieval Bergen has survived. The old harbor area known as Bryggen is home to weathered wooden houses, Hanseatic-era warehouses, and cobbled lanes surrounded by no less than seven mountains. The row of 14th-century painted wooden buildings facing the harbor is really charming, and of course it is hard not to be aware of the Fisketorget (fish market). Try an open-face salmon sandwich while you are there. To get a sense of Bergen's medieval trading days, visit the Hanseatiske Museum at Finnegårdsgaten 1A. The museum sheds light on the trading practices of members of the medieval guild known as the Hanseatic League. It is located in one of the oldest and best-preserved of the city's wooden buildings and is furnished in 16th-century style.

## SCANDINAVIAN BEAUTY

All of Norway is a place of natural beauty. More than nearly any other country, this is a land where creation rules and humans adapt. Norwegians seem happy enough about this, with a passion for enjoying outdoor activities, like hiking and cross-country skiing that is virtually unsurpassed anywhere else.

Even those who have never been there know that Norway's unique natural beauty lies primarily in its fjords. North and east of Stavanger are the Ryfylke fjords, the southern end of Norway's famous fjord country. The Ryfylke fjords beautifully meld mountain, sea, and forest.

Hardangerfjorden, Sognefjord, and Nordfjord, near the city of Bergen, are three of the deepest and most popular of the area's fjords and are best enjoyed by a guided boat tour.

*Getting around.* It rains here 275 days a year, so you will probably see rain during your visit. Because of the rain, the gardens are gorgeous, and because much of the city is on the waterfront, it is compact and easy to get around, if you don't mind a few hills. If you are feeling energetic and if the clouds aren't too low, you may want to climb the Rosenkrantz Tower, which was built in the 1560s. But a best city view can be had if you take the funicular to the top of Mount Fløyen or a cable car to the top of Mount Ulriken. The popular Fløyen Funicular, the Fløybanen, located behind Bryggen on Øvregt, climbs 1,070 feet to the top of Fløyen, one of the city's seven mountains. From the top of Fløyen you can walk leisurely down the mountain back to town. Another enjoyable way to get a quick view of the city is to ride the brightly painted Bergen Express miniature train on an hour round-trip.

*Churches.* Two churches vie for the honor of being Bergen's oldest building. The Mariakirke on Dreggen is a Romanesque stone structure dating from the 12th century. In the choir are 15 statues—the 12 apostles, plus Moses, John the Baptist, and Paul. The Fantoft stave church was built in Sognefjord, also in the 12th century and was later moved to the southern end of Bergen on Paradis, just off E39. It was burned down in 1992 and then carefully reconstructed. A little bit younger, but not much, is the Bergen Domkirke, the Bergen Cathedral at Kong Oscar's Gate.

*Flowers.* If you are a flower lover, visit the Rhododendrarium at Stromgarten and Kaigarten and discover why Bergen was named the City of Rhododendrons. It contains 82 varieties.

*Composer Edvard Grieg's home and workshop* is nearby at Troldhaugen and is worth a stop. Grieg is best known as the composer of the *Peer Gynt Suite.*

*Excursions.* From Bergen you can take a boat ride into Sognefjord, Norway's longest and deepest fjord. The walls rise more than 3,000 feet straight up from the water in some places. From Bergen you can also take a one-day excursion called "Norway in a Nutshell," starting with a train trip to Voss, then another train making the steep descent to Flam, then a steamer to Gudvangen, a coach back to Voss, and then the train back to Bergen. What an unforgettable day that is!

**Bodø** The city of Bodø has the distinction of being the last stop on the European rail station and the first major town above the Arctic Circle. The midnight sun is visible in the islands from May 27 to July 17.

Even here are reminders of Christianity's prevalence. The contemporary Bodø Cathedral (Domkirke) at Torv Gate 12 is stunning. The cathedral's spire is actually separated from the main building, which houses rich modern tapestries that are worth seeing. A war memorial stands in front of the building. Two miles east of the town center, at Gamle Riks Vei 68, is the Bodin Kirke, a church dating from the early 13th century. The Baroque altarpiece inside is the building's most elaborate ornamentation, but in spite of its simplicity the Bodin Kirke is the area's most famous and beloved house of worship.

Just north of Bodø are the Lofoten Islands, a 118-mile chain of mountains rising from the ocean floor. The islands' local farms, fishing villages, and fjords are especially popular with tourists during the summer months. The town of Lofotr is home to the Viking Museum of Borg, south of Svolvær on Rte. E10. The museum has a reconstruction of a Viking chieftain's home. Inside, a fireplace and cod liver oil lamps help to bring visitors back to the year 900. Keep your eyes open for the chieftain himself. He can share a wealth of stories of Viking raids and expeditions.

**Drøbak** About 21 miles south of Oslo is this Christmas town. According to Norwegian legend, Julenisse is a Christmas elf who lives in the woods and has magical powers. This elf now has his own post office, Julenissens Posthuset in Drøbak at Julenissens 1440, and responds to about 30,000 letters a year from children all over the world. In the town's central square is the Tregaardens Julehus (Christmas House). It was once a mission for sailors who couldn't get up the fjord to Oslo because it had frozen over. Now it sells Christmas wares and gifts.

**Flåm** There's not much to do in Flåm, but there is a lot to see and many exciting places to go *from* Flåm. One of the most scenic train rides in Europe goes from Myrdal in the mountains down to Flåm. Or you can take a ferry to Balestrand and watch the fjords go by.

**Heddal** The largest stave church in Norway, and the most visited attraction in the Telemark, the region south of Oslo, is three miles west of Notodden in the small community of Heddal. About 85 feet high and 65 feet long, the church was built about 1147. Dedicated to the Virgin Mary, the Heddal Stave Church is considered the architectural wonder of southern Norway.

**Kabelvag** On the spectacular Lofoten islands, the northern islands known for their fishing and art colonies, is this quiet town with one of the largest wooden churches in the country. A century ago, the 1,200-seat church was built to minister to the fishermen, but now there aren't 1,200 people in the entire village. Although the church was built in the 1800s, it has a chandelier dating back to the 12th century and an altarpiece to 1520.

**Kongsberg** This town, about 52 miles southwest of Oslo, was Norway's silver mining center for more than 300 years. The mines are closed now, but the Royal Mint is still going and is worth a visit. The Norwegian Mining Museum and the Royal Mint Museum are in the same building at Hyttegt 3. During the summer children are allowed to pan for silver.

The Kongsberg Kirke in the town center was built in the heyday of the silver mines here and the gilded Baroque building shows it. It seats 3,000. Organ concerts are given Wednesdays at 6:00 P.M. in the summer.

**Kristiansand** This is Norway's summer vacation capital and one of the most prosperous cities of southern Norway. The third-largest church in the country is the Gothic Revival cathedral on Kirkegaten, built in 1885. During the summer there are frequent concerts here and each year in mid-May it hosts a weeklong International Church Music Festival. While you are here, take a look at Oddernes Kirke at Jegersbergeveien 6, one of the oldest churches in the country. A runic stone in the cemetery says that it was built by Oyvind in 1040.

Kristiansand Dyrepark at 4609 Kardemomme By is actually five parks (a water park, a forest park, an entertainment park, a fairy-tale park, and a zoo). The zoo, incidentally, is Europe's largest breeding ground for Bactrian camels, in case you wanted to know. The fairy-tale park is a village replicated from a Norwegian children's book. It has actors playing townsfolk, shopkeepers, pirates, and even a trio of robbers who wouldn't scare anyone. If the kids are enjoying the park so much they don't want to leave, families can stay overnight in apartments or nearby cottages.

**Lillehammer** This popular ski resort town of 25,000 people became world-famous when it hosted the 1994 Winter Olympics. Located at the northern end of the long narrow Lake Mjøsa, Lillehammer can be reached by way of a two-hour train ride from Oslo's central train station (Sentralstasjonen), or if you have more time, consider traveling by water. You can enjoy the area's natural beauty by way of a paddle steamer, the D/S Skibladner, which travels the length of the lake in about six hours, making brief stops along the way. For more information, contact the Lillehammer Tourist Office, at Lilletorget, Lillehammer, Norway, or by phone 61-25-92-99.

It's still possible to view the Winter Olympic sites. The Norwegian Olympic Museum is in Hakosns Hall. Nearby, if you like more excitement, you can try a downhill ski and bobsled simulator ride yourself. For those over 12, the Bobsled on Wheels is a five-minute ride that replicates an Olympic bobsled ride. You may be interested in going through the Maihaugen folk museum at Maihaugenveien 1, which is a collection of historic farm buildings and a stave church. It is one of the largest open-air museums in northern Europe and is popular with children. More than 100 historic buildings have been relocated here. Visitors can see costumed interpreters demonstrating ancient tools and crafts in a variety of re-created workshops. It is also a collection of other odds and ends, begun by a dentist who allowed his patients to bring him whatever they had around the house in exchange for his dental work. Guided tours are available in English.

Eight miles north of Lillehammer is Hunderfossen Park, on Fåberg., an amusement park that claims to have the world's biggest troll. It has lots of other things too, from rides to a petting zoo, an energy center, and a theater.

**Numedal** Numedal is a beautiful and picturesque valley in an inland mountainous range in southern Norway northwest of Oslo. The area is characterized by lovely old farms and scenic stave churches. Torpo Stavkirke, on Rte. 7 in the nearby village of Torpo, built in the mid-1100s is one of the oldest remaining stave churches. The west and south portals are carved with interwoven animal motifs. The vaulting is supported on carved capitals and covered with paintings from the 13th century depicting Christ with the apostles and scenes from St. Margaret's life. Farther into the valley are two more stave churches, one at Uvdal and the other at Nore. They were apparently decorated by the same artist. At Uvdal you see a naive representation of Adam and Eve and on the pulpit you find scenes showing the four Gospel writers, but you may wonder what St. Matthew is doing with a billy goat.

**Røros** About 97 miles from Trondheim is this old coppermining town, which looks a bit more like a German hamlet than a Norwegian farm village. Its main attraction is Old Town with its 250-year-old workers' cottages. Tours through the town end at Roroskirke, (Roros Church), an eight-sided stone building built in 1784. It seats 1,600 even though only 3,500 people live in the town now. Outside of the town is an old copper mine, Olavsgruva, and if you have warm clothing you might enjoy a trip to the depths of the earth.

## NORWAY'S STAVE CHURCHES

Stave churches are unique to Norway and as such are considered a national heritage. Fewer than 30 remain today, although originally there were hundreds of them. These are wooden church structures mainly from the 11th, 12th, and 13th centuries. They were constructed with wooden planks, which were staked vertically into the ground or base. The earliest ones were rectangular, but later ones incorporated different styles. They were richly ornamented with carvings illustrating various animals, some real, some mythological. The top of the gables was often adorned with dragons to guard against evil spirits. Built without windows, the stave churches got their only light from small round openings under the roof. As the first Christian churches in Norway, the stave churches mixed some elements from Viking mythology with Christian symbolism, and this naturally was a problem to leaders of the Scandinavian Reformation.

**Stavanger** This can be a delightful city if you overlook the oil rigs out in the sea. It is a bustling, thriving international city because the oil industry came in at a time when the fishing industry was dying. It used to be called the sardine capital of the world, and if you are interested, you can tour the Norsk Hermetikkmuseum (Canning Museum) at Øvre Strandgt. 88A and see how they managed to get all those sardines in those little cans. If you like trivia, you should know that the inventor of the sardine can key was from Stavanger.

Stavanger's old quarter is still a lovely place to visit, with its narrow, cobbled streets and clapboard houses. It dates from the 8th century, and you can get a taste of those old days at Ullandhaug, a reconstructed Iron Age farm on Grannesvn.

Make sure that you also visit Stavanger Domkirke in the city center that dates from 1125. The pulpit is extremely ornate with woodcarvings illustrating Scripture from creation to the flight into Egypt by Mary and Joseph and the baby Jesus.

If you have a Norwegian heritage, you can trace your lineage at Det Norske Utvandresenteret (Norwegian Emigration Center). It's located on the fourth floor of the Tax Office (Ligningskontoret) at Nedre Strandgt. 31. While you are tracing your roots, your kids will be more interested in going to the Kongeparken Amusement Park, 4330 Algard, which has a 281-foot figure of Gulliver and a dinosaur exhibit in addition to a variety of rides.

North and east of Stavanger are the Ryfylke fjords, which form the southern end of Norway's famous fjord country. The city is a good base from which to explore this beautiful area. Its "white fleet" of sea buses make daily excursions into even the most remote of the Ryfylke fjords. Although its ties to Christianity are doubtful, Pulpit Rock (Prekestolen) is a great place to visit. The views are heavenly. For detailed information contact the city's Visitor Information Center at Rosenkildehuset, Rosenkildetorget 1, or phone them at 51-85-92-00.

**Stiklestad** A turning point in Norwegian history took place here on July 29, 1030. In an attempt to unify and Christianize the country, King Olav Haraldsson fought the superior forces of some local rulers here, and King Olav was slain. Though he lost the battle, his death was looked on as a martyrdom, and he became a symbol of Norway. Soon after his death Christianity spread throughout the country, churches were formed, monasteries started, and the practice of writing in Norwegian became commonplace. Every year on the anniversary of the battle, a pageant is staged in an open-air theater here with 350 participants and 20,000 spectators. It depicts the king's final days and gives an account of his life and beliefs. In the Nasionale Kultursenter an exhibit called Stiklestad 1030 reveals the background of the battle through scenes based on archaeological finds in the area.

The Stiklestad Kirke is a Romanesque edifice dating from about 1150. It replaced an earlier wooden church that was built on the spot where King Olav is believed to have fallen. Frescoes on the walls of the nave show biblical stories. Paintings in the chancel show scenes of Olav's historic battle as well as alleged miracles that have been credited to Olav.

**Tromsø** Most visitors never get as far north as Tromsø, well above the Arctic Circle. The town has named itself "the Paris of the North," referring to its vibrant nightlife aided by the midnight

## OLAV HARALDSSON (995-1030)

As a teenager he was a marauding Viking, raiding Sweden, Denmark, Holland, Spain, and England. At Canterbury, he killed the archbishop, pelting him to death with bones. But then—and no one knows the circumstances—he became a Christian. Returning to Norway, he proclaimed himself king. Reigning from Trondheim, he reorganized the government and sought to establish Christianity as the religion of Norway. However, when he punished piracy and raiding that were the Vikings' way of life, he lost his popular support. His opponents put together a huge army, and Olav's forces were defeated. Olav was slain at Stiklestad, but that is not the end of the story. A year later clergymen and laymen started calling Olav a martyr and a saint, and soon Norway became Christian. Thus Olav accomplished by his death what he could not do in his life.

Sites associated with Haraldsson are located in Trondheim and Stiklestad, Norway, and in Canterbury, England.

sun. The arctic town is surrounded by permanently snow-capped mountain peaks. If you should find yourself in the Far North, be sure to visit the Arctic church on the E78. The stunning church's eastern wall is made entirely of stained glass. The Tromsø Cathedral, on Kirkegata, is one of Norway's largest wooden churches and the world's northern-most Protestant cathedral.

**Trondheim** This city in northern Norway is the country's third largest and the original capital. It is also called the spiritual capital of the country. Founded in 997 by the Viking King Olav Tryggvason, it has a rich medieval history.

Nidarus Domkirke at Kongsgårdsgt. 2 is Scandinavia's largest building dating back to medieval times. The first church here was built by King Olav Kyrre in 1070, and the oldest wing of the present building dates to the 12th century. The west wall is lined with statues of biblical characters and Norwegian bishops and kings. It is where Norway's kings and queens are crowned, and so you can see the crown jewels here in the North Chapel. Olav was canonized in 1164, and afterward pilgrims came to this town for several hundred years. For a good view of the city, climb to the cathedral tower.

The Trondelag Folk Museum at Sverresborg Allé just outside the city has 60 period buildings including a small 12th-century stave church. Also worth a visit are the Museum of Applied Arts, across the Bybrobridge at Munkegata 5, with special collections of arts and crafts, and the Ringve Museum at Lade Allé 60 with a collection of unusual musical instruments. Included are an Amati violin from 1612, a British harpsichord from 1767, and, yes, an American jukebox from 1948.

**Vinterbro** The town of Vinterbro is home to Norway's largest amusement park, known as Tusenfryd. More than 50 attractions include a roller coaster, carousels, shops, an outdoor stage, and a variety of eateries. Kids are sure to enjoy Vikingelandet, or Viking Land, a re-creation of life during the days of the Vikings. Visit trading centers, a boat-building operation, jewelry making, a blacksmith, and farm animals. You can also try your hand at archery, with a little assistance from a "Viking," or join "Leif Eriksson" on a trip into a hidden mountain cave. Tusenfryd is open only during the summer months and is located about 12 miles southeast of Oslo on E18.

# *Portugal*

Portuguese Trade and Tourism Office
  US 212-354-4403
  Canada 416-921-7376
  UK 020-7494-1441
*Web site*
  Entire country www.portugal.org
For a complete list of updated links, visit www.christiantraveler.com

### *Country in a Capsule*

*Size:* About the size of Indiana with twice as many people.

*Population:* About 10 million, with 1.5 million in Lisbon and 350,000 in Porto.

*Religion:* Officially Portugal is 95 percent Catholic, but only about 70 percent are practicing Catholics. The major Protestant groups here are Pentecostals (more than 500 churches) and Baptists (about 70 churches).

*Language:* Portuguese, and proud of it. There are differences in the language between north and south. They love it when you try to say some Portuguese words.

*Money:* Escudos. At this writing, about 200 escudos equal one American dollar.

*Food:* Fish is basic, and cod (bacalhou) is the most common fish. Pork is the favorite meat, and their roast suckling pig is delicious. Most common dessert is flan. Try the pudim flan, a cream caramel.

*Shopping:* Get embroidered linens and cottons along the coast. To the north, filigree work. Antiques anyone? Try the antiques fair on the second and last Sundays of the month at Sao Pedro de Sintra in Sintra.

*Brief history:* When the Roman Empire collapsed in the 5th century, Portugal was conquered first by Germanic tribes (and somewhat Christianized then). Then in 711 it was conquered by the Muslim Moors. Slowly Christian kingdoms of the north began to retake the land. Lisbon became the capital in 1256, and a university was started there in 1288. Portugal's golden age was the time of Vasco da Gama, Magellan, and other explorers in the late 1400s and early 1500s. After a few years of Spanish rule and ups and downs of a monarchy, Salazar headed a dictatorial regime during the middle of the 20th century. Since 1976 Portugal has been recovering from Salazar. It is now a republic with an elected president.

**Lisbon** Like Rio de Janeiro, Lisbon has a huge statue of Christ (*Christo Rei*) overlooking the city. The statue on the Tagus River depicts Jesus with arms outstretched, blessing the city. It was built as a thanks to God for keeping Portugal out of World War II. For a great view, take an elevator to the top.

*The Belém Cultural Center (Centro Cultural de Belém)* hosts a wide range of concerts and exhibitions. Many of the center's offerings are free, including recitals at three Lisbon cathedrals, the Igreja do Carmo, the Igreja de São Roque, and the Sé. You might also ask about the popular annual Early Music and Baroque Festival presented in churches and museums throughout Lisbon every spring. Stop in the office located at Praça do Império or call ahead, 01/361-2400.

*In the center of Lisbon* is the Biaxa, the old business center of town. The city's main square is the Praça Dom Pedro IV. Here's where the entire family can enjoy window shopping as well as eating ice cream cones as you amble down the pedestrian streets.

*Lisbon's Upper Town (Bairro Alto)* consists largely of 18th- and 19th-century buildings, including restaurants, churches, and antique shops. Because this part of town is literally upper—it sits on a hill—you can enter and leave this district by funicular railway (Elevador da Glória) or by street elevator (Elevador de Santa Justa). The railway is on the western side of Avenida da Liberdade by the Praça dos Restauradores, and it offers the best view. The elevator is enclosed in an elaborate Gothic-style tower built in 1902 by Raul Mesnier, a Portuguese student of Gustave Eiffel, who was famous for his own tower. The railway is at Calçada da Glória; the elevator is at Largo do Carmo.

> Sing, choirs of angels, sing in exultation,
> O sing, all ye citizens of heaven above!
> Glory to God, all glory in the highest;
> O come, let us adore Him, Christ the Lord.
>
> KNOWN AS THE PORTUGUESE HYMN, PROBABLY WRITTEN AT THE PORTUGUESE EMBASSY IN LONDON

*Churches.* A narrow walkway from the street elevator (Elevador de Santa Justa) will take visitors under a huge flying buttress of the Carmelite Church (Igreja do Carmo). The 14th-century church lost its roof in a devastating 1755 earthquake, but its Gothic arches remain, as do the sacristy and nave of the church. Inside is the Museu Arqueológico (Archeological Museum). Free recitals take place here regularly—ask at the information area or call the Belém Cultural Center (Centro Cultural de Belém). See entry above.

Don't let the plain exterior of Igreja de São Roque church on Largo Trinidade Coelho fool you. Its interior is not just beautiful, it's stunning. The 18th-century Chapel of St. John the Baptist (Capela de São João Baptista) at Largo Trinidade Coelho is decorated with rare stones and metals and mosaics that appear more like paintings than tilework. It was built in Rome for a Papal Mass, then taken down and shipped to Portugal. Scenes from the Book of Revelation by artists of the Italian School are painted on the wooden ceiling. Note also the first chapel on the left with the paintings *Nativity* and *Adoration of the Magi*. Visit the Museum of Sacred Art (Museu de Arte Sacra) next door to see 16th- to

18th-century religious paintings. Free recitals take place here regularly. For information, call the Belém Cultural Center (Centro Cultural de Belém).

Lisbon's Cathedral (Sé) on Largo da Sé is a stark Romanesque building founded in 1150 to commemorate the defeat of the Moors three years earlier. Visit the beautiful 13th-century cloister and the sacristy, which contains a number of treasures including the relics of the martyr St. Vincent. Free recitals take place here regularly. Call the Belém Cultural Center (Centro Cultural de Belém).

*Museums.* The Gulbenkian Museum at Av. de Berna 45 features masterpieces by Rembrandt, Rubens, Renoir, Rodin, and others, but it also has sections devoted to Egyptian, Greek, and Oriental exhibits. Of the 40 museums in Lisbon, this may be the best.

The Ancient Art Museum (Museu Nacional de Arte Antiga), located at Rua S. Pedro de Alcântara 45, is housed in a 17th-century palace in Lapa, a wealthy district of Lisbon. The museum was founded in 1884 and has a large number of religious paintings, sculptures, and artifacts dating back to the 12th century. It contains works from some of the great European masters like Bosch, van Eyck, and Raphael. The museum's highlights include the St. Vincent altarpiece, created in the late 15th century, and Dürer's *St. Jerome.* There is also a good cafeteria here with seating in a garden overlooking the river.

Portugal is known for its fabulous tile, and the National Tile Museum (Museu Nacional do Azulejo) displays some of the country's finest. Located on Rua da Madre de Deus 4 in the cloisters of the 16th-century Madre de Deus convent, the development of the unique art form is traced from its introduction by the Moors to modern times, spanning the 15th through the 20th centuries. Take a look at the convent's church too. Its 18th-century interior is fabulously decorated and features a rococo altarpiece.

Adults and older children will enjoy displays of beautifully crafted puppets at the Puppet Museum (Museu da Marioneta). Characters range from those in 17th-century operas to knights, princesses, and devils, and the museum also features videos of puppet shows and occasional live performances on a small stage. The puppets feature distorted, gargoyle-like faces that very young children may find scary. The museum is located at Largo Rodrigues de Freitas 19.

Believe it or not, the Museu Nacional do Coches (National Coach Museum) at Plaça Alonso de Albuquerque is visited by more tourists than any other place in Lisbon. Here you will see a 17th-century coach in which Philip II of Spain rode from Madrid to Lisbon to see his new possession.

*St. George's Castle (Castelo de São Jorge)* is a Moorish fortress sitting on the site of a fort used by the Visigoths as early as the 5th century. The inner walls enclose the ruins of a Muslim palace used as a residence for Portuguese kings until the 1500s. The outer walls contain the restored medieval church of Santa Cruz, a few houses and some gift shops. The beautiful grounds and terraced gardens inside the castle offer wonderful views of the city. It's also the home of swans, turkeys, ducks, ravens, and peacocks. The castle is located at Rua da Costa do Castelo, and entrance is free.

*Parks and zoo.* Some three miles northeast of Lisbon's city center is the Park of the Nations (Parque das Nacões), a three-mile-long section of riverfront park that builds on what remains of Expo '98. Included within the park are restaurants, a theater, an indoor stadium, exhibition halls, a marina, a cable-car ride, and Europe's biggest oceanarium.

The beautiful Lisbon Oceanarium (Oceanário de Lisboa) houses 25,000 fish, seabirds, and mammals. It is the first to include various world ocean habitats—North Atlantic, Pacific, Antarctic, and Indian Ocean—within one building. The oceanarium can be reached by footbridge at Doca dos Olivais.

If you enjoy the animals at the Lisbon Oceanarium, consider visiting the Lisbon Zoo (Zoo Lisboa). The zoo doesn't feature the spacious cages that Americans are used to seeing; in fact the animals look a bit cramped. But children may enjoy themselves here anyway. Located in the northwest part of town just off Avenida das Forças Armadas, it is also a major stop on the city's subway line.

*The Tower of Belém* on Av. da India is a great example of Manueline architecture, considered by some to be one of the finest examples. The Manueline style, unique to Portugal, is a richly Baroque style that incorporates maritime and religious themes. Carved stonework may include seashells, ropes, and anchors along with small crosses and saints. The tower was built in the early 16th century on an island in the Tagus River, but over the centuries the river changed course—now it stands near the river's north bank. The tower offers spectacular views of Lisbon, the Tagus River, and the Atlantic.

*Planetarium.* At the Planetario Calouste Gulbernkian, Praça Império, Belém, you can take an imaginary ride through the solar system, take a trip to the moon, and enjoy a journey across the polar regions.

*Boat trips and trolley rides.* Enjoy a boat trip on the Tagus. You will get a good view of Lisbon and also see a variety of craft from Venetian-style boats with triangular sails to larger commercial ships. Riding a trolley or tram in Lisbon can be a unique experience too. Most of these go back to the 1920s.

*Jerónimos Monastery (Mosteiro dos Jerónimos)* at Praça do Império (three miles from downtown in the Belém district) is known for its beautiful display of Manueline architecture, considered one of the best examples in the country. This structure was conceived and planned by King Manuel I in 1502. The profits from Portuguese explorer Vasco da Gama's spice trading in Africa, South America, and Asia helped to finance the project, and King Manuel ordered the monastery's construction to commemorate da Gama's achievements. Highlights of this grand monument to the Age of Discovery include the Cloister and the South Portal with their elaborate stone carvings.

## PORTUGAL'S AZULEJOS

Portugal's architecture is trademarked by the bright, vividly colored *azulejos*, or painted tiles, that decorate the facades of many buildings. The word derives from *al zuleiq*, the Arabic word for a small polished stone. The tile tradition in Portugal dates back to the Moors who lived in the country in medieval times. Highly decorative tiles can be found on many buildings, including churches, palaces, bars, houses, restaurants, railway stations, and Lisbon's subway stations. Many of the tiles depict Christian themes, such as the life of Christ, lives of the saints, or biblical scenes. Others are more secular, portraying the city and landscapes.

The production of *azulejos* has evolved through time, evolving from Manueline to art nouveau to modern 20th-century works of art. In some factories, the great masters of this typically Portuguese art still produce hand-painted tiles, despite the existence of new industrial techniques. The results are beautiful works of art, which continue to be a source of pride and part of Portugal's national heritage.

*Swimming in Lisbon.* The city beach at Costa da Caparica, south of the city, is good for swimming, although it is usually crowded. A better spot is 30 miles farther south at Port Porinho da Arrabida.

**Alcobaça** The Monastery at Alcobaça, built in the 12th century, is the largest church in Portugal and one of the world's first Gothic monuments, although its exterior facade was later changed to Baroque. Enjoy the beautiful halls and cloisters, the intricately carved tombs of Pedro I and Inês de Castro, and the kitchen with its enormous chimney.

**Algarve** The Algarve region is Portugal's answer to Spain's Costa del Sol. If you and your family like sunshine, swimming, and/or fishing, this is the place to go. If you enjoy crowds, go to the central part of the Algarve. The west and east ends are less commercial and less crowded.

The Algarve stretches across the whole of southern Portugal. Its wonderful beaches have attracted both European and American tourists. For families with children, there is a variety of things to enjoy. Zoomarine, The Big One, and Slide and Splash are all in the Albufeira area in the middle of the Algarve. The Aqua Show is farther east toward Quarteira.

**Almansil** Built in the 18th century, St. Lawrence Church (Igreja Matriz de São Lourenço) on N125 in Almansil is a masterpiece of *azulejos,* the uniquely Portuguese decorative tiles. The interior of the chapel, including the dome, is covered with exquisite blue and white tiles and further embellished with generous quantities of gold.

**Alveiro** This is an interesting fishing town of about 30,000 people. Canals, spanned by bridges, crisscross the city. The church and the museum are worth a visit. In the museum is a 14th-century painting of the crucifixion in which Christ's expression changes depending on the angle from which you are looking.

**Batalha** The 15th-century monastery of Batalha is a stunning example of Gothic and Manueline architecture. Its official name is the Monastery of Santa Maria da Vitória and it was built to celebrate a military victory. Its intricate stonework and stunning stained glass windows make this building unforgettable. It is considered one of Portugal's greatest monuments. Entrance to the monastery is through the adjoining church of the same name.

**Braga** About three miles east of town is Bom Jesus do Monte (Good Jesus of the Mountain). An intricately carved Baroque staircase climbs the mountain, representing an upward spiritual journey. Pilgrims and tourists climb, resting in the Chapel of Christ's Agony in the Garden and the Chapel of the Kiss of Judas, among others. They then climb the Staircase of the Five Senses and the Staircase of the Three Virtues. At the top is the church, the Igreja do Bom Jesus, outside of which are eight statues of people who condemned Christ, including Herod and Pilate. Built in the 18th century, the entire Bom Jesus do Monte complex was designed to give Christians a pilgrimage site a bit closer to home than Palestine. You can take a cab or the water-powered funicular if you don't care to walk up the hill. But you'll miss many of the sights if you do.

**Cascais** Once merely a small fishing village, Cascais is today a well-developed resort town. It's an enjoyable stop on the Atlantic, especially in the harbor area and around Largo 5 Outubro. Shop for souvenirs like local lace, or have lunch at a cafe or restaurant. Nearby is the

## BONITO

The Portuguese word for beautiful is *bonito*. Try to remember that word, as it will likely come in handy. Portugal, often left out of European travel itineraries, has more than its share of natural beauty, from its beautiful beaches in the southern Algarve to the remote mountainous region of the north.

Peneda Gerês National Park and the Buçaco Forest offer some of the most scenic hiking you'll find anywhere in Portugal, and both are scattered with bits of Christian history as well. Peneda Gerês is located in the northeastern corner of the country and offers superb mountain vistas, waterfalls, and the Vilarinho das Furnas reservoir, surrounded by hiking trails and good swimming opportunities. The little *espigueiros* located throughout the park—granite tomblike boxes raised on short columns and decorated with crosses—are actually granaries, which keep grain off the ground and out of the reach of hens and rodents.

Buçaco, located north of Coimbra in central Portugal, was a monastic retreat in the 6th century. Today the area is part forest and part arboretum, and the hiking is simply beautiful. The forest's highest point, *Cruz Alta*, recognizable by its large cross, has glorious views as far as the sea.

The Berlenga Islands on Portugal's Atlantic shore feature stunning views of the ocean. People as diverse as monks, fishermen, and biologists have all called the islands home at one time or another. The largest island, Berlenga Grande, is a nature preserve and can be reached from the mainland in about one hour. Enjoy watching seabirds like the guillemot and herring gull as you soak up the sun's rays. Or rent a small boat at the island's jetty to explore the reefs and grottoes around the island. *Bonito!*

253

most popular natural attraction, the Boca do Inferno, or Mouth of Hell. Don't let its evil-sounding name scare you; it's merely a lovely natural grotto where the sea pounds in with great force. Entrance to the grotto is free.

The Church of Our Lady of the Assumption (Igreja de Nossa Senhora da Assunção) on Largo da Assunção features 17th-century paintings by native-born Portuguese artist Josefa de Óbidos.

**Coimbra** This is Portugal's old university city with a school that dates back to 1307. Take time to inspect 16th-century St. Michael's Chapel at the university. You will note the 17th-century Adam and Eve tile paintings flanking the rope archway. The 2,100 pipe 18th-century German-built organ is notable for its horizontal "trumpet" pipes that are unique to Spain and Portugal. King John's Library, with gold leaf everywhere, houses 30,000 books, all from before 1755 and all in Latin, Greek, or Hebrew. The Old University is on Rua José Falcão.

Also in Coimbra is the Old Cathedral (Sé Velha) on Largo da Sé Velha. The chapel to the right is one of the best examples of Renaissance design in the country. Notice the apostles looking at Jesus while musical angels surround them. Also to the left in the Chapel of St. Peter is a carving of Peter being crucified upside down.

A couple blocks south of town across the Santa Clara Bridge is Portugal dos Pequenitos or "Little Portugal." Kids as well as adults love it. The great buildings and monuments of Portugal are shown in miniature. Portugal dos Pequenitos also includes a children's museum.

**Evora** South of Lisbon is the old walled city of Evora with the remains of a Roman temple of Diana on Largo do Conde de Vila Flor; an early Gothic cathedral (Sé) on the same square; and the Church of St. Francis, on Praga 1 de Maio, which is lined with the bones of 5,000 monks.

In the Misericordia church on Rua da Misericórdia is an excellent example of *azulejos,* painted ceramic tiles. Around 1690 these blue and white tiles began to be used as story-telling devices, often telling Bible stories. In this church you will see *azulejos* showing Christ teaching the multitudes and other stories. The Museu Regional (Regional Museum) on Largo do Conde de Vila Flor displays paintings on the first floor showing the life of the Virgin Mary and panels on the altarpiece showing the life of Christ. There is also an interesting 16th-century triptych of the passion of Christ in Limoges enamel.

**Faro** Considering that Faro is the capital of the Algarve, you'd think it would be more heavily touristed than it is. Its Old Town (Cidade Velha) has ornate churches, lovely cafes, restaurants, and souvenir shops. You can also see what's left of the medieval city walls and gates. One of these gates, the Arco da Vila, has a white marble statue of St. Thomas Aquinas at the top. The gate leads to Cathedral Square (Largo da Sé), which is surrounded by orange trees. The Sé has an astonishingly beautiful interior, decorated with 17th-century Portuguese tiles.

The most unusual sight in Faro has got to be the Chapel of the Bones (Capela dos Ossos) in the Carmelite Church (Igreja do Carmo) on Largo do Carmo. The chapel is decorated with human bones taken from the monks' cemetery. The unusual display, while rather grim for modern-day visitors, was created during the time of the black plague, when death was a daily occurrence in the small community. The monks hoped to impress on the living a sense of their mortality.

**Fátima** The town of Fátima is known by Catholics around the world, not as a town but as a Marian shrine. On May 13, 1917, three shepherd children were pasturing their sheep when they claimed to have seen an astonishing vision of the Virgin Mary. That vision was repeated five times over the course of a few months' time, and the children claimed that Mary made known to them various wishes and warnings. Word of the mysterious apparitions passed quickly, and scores of pilgrims made their way to the holy site, many of whom were miraculously cured. Visitors to the area today may join as many as one million people per day who gather to pray, adore the saint, seek healing, and perhaps carry a vessel of holy water home with them. You may see visitors burning wax limbs, which represent their own physical healing.

The site where the little shepherds first saw the Virgin is today marked by a little prayer chapel, the Capela das Aparições, which is in turn completely surrounded by the immense Basilica. Statues flanking the Basilica of Fátima represent various saints. The esplanade out front is twice the size of St. Peter's Square in Rome. For most visitors the most impressive sight in Fátima is the intense emotion and faith of its pilgrims.

*255*

**Lagos** This lovely resort town has pedestrian streets that are lined with interesting shops, cafes, and restaurants. The town is an important fishing port, and its attractive harbor and marina are worth visiting. But the best reason to visit the town is its beaches, the nicest of which is the Praia de Doña Ana, about 30 minutes from town. If you're in town on Sunday, consider worshiping at the Church of St. Anthony (Igreja de Santo António) on Rua General Alberto Silveira, an 18th-century Baroque jewel, known for its extravagant carved and gilt wood interior.

**Mafra** If you enjoy palaces, you may want to visit the Palacio Nacional de Mafra, a 2,000-room building, incorporating a cathedral-size church, monastery, and library (with 38,000 books), besides the palace itself.

**Obidos** Obidos is a walled medieval town that has become Portugal's "wedding city." Even if you're not in a wedding party, it's a great place to take photos.

**Oporto (Porto)** The interior of São Francisco Church on Rua do Infante Dom Henrique is a magnificent example of Portuguese Baroque style, gleaming with elaborately gilded wood carvings. It is this vast quantity of gold that amazes visitors—450 pounds of it, encrusting the high altar and columns and worked into the shapes of angels, garlands, and prancing animals. All the gold ornamentation reaches its peak in the Star of Jesse, carved between 1711 and 1721, showing the genealogy of Christ with his ancestors on the various branches. There is also a good 16th-century painting of the baptism of Christ here. Church and catacombs were begun in the 14th century, but the interior dates from the 18th century. A tour, which includes the church's catacombs, is available.

**Sintra** About 20 miles north of Lisbon, this town has been called "glorious Eden" by Lord Byron in his poem "Childe Harold," because of its fairy-tale castles and beautiful mountain views. It is one of Portugal's oldest towns, and was for centuries the beautiful summer residence of Portugal's kings and aristocracy. Lord Byron's enthusiastic praise of the town and its natural beauties brought many English travelers in the 18th and 19th centuries. Children simply love Sintra, the real-life setting for fairy tales they've heard for years. Several palaces in the area are must-sees, particularly if you're traveling with children—Castelo dos Mouros, Palácio Nacional de Sintra, and Palácio Nacional de Pena.

The Moors' Castle (Castelo dos Mouros) on Estrada da Pena was built in the 8th century. The steep, partially cobblestoned road running up to the ruins offers a scenic but difficult walk. Consider renting a horse-drawn carriage in town if it's too much for you. Once you arrive at the top, you'll understand why the Moors chose this site—the views are fabulous. Admission is free.

Sintra Palace (Palácio Nacional de Sintra) stands in the center of Sintra's Old Town. The building was constructed in the 14th century as a royal summer residence and offers an interesting combination of Moorish and Gothic architectural styles. Visitors today can tour the museum (guided tours only) and enjoy the lovely Moorish *azulejos*. Admission is free on Sunday mornings.

Make sure you also see the Palácio Nacional de Pena, on Estrada da Pena, built in the 1840s by Prince Ferdinand of Bavaria on the site of a 16th-century monastery. It is what you might expect: a Bavarian castle, with Arabic minarets, Russian onion domes, Gothic turrets, Manueline windows, and a Renaissance dome. The grounds include trees and flowers from every corner of the Portuguese empire, which in the 1800s spanned the globe. In the Palácio de Pena, the chapel altarpiece is a 16th-century alabaster and marble work depicting scenes of the life of Christ from the manger to the ascension. Admission is free on Sundays.

For an unusual overnight stay, consider the Capuchin Convent (Convento dos Capuchos), located deep in the Sintra Mountains. Built in 1560 by Franciscan monks, the small cells are carved out of solid rock and lined with cork for warmth and insulation. The convent is four miles northeast of Cabo da Roca, 5.5 miles southwest of Sintra, and is signposted off Rte. N247, phone 01/923-0137.

**Tomar** Built in the 16th century, the Convent of Christ (Convento de Cristo) was the fortress and headquarters for the monk-knights of the Order of Christ, also known as the Knights Templar. The incredibly elaborate 16-sided rotunda and its octagonally shaped altar form the center of the monastery and comprise the original church of the Knights Templar, who also planned crusades from their headquarters here. The most famous architectural feature of the convent is its famous Manueline window, decorated with such intricate stonework that it's difficult to believe it's really stone. Christian symbols are intertwined with objects from the sea, including ropes, curlicues, and shells.

# *Spain*

Tourist Office of Spain
  US 212-265-8822
  Canada 416-961-3131
  UK 020-7486-8077
*Web site*
  Entire country www.okspain.org
For a complete list of updated links, visit www.christiantraveler.com

### Country in a Capsule

*Size:* About 20 percent larger than the state of California both in area and in population. California has four cities with more than a half million people; Spain has six.

*Religion:* Until 1978 Roman Catholicism was the state religion of Spain. Today there is no state religion, but Catholicism is still dominant, with more than 95 percent of the people belonging to the Catholic Church. Among Protestant groups, Plymouth Brethren, Baptists, and Pentecostals have churches in most major cities.

*Language:* The official language is Castilian Spanish. However, in the northeast, including Barcelona, Catalan is spoken; in the northwest, Galician is common; and in the Basque territory, Basque is spoken.

*Money:* The peseta is the Spanish unit of currency. While its value fluctuates, usually about 200 pesetas equal a U.S. dollar.

*Food:* Special dishes are regional, but ham is universal in Spain. Try jamon serran or jamon del pais. In the Andalucian region, the speciality is gazpacho, a cold cucumber and tomato soup. As you get close to the Mediterranean, you find more seafood. Try the king prawns. And for dessert ask for crema catalana, a custard cream with a layer of caramel.

*Shopping:* Spain is known for its leather goods. You can also do well buying porcelain statuary, earthenware pottery, cultured pearls, and handicrafts.

*Brief history:* Christianity came to the Roman province of Spain in the 1st century A.D. (The apostle Paul mentions his desire to bring the gospel to Spain in his Epistle to the Romans.) In the late 4th century Spain was overrun by Germanic tribes and then captured by Muslim invaders (the Moors) in A.D. 711. For the next 700 years Christian Spaniards attempted to reconquer the land. It wasn't until Granada was recaptured in 1492 that the Muslim forces were finally driven out. This began the Golden Era for Spain under Ferdinand and Isabella, with explorers going out and returning with the gold of the New World. But it was also the time that the Inquisition began targeting Moors, Jews, and, later, Protestants.

In 1588 the defeat of the Spanish Armada marked the end of Spain as a sea power. Wars and squandered wealth brought the country down further in the following century until it was no longer a major European power. The key figure in the 20th century was Francisco Franco, the Fascist dictator who ruled for 40 years until 1975. Now a democracy, Spain is rapidly recovering in the post-Franco years, and its economy is among the fastest growing in Europe.

**Madrid** In the center of the country, Madrid is the capital and largest city (about the size of Chicago). Viejo Madrid (Old Madrid) is the part that most tourists visit and it is so large and engaging that you can spend your entire time here if you wish, although there is much to see outside of the Old City.

*Interesting streets.* Plaza Mayor is the architectural center. It was also the place where historically there were bullfights and imperial proclamations and where many Protestants, Jews, and Muslims were executed during the Inquisition. Today you see artists at work, vendors plying their wares, and fascinating shops around the edges. On Sunday mornings a stamp and coin market is held under the arches.

Madrid's best-known square is the Puerto del Sol, with streets radiating outward like rays from the sun and a marker that indicates the point from which all distances in Spain are measured. Walking northeast from the Puerto del Sol is a pedesterian street, Calle de Preciados, where musicians and street mimes fascinate strollers. Ice cream shops are plentiful as are outdoor cafes.

*The Monasterio de las Descalzas Reales,* a very unique convent indeed, is nearby. When you go inside, you are transported into another world. The Convent of the Royal Barefoot Nuns (Convento de las Descalzas Reales) is one of Madrid's best-kept secrets. Over the centuries the resident nuns—daughters of noblemen— have made gifts to the convent of a large collection of royal jewels, Flemish tapestries, religious ornaments, and priceless artwork. The most valuable piece of art here is probably Titian's *Caesar's Money,* but the ten tapestries by Rubens, the works by Bruegel the Elder, and Pedro de Mena's *Ecce Homo* are distinctive too. The convent, located at Plaza de las Descalzas 3, is still a convent today.

*Museums.* Madrid's leading cultural site is the Prado Museum (Museo del Prado), located in the old cobblestone section of the city on Paseo del Prado. The Prado is considered one of the world's most important art museums, so expect crowds and plan to spend two days if you want to see everything. The great Italian painters— Raphael, Botticelli, Fra Angelico, Titian—are well represented here, but the Prado is where the Spaniards, El Greco, Goya, and

Velázquez really stand out. The museum is free on Saturdays after 2:30 and all day Sunday.

Not as famous, but nearly as magnificent, is the Museo Thyssen-Bornemisza, a newer museum very near the Prado with about 800 paintings. On the second floor you will see Buonesegna's *Christ and the Samaritan Woman*, and an outstanding ivory diptych with scenes from the life of Christ. The museum is located at Paseo del Prado 8.

*Churches.* Among Madrid's many historic churches are the Iglesia de San Francisco El Grande on Correra de San Francisco, with its walls and ceiling decorated with 19th-century frescoes; the Catedral de la Almudena, on C. de Bailén, with its psychedelic stained glass windows just south of the 18th-century Palácio Real; the Pontificia de San Miguel on San Justo, interestingly designed in an 18th-century Baroque style; and the Cathedral de San Isidro, not far from the Plaza Mayor at C. Toledo and C. Sacramento.

> Of the Father's love begotten, ere the worlds began to be,
> He is Alpha and Omega, He the source, the ending He;
> Of the things that are, that have been,
> And that future years shall see, evermore and evermore.
>
> AURELIUS PRUDENTIUS OF SPAIN

*Parks and zoo.* Sixteen miles northwest of Madrid is the Aquapolis on the A6 to El Escorial. It has water slides, wave-making machines, and tall spiral slides that give the kids a chance to enjoy themselves. The area also has shops and a barbecue restaurant to make adults feel at home.

Another park for the family is the Parque de Atracciones in Casa de Campo just beyond the Campo del Moro Park and across the Manzaneres River. This park has a variety of rides including a toboggan slide, pony rides, and a roller coaster named 7 Picos. The most pleasant approach to the park is via the Teleferico, a cable car that takes you above two parks, over the Manzanares River, with views of the Royal Palace (in good weather) and on to the Casa de Campo. It takes about eleven minutes and it leaves from Paseo del Pinto Rosales in Madrid's city center.

Madrid has a great zoo (also at Casa de Campo) with about 3,000 animals, and an unusual wax museum (Museo de Cera de Madrid) at Paseo de Recoletas, 41. The wax museum includes a

30-minute recap of Spanish history from the Phoenicians to the present.

If you get exhausted traipsing around the museums and palaces of Madrid, take some time out to enjoy Retiro Park, an island of relaxation in the midst of a busy city. There is a lake where boats can be hired.

Another park that natives enjoy is Parque del Oeste (West Park), a landscaped garden area overlooking the Manzanares River. Located here is the Temple de Debod, an Egyptian temple that once stood along the Nile in Egypt, but when the Aswan dam threatened it, the Egyptian government gave it to Spain. It was taken down stone by stone and then reconstructed here. La Rosaleda is a beautiful rose garden; visitors can also go boating in El Estanque, a lake in the middle of the park; enjoy street musicians and magicians, or just enjoy a stroll past numerous fountains and statues. And speaking of fountains, check out the Monument to the Fallen Angel. Madrid is the only capital in the world to have a statue dedicated to the devil. The park is between C. Alfonso XII and Avda. de Menéndez Pelayo below C. de Alcala.

About 20 minutes south of Madrid on Rte. N401 you will see a large round hill topped by a statue of Christ. This is the Hill of the Angels (El Cerro de los Angéles). Apart from offering a reminder of Spain's Christian heritage, the monument marks the geographical center of the Iberian Peninsula.

**Alcala de Henares** About 12 miles east of Madrid is this city of 165,000 that is known as the city of Miguel de Cervantes, Spain's most famous author, and the city of a famous university. The Plaza de Cervantes is filled with rose bushes and cafes, and just east of it is the Plaza San Diego where the Colegio Mayor de San Ildefonso held classes from about 1508 to 1836, when the university was moved to Madrid. Famous for its teaching of foreign languages, the university published the first polyglot Bible in 1517 with parallel texts in Latin, Greek, Hebrew, and Chaldean.

**Alicante** This city of 275,000 is the tourist capital of the Costa Blanca on Spain's East Coast. An old fortress, Castillo de Santa Barbara, guards the city. It is said that the fortress was built originally by the Carthaginian general Hamilcar. Recently reconstructed, the 650-foot-high fortress has a dry moat, dungeon, and all the other things that an old fortress should have. There is a paved road up to it, but most people take an elevator up the hill to the fortress and walk down. Nearby is the Santa Maria church on Calle Mayor. It was once a mosque and was rebuilt in the 14th century and then enlarged several times. Near the entrance is a painting of John the Baptist with John the apostle.

**Ávila** A few miles northeast of Madrid, this ancient and splendidly preserved walled city is best known as the city of two 16th-century mystics, St. Teresa of Ávila and St. John of the Cross. The writings of both are read by Catholics and Protestants alike. In Teresa's *The Way of Perfection,* she develops the concept of mental prayer, which is "friendly conversation, frequently conversing alone, with One who we know loves us." St. John of the Cross is best known for his *The Dark Night of the Soul.*

The local specialty, by the way, is *yemas de Santa Teresa,* which is candied egg yolk. Try it while you are here; you might like it.

Teresa called the soul "a diamond castle," and if you look at the profile of the cathedral on Plaza de la Cathedral, you can see why. It dates back to the 11th century, although it took a few hundred years to complete. Ávila Cathedral, which resembles a fortress as much as a cathedral, originated during the Romanesque period—those sections can be recognized by their red and white stone—but the cathedral is usually considered Spain's first Gothic cathedral. From the cathedral, go into the museum, which in addition to a display of some interesting paintings has a large display of old hymnals.

The Convent of St. Teresa, just south of the cathedral on Plaza de La Santa, was built on the site of her birthplace and childhood

## TERESA OF ÁVILA (1515-1582)

One of the most famous mystics of 16th-century Spain, Teresa was born in Ávila into a Spanish noble family. Early in life she committed herself to converting the heathen and healing the division with Protestants. When 21, she entered a Carmelite convent. Concerned about the scandalous condition of Spanish monasteries, she traveled throughout the country preaching reform and she started a Barefoot Carmelite order. She also recruited John of the Cross to start a similar order for monks. Teresa sought oneness with God through contemplation and prayer. Her best known works are *The Way of Perfection* and *The Interior Castle.*

Sites associated with Teresa's life and ministry are located in Ávila.

home. The Monasterio de Santo Tomas is also worth seeing. Located outside the city walls on Plaza Granada 1, it was a summer palace for Catholic monarchs and a seat of the Inquisition.

Also outside Ávila's city walls is one of the city's finest Romanesque churches, the Basilica de San Vicente, located on the Plaza de San Vicente. The church was built on the spot where St. Vincent and his sisters Sabina and Cristeta were martyred in A.D. 306, a few years before the Emperor Constantine officially recognized Christianity. The scenes portraying the stripping and torture of the martyrs are graphically presented at the tomb in the west portal.

**Barcelona** The second largest city in Spain, Barcelona is exciting, cosmopolitan, Mediterranean, and much more. It is both modern and ancient, and you will need to soak up both parts while you are here.

*Las Ramblas*, in the heart of the old city, is the pedestrian-only shopping street, but it is more than that; it is an ongoing carnival, with flower vendors in one block and bird cages in another. At the bottom of the Ramblas is the Columbus Monument (Monument a Colom), which holds special meaning to visitors from the Americas. You can ride an elevator to the top of the monument for a lovely view of the city and its famous port. But alas, Columbus is facing the wrong way. He is pointing east, toward Italy. Apparently his navigational skills were superior to those of the monument's creators.

*Churches.* If you don't know the name of Antoni Gaudi already, you soon will. And you will either love his work or hate it; you won't be neutral. His architecture is creatively modern. La Sagrada Família (Church of the Holy Family), which he began in 1883 and is still not finished, will give you a taste of his work. The cathedral, at C. de Mallorca and C. de Provença, may not be Barcelona's loveliest, but it is certainly the city's most famous. The church was far from finished at the time of Gaudi's death in 1926, when he was run over by a tram and killed. He lies buried in the crypt. Work continues on La Sagrada Família. On the outside, the three facades are dominated by four tall spires representing the 12 apostles. The Nativity facade, which is complete, has three doorways, Faith, Hope, and Charity. Visitors can take an elevator to the top of one of the church's towers for a gorgeous view of Barcelona.

The Cathedral of St. Mary of the Sea (Santa Maria del Mar) on Plaça Santa Maria is simply the best example of Mediterranean Gothic architecture anywhere, and it is widely considered Barcelona's most beautiful cathedral. It was built between 1329 and 1383. The beautiful rose window adds to the simple beauty of this church. Ask the information desk about free concerts sometimes held in the cathedral, or contact the City Hall's Saló de Cent for a schedule.

The elaborate Gothic cathedral in Barcelona (Catedral de la Seu, on Plaça de la Seu) was built largely between 1298 and 1450, with the final spire and facade completed in 1892. The elaborately carved choir stalls are a highlight. But while the cathedral is worth a visit in its own right, there's another reason to stop by on Sunday mornings: In front of the church every Sunday, citizens of Barcelona gather to dance the sardana, a symbol of Catalan identity.

*Roman City.* Nearby, beneath the City Museum on Palau Padellàs and Carrer del Veguer is the Roman City, which allows you to discover some of the vestiges of an ancient Roman town. By taking a walk through it, you get a feel for life in the time of the apostle Paul.

*Museums.* Just behind the cathedral on Plaça de la Seu is the Museu Frederic Marès, which has an amazing display, almost overwhelming in fact, of Christ and Calvary figurines carved in wood. The museum, a vast repository of medieval sculpture, is housed in an ancient palace with soaring ceilings and interior courtyards.

One of the most popular museums in the city is the Science Museum (Museu de la Ciencia), a little west of the city center. Its hands-on exhibits make it fun for kids, and there are more than 300 exhibits in all, so you can take as much time here as you want. There is a special area for children, ages three through seven.

*Family fun.* The family will also enjoy the zoo (Parc Zoologic) located in the Parc de la Ciutadella, which ranks as the best in the country. Another site for the family is the Parc d'Atraccions (Montjuic), a fun-park on the south end of the city on a hill called Montjuic. The most enjoyable approach to the park is via the cable car (Telefèric), which runs from the end of Passeig Joan de Borbócan up the hill. Concerts, three dozen rides, and illuminated displays make this an attraction indeed. Another Parc d'Atraccions (Tibidabo) is north of the city. Located on Tibidabo Mountain, the park is reached by a funicular that takes you up

1,600 feet to the top, where there are rides, restaurants, hotels, and even a church. From the park you get a fantastic view not only of Barcelona (it's fantastic at night) but also of the Mediterranean and even the Pyrenees. The name, by the way, is biblical. When, during the temptation of Jesus, Satan took him to a high mountain and showed him the kingdoms of the earth, he said, "All this I will give you." In the Latin Bible, "I will give you" is translated "Tibidabo."

Barceloneta was once the fishermen's quarter in town, built in 1755. Simple fish restaurants abound, as you might imagine. Take a walk out to the end of the rompeolas, or breakwater, which reaches out into the Mediterranean 2.5 miles where you can enjoy a lovely view of the city and breathe in the salty air. The modern port is home to one of Europe's best aquariums, the Maregmagnum shopping center, an IMAX cinema, and numerous restaurants. The giant gold fish sculpture next to the Hotel Arts distinguishes a hot tapas and nightlife spot. It was once the home of the 1992 Olympic Village. Barceloneta is located below Estaciá de França and Ciutadella Park.

Park Güell, in the upper part of town on C. D'Olot, was created by Barcelona's famous designer and architect, Gaudi. This was his attempt at creating a garden city, and you have to marvel at the architect's imagination. As you enter, you have the feeling that you are walking into an enchanted forest filled with mushroom-shaped pavilions. The way he combined architecture and nature into a fantasy park is amazing.

**Burgos** About 150 miles north of Madrid is this historic, conservative city with a magnificent cathedral on Plaza del Rey San Fernando, the third largest cathedral in Spain. In addition, much of the life of El Cid, Spain's real-life folk hero, centers around this city. Although he was anything but a chivalrous knight, his ashes are interred in the cathedral. One of the unique features of the cathedral is what is called its Flycatcher Clock on the center aisle near the main door. When it tolls the hours, it opens its mouth and appears to be gulping flies.

**Carmona** This lovely Andalusian town has its roots in the times of the Romans and the Moors. Mudéjar (a uniquely Spanish Arabic style) and Renaissance churches and whitewashed houses are the rule here. At the town's entrance stands the church of San

Pedro. It was begun in 1466, and its interior exhibits nonstop sculptures and gold.

**Córdoba** This city, east of Sevilla, dates back to Roman times. The famous Roman philosopher, Seneca, who became Nero's tutor, was born here. In the 10th century a university was founded by the Muslims that was remarkably tolerant, allowing Muslims, Christians, and Jews to live and thrive side by side—at least for a while. Maimonides, perhaps the outstanding Jewish theologian of the Middle Ages, was from Córdoba, although he had to flee because of persecution. The time of tolerance had ended.

In a strange way, the three religions are still seen in Córdoba. La Mezquita at Torrijos and Cardenal Herrero was built on the site of a previous Visigoth church and was intended to be the largest of all mosques. For years it was enlarged again and again. But when Christians reconquered Córdoba in 1236, they began converting it back into a church again, and so the center of the building was cut away and a cathedral rose out of the center of the mosque. Just northwest of the cathedral is the old whitewashed Jewish quarter (Juderia), where there is a 14th-century synagogue on C. Judíos, one of only two major synagogues remaining from medieval Spain. It is decorated with Hebrew inscriptions from the Psalms. A statue of Maimonides stands beside it.

One of the most famous religious shrines in Spain is Cristo de Los Faroles (Christ of the Fountains). Located in Plaza Capuchinos, the shrine has a large cross surrounded by wrought iron lanterns. Faithful Catholics come here for all-night vigils.

**El Escorial** Some 30 miles northwest of Madrid, the palace dominating the town of the same name is not elegant, but it is awesome. Built between 1563 and 1584, when Protestantism was on the rise in northern Europe and Spain was bringing back tons of gold from the New World, El Escorial started out as a monastery to remember St. Lawrence. But since King Philip II wanted it to serve also as a royal palace and a pantheon, it has both palatial grandeur and monasterial austerity. The building is 676 feet by 528 feet, has 1,200 doors and 2,600 windows; it contains a basilica that is 300 feet high and has four organs and a dome based on Michelangelo's drawings for St. Peter's; and a 60,000-volume library, one of the most priceless in the world. Then there is the Museo de Pintura (Picture Museum) with works on religious themes done by artists like Ti-

## THE PYRENEES

The jagged green mountains of the Pyrenees in Spain's northeastern corner move even the most seasoned travelers. Ordesa National Park (Parque Nacional de Ordesa) encompasses the area's high points, like snow-covered peaks, steep rock faces, rushing rivers, and thundering waterfalls. What more could you want? Hiking through the well-maintained trails is the best way to get up close to God's creation here. Favorite trails include the Soaso Circle, the Circo Cotatuero and the Circo Carriata, which take between two and five hours to hike. If you don't want to walk that distance, just head out and turn around when the mood strikes you. Detailed maps and information on other hikes can be picked up at the visitor center *El Parador,* just beyond the park's entrance.

The Pyrenees are also a popular place for skiing. Val d'Aran sits at the center of the area's most dazzling peaks and is home to some of its most chic ski resorts. Nearby Vielha is the biggest town in the valley, offering more affordable amenities. Skiing is big here in winter too, and in summer the town makes a great base for all kinds of outdoor activities. Contact the Oficeria de Baquiera-Beret (phone 973/64-44-55) in Val d'Aran for skiing information. Contact the tourist office in Vielha (phone 973/64-01-10) for skiing or other outdoor information in that town.

tian, Veronese, Tintoretto, Van Dyck, Rubens, and El Greco.

Valle de los Caidos (Valley of the Fallen) is five miles north of El Escorial on the C600. Built by Francisco Franco as a monument to those who died in Spain's Civil War between 1936 and 1939, the basilica is larger than St. Peter's in Rome and St. Paul's in London. As you enter, you will note eight huge tapestries showing scenes from the Book of Revelation. High above the basilica is a cross (La Cruz) on a mountain, overlooking the basilica. The cross itself is 410 feet high, and it is surrounded by gigantic statues of the four Gospel writers. You can get to the base of La Cruz by a funicular. Incidentally, Franco is buried here, but none of the literature mentions his name. Modern Spain would like to forget him.

**Granada** When Granada was captured by the Spanish Christian monarchs, it symbolized the triumph of Christianity over Islam in Europe. One of the last bastions of Muslim Spain was this beautiful, old city. Its Alhambra, built by the Muslims, remains one of the most remarkable fortresses ever built. As Christians took it over in 1492, they added their touches, as Carlos V did when he added to the complex a palace, one of the finest Renaissance buildings in Spain. It was in Alhambra's Hall of the Ambassadors where Christopher Columbus met with King Ferdinand to discuss the route he would take to find India. The summer palace of the Moorish sultans was El Generalife, but the gardens are more to be admired than the palace itself. El Generalife is located on the Cerro del Sol (Hill of the Sun) adjoining Alhambra. Tickets include entrance to both complexes.

In the Old City on Oficios is the Cathedral and next to it the Capilla Real (Royal Chapel), built by Fernando and Isabel. About a quarter of their royal income was spent on this memorial chapel where they were buried. The queen's royal crown and scepter and the king's sword are on display. The cathedral is the second largest in Spain, and the only Renaissance church in the country.

**Guadalupe** Located in western Spain, this ancient village is where the Virgin Mary is said to have appeared to a cowherd in 1300 and left him with an icon. A shrine was built on the spot, and a generation later, a large monastery was established, which soon became the focal point of Catholic pilgrimages. Christopher Columbus named a West Indian island after this shrine, and when the first American Indians were converted to Christianity by Catholic missionaries, they were brought to this church for baptism. The monastery, which has been restored in the last 150 years, dominates the village and contains valuable art in both its sacristy and its painting and sculpture museum.

**Málaga** Built between 1528 and 1782 on the site of a former mosque, the Málaga cathedral on C. de Molina Larios remains unfinished. Its construction funds never came through. No one seems to know just what happened, although rumor was that the money went instead to the American Revolution. Because the cathedral is missing one of its twin towers, the building is sometimes called, *la Manquita,* the one-armed lady. The adjoining museum has interesting religious art and artifacts.

**Mérida** Mérida is the place to go in Spain for Roman ruins. Beginning in 25 B.C., the Romans built temples, a theater, an amphitheater, bridges, aqueducts, and even a race course here. The Roman theater, built by Agrippa, was large enough for 6,000 people; the amphitheater, built in 8 B.C. to hold 16,000, was designed for gladiator combat, and combat between men and animals; and the hippodrome, with a 30,000-seat capacity was designed for chariot races. Nearby, a church commemorating St. Eulalia on Rambla Mártir Santa Eulalia was being repaired in 1990, and workers found, underneath its earliest construction, remains of Roman houses dating back to the time of Christ. A museum and basilica are open daily and the church is open during morning and evening services. During the summer the Festival de Teatro Clasico presents theater and dance performances among the ruins of Mérida.

## PILGRIMAGE

Medieval European Christians viewed pilgrimage as an important goal of their Christian lives. The faithful would leave the care of their businesses or farms to others as they headed to pilgrimage sites, like Rome, Canterbury, and Santiago. The impulse to travel to the shrine of a saint, which probably housed his or her relics, was rooted in the need to obtain physical or spiritual healing or in the desire for spiritual enlightenment.

Because the journey lasted so long, pilgrimage was often limited to the wealthy or to those who felt a strong need for penance. The road was difficult and dangerous, stretching for hundreds of miles from points throughout Europe. Travelers generally journeyed in groups for safety and camaraderie. Hostels and monasteries located along the route offered food and lodging to the pilgrims and also cared for those who became ill, injured, or exhausted along the way.

A special pilgrim's card was often issued and marked by monks along the way to prove that the traveler had indeed completed the entire journey. The faithful could also be recognized by their clothing, a costume consisting of a heavy cape, an 8-foot staff with a gourd attached for carrying water, sturdy sandals, and a broad-brimmed felt hat turned up in front and marked with three or four scallop shells.

Pilgrims were typically in no great hurry to reach the final pilgrimage site. They frequently made detours along the way to visit minor shrines and other religious sites, detours that could add weeks or even months to the journey.

But pilgrimage was not without its pleasures. Family members traveling together strengthened relationships, pilgrims forged new friendships, and the cares of home could be forgotten for a time. When the travelers reached their destination, they were certain to pick up a souvenir before they left—perhaps a shell, a feather, or a container of holy water—to always remind them of their experience.

**Montserrat** Not far inland from Barcelona is the monastery of Montserrat, started by the Benedictines in the 9th century. Set in the mountains, the monastery enjoys spectacular scenery. The Montserrat Escolania (choir school) was started almost a thousand years ago and may well be the oldest music school in Europe. Fifty boys who study in the monastery compose the choir, which can be heard daily at 1:00 and 6:45. The top attraction here is the Black Virgin icon, the most revered symbol in the province. You can take a train or drive to the base of Montserrat, but you will need to take a funicular up the mountain.

**Port Aventura** About 70 miles south of Barcelona and six miles from Tarragona is this 627-acre amusement park. Divided into five different geographical zones—Mediterranean, Polynesian, Chinese, Mexican, and the American Far West—the park has rides, entertainment, atmosphere, and food appropriate to each one. Of course, you probably didn't come to Spain to go to a Far West theme park and ride on a Union Pacific steam engine, but who knows?

**Ripoll** The most unusual thing about the Monastery of Santa Maria around which the town is centered is not that it was founded in the 9th century by a count of Barcelona named Wilfred the Hairy. A thousand years ago its library was one of the greatest in all of Christendom, complete with Scripture texts and theological commentaries. Not too much remains, but there is enough to let you see how the builders of the church were concerned about biblical education. Note the systematic way of teaching the Bible through artwork on the church portals.

**Salamanca** Salamanca is a beautiful medieval city. Looming over the 15-arch Roman bridge are the city's golden stone walls, turrets, and domes, and its two adjoining cathedrals, the smaller Old Cathedral (Catedral Vieja) and New Cathedral (Catedral Nueva) on Tentenecio. Don't miss the terrific altarpiece in the Old Cathedral—all 53 panels of it. Students may be interested in the history of the Capilla de Santa Bárbara inside, or Chapel of St. Barbara. The chapel is sometimes called the Degree Chapel, since anxious students frequently fled here to plead for help the night before final exams.

**Santiago** Santiago (St. James) de Compostela ranks as the world's third most important place of Christian pilgrimage after Jerusalem and Rome and has been popular with pilgrims since the Middle Ages. At its height between 500,000 and 2,000,000 pilgrims visited Santiago de Compostela annually to visit the grave of St. James the Greater, the apostle known as the Thunderer on account of his temper.

James is said to have come to Spain to preach the gospel. His boat was beached on the Spanish shore, and James preached to the native people for seven years before returning to Judea. Years later, after James's death, his disciples returned to Spain with the apostle's body and buried it near the original landing site. The grave went unmarked and virtually unrecognized until early in the 9th century when a star is said to have directed local shepherds to the site. (*Campus Stellae* means field of the star.) Over the centuries James has been credited with assisting the Spanish in their defeat of the Moors, thus becoming Spain's patron saint, and with performing miraculous physical and spiritual acts of healing.

## IGNATIUS OF LOYOLA (1491-1556)

Born to a Spanish noble family, Ignatius was going to be a career soldier, but while recovering from leg wounds received at the siege of Pamplona, he began reading stories of the life of Christ and of various saints. He decided to become God's soldier. After a year of prayer and meditation at a monastery, he wrote his classic *Spiritual Exercises*.

After ten years of study in Barcelona, Alcala, Salamanca, and Paris, Ignatius gathered six friends around him and began the Society of Jesus, the Jesuits, vowing total obedience to the Pope. Though Ignatius of Loyola wanted quality, not quantity, his order grew rapidly and in 20 years there were more than 1,000 Jesuits, mostly from Spain, Portugal, and Italy. And 70 years later there were more than 15,000. The Jesuits emphasized education and today Jesuits run about 4,000 schools.

Modern-day visitors to Santiago will want to visit the cathedral on S. Francisco built over the saint's burial site. Although the building looks Baroque, it was constructed between the 11th and 13th centuries. The cathedral's facade was added in 1750, a richly sculpted entrance known as the Obradoiro ("Work of Gold") Facade. Once inside, take note of the Portico de la Gloria in the narthex, a 12th-century, intricately sculpted doorway featuring Christ, the evangelists, the apostles, and the 24 old men of the Apocalypse. The church's high altar bears a statue of St. James, and the crypt beneath the altar bears his remains in a silver coffin. The cathedral's small treasury and reliquary chapel contain the remains of another James—St. James the Minor.

If you're interested in learning more about the *Camino de Santiago* (Road to St. James) visit the Museum of Pilgrimage (Museo das Peregrinacións) on Pl. San Miguel. Exhibits explain the difficult journey of the pilgrim in greater detail.

**Segovia** The town of Segovia is a lovely golden stone medieval town, full of Roman monuments, great cafes, and greater views. Not the least of the town's lovely buildings is Segovia's cathedral on the Plaza Cathedral, the last Gothic cathedral built in Spain (1525). Its golden interior glows with the light from its 16th-century Flemish windows. The cathedral's museum has the first book ever printed in Spain, dating from 1472.

**Sevilla (Seville)** You've heard about Seville because of *The Barber of Seville* or *Carmen* or *Don Giovanni;* and you wonder if you will be disappointed when you get there. Well, you won't be. It may be hot in the summer, and it may be crowded, but it is still charming, beautiful, and romantic.

You should start with the cathedral, which is the largest Gothic building in the world, and the third largest active church in the world (behind St. Peter's in Rome and St. Paul's in London). You will see where Christopher Columbus is buried; you will see in the chancel an immense Flemish altarpiece with scenes from the life of Christ; and in the Royal Chapel (Capilla Real) you will see numerous works of art from noted painters. Seville's cathedral chapter is said to have declared in 1401, "Let us build a cathedral so grand that those who see it will take us for madmen." They apparently meant what they said. The massive cathedral on Plaza Virgen de los Reyes took more than a century to build. Seville Cathedral also has the world's largest carved wooden altarpiece. By the way, evening concerts are often presented here.

La Giralda is the former minaret of the mosque that was once here. Now it's the bell tower for the cathedral. It's a long climb to the top but kids who have lots of energy usually enjoy it.

Next to the cathedral is the Alcazar, built originally by Moorish governors, but made into a Spanish palace by King Pedro the Cruel. It has been a royal palace for 600 years. You may even enjoy the gardens outside more than the palace itself.

Casa de Pilatos (Pilate's House) on Pl. Pilatos is really not Pilate's house, but it is said to have been modeled after the house in Jerusalem where Pontius Pilate governed. Now it houses Renaissance paintings as well as Roman antiquities, and it is one of the most ornate palaces in the city.

Two rides worth taking in Sevilla: (1) a horse-and-buggy ride from the cathedral to the Plaza de Espana; and (2) a rowboat or a pedal boat ride from the Plaza.

El Parque de Los Descurbimientos (Discovery Park) on La Cartuja Island was the site of Expo '92 and is now a theme park. Replicas of Columbus's three ships are docked here. There is also a Children's Park with a variety of puppet shows and water slides.

Maria Luisa Park (Parque de María Luisa) located on Glorieta San Diego was designed in the 1920s to host the 1929 Hispanic-American exhibition. The villas here are the remains of the fair's pavilions. Formal gardens are blended with wild plants, and the park's shady nooks offer welcome relief from a hot sunny day. At the southern end of the park, you and your kids can feed hundreds of white doves drawn to the fountains around the Plaza de América.

**Tarragona** The Bible says that the prophet Jonah boarded a boat bound for Tarshish. No one knows where that Tarshish was, but most scholars believe it was somewhere in Spain. It could have been Tartessos, a lost city supposedly near Gibraltar, or maybe it was Tarragona near Barcelona. Tarragona was founded by Phoenicians before the time of Jonah, and by the time of the Romans it had developed into a major city and overseas capital. According to local legend, Pontius Pilate was born here, and the apostle Paul came here to evangelize the people.

The Archaeological Museum on Passeig Sant Antoni displays mosaics from the Roman period. The Roman Circus, which was originally designed for chariot races, is mostly buried today, although some sections are still visible. But the Amphitheatre is perched on the water's edge and is still impressive. At least three early Christians, Fructuosus, Augurius, and Eulogius, were martyred here in 259.

The cathedral on the Plaza de la Seu was begun in 1174 on top of a temple to Jupiter. The most notable piece of art is the altarpiece of Santa Tecla. Santa Tecla, the patron saint of the city, was converted to Christ by the apostle Paul. Reliefs recounting her life story can be seen in the Capilla de Santa Tecla in the nave.

**Toledo** When you come to Toledo, you come to the heart of Don Quixote land and the home of the great Spanish painter El Greco. The cathedral on a small square at the end of C. del Comercio is worth seeing if for no other reason than to see the 18 El Grecos and the two Van Dycks in the sacristy, but before long you will see why this cathedral is considered one of Spain's greatest. You will probably want to take a peek into the Tesoro (Treasury), which has a 13th-century Bible given to Ferdinand III of Castille and the 400-pound monstrance (receptacle for the mass), which is paraded through the streets when Corpus Christi is celebrated.

Also worth seeing is the art in the Capilla Mayor, which displays a virtual synopsis of New Testament history. The elaborate church houses bejeweled chalices, stunning religious vestments, and priceless tapestries, as well as 750 stained glass windows and artwork by such masters as Titian, Tintoretto, and Goya. Don't miss the unusual Transparente, an ornate Baroque roof that allows the sun to shine through a hole onto a mass of clouds and figures. The Mozarabic Chapel takes its name from the ancient Mozarabic rite, dating from the days of the Visigoths, and Mass is still celebrated here in that ancient style.

Another interesting church in Toledo is the church of St. Mary the White (Santa María la Blanca). Located at Reyes Católicos 4, the church was originally founded as a synogogue in 1203. In the early 15th century the building was taken over by Christians and consecrated as a church. About the only thing originally Christian in this church is the lovely 16th-century altarpiece. The architecture is actually Moorish, with its five naves, horseshoe-shaped arches, and texts from the Koran displayed throughout.

The beautiful Gothic church of San Juan de los Reyes on Reyes Católicos was founded by Ferdinand and Isabella in 1476. The outer walls are decorated with iron manacles, placed there by Christians who were freed by the Moors.

Since El Greco lived most of his life here, you find his works almost anywhere in town. Many of them are in the Prado in Madrid, but in Toledo you can see them in the Iglesia de Santo Tomé on C. de Santo Tomé, the Museo de la Santa Cruz on Plaza de Zocodover, the Hospital de Tavera on Cardenal Tavera (where his last work *Baptism of Christ* is displayed), and in the Casa y Museo de El Greco off Calle de San Juan de Dios, which has 19 of his works.

**Valencia** Spain's third largest city is a cosmopolitan, business town, but also a place with a historic past and a people who love fiestas. Las Fallas, celebrated from March 12 to 19, is Valencia's most celebrated event with parades, bullfights, fireworks, and street dancing, climaxed by the contest between communities to see who can build the biggest and best papier-mâché effigy. Then on the final night, which is called fire night, all the effigies are burned in one glorious bonfire.

The cathedral on the Plaza de la Virgen is fascinating because of the various architectural styles it exhibits. Three different entrances are in Gothic, Baroque, and Romanesque styles. Near the cathedral on the same plaza is the Palácio de la Generalidad, a 15th-century Gothic palace. As you enter, you see a sculpture of Dante's Inferno.

One of the biggest markets in Europe is the Mercado Central on Plaza del Mercado. It has an amazing display of fruit, fish, and vegetables. It closes at 2:00 P.M., so make sure you get there in the morning.

Just outside the historical district are a series of parks. The Jardin Botanico at Beato Gaspar Bono 6 has 43,000 plants from 300 different species. And just beyond that is a public recreation area that children will enjoy. They can climb up a huge model of Jonathan Swift's Gulliver in Lilliput. Of course, the beach is never far away. The beaches here are good but, as you would expect, crowded in summer.

# Sweden

Swedish Travel and Tourism Council
  US 212-885-9700
  UK 020-7870-5600
*Web sites*
  Entire country www.visit-sweden.com
  Scandinavia www.goscandinavia.com
For a complete list of updated links, visit www.christiantraveler.com

### Country in a Capsule

*Size:* You can think of Sweden as a colder version of California. It has about the same area and shape, but only a third of the population, which is understandable when you realize that 15 percent of the land is north of the Arctic Circle. Its largest city is Stockholm with about 650,000 people in the city proper, but 1.4 million living in the metropolitan area. In the northern half of the country, only two towns have more than 50,000 residents.

277

*Religion:* **87** percent are officially members of the state church (Evangelical Lutheran), but church attendance is only about 10 percent. There are about 120,000 Roman Catholics and about the same number of Pentecostals. The Mission Covenant, Baptists, Methodists, and the Salvation Army are also relatively strong here.

*Language:* In most tourist areas, the Swedes speak and understand English because it has been taught in schools as the second language for 50 years. Swedish is related to, but distinct from, Norwegian and Danish.

*Money:* The krone is worth about 11 cents.

*Food:* While you are here, you will have to have some Swedish meatballs (kottbullar) with lingonsylt (something like cranberry sauce). But the staple of Swedish food is fish, and the favorite has long been herring (smoked, pickled, or what-have-you). Smorgasbord, of course, is the Swedish word for their lavish buffet spread.

*Shopping:* Sweden is known for its glassware, pewter, and wooden handicrafts. A Dalarna painted wooden horse is typically Swedish. The major Stockholm department stores carry excellent lines of Swedish glassware.

*Brief history:* It was a missionary named Ansgar who first brought Christianity to Sweden in the middle of the 9th century in the heyday of the Viking age. But conversions were few and it wasn't until two centuries later—when a missionary from England, Sigfrid, converted King Olaf—that Christianity took root in the country. That date is also the beginning of Sweden's modern history. In the Middle Ages (1000–1500) two women left their mark on Sweden: the charismatic and forceful St. Bridget, who founded the Bridgettine order, and Queen Margareta who united Sweden, Denmark, and Norway, and ruled with strength and wisdom. After a time of Danish rule, Gustav Vasa brought both independence and the Protestant Reformation to Sweden, and a century later it was Gustavus Adolphus who made Sweden a world power. After World War I, the Social Democratic party began its control of the country's economy, and the nation has been increasingly a welfare state.

**Stockholm** Built on 14 small islands, Stockholm is often called the "Venice of the North." But one big difference between Stockholm and Venice is the cleanliness of the water around Stockholm. The Scandinavian water is so clean and clear you can fish or swim right in the heart of the city. Touring the islands by boat is a great way to see Stockholm. Tickets can be purchased from the Strömma Canal Company (Strömma Kanalbolaget) at the Stockholm City Hall Bridge, 08/58-71-40-00, or from the Waxholm Steamship Company (Waxholmsbolaget) on Strömkajen, in front of Grand Hotel, 08/67-95-830.

*An old and new city.* Because most of its main attractions are in a relatively small area, Stockholm can be viewed quite easily. Another way, besides the boat tour, to get a good look at the city, is to go to the City Hall (Stadshuset) at Hantverksgatan 1 and take the elevator to the top. You will see that it is both a modern city and an old city with parts of it dating back to the Middle Ages.

Top priority should be given to Gamla Stan (Old Town) with its medieval streets. A good place for you to start is the Riddarholm Church (Riddarholms Kyrkan) on Riddarholmen, where most of Sweden's royalty ended up. (They're buried there.) The church, originally a Greyfriars monastery, dates from 1270.

Also in Gamla Stan is the Storkyrkan (Great Church), on Källargränd, which was consecrated in 1306 but dates back farther than that. It is now Sweden's national church where royal marriages are celebrated. To the left of the entrance is a candlestand with 49 candles. Why 49? Well, the designer, remembering Christ's words to forgive seventy times seven, wanted to put 490 candles on it, but space allowed for only one-tenth that number. Inside you can see the painting *Parhelion*, the oldest painting of Stockholm in existence, dating from 1520. The cathedral's treasure is Bernt Notke's masterpiece *St. George and the Dragon*, more than ten feet high. It was dedicated in 1489. Also worth seeing is Ehrenstrahl's *Last Judgment*. Under the pulpit lies the grave of Olaus Petri, the driving force in the Swedish

> Thanks for roses by the wayside,
> Thanks for thorns their stems contain!
> Thanks for home and thanks for fireside,
> Thanks for hope, that sweet refrain.
>
> AUGUST LUDWIG STORM,
> OF STOCKHOLM, SWEDEN

Reformation. One of Luther's pupils, he translated the New Testament in 1526, and by 1541 most of the Old Testament, into Swedish. In his spare time, he wrote hymns, sermons, history, and a play.

*Royal palace.* Not many active residences of European monarchs are open to the public, but Kungliga Slottet, Sweden's royal palace, is. If you don't happen to see Sweden's king and queen, they are probably at another palace, Drottningholm, about seven miles away.

*Family fun.* If you have kids with you, you will want to take time for Gröna Lund Tivoli, Stockholm's answer to Copenhagen's Tivoli. It's a favorite family attraction for Swedes as well as for tourists. It's located on Djurgården, which is known as Stockholm's fun island. Considered a family favorite, the park offers traditional rides as well as new attractions on the waterfront each season. Gröna Lund is open from mid-April to late September.

Another favorite destination for children is Junibacken, a fairytale house on Galärvarsv. Small carriages transport visitors through the world of Pippi Longstocking, the indomitable girl created by the Swedish children's book writer Astrid Lindgren.

Young and old alike will enjoy Skansen (Djurgården 49–51). More than 150 reconstructed traditional buildings from all over Sweden form a popular open-air folk museum. In addition to touring the historic buildings, visitors can spend time at various handicraft displays and demonstrations, an aquarium, an old-style *tivoli,* or amusement park, and a zoo, including native Scandinavian lynxes, elks, and wolves. With a restaurant and snack kiosks on location, you'll find it easy to spend an entire day.

*Botanical garden.* North of Stockholm's city center on Frescati is the Bergianska Botanical Garden (Bergianska Botaniska Trädgården). The garden claims to have the world's largest display of water lilies. Plants from all over the world are on display at the Victoria House.

*Boat trips.* If time permits, take a boat trip to Skokloster Palace, about 44 miles from Stockholm in Bålsta. An alternative destination might be Sigtuna. Sigtuna's main street is lined with colorful 19th-century wooden buildings, picturesque shops, and cafes; it is said to be the oldest street in Sweden. The town has three churches that have been in ruins since the 11th century, so the town existed before that.

About 20 minutes by boat outside Stockholm's city center lies a group of four islands known as the Feather Islets (Fjäderholmarna). Formerly a restricted military zone, the islands have been transformed into a vacationer's dream, and include restaurants, cafes, handicraft studios, shops, an aquarium featuring Baltic marine life, a museum depicting life in the islands, and a pirate-ship playground. Boats leave from Slussen, Strömkajen, and Nybroplan from late-April to mid-September. Tickets can be purchased from the Strömma Canal Company (Strömma Kanalbolaget, see p. 279).

*Gripsholm Castle.* Some 42 miles southwest of Stockholm is Gripsholm Castle, a 16th-century fortress that is one of the best-preserved castles in Sweden. Gripsholm is located on an island in Lake Mälaren near the attractive village of Mariefred.

**Birka** It is not much to look at today, but Birka on the island of Björkö in Lake Mälaren was once the major Viking market-place. It was here that Ansgar, the first known Christian missionary to Sweden, came in 829 to convert the people of the island. He stayed for 18 months with only modest success. To get to Birka you can take either a ferry from Rastaholm or a two-hour boat trip from Stockholm's City Hall. Once there, you can see the fort, the small Ansgar Chapel with three sculptures and several paintings, as well as several archaeological sites.

**Dalarna** Steeped in tradition, this province is the folklore center of the country, and it will give you a feeling of Sweden as it used to be. Here in the various villages you will see the regional costumes, with each village having its own colors and patterns. If you are fortunate enough to be here during a special festivity, you will see almost everyone in colorful outfits. You will hear folk music with fiddle, keyharp, clarinet, and accordion, and you will see local Dalarna painting on cupboards and chests, often including biblical scenes. You may even witness the church boat races across Lake Siljan. It's an old custom. In the old days it was customary for church members to row to church across the lake. When two boats met on the lake, they raced each other to church. During the month of July this custom continues.

**Dalby** This small town near Malmö has the oldest stone church still in use in Scandinavia. Founded by King Sven Estridsen in

1060, the church was a cathedral for six years and at one time was twice as long as it is today. In a showcase are copies from the *Book of Dalby,* one of the oldest Scandinavian manuscripts. The church is located between the cities of Malmö and Lund just off Road 11.

In Torna Hallestad, three miles west of town, the village church has vault paintings (from 1460) that depict the events of Passion Week with a flair. *The Entry into Jerusalem* has Herod waiting at the city gate and Zacchaeus in his sycamore tree, Christ washing his disciples' feet in a large basin, and Judas at the Last Supper looking as if he were one of the Three Stooges. Three runic stones built into the rear wall of the church are dated from around 1000.

**Drottningholm** Drottningholm's Slott (Queen's Island Castle) has been called a miniature Versailles for good reason. It is one of Europe's most delightful palaces with interiors from the 17th, 18th, and 19th centuries.

**Göta Canal** Built between 1810 and 1832, this navigable waterway connects Gothenburg on the west coast with Stockholm on the east, so ships don't need to use the Baltic Sea to get to the other city. In earlier centuries, the Swedes feared the Danes and the canal made it possible for ships to avoid proximity to Denmark. Today, since the Danes don't pose a threat, the canal is used mostly for leisure. There are several possibilities available for vacation travel from Gothenburg to Stockholm (or vice versa) (a) on a historic steamer, stopping at towns and villages along the way, (b) a shorter day trip, (c) hire a smaller boat yourself, or (d) rent a bicycle and go as far as you want on a towpath.

## Bridget of Sweden (1303–1373)

Though she was raised to be a lady-in-waiting to the queen of Sweden, Bridget became a mother, a nun, an advisor to Swedish royalty, the founder of a religious order, a pilgrim preacher, an organizer of charities, a nag to the Pope, and a mystic visionary. Married at 13, she had eight children, but when her husband died, she pursued the visions she had been having and founded a religious order for both men and women in Vadstena, Sweden. She went to Rome to get her Bridgettine order approved. While there, she organized charities for the poor and criticized one Pope, whom she denounced as "a murderer of souls, more unjust than Pilate and more cruel than Judas."

Canonized 20 years after her death, Bridget was named the patron saint of Sweden.

Sites associated with Bridget's life are located in Vadstena, Sweden; Rome, Italy; and Downpatrick, Northern Ireland.

**Gothenburg (Göteborg)** The second largest city in the country, Gothenburg is the country's major port and is generously scattered with parks and gardens. Gothenburg was once known as "Little London" due to a heavy British influence during the 19th century, but it more closely resembles a "Little Amsterdam," and with good reason. Dutch architects laid out the city plan two centuries earlier, giving it a network of straight streets divided by canals. Only one of the major canals survives, and visitors explore the canal by sightseeing boats. Passengers can buy one-hour tour tickets at the Paddan terminal on Kungsportsplatsen.

The Paddan sightseeing boats are an attraction in themselves. They tour the canals and go to Liseberg, the amusement park that is the most visited attraction in Sweden. Besides the Paddan boats, you can also have an enjoyable ride here via the vintage trams. The Liseberg amusement park, at Öregrytev. 5, is open from May through August and on weekends in April and September. It is well-managed and provides everything from concerts to rides for all ages. With gardens, trees, and flower beds, it is also pleasant to walk through.

On leaving Liseberg you can see Örgyryte Old Church, the oldest church in the city. It dates from 1250.

> Neither life nor death shall ever
> From the Lord His children sever.
> Unto them His grace He showeth,
> And their sorrows all He knoweth.
>
> LINA SANDELL BERG OF SWEDEN

The Konstmuseum (Art Museum) is certainly one of the best in the country and holds works not only by Scandinavian artists but also Rembrandt's *Knight with Falcon* as well as paintings by French, Italian, and Spanish artists.

You'll find a little bit of everything in Gothenburg's Garden Association (Trädgårdsföreningen), just off Kungsportsavenyn, from its Rosarium with 3,000 species of roses to its Fjarilhuset (butterfly house) with 200 to 300 butterflies flitting around. Also in the area is Slottsskogen on Vegagatan, a zoological park where royal animals once grazed.

A museum and church in southwest Gothenburg (the Masthugget section) are also of interest. The museum is the Sjofahrtsmuseum (Maritime Museum) at Stigbergstorget, built on the site of an old shipyard. It gives you the history of shipbuilding from the time of the Vikings; on the ground floor is a well-stocked aquarium. The church, Masthuggskyrkan, is unusual because it follows the shipbuilding theme of the area. Its tower is capped by a typical helm. Inside, the ceiling reminds you of a Viking ship. The organ is carved with angels playing musical instruments.

Nineteenth-century hymn writer Lina Sandell (Berg) was from this area. When she was 26, she was accompanying her father aboard a ship across Lake Vättern to Gothenburg. Suddenly when the ship lurched, her father was thrown overboard and drowned. Afterward, Lina Sandell wrote the hymn "Day by Day and with Each Passing Moment."

**Grönklitt** Bring your binoculars when you come to the bear park (Byornpark) here, about ten miles from Orsa. It claims to be the largest bear park on the continent. The bears are in enclosures in a natural environment, but walkways allow you to get close enough to take pictures.

**Halmstad** On the first floor of the museum here you will find a fascinating display of folk art. Between 1700 and 1850, people decorated their cottage walls at Christmastime with their homemade paintings. Some were done on cloth, others on paper. Favorite themes were the three Wise Men, the wedding in Cana, and the parable of the ten wise and foolish virgins. On the top floor are professional works done by the Halmstad school of artists.

**Helsingborg** If you're in this city (population 82,000), you are probably going someplace else, but take a look at the city before you go. Helsingborg is only three miles from Denmark and during the summer, ferries cross every 15 minutes. An ultramodern traffic terminal unites the railway station with the port, the bus terminal, and the car parks. The complex with its shops and restaurants is worth a visit in itself.

Not far away is a monumental staircase (an elevator is also available) that takes you up to King Oskar's Terrace, part of Sofiero Slott (castle) on Sofierovägen, and from the top you get a good view of not only the town but also across the sound into Denmark, where you can see Elsinore (Hamlet's castle, actually called Helsingborg).

Then after coming down from the staircase make a left turn into Sankt Maria Kyrka, built in the 15th century on the site of an older church. On the left as you enter you will see a portrait of Martin Luther and on the right a painting of the parable of Lazarus and the rich man.

About ten miles north of Helsingborg in Brunnby is an unusual medieval church. As you go in, you will see paintings of eight Old Testament figures, then eight male saints, then eight female saints, followed by apostles and church fathers, all labeled with their names. In the churchyard you will see a rare tithe barn, which is where the area farmers brought the produce that they were tithing.

**Husaby** King Olav Skotkonung was baptized here by St. Sigfrid, an English missionary, and became the first Swedish king to abandon the Viking gods and embrace Christianity. The date was 1008. Just east of the church is a well where the baptism took place. The present church dates from the mid–12th century.

**Karesuando** Here is Sweden's northernmost church, about 150 miles north of the Arctic Circle. Alongside the church is a small wooden cottage (open to visitors) where Lars Levi Laestadius, a fiery evangelist, lived in the 1800s. Though he had established a reputation in Sweden as a renowned botanist and had received from France the Légion d'honneur, he became an evangelist, transforming his local parish and also having a major impact on other churches in Finland and Norway as well as Sweden.

**Karlstad** As a lumber town it was prone to fires, so the modern city with its lovely squares and wide streets dates only to the second half of the 19th century. Its cathedral on Norra Kyrkogaten, however, goes back to 1730. At times the many symbols in the cathedral seem to conflict with each other. The gilded coat of arms on the porch is surrounded by symbols of Christ, but other symbols refer to various religions.

South of the city is Mariebergsskogen in Mariebergs Park, an open-air park that includes a children's zoo, a fun-fair, a museum, and more. Still farther south on the peninsula of Hammaro is a 14th-century church that has some 15th-century paintings and an 18th-century altarpiece.

**Luleå** This is Arctic Circle and reindeer-breeding country, but you might be surprised as to what else you will find here. With 43,000 people it is the administrative capital of the province of Norrbotten. Gammelstad (Old Town in the original Luleå) is a few miles away and boasts a stone church in the town center that was built at the end of the 15th century. Around the church are some 500 church cottages, owned by the church. Because people came from such distances to attend church, cottages were built so that church members could stay overnight and they are still used by parishioners today during important religious holidays. Church stables were provided for the horses and a tithe barn to collect the offerings of produce was available.

**Lund** In 1103 the Pope declared that Lund would be the seat of an independent archbishop over the entire area of Denmark, Sweden, Norway, Finland, Iceland, and Greenland, making it the largest archdiocese in Europe. Today it is best known for its university, the largest in Scandinavia with more than 20,000 students, as well as its major industrial companies. The cathedral on Kyrkogatan was completed in 1160. The 19th-century bronze doors show biblical history from Adam onward, the first three rows being the Old Testament and the next four the childhood of Christ.

**Malmö** The third largest city of Sweden, Malmö is closer to Copenhagen than to Stockholm and consequently many of its sites have a Danish flavor. When the Reformation began, Malmö was under Danish rule. Then the mayor, Jorgen Kock, got a printing press, and a local clergyman, Claes Mortensen, translated the Bible into Danish. Shortly thereafter, Kock negotiated a treaty between the Swedes and the Danes, and the province of Skane, including the city of Malmö, became Swedish. In the center of the main square, Storforget, stands the equestrian statue of the Swedish king who signed the treaty in 1658. The town hall, Radhus, was originally built by Mayor Kock, but was redone in the 1860s. The house of the dynamic mayor built in 1522 is at the northwest corner of the square.

On the other side of the town hall is St. Peter's Church (Sankt Petri Kyrka), which was built in the 14th century, probably on the site of an even earlier church. Though many of the paintings in the church are not in good condition, of interest are the paintings on the south wall of the Church Fathers, Gregory, Ambrose, Augustine, and Jerome, along with Christ in the winepress. The pulpit itself is supported by a statue of Moses, and on it are reliefs depicting the annunciation, Christ's birth, the Last Supper, the crucifixion, the resurrection, and the ascension. In the floor of the nave near the pulpit is the grave of Mayor Kock. Pastor Mortensen's grave is also in the sanctuary. The organ is worth seeing. Built in 1951, it has 5,935 pipes.

The historic medieval organ, which dates at least to 1500 and is still playable, is now in the Malmö Museum. The museum was once Malmöhus Castle and is located on Malmöhusvägen. Across from the organ in the museum is Joakim Skovgaard's *Christ in Majesty.*

**Njupeskär** Toward the Norwegian border is one of Sweden's highest waterfalls, with a total drop of about 400 feet. A footpath goes from the car park to the waterfall.

**Rättvik** At midsummer hundreds of people flock to Rättvik to attend church. But this is no ordinary church service—it marks the midpoint of summer, and those in attendance arrive in longboats dressed in traditional costumes, a tradition that has continued for centuries.

> When through the woods and forest glades I wander
> And hear the birds sing sweetly in the trees,
> When I look down from lofty mountain grandeur
> And hear the brook and feel the gentle breeze
> Then sings my soul, my Savior, God to Thee,
> How great Thou art, how great Thou art.
>
> CARL BOBERG OF KALMAR, SWEDEN

**Storuman** In northern Sweden, you will find many large wooden churches, but this church, located 2 miles east of town in the little village of Stensele, built in 1886, may be the biggest. In this large church is one of the smallest books. It has a copy of the Lord's Prayer in seven languages and you will need a magnifying glass to read it. The church also has a good facsimile of Queen Christina's 1646 Bible.

**Uppsala** Uppsala is located in the area commonly known as Sweden's "Folklore District." The city is home to Uppsala University on Akademig., Scandinavia's oldest, founded in 1477, and to Linni Trädgården at Svartbäcksg. 27, the gardens and home of Carl von Linné. Known as Linnaeus, in the 1740s the botany professor developed the system of plant and animal classification still used today. The Carolina Rediviva (University Library) has more than two million volumes, but the one manuscript that draws the most attention is its Codex Argenteus (the Silver Bible) on display to the right of the entrance. It is a translation into the now extinct Gothic language, and dates from before A.D. 526.

Uppsala Castle (Uppsala Slott) is strategically positioned on a hill (Borggården) and is easily visible. The castle was built during the 1540s by King Gustav Vasa, who was known for his split with the Vatican. In an effort to show his disdain for the Catholic Church, he arranged to have the castle's cannons aimed directly at the archbishop's palace.

The impressive twin towers of Uppsala's cathedral (Domkyrka) on Domkyrkoplan dominate the city's skyline. For 700 years, this cathedral has been the seat of the archbishop of the Swedish church. In the north tower is a cathedral museum, where a collection of Europe's finest ecclesiastical textiles is on display.

Gamla Uppsala is Swedish for Old Uppsala, and this area of town is indeed old. The area is dominated by three huge burial mounds, which date back to the 5th century, the resting places of the first Swedish kings, Aun, Egil, and Adils. Next to the burial mounds is a Christian church, the seat of Sweden's first archbishop, built on the site of a former pagan temple.

**Växjö** The cathedral in Växjö on Linnégatan was founded by the English monk St. Sigfrid. When he baptized King Olav at nearby Husaby in 1008, it marked the beginning of the Christian church in Sweden. There is a large brass *S* in the floor of the nave where Sigfrid is said to have been buried. The church was rebuilt about 40 years ago to restore its medieval appearance. The artwork is mostly modern. The mosaic in the south transept takes its themes from the Book of Revelation, with the 12 gates of the new Jerusalem and the seven angels with trumpets. In the north transept, however, is an 18th-century painting of the Last Supper.

The famous botanist Carl von Linné (Linnaeus) and the father of Swedish gymnastics, Per Henrik Ling, both went to school here. Beside the cathedral in the Linnepark is a bust of the botanist.

Across the bridge is the Swedish Emigrant Institute (Utvandrare Hus), a building that makes this city a popular stopping point for Swedish-Americans. Today it has the largest European archives on emigration and a library of more than 25,000 volumes. Between 1846 and 1950, 1.3 million people (about one quarter of the country), left Sweden for America. More than 250,000 of these came from this province.

One room in the institute is the study of Vilhem Moberg, the writer who told the story of the emigrants in his four "Emigrant" novels. On the second Sunday in every August, Växjö celebrates "Minnesota Day," when Swedes and Swedish-Americans come together to remember their common heritage with—believe it or not—square dancing. Utvandrareshus (Emigrants' House) is on Vilhelm Mosbergsg. 4 in the town center.

Växjö is also the center of Sweden's glass country. Glassmaking dates back to about 1550, when Venetian glassblowers were invited to the Swedish court. All of Sweden's major glass companies still operate in this area. Orrefors celebrated its centennial in 1998, and both it and Kosta Boda open their plants to the public. Tour information can be had from Orrefors at 0481/34000 and from Kosta Boda at 0481/34500. Check out their factory shops, which sometimes offer huge discounts.

**Visby** On the island of Gotland in the Baltic Sea is this medieval city, enclosed almost completely by a town wall. There are buildings from the Middle Ages on narrow streets, framed with climbing roses. Christianity came here in the 11th century but now ten of Visby's old churches are in ruins. Sankt Maria Kyrka, on Norra Kyrkogatan, consecrated in 1225, is the only one in use. Above the reddish limestone baptismal font is a 13th-century wooden figure of the risen Christ. When you see the grandeur of this church, you are impressed with what the city must have looked like when all the churches were active.

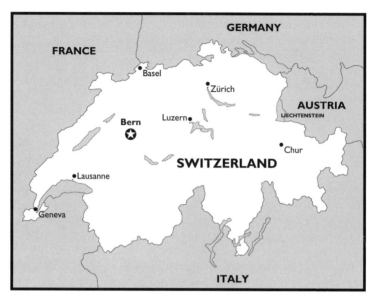

# Switzerland

Switzerland Tourism
  US 212-757-5944
  Canada 416-695-2090
  UK 020-7734-1921
*Web site*
  Entire country www.switzerlandtourism.ch
For a complete list of updated links, visit www.christiantraveler.com

### Country in a Capsule

*Size:* Switzerland is about two-thirds the size of West Virginia, but has three times as many people. Like West Virginia, it is landlocked and mountainous. Ten cities in Switzerland have populations over 100,000; West Virginia doesn't have any.

*Religion:* About 44 percent claim to be Protestant, about 47 percent Roman Catholic. The Jewish percentage is less than 1 percent. Most of French-speaking Switzerland around Geneva is Protestant, as are the northern and eastern sections. The central and southern sections are predominantly Catholic.

*Language:* Four languages are spoken in Switzerland. Nearly two-thirds of the country is German-speaking. About 18 percent is French-speaking, 11 percent Italian, and 7 percent Romansh, a language of Latin origin. In major cities and tourist areas, you will have no problem being understood in English.

*Money:* The Swiss franc is equivalent to about 54 cents.

*Food:* Try a Swiss fondue while you are here. Another Swiss specialty is geschnetzeltes Kalbfleisch (veal bits in cream sauce with mushrooms). Besides Swiss chocolate, of course, you will want to try leckerli, which is a spiced bread made with honey and almonds.

*Shopping:* Watches and chocolates are naturals, but also think of handicrafts and linens.

*Brief history:* Switzerland dates its founding to 1291 when three "forest states" signed a treaty of mutual assistance "to last, if God will, for ever." The legend of William Tell is loosely (very loosely) based on that declaration of independence from outside interference. In the 1500s the preaching of Reformation leaders Ulrich Zwingli (in Zurich) and John Calvin (in Geneva) added to the independent fervor of this little country. The French wanted to impose a centralized republic on the Swiss people, but the Swiss chose instead to copy the American model of states (or cantons) federating together, and this was shown in their constitution of 1848. Since then, Switzerland has maintained neutrality in European conflicts, and its people have worked for peace. The International Red Cross was founded here in 1863.

**Geneva** It's not the capital of Switzerland nor is it the country's largest city, but it is a lovely cosmopolitan city, and perhaps more than any other city in the country it has affected the entire world. This is partly because it is the headquarters of the Red Cross, partly because it was the second seat of the United Nations, housing several international organizations, but mostly because it was John Calvin's city and several Protestant denominations have their roots here.

*The waterfront.* Geneva's landmark is its harbor and its Jet d'Eau, the highest fountain in the world. The entire waterfront area is a never-to-be-forgotten scene. The Jardin Anglais (English garden) on the south bank is dominated by a floral clock and next to it is the Parc de la Grange, arguably the finest rose garden in the country. A couple blocks south is Old Town with the Cathédrale St-Pierre, where John Calvin preached and where the Reformation Monument stands.

*Calvin and Knox.* In the 16th century John Calvin and John Knox fled here. Because of their preaching and teaching, Geneva rejected Catholicism and became a stronghold of Protestantism. The Protestant Lecture Hall (Auditoire de Calvin) on Pl. de la Taconnerie is a Gothic chapel that had been Catholic until Calvin arrived on the scene. In the 16th century Calvin taught from the Lecture Hall and founded what became Geneva's university. The Scot reformer John Knox also preached here for three years beginning in 1556. Today worshipers can enjoy English, Dutch, and Italian services here every Sunday.

The Gothic St. Peter's Cathedral (Cathédrale St-Pierre), begun in 1160 and located on Cour St-Pierre, also became Protestant under the influence of Calvin. Calvin's seat is on the north aisle, just before the transept crossing. The simplicity of the nave reflects the change to Protestantism, as the church was stripped of its icons. Visitors can climb the

---

## JOHN CALVIN (1509-1564)

John Calvin and Martin Luther were the two spark plugs of the Protestant Reformation, but they were quite the opposite in personality. Luther was outgoing and talkative; Calvin was quiet and sensitive. Born in Noyon, France, Calvin was introduced to Luther's teachings while a student at the University of Paris. When 24, he experienced a sudden conversion. After attending a Protestant meeting, he found himself a hunted man and fled to Switzerland. He was expelled from Geneva and went to Strasbourg, in France, where he pastored a congregation of refugees, found a wife, and then was invited back to Geneva. He spent the rest of his life leading the Reformation there.

A systematizer, Calvin codified the city's laws, making Geneva the Rome of Protestantism, and codified the Reformed faith with his *Institutes.*

Sites associated with Calvin's life and ministry are located throughout the city of Geneva, Switzerland, and Noyon and Strasbourg, France.

---

north tower for a lovely view of the city. Underneath the Cathédrale St-Pierre are archeological remains (Site Archéologique)
unearthed in 1976. Excavations continue still, but many intriguing remains are already visible, including the remnants of a 4th-
century Christian sanctuary, 5th-century mosaic floors, and an
11th-century crypt.

Erected between 1909 and 1917, the Monument of the Reformation (Monument de la Réformation) is a huge wall, 329 feet
long, with larger-than-life statues of 16th-century Reformation
leaders: William Farel, who brought Calvin to Geneva; John
Calvin, who preached in St. Peter's Cathedral and organized a
church-state in the city; Theodore Beza, who succeeded Calvin as
leader of the Swiss Reformation; and John Knox, who learned his
doctrine from Calvin and then returned to Scotland to spread the
Reformation there. Memorials to two other leading reformers,
Ulrich Zwingli (of Zurich) and Martin Luther (of Germany), flank
the statues. The monument is located in the Parc des Bastions.

*Two other churches* in the area make for fascinating stops: the
Russian Orthodox St. Croix church on rue Toepffer, with its
golden domes and its interior adorned with Byzantine paintings,
and the St. Paul church (Eglise St-Paul), which features contemporary religious art including 14 stained glass windows and a canvas illustrating the life of the apostle Paul.

*Museums.* The south bank also houses some wonderful muse-
ums, including the Museum of Art and History at 2 Terrasse St-
Victor and the Petit Palais Museum of Modern Art at 10 rue des
Vieux-Grenadiers.

*Parks.* On the north bank of Lake Geneva are three beautifully
landscaped parks. One of them, La Perle du Lac off rue de Lausanne, contains the Musée d'Histoire des Sciences, impressive for
its murals as well as for its display of scientific equipment.

*Festivals.* Geneva is host to two great festivals each year. The
International Motor Show comes in early March and is headquartered in the International Museum of the Automobile located
at the Palexpo, Halle No. 7, which displays 400 vehicles in chrono-
logical order including a Ferrari owned by Elvis Presley.

In December Geneva celebrates Escalade Day, remembering
when the city beat back the invasion of the Catholic Savoyards
who were attempting to scale the walls (l'escalade) and take back
the Protestant city. The celebration culminates with a religious

service in the cathedral, but it is accompanied by fireworks and cauldrons of Swiss chocolate.

*Tour boats.* One of the very best ways to enjoy Geneva's stunning natural beauty is by boat on Lake Léman. Many tour operators ply the Alpine waters, offering trips from as brief as 30 minutes to daylong cruises to Montreux and back. Consider Mouettes Genevoises (022/732-29-44); Compagnie Générale de Navigation (022/312-52-23); or Swissboat (022/732-47-47).

**Aarau** Three miles southwest of town in Schönenwerd on Olten Rd. is the Bally Schuhmuseum. Maybe you didn't come to Switzerland to look at shoes, but the collection from all periods of history and all kinds of people is both fascinating and educational. The town of Aarau has a delightful old town section and a parish church on Kirchgasse with a 17th-century belfry.

**Altdorf** In the town's square stands a statue in honor of William Tell, the famous archer. The town is a crossroads community. Going south will take you into Italian Switzerland, going north into German Switzerland; and here you feel the influence of both.

**Andermatt** South of Altdorf is the ski resort community of Andermatt, and farther south yet is the beautiful St. Gotthard pass. The pass gets its name from a chapel built in about 1300 in honor of St. Gotthard, bishop of Hildesheim.

**Appenzell** This fascinating community is full of embroidery shops and bakeries. Its Baroque church and the museum, both at Hauptgasse 4, are both worthwhile stops. (Incidentally, so are the bakeries.) But four miles southeast is the cable car ride up Hoher Kasten, from which you can see both Lake Constance in the north and the Liechtenstein Mountains in the south.

**Augst** Seven miles southeast of Basel are the Roman ruins that reveal the traces of an ancient town of about 20,000 people. The excavated theater with a seating capacity of 8,000 is the largest Roman ruin in the country. Outdoor concerts are held here in the summer. You may also be interested in seeing the reconstruction of a Roman house and the adjoining museum (the Römermuseum) at Giebenacherstr. 17. A variety of exhibits are on display, including "the silver hoard," discovered about 40 years ago. The "hoard" is a 68-piece sumptuous table set.

**Baden** Not to be confused with Baden in Germany, this is an old spa that dates to Roman times. Its hot sulphur springs make it a popular health resort today for people with rheumatism and respiratory disorders. Two miles south of Baden is Ehem, a former Cistercian abbey, which now houses a school. The abbey church was rebuilt in 1517, and its sophisticated interior makes it a worthwhile visit. The abbey is located between the railroad station and the Limmat River.

**Basel** This city of 180,000 people is not just another big city. Its Old Town will capture you. Its 12th-century Münster (cathedral) on Münsterpl. with two Gothic towers is full of intriguing art. The old 16th-century streets and houses transport you into another time frame. The Kunstmuseum (art museum) at St. Alban-Graben 16 is outstanding with a great deal of biblical art including Grunewald's *Christ on the Cross* and Rembrandt's *David before Saul*. The first floor contains 15th- and 16th-century art, while the second has 20th-century art, including works by Chagall and Klee.

The Zoologischer Garten at Binningerstr. 40 is an internationally regarded zoo with 5,600 animals from all continents. The children's zoo and play areas will be enjoyable for younger members of the family.

Basel was home for Erasmus, the philosopher with whom Luther dialogued. Mementoes of Erasmus are contained in the Historical Museum on Barfüsserpl. Because the building was once a 14th-century Franciscan church, it is also full of altarpieces and liturgical objects from that period. Incidentally, the square takes its name, "Barefoot Square" from the Franciscan friars who went without shoes.

Neoorthodox theologian Karl Barth was born in Basel and spent his final years, after being expelled from Nazi Germany, at the University of Basel.

**Bern** The capital of Switzerland, Bern has much to offer the tourist even though it is usually not regarded as highly as Geneva, Zurich, Lucerne, or Basel. Old Bern is a pedestrian zone and its monuments are floodlit from Easter through October. The

Heiliggeist Kirche is not in the best of neighborhoods but is worth seeing in the daytime. Its large Baroque facade contrasts with modern and medieval buildings in Bern. Located at Spitalg. 44, the church was finished in 1729.

However, a better stop is Bern's famous cathedral (Münster) at Münsterpl. 1. This great Gothic cathedral was begun in 1421 but it took over a century to complete. Its floorplan is so spacious that when it was constructed half the population could worship in it at one time. Take special note of the fabulous, brightly painted portal, completed in 1490, depicting the last judgment. There are beautiful stained glass windows in the church, some original and some reproductions. The steeple was added in 1893, and at 328 feet is the tallest in Switzerland. If you want to climb a few steps, 270 of them will take you into the tower to a great panorama of the town.

> For why? The Lord our God is good,
> His mercy is forever sure;
> His truth at all times firmly stood,
> And shall from age to age endure.
>
> WILLIAM KETHE, GENEVA, SWITZERLAND

The Fine Arts Museum at Hodlerstr. 12 has a great collection of paintings including Fra Angelico's *Madonna and Child*. Lutherans especially will be interested in seeing Cranach's portraits of Martin Luther and his wife Katharine.

The Historical Museum (Historisches Museum) at Helvetiapl. 5 houses a wide variety of items crossing a similarly wide span of time. A prehistoric collection contrasts with 15th-century Flemish tapestries as well as 15th- and 16th-century stained glass. Protestants will especially enjoy the three-way portrait of reformers Calvin, Zwingli, and Luther.

Bern is known for its bears. According to legend, Berchtold V named Bern after the first animal he killed when hunting: a bear. At that time there were plenty of bears. Today your best bet at seeing a bear is at the Bear Pits (Bärengraben) on the south side of Nydeggbrücke. Specimens of the live mascots have been on display here since the late 15th century, fat and well-fed on carrots. They can be viewed year-round.

The ancient Nydegg Church (Nydeggkirche) on Nydegg. marks the founding place of the city of Bern. It was constructed between 1341 and 1571 on the foundations of Berchtold V's ruined fortress.

Bern's Clock Tower (Zytglogeturm), located on Kramg. between Theaterpl. and Kornhauspl., is the city's oldest building. The massive landmark was built as a city gate in 1191 and received its astronomical clock in 1530. At four minutes to the hour every hour mechanical figures parade out of the clock. A knight circling above the figures hammers out the hour, and Father Time, seated in the middle of the group, beats time with a scepter in one hand and an hourglass in the other.

**Chillon** Ever since Lord Byron wrote his poem "The Prisoner of Chillon," the castle on the banks of Lake Geneva has been the most popular monument in Switzerland. François de Bonivard had tried to introduce the Reformation but was arrested and thrown into the dungeon at Chillon where he was chained to one of the pillars. He was freed by the Bernese in 1536 after four years. The castle as well as the dungeon are worth seeing.

**Disentis** This small town, the center of Romansh culture, was colonized by Benedictine monks in the Middle Ages. Today it is a great place for skiing in the winter and delightful walks in the summer. The foundations of the Benedictine abbey date from the 8th century, but the present buildings are more recent. The church was built between 1695 and 1712.

**Einsiedeln** It is just a small town with a population of about 10,000, but it is a famous pilgrimage destination for many. On September 14 a torchlight procession leads to the Great Festival of the Miraculous Dedication at the Abbey Church in the town square. In addition, every five years performances of *The Great Theatre of the World* by Calderon de la Barca take place here (the next one in 2005). The abbey church on Kreuzwig, built in 1719 to 1735, is 370 feet long (longer than a football field). The style is Baroque, and the artwork is an exuberant display of paintings, frescoes, and stuccowork.

Incidentally, Ulrich Zwingli, the Protestant reformer, served two years at the church here before moving on to Zurich where the Swiss Reformation began.

**Fribourg** This large town southwest of Bern has been a Catholic stronghold despite the Protestant Reformation that swept Geneva to the south and Zurich to the north. In the 1600s, it became the

Catholic capital of the country as Franciscans, Jesuits, and others came to build in it. Located on the dividing line between the French-speaking and German-speaking parts of the country, you will find street signs in French on the west bank of the Sarine River, and street signs in German on the east bank.

Old Town is worth a visit. The Baroque-style Eglise des Augustins near the Pont de Zähringen displays religious scenes from the life of the Virgin Mary. Nearby is Rue de la Samaritaine and on it is The Samaritan's Fountain with artwork by Hans Gieng depicting Christ with the Samaritan woman. The New Town area has the magnificent Cathédrale St. Nicholas on the Pl. de l'Hôtel de Ville, which dates from 1283, and the Franciscan church, Eglise des Cordeliers on rue de Morat, filled with notable pieces of art. While you are in town, visit the Museum of Art and History with its plethora of religious art.

**Grindelwald** If you are driving, you should know that this is the only mountain resort in the Jungfrau area that you can reach by car. And it is also a great jumping-off place (if you will pardon the expression) to get to other famous resort areas. Two early morning trains can take you up the Jungfrau peak (which means "virgin" in English, in honor of Mary).

**Interlaken** Twelve miles northwest of Grindelwald is this famous resort area. Besides the rides via rack-rail, cable car, or funicular, boat trips are also available on Thun Lake and on Lake Brienz. The town is known for its aquatic sports availability as well as its skiing, and just plain old sightseeing.

**Lausanne** This is a gorgeous, cosmopolitan city on the northern shore of Lake Léman. The first cathedral was built here around the end of the 8th century and it was a major Catholic center until the Reformation. When Bernese troops occupied it in 1536, it became a Protestant territory. Through the years it has also achieved a great reputation for its culture; many of the famous British poets of the 1800s spent time here. More recently, when Billy Graham chose a site for the Congress on World Evangelization in the 1970s, he chose Lausanne. Meetings were held at the Palais de Beaulieu on av. des Bergières.

Ouchy is the small community that is Lausanne's port, and it is linked to Lausanne by what has been called the world's shortest subway system. Actually, it is not much more than a funicular, but you will enjoy the experience.

Lausanne's Cathedral on Pl. de la Cathédrale was begun in the mid-1100s and completed 100 years later. It has been called the finest Gothic building in Switzerland.

If you have time, take one of the lake steamers from Ouchy-Lausanne and enjoy a leisurely cruise of upper Lake Geneva.

**Locarno** This Italian-speaking town—not to be confused with Lugano, a few miles south—has not only a fascinating castle, Castello Visconti on ripa Canova, but also a very interesting church, Madonna del Sasso. The church is on top of a hill overlooking both the city and Lake Maggiore, and you can get there by car or better yet by a six-minute funicular ride from the station on Via Ramogna. Notice the altarpiece by Bramantino from 1522 *Flight into Egypt*. It's at the end of the south aisle of the church. Then, out of the church, take a ten-minute cable car ride up Alpe di Cardada, where the view is better yet. If you aren't satisfied, take a chairlift to the top of the Cimetta, and that will get you up 5,482 feet. And that's quite a view!

**Lucerne (Luzern)** This is one of those places where you keep running out of film.

*Bridges.* One of the most charming features of Lucerne is its compactness, making it easily navigable by foot. As you explore the city, be sure to walk across the Chapel Bridge (Kapellbrücke), synonymous with Lucerne itself. The bridge was originally constructed in the early 14th century and crosses diagonally over the Reuss River near its junction with Lake Lucerne (Vierwaldstättersee). The bridge, its shingled roof, and water tower are nearly entirely wood. Tragically, it was all but destroyed in a fire in 1993, including many of the lovely 17th-century paintings inside it. The original 111 gable panels, painted by Heinrich Wägmann, have been replaced with replicas that depict scenes from the history of Lucerne and Switzerland. There are also paintings of the legendary exploits of the city's patron saints, St. Leodegar and St. Mauritius. The bridge is located between Seebrücke and Rathaus-Steg bridges, connecting Rathausquai and Bahnhofstr.

Another beautiful footbridge is the narrow, weather-beaten, all-wooden Spreuer Bridge (Spreuerbrücke), a covered bridge dating back to 1408. Like the more famous Kapellbrücke, its interior

## THE SWISS ALPS

Switzerland is known and loved for its Alps. Even the most well-traveled visitors are reduced to monosyllables in the midst of Switzerland's tremendous natural beauty. To really get a good eyeful of God's creation, take one of the ubiquitous incline railways throughout the country—just look for the —|—|—|—|—|—|— symbol on your map. Not to be missed in the Lucerne area are Mount Pilatus, which can be reached by ferry, train, or car to Alpnachstad; or Mount Rigi Kulm, which can be reached by ferry, train, or car to Vitznau. In Interlaken climb Mount Harder Kulm by funicular, which ascends from the Ostbahnhof train station. And near Zermatt, the cog railway, the Gornergratbahn, serves both skiers and sightseers. It connects out of the main Zermatt train station.

Boat cruises are popular ways to enjoy both the scenic beauty of the Alps and the crystal clear water of the Alpine lakes. Two of the most popular places to cruise are in Lucerne and Geneva. Lucerne's cruise ships run on a standardized, mass-transit schedule, crossing the lake regularly and stopping at scenic resorts and historic sites on the shore (phone, Schiffahrtsgesellschaft des Vierwaldstättersees at 041/367-67-67).

Geneva's stunning natural beauty is complemented by Lake Léman. Many tour operators cruise the local waters, offering short trips or daylong cruises to Montreux and back. Consider Mouettes Genevoises (022/732-29-44); Compagnie Générale de Navigation (022/312-52-23); or Swissboat (022/732-47-47).

gables bear well-preserved paintings, although these are a bit gloomier. The artist, Kaspar Meglinger, created the *Dance of Death* series during the 17th century. But the pictures have a more medieval style, depicting scenes from the plague that devastated Lucerne and all of Europe during the 14th century. In the center of the bridge is a charming 16th-century chapel that offers a view back to the Old Town. The Spreuer Bridge is located between Geissmattbrücke and Reussbrücke bridges, connecting Zeughaus Reuss-Steg and Mühlenpl.

*Churches.* A Baroque masterpiece, the Jesuit Church (Jesuitenkirche) on Bahnhofstr. was constructed between 1667 and 1678. The church's lovely interior has been painstakingly restored, a rococo fireworks display of gold, marble, and frescoes. The two onion-dome towers flanking the entrance were added in 1893.

The beautiful Collegiate Church (Hofkirche) at St. Leodegarstr. 13 was actually founded as a monastery, well over 1,000 years ago, in 750. The building was destroyed by fire in 1633 and rebuilt in the late-Renaissance style. Ask about organ recitals. The church's 80-rank organ, built in 1650, is considered one of Switzerland's finest.

The Franciscan Church (Franziskanerkirche), located on Franziskanerpl. just off Münzg., was built more than 700 years ago but like most buildings has undergone occasional modernization efforts. Its choir stalls and carved wooden pulpit were added in the 17th century.

*Transportation museum.* Visitors of all ages enjoy the Verkehrshaus, a museum showing the history of transportation in Switzerland. You will see automobiles from all decades of the past century, locomotives and steam trains, cable cars, airships, rockets, and paddlewheel steamships.

*Boat tours.* The beautiful city of Lucerne and its shoreline ought to be seen from aboard a boat on the Vierwaldstättersee (which is quite a mouthful. You may prefer the English, Lake Lucerne). The cruise ships that ply the lake's waters run on a standardized, mass-transit schedule, crossing the lake regularly and stopping at scenic resorts and historic sites on the shore. Visitors can contact the boat company Schiffahrtsgesellschaft des Vierwaldstättersees at 041/367-67-67.

In addition, take the opportunity to travel up Mount Pilatus while you are here. You can take a boat to the base of the mountain and then take the rack-rail up the mountain, or you can drive to Alpnachstad and pick up the rack-rail there.

**Lugano** Now you are almost in Italy, and you can feel it in the atmosphere. You are also in a delightful center from which you can visit three famous lakes—Maggiore, Lugano, and Como. During the summer, you can enjoy open-air concerts in the Parco Civico, which is worth enjoying for its fountains and statues, even when you can't hear a concert.

Swissminiatur, 4.5 miles south of town at Melide, is an area that kids as well as moms and dads will enjoy. On 2.5 acres it shows in miniature the main attractions of each of the Swiss cantons. To help your family enjoy it more, there are miniature cable cars, boats, and trains that take you from place to place.

The Cathedral of St. Lawrence (Cattedrale de San Lorenzo) has a graceful Renaissance facade. Inside, enjoy stunning frescoes, and outside, a lovely view. The church is located on Via Cattedrale.

The stunning Church of St. Mary of the Angels (Chiesa di Santa Maria degli Angioli) was constructed in 1455. Located on Piazza

Luini, it houses many beautiful works of art, including the frescoes *Passion* and *Crucifixion* by Bernardino Luini.

The lovely Town Park (Parco Civico) has an aviary and a tiny deer zoo, which is especially popular with children. In addition to the fauna, the park has some interesting flora, including exotic plants, cacti, and over 1,000 varieties of roses. The view of the bay from the peninsula within the park isn't bad either. Musical events are frequently staged here during fair-weather months. The park is located south of Viale Carlo Cattaneo and east of Piazza Castello.

**Meiringen** You probably don't have a clue as to why there is a statue of Sherlock Holmes and a Sherlock Holmes Museum in the middle of Switzerland. Elementary, my dear Watson. Arthur Conan Doyle, author of the Sherlock Holmes books, loved Switzerland so much that he was made an honorary citizen. The museum reconstructs Holmes's drawing room and includes memorabilia of his faithful assistant, Doctor Watson. It is located on Arthur Conan Doyle Sq.

Not as many people go into the upper part of the village to the old church here. It is actually the fifth church built on the spot, the first one having been built in the 11th century. A series of Romanesque frescoes showing scenes from the Old Testament were recently discovered in the church.

**Montreux** At the other end of Lake Geneva (or Lake Léman, if you prefer) from Geneva is Montreux. It is a beautiful spot and it takes advantage of its setting to host a variety of festivals and musical events. The International Choral Festival meets the week after Easter, a jazz festival is held in July, and a Classical Music Festival in September.

**St. Gallen** Gall, a missionary from Ireland about a hundred years after St. Patrick, brought Christianity to Switzerland and established a monastery that became one of the outstanding educational institutions in the area during the Middle Ages. When the Reformation came to St. Gallen, the abbey lost its influence and not until 1750 did it begin to expand again.

The Cathedral on Klosterhof built from 1755 to 1768 on the site of an earlier church is remarkable, especially the chancel. Note the paintings illustrating the Beatitudes in the central dome. The former abbey is attached to the cathedral.

Even if you aren't interested in books, you should go into the library (Stiftsbibliothek) on Klosterhof. The painted ceilings, the rich woodwork, and the parquet floor are memorable. The library contains about 100,000 volumes, including 2,000 rare manuscripts that go back as far as the 8th century, and 1,650 pre-1500 books.

**St. Maurice** South of Montreux is this picturesque little town with a long history. Maurice was a Roman centurion at the end of the 3d century who led his African troops—the Theban Legion. On arriving near this spot, he and his forces were commanded to worship the Roman gods. When they refused to do so, he and his men were massacred. The Abbey of St. Maurice was founded in 515 by King Sigismund of Burgundy to perpetuate his memory. Thoughout the Middle Ages many of the faithful made pilgrimages here, often leaving gifts at the abbey. On September 22, St. Maurice and the other soldier-martyrs are still remembered. The Abbey Church on the north end of town dates from the 17th century, though the belfry itself goes back to the 11th century. The Treasury is an amazingly rich storehouse of gold and jewelry, brought by kings like Charlemagne as well as by peasants. Near the belfry is the Fouilles de Martolet, an intriguing excavation where foundations of buildings that go back to the 4th century have been discovered. The plan of the church is clearly seen. You can also visit the catacombs, leading to the crypt and tomb of St. Maurice.

**Tellsplatte** South of Brunnen on the shore of Lake Uri is the small chapel known as the Tellskapelle, commemorating an episode in the life of William Tell. After the "apple" incident, Tell was taken prisoner and thrown into a boat. When a sudden storm arose, he took advantage of the situation, leaped onto the rocky shoreline and escaped, kicking the boat back into the stormy sea. This is supposedly where it all happened.

**Villars** In the little village of Huemoz, near Villars, Francis and Edith Schaeffer established L'Abri, a refuge or shelter for young people seeking answers to the confusions of life. The place drew young people from many countries and they sat at the feet of this evangelical philosopher and his wife. Villars itself is a lovely mountain resort not far from Montreux. Though Schaeffer died in 1984, the work continues.

*303*

**Zermatt** The Matterhorn is practically synonymous with Switzerland, right up there with cheese and yodeling. And Zermatt is the place to see it best. An exhilarating cog railway, the Gornergratbahn, serves both as a ski transport and a sightseeing excursion. Completed in 1898, it is the highest exposed rail system in Europe, connecting out of the main Zermatt train station and then climbing slowly up to the Riffelberg, an impressive peak in its own right at 8,471 feet. You can also enjoy a great view from the top of the Rotenboden, at 9,248 feet. A short walk downhill from there will take you to the Riffelsee, a lake with outstanding reflections of the Matterhorn and tremendous photo opportunities. At the end of the cog railway line, passengers empty out onto the observation terraces of the Gornergrat, the highest of the three peaks at 10,269 feet. You can view some of the best the Swiss Alps have to offer, including the Matterhorn and scores of other peaks. If you don't feel close to God up here, it's your own fault. Be sure to bring warm clothes, good walking shoes, and sunglasses. If you like, you can purchase a one-way ticket and hike or ski down. Excursions depart from Zermatt Train Station every 24 minutes, from 7:00 A.M. to 7:00 P.M.

**Zillis** Admittedly, most visitors to Switzerland don't stop at Zillis. It's not that easy to find. Located south of Chur, not far from Via Mala, the Zillis church has a ceiling that is beautiful to behold. It is one of the finest pieces of painting by Romanesque artists that you will find anywhere in the country. Probably dating from the 12th century, 153 panels depict scenes from Revelation on the outer perimeter and scenes from the life of Christ on the inside panels.

**Zurich** It's the largest city in Switzerland, the financial and commercial center, and also the city where the Swiss Protestant Reformation first hit. Ulrich Zwingli, whose debates at the Zurich Town Hall on Limmat-Quai in 1523 sparked the Reformation, was minister of the Grossmünster on Zwinglipl. along the Limmat River. Built between the 11th and 13th centuries, it is still an awesome place to visit. In the 3d century St. Felix and his sister Regula were martyred nearby by the Romans. According to one legend, once the two were beheaded, they walked up the hill carrying their heads and collapsed on the spot where the Large Church now stands. A statue of Charlemagne can be seen on the church's south tower. According to another legend, which is a bit more likely, Charlemagne founded the church here when his horse stumbled on the very same spot. The existing church was actually erected in the 11th century.

While Zurich's skyline includes a number of church spires, that of the Church of Our Lady (Fraumünster) is perhaps the most lovely and graceful. Located on Stadthausquai, the church is worth viewing up close as well, especially the pre-Gothic Romanesque choir. Its stained glass windows were created by Chagall.

St. Peter's Church (St. Peters Kirche) on St. Peterhofstatt is Zurich's oldest parish church. Its tower was constructed in the 13th century, and the building sports the largest clock face in Europe.

The Water Church (Wasserkirche) at Limmatquai 31 is one of Switzerland's most delicate late-Gothic buildings. Note the stained glass windows, designed by Giacometti.

The Lindenhof comprises the remains of the original Roman fortress and customs house here, as well as the imperial medieval residence. The fountain in the quiet square commemorates the day in 1292 when the city was saved from the Hapsburgs by Zurich's women. Legend has it that the town was facing military defeat when its women dressed themselves in armor and marched to Lindenhof. When the enemy saw them, they thought they were facing another army and promptly retreated. The palace is bordered by Fortunag. on the west and intersected by Lindenhofstr.

The Swiss National Museum (Schweizerisches Landesmuseum) is located at Museumstr. 2 in a gigantic neo-Gothic build-

## ULRICH ZWINGLI (1484–1531)

Zwingli, though not as well known as Luther and Calvin, was also a major force in the Reformation. Zwingli began to develop his evangelical theology about the same time that Luther did, and their beliefs were much the same, except in their views on holy communion. In 1518 Zwingli was called to be the priest at the Great Minster (Grossmünster) Church of Zurich, began lecturing on the New Testament, and worked with the city council to reform the society. He broke with Rome in 1523, but two years later some of his followers, the Anabaptists, broke with him. Anabaptists (predecessors of the Mennonites) disagreed on at least two matters: that infant baptism was a valid baptism and that the church needed to wait for the city council's approval before initiating reforms. Zwingli died in battle, when five Catholic Forest Cantons went to war against Zurich.

Sites associated with Zwingli's life and ministry are located in Zurich and Einsiedeln.

ing, and has a collection just as large. The museum has objects dating from the Stone Age to modern times, such as furniture, costumes, watches, and thousands of toy soldiers reenacting military history.

In Zurichberg is the Zoo Dolder, an attractive setting for more than 2,000 animals that live there. Speaking of zoos, you can go by boat from Burkliplatz in Zurich to the end of Lake Zurich to Rapperswil, which is known for its Kinderzoo, featuring Noah's ark. Rapperswil also has a fascinating castle, if you don't care for zoos.

# United Kingdom

British Tourist Authority
  US 212-986-2200 or 800-462-2748
  Canada 416-925-6326 or 888-847-4885
  UK 0800-192-192
  Australia 02-9377-4400
*Web sites*
  Entire country www.visitbritain.com
  England www.travelengland.org.uk
  Northern Ireland www.ni-tourism.com
  Scotland www.holiday.scotland.net
  Wales www.visitwales.com
For a complete list of updated links, visit www.christiantraveler.com

### Country in a Capsule

*Size:* When you put England, Northern Ireland, Scotland, and Wales together, you have an area equivalent to that of New York and Pennsylvania combined, but the population of the United Kingdom is about twice that of the two states.

*Religion:* The population is 70 percent Protestant and 10 percent Catholic. About 80 percent of the Protestants are Anglican (Church of England), 6 percent Methodist, 4 percent Presbyterian (Church of Scotland), 2 percent Baptist. However, the percentage who attend regularly may be only about 20 percent, with higher percentages in Northern Ireland and Scotland.

*Language:* English.

*Money:* At press time the British pound was worth about $1.45.

*Food:* The British aren't known for their food, but the English breakfasts can't be beat. Their cottage pie, steak-and-kidney pie, Cornish pasties, and fish and chips are good. But also try Yorkshire pudding, scones with jam and clotted cream, Stottie cakes, and mint cakes.

*Shopping:* Antiquing is big in Britain. It is also a good place to buy woolen goods, china, and books. And of course when you get to Scotland, look for tweeds, woolens, and tartan rugs and fabrics.

*Brief history:* Julius Caesar made brief forays in the area in 55 and 54 B.C. The Romans built Hadrian's Wall in the north and occupied the land for 400 years, building a fine road system. Christianity filtered in quite early, but Christian Britons were pushed into Wales by the invading Saxons. From Wales Christianity went to Ireland, and then St. Columba brought the faith from Ireland to Scotland, and St. Augustine of Canterbury came to southern England from Rome. The Vikings wreaked havoc, but it was a Viking descendant, William the Conqueror, who laid the foundations for England's future in 1066.

Two devastating wars, the Hundred Years' War with France and the War of the Roses, brought 150 years of strife from 1338 to 1485. Finally the Tudor dynasty was established with Henry VIII, and his reign and that of Elizabeth I were years of dynamic development. Henry declared the dissolution of the monasteries and himself as head of the church. After the death of Elizabeth I, James took the throne, bringing England and Scotland under one king. A civil war and the London fire in the middle of the 17th century were major setbacks to progress.

The 18th century saw the beginning of the Industrial Revolution, the expansion of the empire, but also the loss of the American colonies. Through the 19th century and Queen Victoria's reign, England struggled with social issues, trying to reform the old while still preserving it. In the 20th century, with two devastating World Wars, the United Kingdom has dismantled much of its empire and struggled with the problem of Northern Ireland.

# ▲ ENGLAND

**London** London is like no other city. It is rich in history and yet thoroughly modern. It is filled with churches, museums, parks, palaces, street markets, theaters, excitement, and confusion. Most major cities may have the same elements, but not to the degree that London has.

*Buckingham Palace* on Buckingham Palace Rd. reigns supreme among Britain's royal must-sees. The British monarchy has ruled from Buckingham only since 1837 when Victoria moved from Kensington Palace. The Palace is the queen's London home for most of the year, excluding January, June, August, and September. If she's home, you'll know by the royal standard located over the east front. Parts of Buckingham Palace have recently been opened to visitors during August and September. Be sure to confirm whether the Palace is indeed open during your travel dates— the queen has the final word. You can phone the information line at 020/7839-1377, and purchase tickets via credit card at 020/7321-2233. Tourists often flock to Buckingham Palace to see the always popular Changing of the Guard, which takes place in front of the palace at 11:30 daily from April through July, and every other day of the week during the rest of the year.

*The Houses of Parliament* on St. Margaret St. are among London's most famous and often photographed sites. The building is also known as the Palace of Westminster, as it was the home of the monarchy from the 11th to the early 16th centuries. The palace's most famous features are its bell towers. The 336-foot tower on the south end is Victoria Tower. On the north end is St.

Stephen's Tower, or the Clock Tower, better known as Big Ben. The name is actually inaccurate: Big Ben is the name of the 13-ton bell in the Clock Tower that is sounded on the hour.

*Churches.* Start your tour with St. Paul's Cathedral on St. Paul's Churchyard. It's a Christopher Wren church, and you will be hearing a lot about Wren in London. Right after the Great Fire of London ravaged the city and burned down 76 of the city's 87 churches, Christopher Wren got to work and started rebuilding them. Today, 300 years later, after the blitzkriegs of World War II, there are still 23 Wren churches in the city. One of them is the majestic St. Paul's. It was the setting for Winston Churchill's funeral in 1965 and the wedding of Prince Charles and Lady Diana Spencer in 1981. There is plenty of beautiful art throughout the church, including fabulous ceiling mosaics. Take special note also of the stunning *The Light of the World* by William Holman Hunt, located in the south aisle.

The cathedral's dome is its greatest architectural glory. It is among the world's largest and consists of three sections: an outer timber-frame dome covered with lead; an inner dome built of brick and covered with frescoes of the life of St. Paul; and linking the two a brick support system. This brick support also holds a massive 850-ton lantern that shines through an opening in the inner dome. You can get a great view of the church below from high up in the inner dome's "Whispering Gallery," so called because of its remarkable acoustics. Words spoken on one side can clearly be heard on the other side, over 100 feet away. Above this gallery are two external galleries, which offer great views of the city. A guided tour is worth it, because guides take you to parts of the cathedral you can't see on your own. Evensong or vespers is at 5:00 every day

## WILLIAM WILBERFORCE (1759-1833)

Best known for his campaign against the slave trade in England, William Wilberforce was converted at the age of 25, entering politics shortly thereafter and serving in the British parliament for nearly 40 years. Frequently he made parliamentary resolutions to abolish the slave trade, and eventually in 1807, a bill abolishing traffic in slaves became law. He also helped to open India to missionaries in 1813 and fought for child labor restrictions and for prison reform. His influential book, *A Practical View,* on the application of Christianity to politics was published in 1797.

Sites associated with Wilberforce are located in Kingston-upon-Hull and London, England. He is buried in Westminster Abbey.

## How to Visit a Cathedral

There are 48 Anglican cathedrals in England and Wales, each one a unique kaleidoscope of historical and artistic interest. But a cathedral is not a museum! Its vibrant religious life, reflecting centuries of faithful devotion, continues today.

To make the most of your visit:

1. As you enter the cathedral, pick up a leaflet highlighting the main features or purchase a souvenir pictorial guidebook at the cathedral shop (some have tour folders for children too). Sit awhile planning your tour. Absorb the spirit of quiet reverence in this house where prayer has been offered for centuries. Thank God for thousands of dedicated Christians who have worshiped here.

2. Ask questions of a guide if one is available.

3. Remember that, even with volunteer guides and bookshop attendants, building maintenance and basic services can cost up to $4,000 a day. Some cathedrals now charge admission; most request, and deserve, generous donations.

4. Time your visit to attend a service: Sunday morning worship (some Saturday newspapers publish cathedrals' Sunday schedules) or the uniquely Anglican Evensong (late afternoons; earlier on weekends). You'll sit very near the choir. And watch for special events while you're there (concerts, exhibits, dramatic performances, or the pomp of a civic ceremony).

5. Relive British history as reflected in the cathedrals' stories. Some preserve remnants of Roman occupation and Celtic Christianity. You can see where Hereward continued resisting the Normans after most of England had been conquered (Ely and Peterborough), where Archbishop Thomas à Becket was assassinated (Canterbury), where the barons vowed to make King John sign the Magna Carta (St. Edmundsbury), where Charles I took refuge during the Civil War (Oxford), where the Young Pretender worshiped (Derby) on the day in 1745 he gave up his march on London.

Imposing tombs call to mind saints and royalty, heroes, statesmen, and ordinary folk. At Winchester you walk over the slab marking Jane Austen's grave. Windows commemorate the poets Herrick (Leicester) and Herbert (Salisbury) and the angling enthusiast Izaak Walton (Winchester). John Donne stands in St. Paul's, sculpted in his shroud, a reminder of mortality. Tennyson sits in the garden at

continued on page 313

except Sunday when it is at 3:15. There are many monuments, but one of the most interesting is to Christopher Wren himself, who is buried here. It says simply (in Latin), "Reader, if you seek his monument, look around you."

St. Martin-in-the-Fields is also located on Trafalgar Sq. If the church looks familiar to Americans, it may be because the classical design became a pattern for churches in early colonial America, and as such can be considered one of the most influential churches architecturally of all time. The church has a notable history of helping society's downtrodden. From 1914 to 1927 the crypt was used as a shelter for homeless soldiers and other unfortunates. During World War II it served as a bomb shelter. And even today the church helps the homeless through a lunchtime soup kitchen. The church houses a cafe and a religious bookstore, as well as the London Brass Rubbing Center, and a good craft market in the churchyard. The church is also known for its music. Handel played on the church's first organ, Mozart gave a concert here, and the Academy of St. Martin-in-the-Fields orchestra was founded in 1726. Free music recitals take place Mondays, Wednesdays, and Fridays at 1:05; evening concerts usually feature big-name ensembles. For information about evening concerts phone 020/7930-0089.

The dome of St. Stephen Walbrook on Walbrook St. was considered Christopher Wren's practice run before building his more famous St. Paul's Cathedral. He seems to have succeeded beautifully. Although the exterior of the small church looks rather plain, the interior of St. Stephen is a lovely surprise. Its columns and dome give the sanctuary a bright and airy look. Take special notice of the intricate carvings on the pulpit and font cover. Organ recitals are held here on Fridays.

St. Paul's Church on Bedford St. in Covent Garden was built in 1633 and is commonly known as the Actors' Church. Inside are memorials to numerous people connected with the theater. St. Paul's eastern portico is essentially a fake door (the portico is a common spot for outdoor entertainment). The real entrance to the church is on its west side, through the churchyard.

Westminster Abbey on Broad Sanctuary is the most ancient of all of London's churches, and the most important. The abbey contains some of the most glorious architecture of medieval London, it houses the most impressive collection of monuments and tombs in the world, and it has been the site of every British coronation continued from page 312

Lincoln, larger than life, and Southwark (a stone's throw from the Globe Theatre) has a modern monument to Shakespeare. Equally stirring are memorials to ordinary folk, otherwise forgotten but living now in the Church Triumphant, the communion of Saints. Sometimes we may glimpse tragedy—shipwreck, children dying, beloved wives lost too soon.

6. Grasp the basic architectural layout, a cross-shaped floor plan west to east (facing Jerusalem), nave through choir to high altar. Beyond that, the retrochoir (a few retain the old semicircular apse, but most have squared off and enlarged the eastern end, adding small chapels). The "arms," north and south transepts, meet at the crossing (and sometimes there is another pair farther east). Above the crossing, there is usually a tower, weighing tons: at Salisbury, whose spire reaches 404 feet, notice how the supporting pillars bend. A tower with windows is a lantern (Ely's is octagonal). And watch for variations (each cathedral is unique). Beneath the choir is the crypt, typically the oldest part. Outside the cross-shape are, typically, cloisters (a covered walkway surrounding a garden), chapter house (for meetings of the cathedral's governing body, the "chapter"), sometimes a bell tower. Medieval monastic outbuildings, perhaps in ruins, may illuminate the monks' daily lives.

7. Be alert to how differing architectural styles handle space, light, mass, and decoration. Most cathedrals exhibit a blend of styles. Ripon's crossing and Rochester's nave demonstrate remodeling abandoned for lack of funds. Initial construction often took years; there were subsequent enlargements, adaptation to new fashions, restorations (sometimes misguided), and repairs following fire, earthquake, war damage, vandalism, insect infestation, neglect, or structural collapse. Restorers might undertake faithful replication or seize the occasion for creative new work in a different style.

8. Appreciate practical engineering solutions: buttresses to keep the walls from buckling outward (called flying if separated from the wall by a half-arch); gargoyles at the roof, diverting rainwater from the foundations; a clerestory (the highest row of arches) to admit daylight to the nave.

9. Rejoice in the artists whose talents have contributed to the cathedral's beauty. Study the windows, their delicate stone tracery,

continued on page 315

since 1066. Both national church and national museum, Westminster occupies a special place in most Britons' hearts.

Most of the abbey dates from the 13th century, and its nave is the highest in all of Britain. There is plenty to see here. Take special note of the Lady Chapel, built in the early 16th century; the octagonal Chapter House; Poets' Corner with its memorials to numerous literary giants like Chaucer, Shakespeare, and Dickens; and the Cloisters with its brass rubbing center. Visitors are invited to create a rubbing of brass tomb effigies to take home as a souvenir. Westminster has been so overwhelmed by crowds in recent years that they've begun charging admission, but the church is always free to those who wish to attend a worship service.

It is the highest honor to be buried here. One who received the honor was David Livingstone, the missionary/explorer. There are memorials to Shakespeare and to Handel. There is also a tablet in memory of Bible translator William Tyndale; the grave of William Ussher, who gave us Ussher's chronology of the Bible; a stained glass window in memory of John Bunyan, who couldn't be buried here because he wasn't Anglican; a tablet in memory of Henry Francis Lyte, who wrote "Abide with Me"; and tablets in memory of Gerard Manley Hopkins and T. S. Eliot.

Don't get confused by the various Westminster churches. Westminster Cathedral on Asley Place was completed in 1903 and is the headquarters of the Roman Catholic Church in England. An organ festival is held every second Tuesday at 7:00 P.M. during the summer. And then there is Westminster Chapel, about three blocks south of the Abbey on Queen Ann's Gate. The Chapel is not distinguished by its architecture but by its preaching. Evangelical preachers like G. Campbell Morgan and Martyn Lloyd-Jones have been ministers of this church.

Other noted evangelical churches in London include All Souls, Langham Place, where John Stott was rector for many years; St. Helen's Bishopsgate; and Holy Trinity, Brompton. John Foxe (author of *Book of Martyrs*) and the poet John Milton are both buried in St. Giles Cripplegate Church on Fore St. On King William St. is the Church of St. Mary Woolnoth, where John Newton was rector from 1780 to 1807. He and his wife were buried here, but in 1893 their remains were moved to Olney where he had previously ministered. Bible translator Miles Coverdale is buried near the altar of St. Magnus the Martyr Church on Lower Thames St.

continued from page 314

rich medieval colors, traditional symbolism, and the stories they tell from the Bible or saints' lives ("books for the illiterate"). Besides medieval glass (fullest at Canterbury) there is much good newer work, Victorian and 20th century. Look for windows by the Pre-Raphaelites (Birmingham, Bradford, Oxford), Marc Chagall (Chichester), and others. At Ely, visit their stained glass museum. Let tomb sculpture and memorial tablets reveal how people have handled death, with faith and hope but sometimes, depending on the age's taste, gruesomely (worms consuming bodies) or sentimentally.

Enjoy the skill of wood- and stonecarvers and their humor. Carvings appear on fonts, pulpits, ceiling bosses, capitals of columns, spandrels between arches, corbels (supports projecting from the face of a wall), choir stalls, misericords underneath choir seats. Some show Bible stories or scenes from daily life, like the "Fruit Stealers" at Wells and Exeter's rugby player. Some depict native foliage; others portray fantastic beings, a pagan "Green Man," or Ely's and Lincoln's "imps." There are contemporary portraits of a loved bishop or maybe the carver himself. Imagine the cathedral as it was in medieval times, with more color than now (though recently the style of richly painted ceilings has been revived). Bits of old wall painting still exist, some discovered only lately on removing plaster or whitewash. Other media also lend color: mosaics, tapestries (like Coventry's huge modern "Christ in Glory"), embroidery, floor tiles.

10. View artistic and cultural masterpieces found in cathedral treasuries (for example, gold and silver chalices) and libraries (sumptuous handwritten Bibles, illuminated psalters, early music manuscripts, chained books).

11. Experience a cathedral's unique features, like the moat and scissor arches at Wells, the whispering gallery under St. Paul's dome in London, Ely's labyrinth, Exeter's minstrel gallery with its choir of angels, the view from York's roof, or Hereford's famous world map centered on Jerusalem.

CHARLES A. HUTTAR

In Bunhill Fields on City Rd., Finsbury, is a burial ground for Nonconformists—Christians who did not belong to the Anglican Church. Among those who are buried here are John Bunyan (*Pilgrim's Progress*), Daniel Defoe (*Robinson Crusoe*), Susanna Wesley, and Isaac Watts (writer of countless hymns). Across the street is the John Wesley House and the Wesley Chapel. Nearby in Bunhill Row, John Milton finished *Paradise Lost* and wrote *Paradise Regained*.

*Museums.* The British Museum, founded in 1753, is one of the world's greatest historical treasures. Located on Great Russell St., it is sometimes referred to as "Mankind's Attic." Your understanding and appreciation of Scripture will be enhanced when you see treasures from Nineveh, Egypt, Ur of the Chaldees, or Babylon, or when you see an inscription from Corinth with the name of someone whom Luke mentions in passing in the Book of Acts. The museum also has copies of the Gutenberg Bible and the Lindisfarne Gospels, as well as the Magna Carta.

The Tate Gallery on Millbank specializes in British and modern art, but it has a wide variety of European artists as well. Several religious paintings of interest to Christians include John Everett Millais' *Christ in the Home of His Parents,* and Ford Maddox Brown's *Jesus Washing Peter's Feet.*

The National Gallery on Trafalgar Sq. now has the nation's most valuable collection of art with more than 2,000 paintings from early Italian Renaissance to French post-Impressionism. One that stands out is Piero Della Francesca's *The Baptism of Christ,* a tempera on poplar painted in the 1450s. Don't miss Leonardo da Vinci's drawings of the Virgin Mary, Christ, St. Anne, and John the Baptist. Admission is free.

Though the name of the Victoria and Albert Museum on Cromwell Rd. seems old-fashioned, the museum is very creative and lively. It is devoted to fine and applied arts of all countries, so you have a little bit of everything here. Donatello's marble relief *The Ascension* is here, and so is Bologna's *Samson and a Philistine.* The museum contains seven miles of gallery space, so don't feel that you have to see it all in one afternoon.

*Other places of interest.* Shakespeare's Globe Theatre on New Globe Walk is actually a replica of the Bard's original 16th-century Globe Playhouse, where most of the playwright's great plays premiered. The Globe has been built with the use of authentic Elizabethan materials, including the first thatch roof in London since the Great Fire. Plays are performed in the open-air, in natural light (and sometimes in natural rain), to about 1,500 people. The main season runs from June through September. Call 020/7902-1500 for performance schedules, or the box office at 020/7401-9919.

Visitors can also find good shopping opportunities in Covent Garden. The piazza and covered Central Market were once a fruit and vegetable wholesalers' market. Today the building houses a wide array of small shops, selling everything from designer clothes to books and antiques. There are plenty of places to grab a bite to eat, and street entertainment is a tradition that has existed in the area since the 17th century.

If you need a break from churches, museums, and monuments, stroll through Hyde Park or Kensington Gardens. Hyde Park was begun as Henry VIII's hunting grounds—which is difficult to imagine in the midst of such a large city. The park remains a quiet green oasis, with the notable exception of Sunday in Speakers' Corner. Soapbox orators of all types share their ideas for a better society, while the audience heckles them mercilessly.

Next to the park is the more formal Kensington Gardens. Children will especially enjoy the statue of J. M. Barrie's fictional Peter Pan, the boy who never grew up. The Serpentine is an artificial lake that crosses through both parks and is used for swimming and boating. The Round Pond, in the center of Kensington Park, is often full of model boats operated by both children and adults, and in the winter the pond is sometimes used for skating. In the north, near Lancaster Gate, is a dogs' cemetery.

North of Kensington Gardens is the Notting Hill district, with a nice variety of restaurants and cafes. Portobello Road, which runs through the district, is a favorite attraction with its lively antiques market held each Saturday beginning at 6:00 A.M. The southern end is a good place to shop for antiques; you can find food, flowers, and secondhand clothes on the northern end. The street is also lined with more traditional antiques shops that are open most weekdays.

The British take gardening seriously, so it's little wonder that London is home of the granddaddy of all gardens—the Royal Botanic Gardens at Kew, the largest and most complete gardens in the world. Begun in the 18th century, the gardens were handed over to the public in 1841 and now contain about 40,000 different kinds of flora. Kew is also a center for scholarly horticultural and botanical research. Garden enthusiasts will find it easy to spend the whole day.

The Millennium Dome was constructed for the advent of the year 2000, as its name indicates, and is probably the biggest monument to the new century. The dome looks like a futuristic sports arena. It is more than 2.5 miles in circumference and its roof is 1 mile high. The dome is supposed to provide the ultimate look at what life will be like in the next century and is organized into sections like Learning, Play, and Work. The Body Zone is perhaps the most unique. A model human larger than the Statue of Liberty allows visitors to journey through various passageways to see how bodies function. In the performance area a cast of 200 performs acrobatics and musical routines up to six times a day. Most of the year tickets will be for the day, but during peak summer seasons, tickets will be available for half-day sessions. You cannot buy tickets to the dome on site. You need to purchase them from lottery tickets agents, newsstands, stores throughout London, and by telephone, 0870/603-2000.

*For the kids.* It depends on how adventuresome your children are, but you might try the London Dungeon on Tooley St. (not permanently, you understand); Bethany Green Museum of Childhood on Cambridge Heath Rd.; the Natural History Museum on Cromwell Rd., with its 13,000-square-foot dinosaur exhibit; the London Zoo, one of the best zoos in the world; or the Unicorn Theatre for Children on Great Newport St., which is the city's only theater just for children.

There are several great ways to get an overview of the city of London. Perhaps the most popular is via the red double-decker buses of the Original London Sightseeing Tour (phone 020/8877-1722). Tours run daily every 12 minutes, departing from Baker Street, Marble Arch, Piccadilly, or Victoria. The bus stops at 21 different locations, and includes all the major sights. If you want, you can get off the bus at any of the stops to look around, and hop back on the next bus.

Another good view of the city's skyline can be had via the River Thames. Boats ply the waters here year-round. Contact Catamaran Cruisers (020/7839-3572); Westminster Passenger Boat Services (020/7930-4097); City Cruises (020/7488-0344); or Thames Barrier Cruises (020/7930-3373).

For a unique tour option, the Original London Walks can't be beat. The duration of the walks vary, generally lasting between one and three hours. The themes of the walks vary as well, covering everything from "The Westminster Nobody Knows" to "Princess Diana's London." Walks are held daily at various times, and reservations are not required unless you're traveling with a group. London Walks will customize tours and also conduct tours for children. You might phone ahead if you want a fun walk with your children that emphasizes a particular curriculum. Phone them at 0171/624-3978; e-mail them at london@walks.com; or find them on the Internet at www.walks.com.

**Ambleside** If Shakespeare is associated with Stratford-upon-Avon, then William Wordsworth is associated with England's Lake District. His home was Rydal Mount, 1 mile northwest of Ambleside, from 1837 until his death some 40 years later. Wordsworth moved here at the height of his career, and his descendants still live here. The poet's study ceiling is still covered with the Renaissance paintings he copied on a trip to Italy. Nearby is Dove Cottage in Grasmere, Wordsworth's home from 1799 to 1808. The cottage still contains many of his personal belongings. While Wordsworth lived here, Dove Cottage was a magnet for other Romantic writers, including Samuel Taylor Coleridge and Robert Southey. A small museum behind the cottage contains manuscripts and memorabilia.

**Ashby de la Zouch** Believe it or not, there was a popular hit song during World War II with the name "Ashby de la Zouch Castle Abbey." But just as unbelievable is that this town was where Charles Jennens wrote the libretto to Handel's *Messiah*.

The town is famous as the setting for the tournament in Sir Walter Scott's novel, *Ivanhoe*. Ruins of the old castle with its underground passages can still be seen. Also to be viewed are the ruins of St. Helen's Church with its "finger pillory," which was once used to punish anyone interrupting a sermon.

**Bath** This is a much photographed city and rightly so. Founded in Roman times, there is a bit of ancient Rome still here. In 944 a monastery was built, and you can still see traces of the medieval town wall. In the 18th century it became a popular health resort and many of its picturesque buildings date from that time.

Although the first church was built here in the 10th century, the present Gothic Bath Abbey on Abbey Churchyard dates from the 15th century. Stained glass windows on the east end of the church show the life of Christ. On the west end you see angels climbing up and down stone ladders. All told, there are 640 wall monuments. Its fan-vaulted ceilings in the nave are considered superb, a product of two of the designers who worked on Westminster Abbey. A multimedia show about the abbey's history is available in the Heritage Vaults next door.

In the Royal Victoria Park, south of Royal Crescent, there are free concerts in the summer, and all year around the botanical gardens on the east side of the park are open.

Sally Lunn's Kitchen Museum in North Parade Passage is a small basement museum, telling you how Sally Lunn, a Huguenot refugee in the 17th century, baked brioches. Brioches are on sale in the cafe upstairs.

Although Bath is a city of more than 80,000, it has lots of area for walking and biking. Bicycles can be rented, so can rowboats and punts if you are interested in exploring the Thames.

**Bedford** This city of 77,000 in England's Midlands region is associated with John Bunyan, the 17th-century Baptist preacher and author of *The Pilgrim's Progress*. The Bunyan Meeting on Mill Street was built in 1849 and so is not the same meetinghouse where Bunyan preached but it is built on the site of the barn were Bunyan preached from 1671 to 1678. The prison where he was confined can also be seen. At the public library on Harpur Street is an exhibition devoted to Bunyan and at the corner of St. Peter's and Broadway is a bronze statue of the noted author. Less than two miles south of Bedford in the village of Elstow, you can see Bunyan's birthplace and the village church where he was baptized.

Nearby at Woburn is the Woburn Safari Park, the country's largest drive-through animal reserve, and in nearby Whipsnade is the Whipsnade Wild Animal Park, a branch of the London Zoo with 2,500 animals on a 600-acre site. The park has a railway to transport you around or you can see it by car.

**Brighton** In this seacoast town, Charlotte Elliot wrote the hymn "Just as I Am without One Plea." She was 45 years old at the time and in poor health. Discouraged by her inability to serve the Lord in a meaningful way, she wrote this hymn while confined to her bed.

With its palatial waterfront hotels, Brighton is England's largest coastal resort. St. Bartholomew's Church on Ann Street is unusual to say the least. It was built to the exact dimensions of Noah's ark, and though it was initially laughed at, it is an experience to visit. Note its Byzantine altar and the rose window. (Did Noah's ark have a rose window?)

Be sure to see the Royal Pavilion on East St., built by the Prince Regent, George III's son, in extravagant Indian palatial style. The museum here has an interesting collection of musical instruments.

**Bristol** With more than 400,000 residents, Bristol is southwestern England's largest city. Though World War II bombing raids destroyed much of the city center, there is still much to see and do.

St. Mary Redcliffe on Redcliffe Way, the Lord Mayor's Chapel and the Cathedral, both on the College Green are Bristol's best known churches. Queen Elizabeth called the first one "the fairest, goodliest and most famous parish church in England." An English poet called the second, "for its size one of the very best churches in England." And the third was praised by a British poet laureate.

But don't overlook the New Room, almost hidden in the Broadmead Shopping Center on Broadmead. It opened in 1739 as the world's first Methodist chapel. In the courtyard is a statue of John Wesley on horseback. Upstairs you can visit the old living quarters with rooms for John and Charles Wesley and for Francis Asbury.

Bristol was George Whitefield's base of operations, and it was here that Whitefield introduced John Wesley to "preaching in the fields." At first shocked by it, Wesley said afterward, "I should have thought the saving of souls almost a sin if it had not been done in a church."

It was also in Bristol that George Müller established his orphanages, operating them on faith for more than 60 years in the 19th century.

**Brockhole** In the town of Brockhole, three miles northwest of Windermere on A591, is the Lake District National Park Visitor Centre, which is housed in a magnificent lakeside mansion. A wide array of exhibitions are offered, including displays about the local ecology and plant and animal life. The center's gardens are lovely in their own right, as daffodils and azaleas flood the grounds with springtime color. Brockhole is also a good place to take Windermere Lake Cruises for a lovely view of the Lake District's best scenery. Regular service is offered to other lakeside towns, including Ambleside, Bowness, and Lakeside. If you'd like to use the boats as a ferry service, purchase a Freedom of the Lake ticket, which offers unlimited travel for a 24-hour period.

**Cambridge** Cambridge is home to the second of Britain's greatest universities, the other being Oxford. Cambridge is younger than its rival, but not by much. Its first college, Peterhouse, was founded in 1284. The university is actually a collection of 31 independent colleges. Emmanuel College was an early center of Puritan learning. One of its famous alumni is John Harvard, founder of Harvard University in Cambridge, Massachusetts. Trinity College is the university's largest. It is the home of the massive clock known as Great Tom, which strikes each hour. Great Tom figured in the famous race around the quadrangle in the movie, *Chariots of Fire.*

The city is relatively small and compact, and hence quite walkable, but the 31 colleges of the university are spread out. King's College Chapel, completed in 1536, looks like a cathedral. It is 289 feet long, almost as long as a football field. Public recitals are often held here during the summer. One of the chapel's most beloved annual activities is the performance by the college choir of the *Festival of Nine Lessons and Carols,* a Christmas Eve concert, which is broadcast all around the world.

Christ's College on St. Andrew's St., founded in 1505, was attended by the poet John Milton, who wrote his "Hymn on the Morning of Christ's Nativity" here. His rooms can be visited. The gardens here are open to the public.

## THE LAKE DISTRICT

England's largest national park is the Lake District, some 866 square miles of dramatic mountainsides and water wherever you look. Poets, authors, and philosophers have flocked to the Lake District for centuries, and little wonder. The beauty of creation here can't help but put you in a thoughtful frame of mind. The park's visitors center is in the town of Brockhole, which is also a good place to board Windermere Lake Cruises for the best viewing of the Lake District's scenery. Regular service is offered to other lakeside towns, including Ambleside, Bowness, and Lakeside.

The Round Church (St. John's and Bridge Sts.) built in the 12th century is one of four remaining round churches in England. In the church is the Cambridge Brass Rubbing Center, where you can make rubbings of medieval church brasses in gold, silver, and bronze wax.

C. S. Lewis was associated with Oxford most of his life, but in his last years he taught at Cambridge's Magdalene College as professor of medieval and Renaissance English.

Fitzwilliam Museum on Trumpington St., with its excellent collection of antiquities from Greece and Egypt in its Lower Galleries and its fine exhibits of art by the great masters in the Upper Galleries, is a first-rate museum.

Queen's College has an interesting story attached to its Mathematical Bridge, an arched wooden span that was originally held together only by gravitational force. When it was disassembled to see how Isaac Newton accomplished his feat, no one was able to reassemble it correctly. It is today securely nailed together.

Robert Robinson, pastor of the Baptist church here, wrote the hymn, "Come Thou Fount of Every Blessing," when he was only 23 years old.

**Canterbury** Canterbury's Christchurch Cathedral at Cathedral Precincts is the headquarters church of the worldwide Anglican (Episcopalian) communion. It has been the spiritual center of Christianity in England since St. Augustine arrived here in 597. Augustine had been dispatched here to bring the gospel to the pagans of England. By all accounts, he was extraordinarily successful. When Augustine's church burned, a new church was erected in 1070, and when that proved too small, a larger building was consecrated in 1130.

Thomas à Becket was murdered in the Christchurch Cathedral in 1170 by four of King Henry II's knights. A marker in the northwest transept shows the spot where Thomas fell. Behind the chapel is the crypt where Thomas à Becket was first buried and where Henry II completed his penance for the murder. Notice the nine windows in Trinity Chapel depicting the life of Thomas à Becket. In St. Anselm's Chapel note the wall painting of the apostle Paul and the viper. Choral evensong is at 5:30 and 3:15 on Saturdays and Sundays.

The remains of St. Augustine's Abbey (on Monastery Street) and also the 7th-century St. Pancras Church can be seen at St. Augustine's College. Enter through the 13th-century Fyndon's Gate.

## PERIOD STYLES

English churches and cathedrals reflect changing taste through the centuries.

*Saxon* (before the Norman Conquest in 1066), is plain and simple. Only bits survive, for example, at Ripon and Rochester.

*Norman* (beginning late 11th century; also known as Romanesque), is typified by massive columns and round arches cut in geometrical designs. Durham is an outstanding example, also Peterborough and Norwich (which retain the apsidal east end), Ely, the towers of Exeter and St. Albans, and several fine crypts.

*Early English* (13th century, beginnings of "Gothic"), with slender pillars and pointed arches, gives a sense of height and elegance: Lincoln, Salisbury, the "Five Sisters" window in York's north transept, the west fronts of Wells, Peterborough, and Ripon.

*Decorated* (14th century). This style has more delicate stone tracery in the windows, stone carving in natural forms, and other adornment: Exeter's west front, York's nave (widest and highest in England), Ely's lantern, Salisbury's spire, Wells's chapter house, and Hereford's tower.

*Perpendicular* (late 14th to early 16th century) is a uniquely English development, contrasting with the contemporaneous Continental "flamboyant," having greater open space, larger windows, intricacy of fan and lierne vaulting and ceiling bosses where ribs of the vaults meet: the Worcester, Canterbury, and York towers, Gloucester's cloisters and east window, Norwich's bosses, Canterbury and Winchester naves, York's choir, St. Edmundsbury, Manchester, and Chelmsford.

*Renaissance and Baroque.* Christopher Wren's St. Paul's in London, built after the 1666 fire, is the finest example, with its classical dome where medieval cathedrals had a tower. Derby and Birmingham exemplify 18th-century work.

*Victorian,* the period of the gothic Revival. This is a period of restoration (sometimes involving major alterations) and new building patterned after the medieval: Newcastle, Bristol, Leicester's spire, Worcester's west window, Southwark's nave, Truro (influenced by Continental Gothic), Liverpool (begun in 1904 though not completed until 1978).

*Modern.* Coventry and Llandaff (both rebuilt after extensive war damage), Portsmouth, St. Edmundsbury, and Guildford.

CHARLES A. HUTTAR

It was because so many pilgrims came here to do penance at the shrine of Thomas à Becket that Chaucer wrote *The Canterbury Tales* in the 14th century. In the 20th century, T. S. Eliot's *Murder in the Cathedral* was first staged here in the Chapter House.

Geoffrey Chaucer's *The Canterbury Tales* recounts the stories of a number of travelers making a pilgrimage from London to Canterbury Cathedral, which became the most important center of pilgrimage in northern Europe. The Canterbury Tales on St. Margaret's St. simulates the journeys of those pilgrims in a museum. Besides enjoying the artifacts, you will be treated to a modern English version of the tales.

At the Independent (Congregational) Chapel here Edward Perronet wrote the hymn, "All Hail the Power of Jesus' Name" in the 18th century. The tune, Miles Lane, was composed by William Shrubsole, only 19 years old at the time, who had been a choir boy at the Canterbury Cathedral.

**Chester** This old walled city, like York, is a must on most people's itineraries. The walls were built around A.D. 70, and if you take a walk on the walls around the two-mile circumference, you can get a good introduction to the city. The Roman sites are fascinating, particularly the Roman amphitheater just outside the Newgate on Victoria Rd., probably the largest in the country. The Chester Cathedral on St. Werbergh St. dates back to medieval times. Choral evensong is sung Sundays at 3:30, Tuesdays, Wednesdays, and Thursdays at 5:15, and Saturdays at 4:15. The Chester Zoo, 2 miles north of town on Victoria Rd., is the largest in the country and is noted for its natural setting.

**Chichester** The cathedral at West and South Sts. was built between 1088 and 1148 replacing an earlier cathedral founded in 681. Among the notable works of art are sculptures of Jesus at Bethany and paintings of Christ with Mary Magdalene. The cathedral is known for its outstanding choir, which sings daily at evensong, 5:30, Monday through Saturday, and 3:30 on Sundays.

**Colchester** This is England's oldest recorded town; its medieval town plan still remains intact inside the Roman walls. The town's most distinctive area is the Dutch quarter, founded by Dutch Nonconformists and Quakers.

Charles Haddon Spurgeon was converted in a Primitive Methodist church in Colchester. He was born in Kelvedon, Essex, and at the age of 18 became pastor of a little Baptist church in Waterbeach, six miles from Cambridge.

If you're interested in trivia, "Twinkle, Twinkle, Little Star" was written here in about 1806.

**Cotswolds** About two hours west of London is the delightfully scenic area of rolling hills dotted with picturesque villages like Stow-on-the-Wold, Wotton-under-Endge, Moreton-in-Marsh, Chipping Campden, and Shipton-under-Wychwood. It is a great place for the family to do things together. Several companies provide suggested walking tours or bike tours of the region. Here are a few places to consider.

Check out Birdland in Bourton-on-the-Water with 1,200 birds of 361 species. St. James Church in beautiful Chipping Campden is a good example of a Cotswold wool church. (Wool churches, which are unique to the Cotswolds, were constructed of local materials purchased as a result of generous endowments from the area's wealthy wool merchants.) The medieval Berkeley Castle in Berkeley is surrounded by terraced Elizabethan gardens and lovely lawns. Castle Combe, a tiny village with one street—which is called The Street—a brook, and little stone cottages, has the well-deserved reputation of being England's prettiest village. Cheltenham is really too large to fit with the Cotswold villages, but it has the most going on, including its International Festival of Music in early July. St. John's Church in Cirencester is one of England's largest. And the list could go on and on.

**Dover** The white cliffs of Dover are famous, but there is a bit more to see in this famous seacoast town. Pharos, the world's only existing Roman lighthouse, built about the time of Christ, is here. The impregnable Dover Castle on Castle Rd. dates from the 12th century. Richard the Lionhearted left from here on his third crusade in 1189.

**Durham** The castle and the cathedral are the reasons people come to Durham. The castle on Palace Green dates back to the 11th century. The cathedral, also on Palace Green, was built between 1093 and 1279. Its 15th-century Galilee Chapel has the tomb of the Venerable Bede, the historian-scholar, who wrote the

# John Wesley (1703-1791)

Born and raised in the Epworth rectory, the 15th of 19 children, John Wesley went to Oxford, was ordained an Anglican priest, and went, along with his brother Charles, to Georgia in America as a missionary. But it wasn't until after he returned to London in 1738 that he had his Aldersgate Street experience and his heart was "strangely warmed." Immediately, the Wesley brothers became evangelists. John preached over 40,000 sermons and traveled more than 225,000 miles before he "first began to feel old at 85." Charles wrote hymns (more than 7,000 of them) that the masses loved to sing.

In Bristol, John founded the first "society" and erected a chapel. Because churches were often not open to them, they preached outdoors; thousands of working people and the poorer classes were converted. Although John never left the Anglican Church, the Methodist Church was soon formed.

The new converts were not only enthusiastic about their faith; they were also enthusiastic about transforming society. Encouraged by Wesley, Wilberforce campaigned against slavery, and John Howard urged prison reform; others sought to end decadent practices in the workplace.

Sites associated with Wesley are located in Adare, Ireland, and in London, Bristol, Epworth, and Oxford, England.

---

first historical text in English in the early 8th century. For a good view of the city, climb the 325 steps to the tower.

Near Durham (about eight miles northwest) in the town of Beamish is a huge 200-acre area that re-creates life in the early 1900s. It is called the Beamish Open-Air Museum. A costumed staff helps you explore life of a century ago.

**Epworth** About 11 miles southwest of Scunthorpe is the Old Rectory at Epworth, the childhood home of John Wesley. In the Borough Museum Art Gallery of Scunthorpe (on Oswald Road) is a John Wesley collection. Frodingham Vicarage, a mile or two north of Scunthorpe, also has a Wesley collection.

**Glastonbury** This village of 7,000 is England's New Age capital, so you might want to avoid it. On the other hand, there are some interesting Christian traditions associated with it as well. According to one legend, Joseph of Arimathea brought the Holy Grail here and began a church. Another legend, even more famous, is that King Arthur and Queen Guinevere were buried here. The folks at the visitors center will explain everything to you.

**Hawkshead** Just outside of the Lake District village of Hawkshead is Hill Top, the home of the perennial favorite children's author and illustrator Beatrix Potter. The tiny house in which the Peter Rabbit stories were created is very popular with children, and while that may be good news for your children, you may want to avoid coming during weekends and local school holidays if you want to get a good look around. The house can be reached by B5285 or by car ferry from Bowness-on-Windermere.

**Keswick** This Lake District town was the site of the famous annual Keswick Conference, begun in the 19th century to promote the deeper spiritual life. It is still going strong and has spawned several Keswick Conference grounds in North America in this century.

**Kingston-upon-Hull** Wilberforce House, birthplace in 1759 of William Wilberforce, the remarkable Christian antislavery crusader who halted the slave trade in England and affected the abolitionist movement in America, is here. The museum, which is contained in several Georgian houses, tells of Wilberforce's remarkable campaign against slavery.

**Lincoln** The big attraction in this city of 80,000 is its 900-year-old Cathedral of St. Mary, the third largest in the country. Its tower is 271 feet high, but it was twice as high as that until a storm toppled it in 1547. Evensong is at 5:15 each afternoon (3:45 on Sundays), and matins are sung at 11:15 each Sunday. While you're here, don't miss the Lincoln Castle on Castle Hill, begun in 1068, four years before the cathedral. A copy of the Magna Carta is on display in the same building at the chapel. A statue of the poet Alfred Tennyson stands outside the cathedral. In nearby Somersby you can see the house in which he was raised. His bust is in the Somersby Church.

**Lindisfarne** That's the Celtic name, but the name most people use today is Holy Island and it is known as the cradle of Christianity in Britain. In 635 Aidan, a missionary from the Scottish island of Iona, founded the now ruined Lindisfarne Priory. In 1082 the priory became a Benedictine monastery, and the faith spread from here across northern England. A museum on Holy Island tells the history of Lindisfarne. In 698, monks produced the Lindisfarne Gospels, a gorgeous illustrated text of Scripture that you can see in the British Museum. The ruins of the priory are not much to look at, but there is an adjoining museum. While you are here, you can also explore the 16th-century castle. All of Lindisfarne's attractions are located within walking distance of one another.

About 14 miles away, Berwick-upon-Tweed on the Scottish border is where Reformer John Knox retreated to get away from Scottish intrigue and it was here that he found a wife. It is a delightful town whether you are looking for a wife or not.

**Liverpool** This major city is trying to recover its past grandeur. The Liverpool Anglican Cathedral on St. James's Rd. is not old but it is large. It was completed in 1978, and the only larger cathedrals in Europe are in Vatican City, Milan, and Seville. From the top, you can get a great view of the city, but it takes you two elevator rides and a 108-step climb to get there. The modern Roman Catholic cathedral (the Metropolitan Cathedral of Christ the King) on Mount Pleasant does not measure up to other cathedrals in the country.

**Lutterworth** In this small market town, John Wycliffe, the Bible translator, served as parish priest and worked on his translation. A white marble memorial erected under the east window of the town's church on A426 shows Wycliffe preaching. He was buried in the churchyard, but 44 years later he was condemned as a heretic and his ashes were thrown into the river.

**Manchester** You might be tempted to skip Manchester, and we could hardly blame you because it's an industrial city (severely damaged in World War II) of about a half million people. But here is what you would be missing. The John Rylands Library at 150 Deansgate is here with its Gutenberg Bible, several Caxton Bibles, and other manuscripts that go all the way back to 2000 B.C. (Abraham's time). The Manchester Museum and Whitworth Art Gallery on Oxford Rd. are part of the University district. The museum specializes in Egyptology, and the gallery does a good job with English watercolorists. The cathedral on Deansgate suffered major damage from air strikes; it has been restored, but it just isn't quite the same.

**Norwich** The cathedral on The Close is amazing with its 315-foot spire, its medieval frescoes in the treasury, and its stained glass windows. In the vaulted ceiling are more than 300 ornamental projections, "bosses," depicting Old Testament scenes. Edith Cavell, an English nurse put to death by the Germans in World War I, is buried on the cathedral's Life's Green. Her last words were, "Patriotism is not enough. I must have no hatred or bitterness towards anyone."

An alley off King St. leads to the church of Julian of Norwich. Julian of Norwich was a mystic who wrote *Revelations of Divine Love* in her small cell here. The work has been called "the most beautiful of all English mystical works."

## JULIAN OF NORWICH (1343-1413)

We know very little about Julian of Norwich. We don't know if she was a laywoman or a nun, and we don't even know her name for certain. She is called Juliana or Julian because she was attached to the church of St. Julian in Norwich. When she was 30, she became so ill that she was given last rites.

Julian prayed that she might be given a "bodily sight" of Christ's passion to help her share in his sufferings. In the next two days she received 16 visions, after which she recovered her health quickly. She wrote of her visions in a short form immediately, and then after 20 years of meditation on them, she wrote an 86-chapter version called, *Revelations of Divine Love,* emphasizing the Trinity, God's love, and the delight of knowing God.

Sites related to Julian are located in Norwich, England.

**Nottingham** Okay, so Robin Hood wouldn't recognize it today, but there is still enough to see and do to make a stop worthwhile. Twenty miles north of the city, the 450-acre Sherwood Forest Country Park attracts a quarter million visitors a year, even though the forest has been open grassland since the 14th century. So you have to have a bit of imagination to think of Robin Hood in surroundings like this. Frankly, the amusement ride called Tales of Robin Hood (on Maid Marian Way) may also disappoint. In the city itself Nottingham Castle, on the edge of the city center, with a statue of Robin Hood outside, is more a mansion than a castle, but the site was the administrative center where the high sheriffs lived who watched over Sherwood Forest. The history of Nottingham, which is told here, is interesting.

Just below Castle Rock is the Brewhouse Yard where religious dissenters in the early 1600s found refuge. A visit here is fascinating although some of it may seem a little hokey.

At the Baptist Chapel on Friar's Lane in 1792, William Carey preached his famous sermon that launched the modern era of foreign missions.

**Olney** This small town with a large 14th-century church is known for two things: its Shrove Tuesday pancake race, and as the home of John Newton. Newton, the former slave trader who was amazingly converted, became a Christian minister and hymn writer. Among his hymns are "Amazing Grace, How Sweet the Sound" and "Glorious Things of Thee Are Spoken." William Cowper, the noted 17th-century British poet, became a close friend of Newton and was encouraged by Newton to write hymns as a therapy for his depression. Among Cowper's hymns are "God Moves in a Mysterious Way" and "There Is a Fountain Filled with Blood." Cowper's former home in the market square houses the Cowper and Newton Museum.

> Ye fearful saints, fresh courage take;
> The clouds ye so much dread
> Are big with mercy, and shall break
> With blessing on your head.
>
> WILLIAM COWPER, OF OLNEY, ENGLAND

**Oxford** England's oldest university, Oxford was developed around a nunnery, now Christ Church Cathedral. The university began around 1200, and its unique blend of history and scholarliness can best be appreciated by walking the grounds. The university is actually a collection of 35 independent colleges, with magnificent chapels and dining halls that are opsen to visitors (although many are open only in the afternoon). To get a good look at the university, you may choose to join a walking tour, which you can do at the Tourist Information Centre. Like Cambridge, the colleges and halls are spread throughout the town, rather than being clustered around one campus. All the colleges have illustrious alumni. Christ Church College, for instance, boasts John Wesley, William Penn, W. H. Auden, and Lewis Carroll, to name a few. C. S. Lewis taught for many years at Magdalen College. Evangelical theologian J. I. Packer studied at Corpus Christi College here.

On St. Giles St. is the Martyrs' Memorial showing the Protestant martyrs Cranmer, Latimer, and Ridley, all burned at the stake nearby. Cranmer had been taken to Radcliffe Square and was asked to recant publicly. He was chained to a pillar in what is now the University Church of St. Mary's; a stone cross in Broad St. marks the spot of his execution. A somewhat more gruesome sight are the doors between the inner and outer quadrangles of Balliol College. They still bear the scorch marks from the flames that killed Cranmer, Latimer, and Ridley in 1555.

## JOHN WYCLIFFE (1329-1384)

Called "the Morning Star of the Reformation," Wycliffe is perhaps best known for his translation of the Bible into English, but he did much more than that. Born in Yorkshire, he studied at Oxford, where he became a leading philosopher. A religious reformer, he preached against the Pope's secular sovereignty and infallibility, acknowledging the Bible as the only source of truth. The church, he said, consisted of God's chosen people, who did not need a priest to mediate with God for them. When prohibited from preaching, he retired to Lutterworth in England's Midlands. While there, he began his translation of the Bible, the first systematic translation of Scripture into English. His translation set a standard for English prose, and his tracts, read by Jan Hus, sparked a reformation in Bohemia.

Sites associated with Wycliffe are located in Lutterworth, Oxford, and Yorkshire, England.

Both the Bodleian Library on Catte St. and the Ashmolean Museum of Art and Archaeology on Beaumont St. are outstanding. John Keble, early 19th-century professor of poetry at Oxford University, is best known for his simple hymn, "Sun of My Soul." It is based on the Gospel story of Christ's walk to Emmaus with two disciples after his resurrection. William Holman Hunt's famous painting *The Light of the World*, depicting Christ knocking on the door is in Keble Hall here. Another rendering of the same painting is in St. Paul's Cathedral in London.

C. S. Lewis lived in The Kilns in Headington, just east of Oxford. This is also where he is buried.

**Plymouth** In 1620 the Pilgrim Fathers set sail on the Mayflower from the Barbican quarter of the harbor. Many of them spent their last night on British soil in the Island House, 9 The Barbican. On the "Mayflower Steps" is a sign listing the passengers on the pilgrimage.

Plymouth is also a city famous in British history. In 1577 Francis Drake set out from here in the Golden Hind and sailed around the world. Eleven years later the English fleet with Drake as vice admiral sailed from Plymouth in the defeat of the Spanish Armada.

**Salisbury** No question about it; the Salisbury Cathedral is one of the most beautiful in England, with a spire stretching 404 feet in the air. The church was built in the 13th and 14th centuries. The beautiful Gothic Chapter House of 1263 to 1264 holds one of the four surviving originals of the Magna Carta, drafted in 1215. Around the room is a frieze recounting Old Testament stories. In the Cathedral Cloisters is a brass rubbing center where staff members will help you in the art of brass rubbing of various designs.

John Foxe, who wrote the classic *Book of Martyrs* in 1563, became the Canon of Salisbury the year the book was published.

In Bemerton, a small village just outside Salisbury, the 17th-century poet George Herbert served the small parish church. He would walk across the meadow to attend evensong at the large cathedral.

Stonehenge, nine miles north of Salisbury, may be the most important prehistoric monument in Britain. New Agers make pilgrimages here believing that the circles of stones were the work of Druids. Scientists now believe it was built before the Celtic Druid cult arose, and that it was probably an astronomical observatory, built to help early man predict eclipses.

**Somerset** In the village of Burrington Combe, near Glastonbury, a limestone crag rises 70 to 80 feet in the air. Near the center of this huge rock is a deep fissure. According to local tradition, Augustus Toplady was caught one day in a thunderstorm and took refuge in the rock. There he wrote the hymn "Rock of Ages, Cleft for Me." True, the crag is in walking distance of a church Toplady had served, but he left there in 1764, and the hymn was not published until 1773. Even if he didn't write it there, it may have been his inspiration for the hymn.

**Stourhead** Stourhead is considered one of the finest examples of English gardening today. The garden was actually designed by a banker, Henry Hoare II, in the 18th century, using as inspiration the landscapes he saw on his travels. The garden has a number of interesting features, including a triangular lake, a grotto, reproductions of ancient buildings, and, of course, lots and lots of plants.

**Stratford-upon-Avon** Were it not for the city's most famous son Stratford-upon-Avon would still be worth visiting, with its lovely 16th-century timbered buildings. But it is William Shakespeare who reigns supreme in this city. The main sites associated with Shakespeare are run by the Shakespeare Birthplace Trust (phone 01789/204-016). All of the sites have similar opening times, and if you plan to see many of them it may be worthwhile to purchase a combination ticket for them all. Tickets can also be purchased individually.

Anne Hathaway's Cottage on Cottage Lane is always a favorite. The early home of Shakespeare's wife, the cottage has the thatched roof that visitors hope to see in Britain and is considered one of the most picturesque buildings in all of England. Shakespeare's birthplace is across town on Henley Street. The building contains an exhibition of the playwright's life and work, and also houses a small museum with Shakespeare memorabilia.

Other buildings associated with Shakespeare's life include Hall's Croft on Old Town, the home of Shakespeare's daughter Susanna; Holy Trinity Church on Trinity St., where Shakespeare and Anne Hathaway are buried; and Mary Arden's House in the nearby village of Wilmcote, Anne's girlhood home. At Holy Trinity Church you can see copies of Shakespeare's baptism and burial records. If the children want to know where Shakespeare went to school, take them to King Edward VI School near the corner of Chapel Land and Church St.

As you might expect, visitors also have the opportunity to see the Bard's plays performed in Stratford-upon-Avon. The Royal Shakespeare Theatre, the most famous of all the world's Shakespearian theaters, performs several plays each season, as well as works by other playwrights. Backstage tours are offered twice daily. It's best to book seats well in advance of attendance. Contact: The Royal Shakespeare Theatre, Stratford-upon-Avon, Warwickshire, England CV37 6BB, phone 01789/295-623.

**Wakefield** Sabine Baring-Gould, minister of the church at nearby Horbury Bridge, wrote "Onward Christian Soldiers" as a marching song for children of his parish to sing as they walked a few miles to a nearby parish, for a festival. He also wrote "Now the Day Is Over" for children of his parish.

**Wells** With a population of less than 10,000, England's smallest cathedral city possesses one of the country's most beautiful cathedrals, the Cathedral Church of St. Andrew. Begun in 1175, it wasn't finished until 1508. What the cathedral experts appreciate is that it has everything that a cathedral complex should have: bishop's moated palace, cloisters, church, exciting clock, ten bells, octagonal chapter house. The west front has one of the richest collections of 13th-century sculpture in England. Be sure to visit the astronomical clock in the north transept, which has displayed a knights' tournament every quarter of an hour since 1390. The street known as Vicars' Close is called one of the most beautifully preserved streets in Europe. There are lunchtime recitals and evening concerts year-round so you have a good opportunity to hear the historic cathedral choir.

For a little variety you might want to investigate the Wookey Hole Caves and the Cheddar Show Caves, just west of town. Wookey is a series of attractions combining an ancient handmade papermill, an Edwardian fairground, a maze of mirrors, and a bunch of old penny arcade machines. The Cheddar Caves adventure will show you how Cheddar cheese is made and will take you deep underground to explore the caves.

**Whitby** This town is remembered for two things—the birthplace of Captain James Cook, intrepid explorer who charted the Pacific, and the site of the Synod of Whitby, which shaped the medieval English church. St. Hilda established a monastery here in 657, and in 664 leaders of the Celtic church met with Roman church leaders at the abbey to resolve their differences. The abbey was later destroyed but ruins of a Benedictine abbey on the same site on Abbey La. and a lovely St. Mary's Church on Church La. remain high on a clifftop overlooking the city.

However, the most popular tourist attraction these days in Whitby is none of the above, but rather "The Dracula Experience." Visitors can pick up a brochure at the local tourist office that will direct them along a Dracula Trail through the graveyard and along a cliff side. The story of Dracula was written while Bram Stoker was staying at a local bed and breakfast.

**Winchester** The city of Winchester was England's capital from the 9th century through half of the 12th century, so it is only fitting that a grand cathedral be located here. Winchester Cathedral on The Close is the longest Gothic cathedral in Europe. Construction began in 1079, but the building wasn't completed until nearly 450 years later. The cathedral's stone comes largely from the Isle of Wight. Take notice of the 12th-century black Tournai marble baptismal font and the canopied choir stalls, decorated with little smiling faces. Evensong is at 5:30 on Monday through Saturday and at 3:30 on Sundays.

In the church's library is an illuminated 12th-century copy of the Winchester Bible, a copy of Bede's 8th-century *Historia Ecclesiastica,* and a unique Bible, dating from 1661, in the Algonquin Indian language. It was translated by John Eliot of Massachusetts and printed in Cambridge.

> The Church's one Foundation is Jesus Christ her Lord;
>
> She is His new creation, by water and the word;
>
> From heaven He came and sought her to be His holy bride;
>
> With His own blood He bought her, and for her life He died.
>
> SAMUEL STONE OF WINDSOR ON THE THAMES, ENGLAND

**Windsor** Windsor Castle has been a royal residence since the 11th century, although nearly every monarch since then has revamped or added to the palace. A devastating fire in 1992 destroyed much of the State Apartments, but subsequent work has restored the rooms to their former grandeur. All of the restored rooms, except the private chapel of the royal family, are open to the public. But be forewarned that the State Apartments are closed when the queen is in residence. Of special interest is St. George's Chapel—230 feet long, lots of windows, and hundreds of gargoyles and buttresses. This is a remarkable building. Many monarchs are also buried here, including Henry VIII and George VI, father of the present queen.

Art lovers will be fascinated by the magnificent art collection, including works by Rubens, da Vinci, and Van Dyck. And children will enjoy Queen Mary's Dolls' House, a toy country house that was created in exquisite detail, including electricity and running water. It was built in 1921 for the present queen's grandmother. You can purchase tickets to the castle individually or buy a family ticket. Tickets are required to visit the Dolls' House, unless you purchase the family ticket, in which case admission is included.

Just outside of Windsor on B3202 is Legoland, which children love. Located in a wooded area, the park includes lots of hands-on activities, most of which involve the popular building bricks, as well as driving and boating.

The hymn "The Church's One Foundation" was written by Samuel John Stone, when he was just beginning his ministry as an assistant in Windsor. He began working in a mission chapel here and spent all his life working with poor people both in Windsor and in London.

**Worcester** This city of 75,000 is famous as the home of magnificent bone china, the location of a grand cathedral, and the birthplace of composer Edward Elgar. The Royal Worcester Porcelain Factory (Severn St.) is the oldest in Britain, and they will show you how they do it. Next door is a seconds shop with discounted porcelain. The present cathedral on High St. dates back to 1084, although there has been a church here since 680. The tomb of King John is buried in the choir. The cathedral choir sings evensong at 5:30 daily except Thursdays. On Sundays evensong is at 5:00. Best-known for his "Pomp and Circumstance," Edward Elgar was born three miles west of the city, and the cottage on High St., facing the cathedral, in which he was born is now a museum of Elgar memorabilia.

**York** York's crowning glory is the York Minster on Duncombe Pl., the largest Gothic church in England and considered one of the finest in Europe. The rose window is a memorial to the marriage of Henry VII and Elizabeth of York, and is one of 128 stained glass windows in the minster. If you're up for a climb, take time to climb the 275 stairs to the top of the Central Tower for a remarkable view of the city and surrounding countryside. The crypt contains some of the cathedral's oldest and most treasured items, including a 12th-century statue of the Virgin Mary. The present building dates to the 13th century, but previous churches were here since 627. The west aisle windows have some of the oldest glass in England, dating from 1150, and the Great East Window with medieval stained glass, depicts scenes of creation, redemption, and the second coming. More than half of England's glass from medieval times is right here. While you are here, explore the Foundations and Treasury. It is a surprising museum. York had 41 pre–16th-century churches and 20 of them still survive. The finest may be All Saints, North Street.

Two sites in York are likely to be of interest to children. The Castle Museum on Clifford St. was a debtors' prison during the 18th century, but has been rebuilt to house a museum, with a number of historic exhibitions and re-creations. Its Victorian cobblestone street with a variety of craft shops is popular, as is the working water mill.

It may surprise you that there is Viking history in York, but you'll learn just how much there is at the Jorvik Viking Centre on Coppergate. Little "time cars" escort travelers back to the sounds, sights, and smells of a Viking street. The remarkable detail of the authentic re-creation was based on archaeological finds.

# ▲ NORTHERN IRELAND

**Antrim** Every St. Patrick's Day Slemish Mountain, about 20 miles northeast of town, becomes a place of pilgrimage. According to tradition, St. Patrick herded swine here for six years for the local chieftain.

**Armagh** In 445 St. Patrick chose this area to be the center for operations in his Christian outreach to Ireland. Today there are two St. Patrick Cathedrals in town. One is called St. Patrick's Cathedral (Anglican) and the other St. Patrick's Cathedral (Roman Catholic). Both are worth seeing. The most impressive cathedral visually is the Catholic cathedral on the northern end of town, with its twin spires and nearly every inch of interior wall space covered in mosaics. The Protestant cathedral in the town center is the older of the two, dating back to medieval times. It is well-known for its 11th-century High Cross.

**Ballymena** This area was settled by several different religious communities. Moravians settled in Gracehill in 1746, bringing their skills in lace making and clock making. Huguenots came to Newtown Crommelin in the late 17th century, bringing their skills in making Irish linen.

At Portglenone, Roman Catholics founded the Cistercian Abbey in 1951, making it the first abbey founded in Northern Ireland since the Reformation.

**Bangor** The first abbey founded here was in 552, after which the city became known as a famous seat of learning and a "city of saints." King Alfred of England got professors from the seminary here to help him get Oxford started. The Bangor Castle is still in good condition. Cultra Manor, which houses the Ulster Folk and Transport Museum, is also worth some time. On its 180 acres are a number of old buildings that have been brought from various parts of Ireland. You will also see demonstrations of weaving, spinning, and thatching here. The Transport Museum has a remarkable collection of bicycles as well as dog carts, monoplanes, and even a merchant schooner.

**Belfast** Check out the interesting Sinclair Seaman's Church in Corporation Square. The pulpit is shaped like the prow of a ship, and the organ is decorated with nautical clocks and port and starboard lights. At Lady Dixon Park there is an internationally known rose garden (20,000 roses), as well as a good children's play area.

The oldest church in Belfast is the First Presbyterian Church on Rosemary St. (known as the Oval Church, and once you see it you will understand why). It was built in 1783.

St. Anne's Cathedral on Donegall St. doesn't look terribly imposing from the outside. But step inside the Protestant cathedral for a treat. Of special interest are the cathedral's immense mosaics, crafted by two sisters in the 1920s. One mosaic depicts St. Patrick's voyage to Ireland. The one over the baptistery contains over 150,000 pieces.

**Devenish Island** In the 6th century the tiny island of Devenish became home to a monastery under St. Molaise. Thus began the long Christian history of the island, which remained an important religious center up until the early 17th century. There are several buildings that have survived, including Teampall Mor. Built in 1225, this church is considered important architecturally for its mixture of Romanesque and Gothic styles.

St. Mary's Priory stands on the island's highest ground. The Augustinian church was erected in the 15th century, and an intricately carved stone cross nearby dates from about the same time period. The most important structure on Devenish Island is considered to be the 12th-century round tower. Standing over 80 feet tall, the tower is immaculately preserved. The five floors are still accessible by internal ladders. Notice the four carved stone faces above each of four windows at the tower's top. A museum on the island explains its history and architecture and also displays a collection of local artifacts. You can reach the island by ferry from Enniskillen in the summer months.

*339*

**Downpatrick** The Down Cathedral on The Mall was built on the site of an earlier cathedral, which had been one of the earliest religious buildings in the country. The earlier structure, which was destroyed by the Danes, is said to have housed the remains of St. Patrick and St. Bridget. The present cathedral dates from 1790. Next door is the St. Patrick Heritage Centre, a museum focused on the Emerald Isle's patron saint.

Just east of town in the village of Saul are the remains of Saul Abbey, a barn that the local chief gave to St. Patrick to use as a church. A newer church here commemorates St. Patrick's coming to the area on his first missionary journey. Some believe that this is also the place where Patrick died in 461. A path from the church goes up to a large granite monument of St. Patrick.

**Londonderry** The city walls date back to 1613 and have withstood two long sieges. The Protestant St. Columb's Cathedral on St. Columb's Ct. was the first cathedral to be built in the British Isles following the Reformation. Constructed between 1628 and 1633, its style is known as "Planters' Gothic." The cathedral's stained glass windows depict the life of St. Columba and incidents from the siege of Derry in the late 17th century. The heads carved in the cathedral's corbels represent former bishops and deans of the church.

The oldest Roman Catholic church in the city is the Long Tower Church, also known as The Church of St. Columba, on Bishop St. The church dates from 1784, although it is on the site of a much older church. A newer Roman Catholic cathedral, St. Eugene's, is northwest of the city center in Brooke Park.

**Omagh** The Ulster American Folk Park, three miles north of town, was built by the Mellon family of Pittsburgh and is a reconstruction of rural life in Ulster from the time when many northern Irish were emigrating to America. It also shows what pioneer life was like in America at the time.

# ▲ SCOTLAND

**Aberdeen** St. Machar's Cathedral is located on Chanonry. It is difficult to place the age of the church, which has gone by turns through one reconstruction—and deconstruction—after another.

It is said that the first church in this location was planted in 580 by St. Machar himself on instructions from St. Columba in Iona. Nothing is left of the original foundation, but reconstruction of the nave is thought to have begun in the 14th century and finished in the 15th century. The twin octagonal spires date from the first half of the 16th century. The lead and church bells were stripped off the church during Reformation battles, and Oliver Cromwell's troops removed stone in the 17th century. A restoration program in the 19th century finally restored the cathedral to its former grandeur.

If you need to stretch your legs and enjoy some great scenery, visit Seaton Park just beyond St. Machar's Cathedral. The park is usually beautifully colored with flowers and shaded with tall trees. In the spring the daffodils are terrific. A single-arch bridge, the Brig o' Balgownie, spans the River Don in Seaton Park. The bridge was built in 1314.

The Adventure Playground on the Beach Esplanade follows a fishing village theme and includes model houses, fishing nets, and a paddling pool. The Rosemount Celebration Centre (on Rosemount Pl.) has a museum and learning center called Jonah's Journey, which is based on life in a 2,000-year-old Israelite village. Very popular also is Duthue Park and Winter Gardens with its boating pond and trampolines, and also Storybook Glen, a 20-acre park on a fairy-tale theme.

There are no less than nine castles in the countryside surrounding Aberdeen. Drum Castle on A93 was built in the 13th century. Since it lies largely in ruins, it makes for great exploring with the kids. There are wooded grounds to run through too. Balmoral Castle, also on A93, is the residence of the British royals when they're in the area. The grounds are beautiful, and there are plenty of walking paths, but you won't be able to see much of the castle. Only the ballroom with its displays of royal artifacts is open to the public. Kildrummy Castle on A944 may be the most interesting of the area's fortresses. Built in the 13th century, the castle's well-preserved facilities make it a good bet.

**Blantyre** Southeast of Glasgow in Blantyre is the David Livingstone Centre on A724. The center features a park around the tiny apartment where the medical missionary to Africa was born in 1813. Exhibits in the center tell of his explorations of Africa, his famous meeting with Stanley ("Dr. Livingstone, I presume?"), and the industrial heritage of the area. Livingstone's body is buried in Westminster Abbey in London. The mill where he worked as a boy can still be seen.

**Dollar** Just beyond this little town is Castle Campbell, once known as Castle Gloom. Its setting is one of the most dramatic of any castle in Scotland. It is associated with John Knox who preached here in the 16th century and with Oliver Cromwell who captured it in the 17th century.

**Edinburgh** Visually exciting and historically fascinating, the city is loaded with Christian significance. Edinburgh's symbol is the massive stone Edinburgh Castle. Perched on an extinct volcano, the castle dominates the city. Of special interest are St. Margaret's Chapel, an 11th-century building; the Crown Room, where Scotland's royal treasures are displayed; and Queen Mary's Apartments, residence of Mary, Queen of Scots. The Castle Esplanade, the parade ground at the entrance to the castle, is home to the annual Edinburgh Military Tattoo, an immensely popular military display staged every summer.

*The Holyroodhouse* at the eastern end of Canongate is where the Queen of England hangs out when she's in Scotland. Founded in 1128 as a guest house for the Abbey of Holyrood, it has seen more monarchs than you can shake a scepter at. On the second floor of the King James Tower, which you can visit

## David Livingstone (1813-1873)

Born to a poor family, David Livingstone went to work in a local cotton mill when he was ten. With his first wages, he bought a Latin grammar, and he worked with a book propped up against the machine. Attending night classes, he got a general education, then studied medicine in Glasgow and later theology in London.

Livingstone went to Africa as a missionary in 1840, and through his explorations there, he became one of the world's greatest explorers. He walked farther and recorded his observations better than anyone else. His goals were to make Christ known to Africa, to eradicate the slave trade there, and to find the source of the Nile so that Africa could become economically viable without dependence on the slave trade. Lost to the world for years, he was found by Stanley in 1871. Two years later his African helpers found him dead, but in a posture of prayer on his knees.

Sites associated with Livingstone are in Blantyre, Scotland, and London, England. His body was buried in Westminster Abbey.

when Queen Elizabeth isn't there, are the rooms that Mary Queen of Scots used. John Knox had some of his confrontations with her here. Lord Darnley's rooms are directly below. Behind the place is Holyrood Park, the hunting grounds of early Scottish kings. From the park you can get a spectacular view of the city.

*Churches.* The Greyfriars Kirk on Greyfriars Pl. is built on the site of a medieval monastery. In 1638 the National Covenant was signed here, declaring the independence of the Presbyterian Church in Scotland from government control.

The High Kirk of St. Giles on High St. is built on a site where churches had been standing since 854. In 1633 the High Kirk was declared a cathedral. The spire is dated from 1495, but much of the church is more recent. In the Thistle Chapel is a bronze memorial to Robert Louis Stevenson.

On High St., the Gothic Tolbooth Kirk, which was built between 1842 and 1844, has the tallest spire in the city—240 feet. It is also noted for something else. Built shortly after 1635, the church had an early minister who prayed for his local government this way: "Lord, hae mercy on every fool and idiot, and particularly on the magistrates of Edinburgh." He was frequently quoted for this remark thereafter.

Canongate Kirk on Canongate St. is a nice example of a Presbyterian church, with its box pews and white painted walls. It was constructed in 1688. Its graveyard will appeal to you as well, as it is the final resting place for many notable Scots, including the economist Adam Smith and the poet Robert Fergusson. There is an interesting story associated with Fergusson's marker. The famous poet Robert Burns visited the city and was shocked to find no marker for Fergusson's grave. He commissioned an architect by the name of Robert Burn to design one. Burn took two years to finish the project, so Burns, likewise, took two years to pay.

*Music festival.* For a celebration focused on music, dance, and drama, visit the Edinburgh International Festival, staged each summer in mid-August. The best artists in the world are invited to perform. Advance information and tickets are available from the Edinburgh International Festival Office, Castlehill, Scotland EH1 1ND, phone 0131/473-2001.

*John Knox House* is opposite the Museum of Childhood on High Street. Both are worth a visit. The museum is a delightful celebration of toys. As for the John Knox House, it is not certain whether the noted Protestant reformer ever lived here, but the house still gives you a good glimpse of what his life would have been like if he had. Mementoes of his life are displayed. Near the John Knox House is a Brass Rubbing Center that allows you and your kids to make do-it-yourself replicas of medieval church brasses and other things.

*The National Gallery of Scotland* (just east of The Mound) is an outstanding art museum with paintings by Velázquez, El Greco, Rembrandt, Van Gogh, Monet, and others.

*The Royal Botanic Garden* on Inverleith Rd. provides 70 acres of the largest rhododendron and azalea collection in Britain. See them abloom in season. The sight is awesome!

*The Edinburgh Butterfly and Insect World* is located in Melville Nurseries, near Dalkeith. You can purchase a family ticket to save a little money on entrance to the tropical indoor exhibition. Humid, junglelike conditions provide the perfect atmosphere for scores of brightly colored butterflies and other bugs.

*The Edinburgh Zoo* on Corstorphine Rd. offers traditional animal settings as well as some hands-on animal sessions in the main season. But the zoo's real highlight is its hugely popular Penguin Parade, held daily in the summer.

*At Deep Sea World* an acrylic see-through tunnel offers a great view of more than 5,000 fish. Displays in the exhibition hall and audio-visual presentations explain the local marine life. The aquarium is located in North Queensferry on the Firth of Forth.

*Authors.* A number of celebrated authors hailed from Scotland, including Robert Louis Stevenson, Robert Burns, and Sir Walter Scott. Exhibits on these and other Scottish authors are housed in The Writers' Museum on Lady Stair's Close. Originally known as Lady Stair's House, the building was constructed in 1622 and pays homage to Scotland's literary heritage. Admission is free.

**Gatehouse of Fleet** One mile south of town is a monument to Samuel Rutherford, saintly 17th-century Scottish theologian and covenanter. He took a prominent part in the preparation of the Westminister Confession and is credited with having written the Shorter Catechism.

**Glasgow** Situated on a hill on Cathedral St., the Glasgow Cathedral, dedicated to St. Mungo, the city's patron saint, was begun in the 12th century and completed 300 years later. At the time of the Reformation, when other Catholic cathedrals were damaged by Protestants desiring to rid the churches of graven images, this one escaped harm, because local trade guilds considered it their own church and defended it from defacement.

Don't miss the St. Mungo Museum of Religious Life and Art adjacent to the cathedral. Exhibits describe the many religious groups who have settled in Glasgow and western Scotland over the centuries, and there is a large collection of religious artifacts and paintings. The centerpiece is *Christ of St. John of the Cross,* a magnificent painting by Salvador Dali. Admission is free.

> And from my smitten heart with tears
> Two wonders I confess—
> The wonder of redeeming love
> And my unworthiness.
>
> ELIZABETH CLEPHANE OF MELROSE, SCOTLAND

Cemeteries don't generally top travelers' lists of must-see sights, but the Necropolis just off Cathedral Square is an interesting place to take a walk. The grave sites are marked with elaborately carved Victorian gravestones, and a statue of John Knox keeps an eye on things.

The Tollbooth Steeple is at the intersection of High St., Gallowgate, Trongate, and London Rd. The steeple is seven stories high and topped by an unusual crown. Built in 1626, it marks the old center of town, the spot where the local market was held, where merchants met with one another, and where the tron, or weigh beam, was used to check merchants' weights. The steeple takes its name from its history as the place where travelers entering the city paid tolls.

The Burrell Collection in Pollok Country Park (three miles southwest of the city center) is Scotland's finest art museum. It is also quite a fascinating building, its walls constructed almost entirely of glass. The building is located on Paisley Rd.

For the children, try the Eastwood Butterfly Kingdom, Rankin Glen Park, or the Glasgow Zoo (with attached amusement park) in Calder Park. The zoo's tiger collection is outstanding. Haggs Castle (100 St. Andrews Dr.) has been given over to children and is now a history museum for children. It is a great hands-on learning experience for them.

The Ministry of Education doesn't sound like a fun place to go, but it is. Located at 225 Scotland St. in the Scotland Street School, the classrooms are fitted out in the styles of different historical periods, and the staff is dressed as the teachers would have been in the various eras.

Get out and enjoy the great outdoors at Victoria Park off Airthrey Ave. The park is known for its excellent boating lake and arboretum, as well as an unusual Fossil Grove. The fossilized stumps of trees said to be over 330 million years old are preserved in the grove. Admission is free, but you have to call ahead to see the fossils, phone 041/959-2128.

**Haddington** Four miles east of East Linton is this small town where John Knox was born and reared. It is a lovely village with 129 buildings marked as having architectural or historical interest. You can visit St. Mary's Church where John Knox worshiped as a lad.

**Innelan** In this popular seaside resort town of western Scotland, George Matheson wrote the hymn "O Love That Wilt Not Let Me Go," in 1880. He was a remarkable minister who was blind, and according to one story, just before he wrote the hymn, he had been told by his fiancée that she didn't want to marry a blind man.

**Inverness** At Culloden Manor, northeast of Inverness, one of the most historic battles in Scottish history took place. In 1746, 5,000 Jacobites fought 9,000 British troops. The Jacobites were routed, and British troops patrolled the Highlands. To add insult to injury, it became illegal for anyone to wear kilts. The visitors center provides a moving video presentation of the battle.

**Iona** The island of Iona has a long and rich Christian heritage. In 563 St. Columba and 12 companions arrived by boat from Ireland and founded a monastery on Iona. Christianity had been brought to Scotland nearly 200 years earlier when St. Ninian arrived in 397, but until St. Columba's church was founded, the word had not spread widely. The island served as a base for missionary journeys to the pagan people in the area, and eventually became the mother house of the Celtic church in Scotland and England. The spiritual endeavor came to an unfortunate end when in 803 a Norse raid left 68 monks dead and sent the others running. The existing buildings all date from the early 13th century, when a Benedictine monastery and nunnery were established on the island, but they fell into disuse around the time of the Reformation. The monastery no longer remains, but there is a remarkable collection of stone carvings from this early Christian era. Many find the rich history and the peaceful scenery an ideal place for quiet reflection; in fact its peacefulness is a bit mysterious in light of the large number of visitors that arrive regularly. In addition to the old buildings, there are an abbey gift shop, bookshop, and coffee house.

In 1938 the Iona Community was established, and the restored buildings in the area serve as a spiritual center under the Church of Scotland. The complex is a mix of ancient and modern.

**Kelso** Horatius Bonar served as a pastor in this border town for many years. It was here he wrote "I Heard the Voice of Jesus Say," "I Lay My Sins on Jesus," and "I Was a Wandering Sheep." However, because he allowed only psalms to be sung in his church, his people never had a chance to sing his songs as a congregation.

**Kirkcaldy** In St. Columba's Church near the adjoining village of Burntisland is where James VI announced the new translation of the Bible, now known as the King James Version, published for the first time in 1611.

**Loch Lomond** If you're going to Scotland, you have to take a boat trip on a Scottish loch. There are good opportunities at several of the lochs. Early Scottish Christians used the islands in the lochs as retreat centers. The island of Inchmirrin in Loch Lomund is where St. Mirrin often spent time in meditation.

**Loch Ness** Loch Ness is renowned for its mysterious resident, the Loch Ness monster, an alleged dinosaur-like beast fondly referred to as Nessie. There is an interesting Christian tie to the

## COLUMBA (521–597)

Born in Donegal, Ireland, Columba helped to establish churches and monasteries in Derry and in Durrow, before leaving Ireland in 563 to "go on pilgrimage for Christ." He and 12 companions landed on the island of Iona, off the coast of Scotland, where they opened a monastery as a base for evangelizing the Scots and the Picts. He preached to the Druid opponents of Christianity and founded many churches in western Scotland. His Celtic Church in Britain was not tied to Rome, and he sent missionaries from Iona to the European mainland. He was also a poet, a hymn writer, and a Bible translator.

Sites associated with Columba are located in Kells, Ireland; Londonderry, Northern Ireland; and Aberdeen and Iona, Scotland.

## SCOTLAND'S NORTHERN HIGHLANDS

Scotland's Northern Highlands are magnificent, with much of the country's most fascinating scenery. Much of Sutherland and Wester Ross are built on gneiss, the oldest rock formations in the country, which were gouged and chiseled by glaciers into many lochs. On top of the lower rock layer are intricately shaped sandstone or quartzite mountains, shaped into pinnacles by centuries of erosion. To best enjoy the landscape, rent a car and enjoy the roads that meander through the area. Plan on spending a while; many of the hilly roads narrow to only one lane.

monster: It was a monk who first saw the creature, and you don't think a monk would steer you wrong, do you? Numerous expeditions beneath the dark waters have failed to reveal the identity of the creature, if it exists.

**St. Andrews** It is best known today for its golf, but in previous centuries it was more famous for its cathedral on Pends Rd. begun in 1161, and its university, west of the castle between North St. and The Scores. The university was the first in Scotland, founded in 1412. John Knox lived for a time at the site of St. Leonard's College, now a school for girls, on South St. just east of St. Mary's College.

A little south of St. Andrews is the Craigtown Country Park, a great place for kids. In the Scottish Deer Centre (three miles west in Copar) children can see red deer at close range. Another good spot for kids is the Sea Life Centre at West Sands in St. Andrews.

**Stirling** This town has the most impressive and best-preserved town wall in all of Scotland. The Church of the Holy Rood is the only church in Scotland, still in use, that has witnessed the coronation of a Scottish monarch. James VI was crowned here in 1567.

**Stranraer** Just south of this town on the Mull of Galloway are some of the earliest Christian monuments in Great Britain. Inscribed stones and Northumbrian crosses can be seen at the small church at Kirknadrine at the top of Rhinns.

**Whithorn** The Whithorn Dig and Visitor Centre (45–47 George St.) is home to a number of early Christian crosses found here. The visitors center explains the significance of the finds. In medieval times, pilgrimages were made to St. Ninian's Chapel, which researchers think may have been at Whithorn.

# ▲ WALES

**Bangor** Back in 525 a Celtic monastery was begun here by St. Deinol, making this the oldest diocese in Britain. The present cathedral on Glarafon was built in the 13th century. Inside is an interesting 16th-century carved wooden figure known as the Mostyn Christ. Bishop's Garden, north of the cathedral, is filled with flowers, shrubs, and trees mentioned in the Bible. The town is also the home of the University College of North Wales, which overlooks Bangor from a hilltop.

**Betws-y-Coed** About three miles southwest of town at Ty Mawr is the cottage of Bishop William Moore, who translated the Bible into the Welsh language. That would have been quite a task. Nearby is a one-mile nature trail, if you'd like to take a short hike.

**Caernarfon** It seems every sizable Welsh hill is home to a castle, although many of those castles are now little more than ruins. Caernarfon sits right on the Irish Sea coast in northeast Wales and is in beautiful condition. Constructed in 1283, the castle was the birthplace of Edward II, the first Prince of Wales, and ever since the title has been bestowed on Britain's heir apparent, including the present Prince Charles. Caernarfon, like all the Welsh castles, begs to be explored. Highlights include several turrets and narrow slot windows that allowed archers to hit their targets below with little exposure themselves. Three other castles in Wales that are well worth going out of the way for are Harlech (near the town of Porthmadog), Conwy (in the town of the same name), and Beaumaris (in the town of the same name).

**Cardiff** Just north of the city on Cathedral Road in Llandoff is the Llandoff Cathedral dating from 1130. Inside you will see Jacob Epstein's powerful aluminum sculpture *Christ in Majesty,* as well as some interesting stained glass work.

**Harlech** Children especially love wandering the grounds of abandoned castles, imagining what it was like to live here as princes and princesses. Among the castles that Edward I built in the late 13th century, Harlech has a wonderful mass of secret labyrinths and twisting stairways that are sure to be a hit with kids. It is not the best preserved of Welsh fortresses, which is precisely its appeal. It is in the empty courtyards and towers that children's imaginations can run their wildest, and kids can pretend to be young royals demanding that others do their bidding. But keep a close eye on your little ones. Guardrails are rare. There's a nice public playground next door.

**Hay on Wye** If you're interested in books, have we ever got a town for you! The population of Hay on Wye is only 1,600, but it has more than 30 secondhand book-stores, some specializing in specific areas like religious subjects.

**Llandudno** On a peninsula between two bays, this town is Wales' largest resort. You can enjoy great views of north Wales from the top of Great Orme, reached by the Great Orme Tramway. The Doll Museum/Model Railway on Masonic St. in town has more than 1,000 dolls and a model train filling one room. Eight miles south are the Bodnant Gardens on Tal-y-Cafn in the village of Conwy, featuring rhododendrons, camellias, and magnolias.

## BEAUTIFUL WALES

Each of Great Britain's divisions can lay claim to great natural beauty. A highlight in Wales is Snowdonia National Park located in the northern Gwynedd Mountains. Snowdonia is home to Snowdon, a weath-ered mountain that offers interesting hiking even for young children. A number of foot-paths head up the peak, but the easiest ascent is from the town of Llanberis. No matter how high you climb, it seems you will always find a few sheep waiting for you. Be sure to pack a jacket. Winds can be strong and bitter at the top. Llanberis is also the home base for the Snowdon Mountain Railway that transports visitors who don't care to climb under their own power. On a clear day the view from the top is stunning, encompassing the Isles of Anglesey and Man and the Wicklow Mountains in Ireland.

**Llanfairpwllgwyngyllgogerychwyrndrobwllllantysilio-gogogoch** It's understandable that a town with a name like this has adopted a nickname. The residents of Llanfair P.G., as it's commonly known, wanted the publicity and fame that comes of being the village with the world's longest name and they succeeded. There's little to do here, but children and adults alike get a kick out of seeing the huge village sign at the train station.

**Llangollen** This small town of 2,600 is famous for its International Musical Eisteddfod, a six-day music and dance festival that attracts crowds up to 120,000. Incidentally, *eisteddfod* means a gathering or a gathering of poets and musicians.

If you want something else to do in Llangollen, take a ride on one of their horse-drawn boats at Llangollen Wharf or on the Llangollen Steam Railway that operates for only eight miles from Berwyn to Carrog. If that's too tame for you, try white-water rafting or canoeing, which are also available here.

**Pantycelyn** Wales is known as the "Land of Song," and when religious revivals swept the land, as they have periodically since the Methodist revivals of the 18th century, the towns burst out in hymn singing. Male voice choirs are a hallmark of not only churches but also mines, quarries, and sporting events. William Williams of Pantycelyn, converted under the ministry of revivalist Howell Harris, began writing hymns shortly after his conversion and became known as the "sweet singer of Wales." His best-known hymn is "Guide Me, O Thou Great Jehovah."

> Guide me, O Thou great Jehovah,
> Pilgrim through this barren land.
> I am weak but Thou art mighty;
> Hold me with Thy powerful hand.
>
> WILLIAM WILLIAMS OF WALES

**Rhyl** St. Asaph's Cathedral, just south of town, is the smallest cathedral in Britain. At the Chapter Museum are early Bibles and prayer books.

**St. David's** It's just a small village but it has a fantastic cathedral. Located on Cathedral Close at the end of the Pebbles, it was built in the late 12th century on top of previous churches that date to the 6th century. Unlike many cathedrals, St. David's is built not on a hill but in a hollow for protection. Visitors must descend 39 steps (known as "39 Articles") to enter this, the shrine to Wales' patron saint. Look inside and you can tell it's old. The pillars are atilt, and the floor slopes upward. Services are held at

7:30 and 8:00 each morning, and sometimes at 6:00 in the evening. Choral evensong is held at 6:00 on Sunday evenings.

Next to the cathedral is the Bishop's Palace built by Henry de Gower in the 14th century. Though it is now in ruins, most of the walls stand, and open-air plays are held here during the summer.

**Tintern** Near Monmouth is Tintern Abbey, the Cistercian abbey, founded in 1131, immortalized by Wordsworth's poetry and Turner's painting.

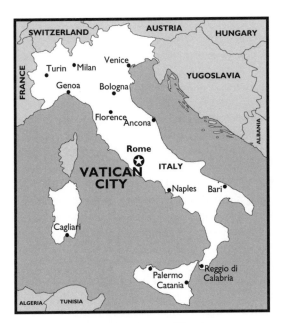

# Vatican City

*Phone number*
  Contact the Italian Government Tourist Board (see page 180)
*Web site*
  Entire country www.vatican.va
For a complete list of updated links, visit www.christiantraveler.com

### Country in a Capsule

*Size:* About 109 acres, so it's the smallest nation in the world. Population less than 800.

*Religion:* Roman Catholic, of course.

*Language:* Italian and Latin.

*Money:* The Vatican lira is tied to the Italian lira in value, and either can be used to make purchases. See Italy for an approximate exchange rate.

*Shopping:* Religious icons and other items associated with the papal residence are naturally quite popular.

> Stamp collectors always enjoy purchasing stamps in
> Vatican City since the world's smallest country doesn't
> circulate much mail outside its borders.
>     *Brief history:* In the 8th century Pepin the Short, king of
> the Franks, recognized that the Pope controlled land.
> How much land? was the question. In the 16th century
> the Papal States included much of central Italy, but as Italy
> came together as a nation, much of that land was incorpo-
> rated into the new nation. Finally, in 1929, Pope Pius XI
> and Mussolini signed the Lateran Treaties recognizing the
> sovereignty of Vatican City on one side and declaring
> Roman Catholicism to be the official religion of Italy on
> the other. However, the privileged position of the
> Catholic Church in Italy was ended in 1984.

Christians, whether Catholic or Protestant, should take the opportunity to visit the Vatican City and its chief attraction: St. Peter's Basilica. It may be the smallest country in the world, but there is a lot to see in it, starting with St. Peter's, which is about 636 feet long and 435 feet high. The church is simply magnificent. The original basilica was built in the early 4th century by the emperor Constantine over an earlier shrine that, according to tradition, marked the burial place of St. Peter. After more than 1,000 years the crumbling church was torn down and replaced by a much larger one, a task that took nearly 200 years to complete. The selling of indulgences to finance the basilica's construction was a turning point in Martin Luther's decision to push for reformation. Master craftsmen like Alberti, Raphael, and Michelangelo contributed to the construction.

Among the most famous works of art in St. Peter's Basilica is Michelangelo's *Pietà,* located in the first chapel on the right as you enter. At the end of the central aisle is a bronze statue of St. Peter. You'll recognize him by his worn foot, eroded by centuries of touching and kissing by the faithful. The bronze throne above the altar in the apse was created by Bernini to contain a simple wooden chair that was believed to have belonged to St. Peter.

The basilica's dome was designed by Michelangelo, who died before it was completed in 1626. At the base of the dome is a Latin inscription beginning, "Tu es Petrus . . ." referring to Matthew 16:18, "You are Peter, and on this rock I will build my church, and the gates of Hades will not overcome it." A fitting inscription. This church is literally built on Peter.

To see the dome and roof of the basilica, take the elevator or climb the stairs in the courtyard near the exit from the Vatican Grottoes. From the roof, visitors can climb a short interior staircase to the base of the dome for a view of the basilica's interior. If you are in good physical condition and are not claustrophobic, consider climbing the narrow stairs to the balcony of the lantern atop the dome. The view of the city of Rome is stunning.

Free 60-minute tours of St. Peter's Basilica are offered daily in English at 10:00 A.M. and 3:00 P.M., and at 2:30 on Sundays. Tours start at the information desk under the basilica portico. Be sure to wear conservative clothing when you visit. Those wearing shorts, miniskirts, sleeveless shirts, or otherwise revealing clothing will be barred entrance to the basilica, the Vatican Museums, and the Vatican Gardens. Women can cover bare arms and shoulders with a scarf. Men should wear long pants.

*St. Peter's Square (Piazza San Pietro)* is as remarkable as St. Peter's itself. Completed in 1667, the huge oval-shaped square in front of the basilica appears to embrace visitors in its massive arms, constructed of quadruple colonnades designed by Bernini. Notice the stone disks in the pavement halfway between the fountains and the obelisk. From these vantage points the colonnades seem to be created from a single row of columns all the way around. The statues atop the columns represent Christian saints. In the center of the huge square is the Egyptian Obelisk, taken from Nero's Circus Maximus and rebuilt in its present place in the 16th century. Pope Sixtux V decorated it with papal emblems. On the very top of the spire is a cross that sits on a reliquary urn, which is said to contain a little piece of Jesus' cross.

If you're interested in attending a mass when the Pope is officiating, you can participate in a Wednesday morning Mass audience at St. Peter's Basilica. Tickets are required and can be obtained in advance by writing the Prefettura della Casa Pontificia, 00120 Vatican City, or by faxing 06/6988-5863. If you'd just like to see the Pope, be in St. Peter's Square at noon on Sunday. When he's in town the Pope appears at the window of the Vatican Palace to bless the crowd below. If you are in St. Peter's Square after dark, you can see the Pope's window, which is the only one that will be lighted up in the dark facade of the palace to the right of the church.

*The grottoes and museums.* Besides St. Peter's, the only other buildings to which you will have access are the grottoes and the museums. The entrance to the grottoes is to the left inside the basilica. What is presumed to be the tomb of St. Peter was found during excavations. You usually need to obtain reservations in advance to be admitted.

Visitors to Vatican City would be ill-advised to skip the Vatican Museums, or Musei Vaticani, home to one of the world's most stunning collections of artistic history. To make the most of your visit, try to visit either early or late in the day, when crowds are not at their peak, and take along a pair of binoculars. Don't take any flash photos of the frescoes.

The Vatican Museum includes the Picture Gallery (Pinacoteca), Sistine Chapel, the Raphael Rooms, the Pio-Clementine Museum, the Tapestry Gallery, the Library, the Raphael Loggia, and a couple others.

The Picture Gallery contains 15 rooms, many of them representing art of various centuries, others showing the works of artists like Angelico, Raphael, and Giotto. The Library (Biblioteca) is really a long, lavishly adorned corridor, and it is easy to be so taken by the decoration that you fail to notice the rare books, including the priceless Vatican Codex of the Bible. In the Raphael Loggia is a series of panels covering most of Scripture from the creation of the world in the first arch to the life of Christ in the 13th arch.

Of course, the Sistine Chapel draws the most attention. While you may think only of Michelangelo in this regard, many other artists were involved as well. Roselli did the fresco *Passage of the Red Sea,* Botticelli is responsible for the dramatic work *Chastisement of Korah, Dathan and Abiram,* and Ghirlandalo for *Calling of the First Apostles.* Most of this work was done a generation before Michelangelo. He received his commission to paint biblical frescoes on the 10,000 square-foot ceiling in 1508. The center one shows the *Creation of Man.* Then in 1534 at the age of 60, he began his large fresco *Last Judgment* to cover the wall behind the high altar with 300 figures.

# Where to Go

Here's where to go to see:

largest carved wooden **altarpiece** in the world—Seville Cathedral, Sevilla, Spain

Europe's biggest **aquarium** (and second-largest in the world)—Genoa, Italy

Scandinavia's largest **aquarium** —Alesund, Norway

world's first modern public **art gallery**—Florence, Italy

**auto races**—Jyväskylä, Finland; Le Mans, France

sites related to Johann Sebastian **Bach**—Arnstadt (near Erfurt), Antoniterkirche in Cologne, Eisenach, Halle, Köthen, Leipzig, Stuttgart, Germany; Naarden, Netherlands

biggest **bear park** on the continent—Grönklitt, Sweden

oldest **belfry** in Belguim—Tournai

tallest **bell tower** in Italy—Cremona

first **Bible** printed in Netherlands—Amsterdam

first **book** printed in Spain—Segovia

only **bread** museum in the world—Ulm, Germany

tallest **brick structure** in the world—Church of Our Lady, Brugge, Belgium

oldest **building** in Berlin—St. Nicholas Church

Europe's northernmost **capital city**—Helsinki, Finland

**car museums**—Canillo, Andorra; Lolland, Denmark; Le Mans, France; Geneva and Lucerne, Switzerland

Denmark's longest **cathedral**—Domkirke, Aarhus

largest **cathedral** in France—Amiens

Sweden's northernmost **church**—Karesuando

oldest **Cistercian monastery** in existence—Fontenay, France

highest **cliffs** on Normandy's coast—Fécamp, France

largest **clock face** in Europe—St. Peter's Church, Zurich, Switzerland

Germany's largest **Christmas fair**—Stuttgart

world's largest **church bell**—Cologne, Germany

tallest **church steeple** in the world—Ulm, Germany

largest **coastal resort** in England—Brighton

sites related to Christopher **Columbus**—Genoa, Italy; Barcelona, Granada, Guadalupe, and Sevilla, Spain;

sites related to Leonardo **da Vinci**—Tongerlo, Belgium; Louvre in Paris; Bückeburg, Germany; Milan, Italy; National Gallery in London; Windsor Castle, Windsor, England

world's largest **flower auction**—Aalsmeer, Netherlands

world's largest **flower gardens**—Lisse, Netherlands

world's highest **fountain**—Geneva, Switzerland

most popular **French attraction** outside of Paris—Mont-Saint-Michel

world's most complete **garden**—Royal Botanic Gardens, London

largest skiable **glacier** in Europe—Les Deux Alpes in France

largest **Gothic cathedral** in England—York

longest **Gothic cathedral** in Europe—Winchester, England

largest **Gothic structure** in Italy (and third-largest church in the world)—Milan

largest **Gothic structure** in the world—Sevilla, Spain

**Gutenberg Bible**—Fulda, Germany; Gutenberg Museum in Mainz, Germany; British Museum, London; Manchester, England

sites related to **Handel**—Halle, Germany; Westminster Abbey and St. Martin-in-the-Fields in London; Haarlem, Netherlands

sites related to the **Huguenots**—Aigues-Mortes; La Rochelle, Poitiers, Tanlay France; Kassel, Nuremberg, Germany; and Bath, England sites related to Jan **Hus**—Prague and Tábor, Czech Republic; Konstanz and Worms, Germany

sites related to **Joan of Arc**—Chinon, Orléans, Poitiers, Reims, and Rouen, France;

world's only existing Roman **lighthouse**—Dover, England

**Legoland**—Billund, Denmark; Windsor, England

first public **library** in Ireland—Dublin

sites related to Martin **Luther**—the Marble Church in Copenhagen; the cathedral in Helsinki's Senate Square; Augsburg, Coburg, Eisenach, Eisleben, Erfurt, Speyer, Stolberg, Wittenberg, and Worms, Germany; Rome, Italy; Helsingborg, Sweden; Geneva and the Fine Arts Museum in Bern, Switzerland

most striking **manuscript** in the Western world—Trinity College, Dublin, Ireland

world's first **Methodist chapel**—Bristol, England

finest **mosaics** in Europe—Ravenna, Italy

highest **mountain peak** in Europe—Mont Blanc, French Alps

largest **movie screen** in Europe—Poitiers, France

**musical instrument** museums—Turku and Varkaus, Finland; Berlin, Germany; Beethoven's home in Bonn, Germany; Bachhaus in Eisenach, Germany; Handel House in Halle, Germany; Leipzig, Germany; Stradivarius Museum in Cremona, Italy; Genoa, Italy; Utrecht, Netherlands; Trondheim, Norway; Brighton England

village with world's longest **name**—in Wales

Europe's largest **national park**—Hohe Tauern National Park in Austria

Europe's biggest **oceanarium**—Lisbon, Portugal

world's biggest **organ**—Lübeck, Germany

largest **organ** in Ireland—Dublin

largest city **park** in Europe—Kassel, Germany

largest public **park** in Europe—Phoenix Park in Dublin

world's longest **pedestrian mall**—Copenhagen, Denmark

oldest **Protestant church** in France—Temple St-Martin in Montbéliard

world's largest collection of **puppet theater material**—
Lübeck, Germany

highest exposed **rail system** in Europe—Zermatt, Switzerland

only **Renaissance church** in Spain—Granada

tallest **steeple** in Switzerland—Bern

oldest Scandanavian **stone church** in use—Dalby, Sweden

sites related to **St. Patrick**—Cashel, Drogheda, Dublin, Tara,
and Westport, Ireland; Antrim, Armagh, and Downpatrick, Northern Ireland

largest **tower clock** in Germany—Hamburg

oldest **town** in England—Colchester

**toy museums**—Munich, Nuremberg, Rothenburg ob der
Tauber, Germany; Dublin, Ireland; Rotterdam, Netherlands; Edinburgh, Scotland

Malta's most valued **treasure**—St. John's Co-Cathedral in
Valletta

world's largest **troll**—Lillehammer, Norway

only **walled city** in Germany with no modern buildings—
Rothenburg ob der Tauber

world's only **wallpaper museum**—Kassel, Germany

highest **waterfalls** in Germany—Triberg

**UNESCO World Heritage Sites**—Jyväskylä, Finland;
Aachen, Germany

**UNESCO world treasure**—Arles, France

sites related to John **Wesley**—Adare, Ireland; Briston,
Epworth, London, and Oxford, England

sites related to Ulrich **Zwingli**—Bern, Einsiedeln, Geneva,
and Zurich, Switzerland

**Amy Eckert** is a freelance travel writer specializing in Christian destinations. In addition to coauthoring *The Christian Traveler's Companion* series she regularly contributes to www.christiantraveler.com and various Internet sites, newspapers, and magazines. Amy has also led workshops on integrating faith with travel. Amy lives in Holland, Michigan with her husband and two teenage daughters who share her love of travel.

**Bill Petersen** is an author and senior editor of Fleming H. Revell. He has authored more than 20 books in addition to *The Christian Traveler's Companion* series and is the former editor of *Christian Life* magazine, *Eternity* magazine, *Christian Retailing,* and several newsletters. His work has appeared in a variety of Christian and secular newspapers and magazines. Bill and his wife are parents of three grown children, and they reside in Chester Springs, Pennsylvania.

Amy Eckert and Bill Petersen have combined many years of travel experience with many hours of research to provide you with *The Christian Traveler's Companion.* Even so, you may know of destinations that the authors missed. If you would like to submit ideas for the next edition of *The Christian Traveler's Companion: Western Europe,* please share them with us. Would you like to add your name to our mailing list? You will receive free information of interest to Christian travelers as well as advance notice of upcoming *Christian Traveler's Companions.* Send your name and mailing address and any inquiries to:

The Christian Traveler
P.O. Box 1736
Holland, MI 49422
info@christiantraveler.com

Or visit our web site at www.christiantraveler.com for regular updates and additional Christian travel information.